BIRKBECK WORD ASSOCIATION NORMS

Birkbeck Word Association Norms

Helen Moss and Lianne Older

Centre for Speech and Language, Department of Psychology,
Birkbeck College, University of London

Psychology Press

An imprint of Erlbaum (UK) Taylor & Francis

Psychology Press
27 Church Road
Hove
East Sussex, BN3 2FA
UK

British Library Cataloguing in Publication Data

A catalogue record for this book is available from the British Library

ISBN 0-86377-404-0

Cover design by Joyce Chester
Printed and bound by Antony Rowe Ltd, Chippenham, Wilts.

Contents

Acknowledgments

We are grateful to all the members of the MRC Speech and Language group at Birkbeck College, London, and formerly at the University of Cambridge who have contributed to the collection of these association norms. We would also like to thank Paul Warren, Paul Day, and Paul Cairns for writing programs to help compile and sort the results on computer at various stages along the way, and Will Luxton for help with the category index. We are especially grateful to Samantha McCormick for her superhuman efforts in checking and organising the entire set of norms. Finally, we thank the many people who have acted as subjects.

The collection of these norms was partly funded by MRC programme grants to William Marslen-Wilson and Lorraine K. Tyler, SERC and BBSRC studentships to Helen Moss and Lianne Older respectively, and a postdoctoral research fellowship and a small personal research grant from the British Academy to Helen Moss.

Helen Moss is now at the Department of Psychology, University of Glasgow.

Introduction

This book contains free association norms for 2464 words in the English language. Free association norms are collected by presenting a large group of subjects with a stimulus word and asking them to respond with the first word they think of, as quickly as they can. The responses are then compiled to compute the percentage of subjects who produced each response. This percentage is generally referred to as the association strength between the pair of words. So, for example, 67% of subjects in our sample said *dog* in response to *cat*. Thus *cat* and *dog* are very strongly associated. On the other hand only 4.2% generate the responses *flap or mouse,* so that *cat–flap* and *cat–mouse* are only weakly associated. When association norms are collected from a large sample of subjects, the aim is to provide an estimate of the degree of association that exists between pairs of words in the linguistic community as a whole.

Word association studies have played an important part in many areas of psychological research over the years. Earlier this century, word association techniques were often used as a psychodiagnostic tool, with the generation of aberrant associations linked to various kinds of mental disorder (e.g. Jung, 1918). The use of word association in the clinical setting has declined over the years, but interest in association norms enjoyed a revival in the 1950s and 1960s as a key paradigm in the study of verbal learning and verbal behaviour. In these studies the interest was not in the detailed analysis of associations given by individual subjects, but in the general patterns of responses for large groups. As a result many large-scale studies were undertaken to collect association norms (e.g. Palermo & Jenkins, 1964; Postman & Keppel; 1970; see Cramer, 1968 for an extensive review).

The motivation for most of these studies was the belief that word associations provided a direct window onto the underlying structure of semantic memory, and even onto the nature of human thought processes in general (e.g. Deese, 1965). The idea that cognitive processes are based on principles of association had its roots in the work of 17th-century empiricist philosophers, such as Locke. Deese, among others, claimed that not only was association of ideas or concepts a basic principle of learning and memory, but also that qualitative aspects of the structure of semantic memory could be inferred from detailed analysis of word association data. For example, the similarity of the sets of responses to two different words could be used as a measure of the similarity of their representations in memory. A recent discussion of this approach is given by Aitchison (1987).

The claim that word associations reflect the structure of semantic memory fits naturally with the kinds of network models of semantic memory made popular by Collins and Loftus (1975). In these models, concepts are represented as interconnected nodes in a network. When one concept is activated, activation spreads along the links to related concepts. It is often assumed that word associations reflect the links in the network (e.g. de Groot , 1989). The idea is that when the stimulus is heard, its node in the network is activated, and activation spreads to related nodes, thus making them available as responses. The different kinds of relation between stimulus and response that occur in association norms are thought to tell us about the kinds of links in the semantic network (e.g. co-ordination, synonymy, antonymy, etc) and the associative strength of a pair of words is believed to reflect the strength of those links (see Kiss, Armstrong, Milroy, & Piper, (1973) for a computational simulation of such a network).

During the 1950s and 1960s an alternative account of word associations was also popular. This was also based on the assumption that word associations reflect the organisation of the subjective semantic lexicon, but was grounded in linguistic theory (more specifically, generative grammar), rather than an associationist account of cognitive processes. Researchers such as Clark (1970) and Clifton (1967) described the kinds of responses frequently given in association norms in terms of rules that operate on the feature-based lexical representation of the stimulus. This was thought to reflect deep structure relations among dictionary entries for lexical items in the language system. For example the stimulus *man* most frequently produces *woman* because of the minimal contrast rule that changes the representation for man (+ noun + det + count + animate + human + adult + male) into the representation for *woman* by changing the last feature in the list.

In spite of the vast number of association studies that were carried out, the notion that association norms can reveal the structure of semantic memory and human thought processes has declined in popularity over recent years. Several specific difficulties with the associative method have been identified. For example, the associate generated can be affected by the list context in which the stimulus word is embedded (Coleman, 1964). An important limitation, pointed out by Aitchison (1987), is that each subject lists only one response, and so this cannot reflect the variety of semantic links that would presumably exist in their semantic memory. In addition, generating an associative response is a fairly complex mental process that may involve numerous operations over and above a direct read-off of relations encoded in semantic memory. Even when subjects are encouraged to respond quickly, and their response latencies timed, subjects take about one and a half seconds on average to initiate a response (de Groot, 1989).

Most importantly, association strength must reflect something more than the relations among concepts in semantic memory. For example, according to association norms the category co-ordinate pair *cat* and *dog* are strongly associated, but equally similar pairs of animals such as *pig* and *horse* or *goat* and *cow* are only very weakly associated, if at all. It has been suggested that the additional "something" that leads to strong associative links is frequency of co-occurrence between a pair of words in the language. Thus, the reason that *cat* and *dog* are so strongly associated may not just be that they are co-members of the category *animal*, and share numerous semantic features, but also because they are frequently mentioned together in conversation as well as occurring in phrases like *raining cats and dogs*. By the same argument, *goat* and *cow* may fail to generate each other as associates because the words do not often co-occur in the language (e.g. Moss, Ostrin, Tyler, & Marslen-Wilson, 1995; Shelton & Martin, 1992). Several statistical studies of language data-bases provide support for the notion that associated words have a high probability of co-occurrence (e.g. Spence & Owen, 1990). Thus, although word association may be based largely on temporal contiguity, as claimed by philosophers such as Locke, and by associationist psychologists, this may affect relations among representations of lexical form, rather than links among concepts in semantic memory (see Moss, Hare, Day, & Tyler, 1994, for discussion, and de Groot, 1990 for an alternative view).

Although there is now less interest in the analysis of the nature of association norms in their own right, they are still widely used in psychological research. This is because they are valuable as a simple measure of relatedness between two words. Most strongly associated words are also semantically related in one way or another (although it is quite possible to identify relations that are purely collocational and share little semantic overlap, such as *couch–potato* and *pillar–society*). Association norms have been especially useful in studies of lexical access and word recognition. In these studies, the precise nature of the semantic relationship is often not of importance and some form of a spreading activation network is frequently assumed, in which associative strength may be a reasonable estimate of the links among nodes in the network. For example, in the extensive literature on "semantic priming" it has been shown that the recognition of a word is facilitated if it is preceded by a related word presented shortly beforehand. In almost all cases, the measure of relatedness is association strength (e.g. Meyer & Schvaneveldt, 1971; see Neely, 1991 for a review). More recent priming studies have examined the effectiveness of prime–target pairs that are semantically related, both with and without an additional associative connection. Both kinds of relation have been shown to support priming, although there has been debate as to whether the underlying mechanisms are the same (e.g. de Groot, 1990; Fischler, 1977; Lupker, 1984; Moss et al., 1995; Shelton & Martin, 1992). Given the current controversy over possible differences between semantic and associative priming, normative association studies are often as valuable for identifying pairs of words that are *not* strongly associated (but are semantically related in some way) as they are for identifying pairs that *are* strongly associated.

In summary, association norms are still widely consulted as a source of materials for empirical studies of language and memory. This leads to a problem because almost all of the large normative studies were carried out 20 or 30 years ago. Collections of association norms such as Postman and Keppel (1970) still continue to be the primary source, although they are now very out of date. Another drawback for British researchers is that the norms were collected from American college students rather than from a sample of British English speakers. It is likely that much of the data provided by those American students in the 1950s and 1960s are quite inappropriate for the British students of the 1990s and beyond. The fact that subjects of different ages and cultures differ considerably in the nature of the associations they provide was demonstrated in several of the early studies (see Cramer, 1968: Chapter 9). Moreover, the use of existing norms restricts selection of stimuli to the rather limited sets of words that were included in those early studies.

For these reasons we have collected our own association norms over the last seven years. We wanted up-to-date data from the type of young British English adults that researchers typically use in their experiments. The norms here are the combined results from several studies, each carried out on a subset of the stimulus words, as part of the process of selecting suitable items for specific experiments on lexical representation and processing. The resulting set of 2464 words is therefore very heterogeneous, taken from various grammatical classes and many semantic domains, and including words of varying frequency and familiarity. We have provided both an alphabetical index and an index organised by broad semantic and syntactic categories, to aid search through the norms for particular types of words. The norms include many pairs of rhyming stimuli (e.g. *gallery* and *calorie*), words within words (e.g. *caterpillar* and *pillar*), morphologically complex words and their stems (e.g. *defrost* and *frost*, *happiness* and *happy*), blends of two related words (e.g *smog* [derived from *smoke* and *fog*], *brunch* [derived from *breakfast* and *lunch*]), function words (e.g. *now*, *although*), as well as all of the 260 picture names from the widely used Snodgrass and Vanderwart (1980) picture set, with the exception of some that are available from the Postman and Keppel norms. Finally, a small selection of popular or famous first names have been included.

METHOD

Subjects

Subjects were all native speakers of British English between 17 and 45 years old, most of whom lived, worked, or studied in Cambridge or London. All were paid for their participation. Between 40 and 50 subjects participated in each test session.

Procedure

The norms presented here represent the total collected from 14 individual tests, which were each used to generate materials for a particular experiment. Some of the tests were also divided into two versions presented to different groups of subjects, either to reduce the total number of responses given by each subject, or to prevent the presentation of highly related stimuli to the same group of subjects. The smallest number of stimuli presented to any one group of subjects was 50, and the largest was 387. Some subjects participated in more than one test session.

In all cases the stimulus words to be tested were ordered pseudo-randomly, such that semantically related words did not occur consecutively. The mode of presentation of stimuli varied across different tests. In 10 tests the stimulus words were typed in a booklet. The words were typed in a column down the left side of the page, with each word followed by a line indicating where the response should be written. Subjects were allowed to complete the booklet in their own time, but were always encouraged to respond as quickly as possible. Subjects were instructed to write down only their first response to each word.

In the remaining four tests, stimuli were presented auditorily. In two cases, the stimuli were spoken by a female native speaker of standard Southern British English, recorded onto audiotape and then digitised onto computer hard disk at a sampling rate of 20,000kHz. Subjects were tested in groups of up to four at a time seated in separate carrels. The stimulus words were played out over headphones from the stored wave forms, with an interval of 13 seconds between words. Subjects gave their responses by typing them onto the keyboard of a BBC microcomputer in front of them. They were given 12 seconds to type the word, followed by another second to get ready for the next word. In another two tests, the words were recorded onto audiotape by the same speaker, and the stimuli were played to the subjects directly from tape. Groups of up to six subjects at a time were tested in a quiet room. There was an interval of five seconds between words, during which subjects wrote down their responses in a numbered booklet. After each block of 20 words, there was a slightly longer pause for subjects to rest. In both versions of the auditory presentation test, subjects were instructed to give their first response only.

The auditory presentation procedures were used when we were collecting norms for experiments in which the acoustic properties of the stimulus words would be particularly important. In total, 1243 of the stimulus words were presented auditorily. These words are marked in the listing of norms by the symbol +. Stimuli that are not marked in this way were presented visually.

In all tests, subjects were given the following written instructions. In the cases where stimuli were presented auditorily, these instructions were modified to explain the details of presentation and where to enter responses.

> **Instructions**: In this booklet you will find a list of simple words. Please read each word and then write down the first word it brings to mind. Write your response in the space provided. For example, if the word is **butter**, the first word you think of might be **bread** or **milk** or **cup**. Please work through the booklet quickly. Remember, we are interested in the word that comes to mind immediately, not after thinking about it for a while. If you can't think of anything at all, leave the space blank. Don't go back and change your mind about any of the words after you have written your first response. Thank you very much for taking part in the experiment.

RESULTS

Results were compiled by counting how many subjects had given each response and then converting this number into a percentage of the total number of subjects participating. This percentage is the associative strength between the stimulus and the response. The exact number of subjects who gave responses for any given stimulus word varied slightly across different studies. The minimum was 41 and the maximum was 50 subjects. Due to compiling and rounding errors, the percentages may not always add to exactly 100%. However, all totals are between 95% and 105%.

We have used the symbol * to represent missing or completely illegible responses. Obvious spelling mistakes and typographical errors have been corrected, but we did not change possible spelling errors that produced a real word alternative. Morphological variants of a word are treated as separate responses, with the exception that regular singular and plural forms are combined (as in Postman & Keppel). We have indicated cases where singular and plural forms have been collapsed in this way by the use of (s). In a few cases we have tested the same word on more than one occasion. Where this has happened the results have been combined.

The following section lists the full set of association norms in alphabetical order. This is followed by an alphabetical index of stimulus words, and then a categorised list. The stimulus words are listed under syntactic/morphological categories including verbs, adjectives, morphologically complex words, and blends. The nouns are listed under semantic categories including animals, household objects, and proper names. These categories are not necessarily exhaustive.

REFERENCES

Aitchison, J. (1987). Words in the mind. Oxford: Basil Blackwell Ltd.

Clark, H. (1970). Word associations and linguistic theory. In J. Lyons (Ed), *New horizons in linguistics.* Harmondsworth, Middlesex: Penguin Books.

Clifton, C. (1967). The implications of grammar for word associations. In K. Salzinger & S. Salzinger (Eds), *Verbal behaviour and some neurophysiological implications.* New York: Academic Press.

Coleman, E. (1964). Supplementary report: On the combination of associative probabilities in linguistic contexts. *Journal of Psychology, 57,* 95-99.

Collins, A. & Loftus, E. (1975). A spreading activation theory of semantic memory. *Psychological Review, 82,* 407–428.

Cramer, P. (1968). Word association. New York: Academic Press.

Deese, J. (1965). The structure of associations in language and thought. Baltimore, MD: The Johns Hopkins University Press.

de Groot, A.M.B. (1989). Representational aspects of word imageability and word frequency as assessed through word association. *Journal of Experimental Psychology: Learning, Memory and Cognition, 15,* 824–845.

de Groot, A.M.B. (1990). The locus of the associative priming effect in the mental lexicon. In D.A. Balota, G.B. Flores d'Arcais, & K. Rayner (Eds), *Comprehension processes in reading.* Hillsdale, NJ: Lawrence Erlbaum Associates Inc.

Fischler, I. (1977). Semantic facilitation without association in a lexical decision task. *Memory and Cognition, 5,* 335–339.

Jung, C.G. (1918). *Studies in word association.* London: Heineman.

Kiss, G., Armstrong, C., Milroy, R. & Piper, J. (1973). An associative thesaurus of English and its computer analysis. In A.J. Aitken, R.W. Bailey, & N. Hamilton-Smith (Eds), *The computer and literary studies* (pp.153–166). Edinburgh: University Press .

Lupker, S. (1984). Semantic priming without association: A second look. *Journal of Verbal Learning and Verbal Behavior, 23,* 709–733.

Meyer, D.E., & Schvaneveldt, R.W. (1971). Facilitation in recognising pairs of words: Evidence of a dependence between retrieval operations. *Journal of Experimental Psychology, 80,* 227–235.

Moss, H., Hare, M., Day, P., & Marslen-Wilson, W. (1994). A distributed memory model of the associative boost in semantic priming. *Connection Science, 6,* 413–427.

Moss, H. Ostrin, R.K., Tyler, L.K., & Marslen-Wilson, W. (1995). Accessing different types of lexical semantic information: Evidence from priming. *Journal of Experimental Psychology: Learning, Memory and Cognition, 21,* 863–883.

Neely, J.H. (1991). Semantic priming in visual word recognition: A selective review of current theories and findings. In D. Besner & G. Humphreys (Eds), *Basic processes in reading: Visual word recognition.* Hillsdale, NJ: Lawrence Erlbaum Associates Inc.

Palermo, D. & Jenkins, J. (1964). Word association norms. Minneapolis: University of Minnesota Press.

Postman, L. & Keppel, G. *Norms of word association.* New York: Academic Press.

Shelton, J. & Martin, R.C. (1992). How automatic is automatic semantic priming? *Journal of Experimental Psychology: Learning, Memory and Cognition, 18,* 1191–1210.

Snodgrass, J.G. & Vanderwart, M. (1980). A standardised set of 260 pictures: Norms for name agreement, image agreement, familiarity and visual complexity. *Journal of Experimental Psychology: Human Learning and Memory, 6,* 174–215.

Spence, D. & Owens, K. (1990). Lexical co-occurrence and association strength. *Journal of Psycholinguistic Research, 19,* 317–330.

Association norms A-Z

A
* 25.0%
B 16.7%
One 8.4%
An 4.2%
Day 4.2%
Man 4.2%
Pale 4.2%
The 4.2%
2.1% 90, Aardvark, Beast, Bee, Car, Fat, Is, It, Letter, Number, Runner, Thing, Woman, Word

Abandon
Leave 35.5%
Hope 12.5%
Child 6.3%
Baby 4.2%
Children 4.2%
Left 4.2%
2.1% *, Abandon, All, Away, Destroy, Dump, Give-Up, It, Lonely, Loose, Lose, Me, Neglect, Orphans, Ship, Them

Abate
Stop 32.0%
* 8.0%
Debate 6.0%
End 6.0%
Lessen 6.0%
Noise 6.0%
Storm 4.0%
2.0% Abet, Ban, Calm, Can't, Cease, Die, Ebb, Fence, Give, Less, Mild, Over, Quieten, Undecided, Wane, Wind

Abdomen
Stomach 42.9%
Body 11.9%
Belly 7.1%
Guts 7.1%
Pain 4.8%
2.4% *, Appendix, Biology, Bottom, Cut, Filling, Medicine, Middle, Protrude, Tummy, Womb

Abduct
Take 27.1%
Kidnap 18.8%
* 8.3%
Steal 8.3%
Away 4.2%
Person 4.2%
Take-Away 4.2%
2.1% Abduct, Abscond, Aliens, Carry-Off, Child, Children, Criminal, Him, Hold, Keep, Seize, You

Ability
Skill 17.4%
Able 15.2%
Clever 6.5%
Strength 4.3%
Success 4.3%
Talent 4.3%
2.2% A, Act, Adept, Aptitude, Big, Capability, Disability, Draw, Good, Help, High, Intelligence, IQ, Learn, Level, Quick, School, Skilful, Style, Swim, Task, Win

Able
Can 14.0%
To 10.0%
* 8.0%
Capable 8.0%
Bodied 6.0%
Cain 6.0%
Willing 6.0%
Body 4.0%
Table 4.0%
Unable 4.0%
2.0% Ability, Allowed, Competent, Disable, Fit, Known, Maladroit, Man, Manage, Not, Pie, Ready, Seaman, Twistable, Wheelchair

Abrupt
Short 15.6%
Sudden 13.3%
Stop 11.1%
* 9.3%
Rude 8.9%
Cross 4.4%
Manner 4.4%
Sharp 4.4%
2.2% Blunt, Break, Brusque, Caught-Short, Cut, Cut-Off, Departure, Hang-Up, Junction, Quick, Start, Terse, Untimely

Absolute
Total 12.5%
Beginner(s) 8.3%
Fabulous 8.3%
* 4.2%
Definite 4.2%
Final 4.2%
Truth 4.2%
Vodka 4.2%
2.1% -Ly, Actual, Al, Cold, Darkness, Declaration, Divine, Exact, Fear, God, Great, Last, Necessary, Nothing, Outright, Power, Reality, Relative, Remedy, Temperature, Together, True, Very, White, Whole

Accept
Take 25.1%
Give 8.4%
* 8.3%
Deny 6.3%
It 6.3%
Agree 4.2%
This 4.2%
Tolerate 4.2%
2.1% Acceptability, Cheque, Consent, Declare, Get-On-With, Giro, Live, Me, Never, Nothing, Now, OK, Punishment, Refuse, Thank-You, Yes

Accordingly
* 22.7%
So 18.2%
Therefore 9.1%
Likewise 4.6%
Thus 4.6%
2.3% OK, Appropriate, By, Done, Due To, Dutifully, Necessarily, Next, Now, Right, Rightful, Sure, Then, To

Accuse
* 14.3%
Point 11.9%
Blame 7.1%
Charge 7.1%
Court 4.8%
Defend 4.8%
Guilty 4.8%
Trial 4.8%
Victim 4.8%
2.4% ?, Condemn, Crime, Deny, Falsely, Guilt, Innocent, Jodie, Law, Order, Skinner, Stealing, Warn, Who, Wig

Ache
Pain 36.0%
Tooth 16.0%
Back 10.0%
Head 10.0%
Heart 4.0%
2.0% Belly, Creak, Door, Face, Hurt, Leg, Neck, Smith, Tablet, Teeth, Tummy, Yearn

Acre
Field 33.3%
Land 22.9%
Green 6.3%
Hectare 6.3%
Lane 4.2%
Long 4.2%
Mile 4.2%
2.1% Acne, Age, Area, Farmer, Football, Grass, Man, Wheat, Wood

Acrobat
Circus 33.3%
Trapeze 16.7%
Gymnastic(s) 7.1%
Jump 4.8%
Swing 4.8%
2.4% Adobe, Balls, Bars, Clown, Dancer, Daring, Flying, Gymnast, Horse, Juggler, Niagara-Falls, Rope, Somersault, Thin

Active
Passive 21.4%
* 14.3%
Fit 7.1%
Life 7.1%
Bouncy 4.8%
Sporty 4.8%
2.4% Alive, Book, Busy, Energetic, Happy, Healthy, Inert, Lazy, Lively, Man, Mood, Neighbour, Participate, Partner, Play, Slow, Wind

Actor
Actress 22.2%
Stage 20.0%
Play 15.6%
2.2% Acting, Anne, Bard, Boards, Camp, Dancer, Drama, Fringe, Junior, Lines, Man, Mask, Masque, Movie, Punch, Seiyuv, Singer, Sophia, Thesp

Actual
Real 46.0%
Fact 8.0%
* 4.0%
Factual 4.0%
Now 4.0%
One 4.0%
2.0% Actuality, Actually, Age, Bodily, Bodily-Harm, False, How, Make, Manage, People, Precise, Really, Statement, Thing, Very

Acute+
Sharp 26.2%
Angle 9.5%
Pain 9.5%
Obtuse 7.1%
Severe 7.1%
2.4% Accent, Angina, Appendix, Bad, Grave, Harsh, Hurt, Letter, Sensitive, Serious, Sore, Special, Stupid, Tense, Terminal, Tight, Ward

Address
Home 33.3%
Book 19.0%
Name 7.1%
House 4.8%
Speak 4.8%
2.4% Abode, Class, Found, Kings, Label, London, My, Number, Phone-Number, Postman, Site, Speech, Telephone

Admire
Like 22.0%
Respect 10.0%
Envy 6.0%
* 4.0%
Beauty 4.0%
Her 4.0%

Idol 4.0%
Love 4.0%
Them 4.0%
2.0% Admiral, Adore, Appreciate, Beautiful, Book, Fan, Figure, Gaze, Him, Look, Me, Much, No-One, Painting, Praise, Surface, Want, Worship, Yourself

Admit+
Confess 33.3%
* 10.4%
Guilt 8.3%
Deny 4.2%
Lie 4.2%
Nothing 4.2%
One 4.2%
To 4.2%
Truth 4.2%
2.1% Acknowledge, Agree, Claim, Confession, Defeat, Enter, Interrogation, Let-In, Responsibility, Say, True

Adolph
Hitler 73.5%
* 22.5%
2.0% Germany, Parents

Advantage
Tennis 19.0%
Disadvantage 11.9%
* 4.8%
Asset 4.8%
Deuce 4.8%
Set 4.8%
Unfair 4.8%
2.4% Against-The-Odds, Big, Edge, Foolish, Help, Lead, Lost, Lucky, McEnroe, Net, Plus, Prejudice, Priority, Step-Up, Stronger, Success, Top, Use

Aerobicise
Exercise 22.9%
Keep Fit 8.3%
Breathe 6.3%
Fit 6.3%
* 4.2%
Aerobics 4.2%
Work 4.2%
2.1% America, Fonda, Acrobat, Action, Athletic, Cycle, Dance, Fitness, Fun, Hurt, Knackered, Lycra, Muscles, Oxygenation, Run, Sweat, Walk, Women, Work Out

Aeroplane+
Fly 19.0%
Sky 11.9%
Flight 9.5%
Crash 7.1%
* 4.8%
Jet 4.8%
Plane 4.8%
2.4% Airport, Boeing, Comfort, Expensive, Fighter, Flying, Glider, High, Home, Journey, Land, Line, Ship, Take-Off, Up, Whine

Africa
* 8.2%
Bambaata 8.2%
Continent 8.2%
South 8.2%
Country 6.1%
Out 6.1%
Asia 4.1%
Famine 4.1%
Jungle 4.1%
2.0% Aids, Animals, Apartheid, Audy, Beauty, Big, Black, Chad, Dark, Giraffe, Heat, Johannesburg, Larger, Mandela, Nigeria, North, Red, Sand, Toto, Trees, Truck

Age
Old 38.1%
Young 11.9%
* 7.1%
Limit 7.1%
2.4% 18, 20, Ageless, Augustan, Blind, Concern, Era, Man, Middle, Number, One, Size, Stick, Stoop, Youth

Agile
Nimble 15.6%
Fast 6.7%
Quick 6.7%
Supple 6.7%
Clumsy 4.4%
Fit 4.4%
Monkey 4.4%
Swift 4.4%
2.2% Acrobat, Active, Alert, Alive, Bendy, Body, Careful, Cat, Exercise, Flexible, Gym, High, Limp, Lively, Mobile, Runner, Soft, Sport, Sprightly, Stolen

Agree
With 20.9%
Disagree 18.8%
* 10.4%
Yes 10.4%
You 4.2%
2.1% Accord, Acknowledge, Affirm, Approve, Argument, Concur, Consent, Hands, Happen, Help, Like, Me, Muse, No, Not, Okay, To

Airport+
Plane(s) 43.5%
Lounge 8.7%
Fly 4.3%
Runway 4.3%
Terminal 4.3%
2.2% *, Aircraft, Busy, Carry, Convention, Crash, Danger, Gatwick, Line, Marble, Poland, Port, Security, Sleep, Trolley, Warsaw, Wing

Alcohol+
Drink 42.9%
Drunk 9.5%
Booze 7.1%
Abuse 4.8%
Beer 4.8%
Bottle 4.8%
Ethanol 4.8%
Wine 4.8%
2.4% Bitter, Drugs, Drunkard, Fags, Fun, Gin, Poisoning

Alike+
Similar 52.4%
Same 31.0%
Different 4.8%
2.4% Dissimilar, Look, Similar, Together, Twins

Alive+
Dead 26.2%
Living 23.8%
Well 16.7%
Kicking 9.5%
2.4% *, Animated, Breathing, Energy, Exist, Happy, People, Quick, Today, Vital

All
Every 25.0%
Nothing 14.6%
Of 6.3%
Together 6.3%
* 6.2%
None 4.2%
Or 4.2%
Over 4.2%
2.1% Around, Both, Collective, Day, Everyone, Or-Nothing, Out, People, Right, Tall, Them, Things, Us, Whole

Alley
Cat(s) 31.0%
Dark 19.0%
Way 14.3%
* 7.1%
Blind 4.8%
2.4% Bowling, Corridor, End, Fence, Kirsty, Lane, Passage, Rape, Road, Street

Alligator
Crocodile 31.1%
Skin 6.7%
Teeth 6.7%
Bite 4.4%
Handbag 4.4%
River 4.4%
Water 4.4%
2.2% *, Adverts, Animal, Bag, Danger, Eat, Eye, Florida, Heel, Jaws, Lager, Purse, Shark, Sign, Stew, Swamp, Tail

Allow
Let 40.0%
Permit 14.0%
* 6.0%
Give 4.0%
Me 4.0%
Not 4.0%
Rule(s) 4.0%
2.0% Consent, Discipline, Do, Go, Have, More, OK, Okay, Prevent, Refuse, Something, Touch

Alone
Solo 22.2%
Home 11.1%
Lonely 11.1%
Together 6.7%
* 4.4%
Again 4.4%
And 4.4%
Own 4.4%
Single 4.4%
2.2% Attached, Here, Island, Liked, Lonesome, Mountains, Quiet, Rim, Sad, Self, Solitary, Solitude

Also
And 27.1%
* 16.6%
Too 8.3%
As-Well 6.3%
Ran 6.3%
More 4.2%
Other 4.2%
Together 4.2%
2.1% Additionally, Again, Auch, Further, Me, Not-Only, Plus, To, Was, Well, With

Amaze
Surprise 12.5%
Astonish 10.4%
Shock 10.4%
Astound 8.3%
Me 8.3%
* 6.3%
Grace 4.2%
2.1% Awesome, Delight, Exclaim, Expression, Give, Incredible, Lost, Magic, Rats, Really, Shun, Spectacular, Stare, Startle, Us, Wonder, Wow, You

Amazement
Surprise 31.0%
Shock 16.7%
Wonder 9.5%
2.4% *, Bewilderment, Circus, Cure, Dismay, Distress, Eyebrows, Eyes, Good, Grateful, Happy, Stare, Startle, Stunned, Sun, Surprised, Truth, Wonderful

Ambassador
Country 11.9%
* 9.5%
Diplomat 9.5%
Embassy 9.5%
Foreign 7.1%
2.4% America, Car, Carpet, Charge, Dictator, Envoy, Far-East, Fat, France, Front, Important, Iraq, King, Message, Monument, Pomp, Rank, Representative, Rich, Silver-Tongue, Suit, Vendetta

Amble
Walk 34.0%
Along 12.0%
Wander 8.0%
* 6.0%
Ramble 6.0%
Stroll 6.0%
2.0% Able, Aimless, Bramble, Gamble, Happy, Lamb, Meander, Red, Roam, Shuffle, Slowly, Steep, Stumble, Yomp

Ambulance+
Hospital 16.7%
Accident 14.3%
Emergency 11.9%
Driver 9.5%
Siren 7.1%
Strike 7.1%
Brigade 4.8%
Dead 4.8%
Man 4.8%
2.4% Car, Danger, Fire, Fire-Engine, Light, Noise, Patient, Police

America
Usa 10.2%
* 8.2%
Flag 8.2%
Continent 6.1%
Bush 4.1%
South 4.1%
States 4.1%
2.0% April, Australia, Big, Brother, Captain, Church, Country, Far, Free, Great, Immigrants, Large, Mad, Map, Money, National, New-York, North, Ohio, President, Rubbish, Shit, Stars, Stars&Stripes, Strong, Texas, Wolf, Yank

Amount
Money 17.1%
Total 12.2%
Number 9.8%
Quantity 9.8%
Sum 9.8%
* 7.3%
Cost 4.9%
Size 4.9%
2.4% 100, Cash, Heap, Large, Lots, Of, Pay, Pounds, Proportion, Scales, Taken

Amputate+
Cut 31.0%
Leg 26.2%
Remove 11.9%
Limb 7.1%
Chop 4.8%
2.4% Amplify, Break Cut-Off, Head, Kill, Loss, Ouch, Take-Off

Anchor
Ship 26.7%
Boat 20.0%
Butter 8.9%
Weigh 6.7%
Drop 4.4%
2.2% Chain, Deuce, Dip, Down, Fix, Hope, Man, Pub, Rust, Sailor, Salt, Sea, Stay, Stop, Water

Ancient
Old 35.7%
Modern 7.1%
History 4.8%
Rites 4.8%
Rome 4.8%
Time(s) 4.8%
2.4% *, Antiquities, Castle, Chant, Dusty, Egypt, Ghost, Greeks, Ivory, Map, Monument, Order, Pillar, Ritual, Ruins, Western

And
Also 14.0%
Now 12.0%
* 8.0%
Or 8.0%
Then 6.0%
But 4.0%
More 4.0%
Plus 4.0%
You 4.0%
2.0% Add, Again, And, Conjunction, Hand, Happen, I, It, Me, Next, Not, So, Them, Together, Too, When, Where, Word

Anger
Rage 16.7%
* 9.5%
Red 9.5%
Fear 7.1%
Hate 7.1%
Fury 4.8%
2.4% Blood, Emotion, Fist, Forgiveness, Fretful, Help, Hollywood, Irritation, Kenneth, Pleasure, Scream, Sorrow, Stare, Strong, Tears, Temper, Threat, Violence, Write

Animal
Dog 14.6%
Cat 12.2%
Beast 7.3%
Bear 4.9%
Magic 4.9%
Tiger 4.9%
2.4% Ark, Bird, Creature, Excrement, Farm, Fat, Fish, Furry, Horse, Human, Insect, Instincts, Kingdom, Mammal, Man, Nature, Pet, Pig, Rabbit, Rights, Vegetable, Zebra

Animate+
Inanimate 15.2%
Object 15.2%
Alive 13.0%
Cartoon 13.0%
Lively 10.9%
* 6.5%
Animal 4.3%
2.2% Friend, Friendly, Laugh, Life, Moving, Ornament, Panting, Picture, Shape, Solid

Ankle+
Foot 14.3%
Leg 11.9%
Bone 9.5%
Knee 7.1%
Sock 7.1%
Wrist 7.1%
* 4.8%
Broken 4.8%
Chain 4.8%
Enough 4.8%
2.4% Achilles, Bangle, Bracelet, Break, Joint, Line, Rich, Shin, Sprained

Anne
* 27.3%
Frank 18.4%
Princess 8.2%
Marie 4.1%
2.0% Auntie, Bancroft, Berlin, Cousin, Cutler, Diamond, Ford, Green, Hathaway, Karenina, Makanen, Mead, Mum, Nightingale, O'Neill, Oakley, Oliver, Richards, Robinson, Sister, Skinner

Annihilation
Death 25.6%
Destroy 9.3%
Kill 9.3%
End 4.7%
Extermination 4.7%
2.3% *, Anger, Bomb, Bosnia, Carnage, Dead, Destruction, Die, End, Evaporate, Explosion, Go, Holocaust, Nothing, Obliteration, Removed, Robot, Total, Whiteout

Announce
Say 11.8%
Tell 8.6%
Loudspeaker 7.5%
Speak 6.5%
Declare 5.4%
* 4.3%
Shout 3.2%
Speech 3.2%
Announcer 2.2%
Engagement 2.2%
Marriage 2.2%
News 2.2%
Speaker 2.2%
Talk 2.2%
Tannoy 2.2%
Wedding 2.2%
1.1% -Ment, Broadcast, Clap, Compere, Cough, Declaim, Denounce, Dictate, Disco, Explain, Hailer, Hear, Herald, Instruct, Intercom, It, Loud, Loudhailer, Loudly, Loudspeaker, Man, Microphone, Party, Proclaim, Public, Reveal, Station, Suggest, System, Yell, You

Annoyance
Irritation 25.5%
Anger 19.1%
Pain 8.5%
* 4.3%
Angry 4.3%
Hurt 4.3%
Irritate 4.3%
2.1% Aggravation, Agony, Bother, Brother, Cross, Image, Irate, Irritant, Life, Mad, Rude, Tantrum, Tense, Trepidation

Another
One 14.0%
More 10.0%
Also 8.0%
Day 6.0%
Other 6.0%
Way 6.0%
Again 4.0%
Else 4.0%
Time 4.0%
2.0% *, Added, Alternative, Book, Boy,

Broken, Dark-Age, Different, Example, Extra, Mother, Next, Problem, Same, Thing, Two, Word, Year, Yet

Antidote+
Poison 16.7%
Cure 14.3%
* 9.5%
Drug 9.5%
Medicine 7.1%
Remedy 7.1%
Tablet 4.8%
2.4% Dose, Injection, Opposite, Pain, Panacea, Panel, Pill, Prevention, Serum, Snake, Tale, Virus

Anxiety
Worry 38.3%
Stress 14.9%
* 6.4%
Fear 6.4%
Attack 4.3%
Exam 4.3%
Nerves 4.3%
2.1% Depression, Down, Eek, Frightened, Hurt, Nightmare, Restless, Shame, Tiring, Worried

Apathy
Lazy 22.0%
* 7.3%
Sad 7.3%
Boredom 4.9%
Indifference 4.9%
Laziness 4.9%
Sloth 4.9%
Sofa 4.9%
2.4% Apathetic, Bored, Care, Depression, Don't-Care, England, English, Hate, Inertia, Pathetic, Reject, Slack, Sleep, Student, Tired, UK, Unfeeling

Ape
Monkey 35.7%
Gorilla 11.9%
Man 9.5%
Chimp 4.8%
Planet 4.8%
2.4% *, Animal, Black, Chimpanzee, Clown, Copy, Father, Gibbon, Hair, Hairy, Pig, Primate, Shit, Super

Appeal+
Ask 9.5%
Court 9.5%
Sex 7.1%
Plead 4.8%
2.4% *, Argue, Attract, Beg, Charity, Children, Delight, Demand, Donation, Good, Help, Judge, Jury, Like, Liking, Look, Mercy, Nice, Oran, Pleasant, Please, Question, Repent, Sexy, Spaniel, Succeed, Sweet, Take, Try

Appear
See 14.9%
Vision 12.8%
Ghost 8.5%
* 6.4%
Apparition 4.3%
Disappear 4.3%
Magician 4.3%
Seem 4.3%
Show 4.3%
2.1% Angel, Around, Be, Develop, Here, Jesus, Light, Look, Magic, Nice, Now, Puff, Reappear, Soon, Sudden, Transfigurate, Transform

Appease+
* 14.3%
Placate 14.3%
Please 11.9%
Calm 7.1%
War 7.1%
Quieten 4.8%
2.4% -Ment, Appropriate, Befriend, Comfort, Correct, Fair, Give-In, Help, Mend, Pacify, Peace, Peaceful, Peas, Plug, Ply, Satisfy, Span

Apple
Pear 26.2%
Core 14.3%
Orange 11.9%
Eve 9.5%
Pie 9.5%
Green 4.8%
2.4% Adam, Banana, Cart, Computer, Cut, Fruit, Label, Magic, Red, Tree

Applicant+
Job 31.0%
Interview 19.0%
Apply 9.5%
Form 7.1%
Hopeful 4.8%
Supplicant 4.8%
2.4% *, Buyer, Candidate, Contestant, Invitee, Person, Succeed, Successful, Test, Weak

Apricot+
Fruit 25.0%
Jam 14.3%
Peach 9.5%
Apple 6.0%
Pear 6.0%
Orange 4.8%
Stone 4.8%
Plum 3.6%
Tree 3.6%
Computer 3.5%
1.2% Blancmange, Brandy, Dessert, Dried, Eat, Fecund, Fibre, Fish, Fruity, Ice, Mango, Nectarine, Pie, Prune, Summer, Wine, Yoghurt

Apron+
Strings 21.4%
Kitchen 14.3%
Mother 11.9%
Cooking 7.1%
Cook 4.8%
Pinny 4.8%
2.4% Bib, Chef, Cookery, Dress, Flour, Floury, Food, House, Lab-Coat, Matron, May, Pinafore, Plastic, Spoon, Waist

Aptitude+
Ability 31.0%
Test 16.7%
Skill 11.9%
Knack 4.8%
Talent 4.8%
2.4% *, Altitude, Attitude, Brain, Clever, Ease, Gift, Goodness, Height, Intelligence, Knowledge, Strength, Success

Argue
Fight 25.8%
Debate 12.9%
Shout 11.1%
* 8.6%
Discuss 6.5%
Row 4.3%
A 2.2%
About 2.2%
Bicker 2.2%
Cross 2.2%
Disagree 2.2%
Quarrel 2.2%
1.1% Again, Agree, Angry, Complain, Contest, Disagreement, Endlessly, Glue, Guess, Hate, Heated, Parents, Report, Speech, War, Well

Arid
Dry 60.4%
* 12.5%
Land(s) 8.4%
Desert 8.3%
Zone 4.2%
2.1% Landscape, Sand, Smelly

Arise
Sun 12.8%
Awake 10.6%
Get-Up 10.6%
* 8.5%
Morning 6.4%
Sir 6.4%
Bed 4.3%
Up 4.3%
Wake 4.3%
2.1% Above, Afloat, Asleep, Bourne, Down, Elevate, Jump, Make, Sepultura, Set, Shine, Sir-Knight, Sir-Neil, Top, Upwards

Arm
Leg 47.6%
Band(s) 11.9%
Baby 4.8%
Hand 4.8%
Muscle 4.8%
2.4% Big, Blow, Chair, Finger, Hold, In-Arm, Lock, Reach, Sleeve, Wrestle, Wrist

Armistice+
Peace 28.6%
War 14.3%
* 7.1%
Day 7.1%
Truce 7.1%
Poppy 4.8%
Treaty 4.8%
2.4% Agreement, Army, Bismarck, Ceasefire, End, Freedom, Gun, Pact, Remembrance, Sign, Summer

Aroma
Smell 77.8%
Coffee 6.7%
* 2.3%
2.2% Food, Fragrance, Fresh, Perfume, Taste, Therapy

Array+
* 10.3%
Arrange 8.7%
4 4.3%
Disarray 4.3%
Many 4.3%
Spread 4.3%
2.2% Army, Arrangement, Chaos, Colour, Different, Group, Happy, Head-Up, Henry, Index, Joy, Large, March, Matches, Matrix, Of, Order, Parade, Place, Raid, Rain, Range, Sample, Set, Shelf, Show, Sort, Variety, Weapons

Arthritis+
Pain 16.7%
Rheumatism 11.9%
Bone(s) 9.6%
Joint 7.1%
Hurt 4.8%
Knees 4.8%
Old 4.8%
2.4% Ache, Age, Arm, Aunt, Brittle, Cripple, Crippled, Death, Disability,

Disease, Grandma, Granny, Ill, Leg, Mother, Rheumatoid, Wrist

Arthur
Daley 20.4%
* 13.0%
Miller 12.2%
King 6.1%
Scargill 6.1%
Askey 4.1%
Peckham 4.1%
2.0% Andersen, Cat, Church, Colvey, Eastenders, Fowler, Grandpa, Lowe, Merlin, Mo, Mullard, Name, Negus, Parker, Ramane, Rubenstein, Walker

Artichoke
Heart(s) 20.9%
Vegetable 16.2%
Green 9.3%
Food 6.9%
Eat 4.6%
Jerusalem 4.6%
Leaves 4.6%
2.3% *, Asparagus, Bite, Butter, Chuck, Delicious, Flower, Fruit, Garden, Marx, Pizza, Plant, Spears, Yellow

Artist
Paint 23.8%
Painter 11.9%
Brush 4.8%
Easel 4.8%
Picasso 4.8%
2.4% Artists, Artwork, Bohemian, Con, Draw, Drawing, Esoteric, Image, Leonardo, Monet, Musician, Oil, Painting, Palette, Picture, Pretention, Renoir, Room, Sculpture, Sex, Underpaid

Asbestos+
Dust 21.4%
Mat 11.9%
Fire 9.5%
Bad 4.8%
Cancer 4.8%
Danger 4.8%
Dangerous 4.8%
Death 4.8%
Poison 4.8%
Roof 4.8%
2.4% Blue, Breath, Ceiling, Cement, Heat, Hot, Lining, Nasty, Poisoning, Powder

Ascertain+
Find 16.7%
Discover 11.9%
Decide 7.1%
Establish 7.1%
* 4.8%
Check 4.8%
Deduce 4.8%
Determine 4.8%
Guess 4.8%
Obtain 4.8%
2.4% Achieve, Ask, Believe, Certain, Confirm, Evidence, Lawyer, Learn, Meaning, Thinks, Truth

Ashtray+
Cigarette(s) 28.3%
Smoke 17.4%
Fag(s) 13.0%
Ash 10.9%
* 2.4%
2.2% Ashley, Bin, Burn, Cigar, Filth, Filthy, Grey, Joint, Smokers, Smoking, Smoky, Urgh

Ask
Question 30.2%
* 7.0%
Please 7.0%
Request 7.0%
Enquire 4.7%
Order 4.7%
2.3% About, Answer, Find, Forgiveness, God, Help, Lend, Me, More, Now, Polite, Queue, Receive, Speak, Take, Tell, Trust

Asparagus
Soup 20.0%
Green 17.8%
Tips 13.3%
Spears 8.9%
Food 6.7%
Butter 4.4%
Stalk 4.4%
Vegetable 4.4%
2.2% Broccoli, Dinner, Fridge, Gypsy, Hearts, Herb, Leaf, Story, White

Aspirin+
Headache 45.2%
Tablet 11.9%
Medicine 9.5%
Pain 7.1%
Pill 7.1%
2.4% Cupus, Dispirin, Drug, Fever, Paracetamol, Sick, Water

Asset
Money 38.3%
* 6.4%
Good 6.4%
2.1% Assent, Bank, Best, Capitalism, Car, Cash, Debit, Deficit, Down, Face, Fund, Gain, Goods, Have, Help, House, Looks, Object, Possession, Save, Shares, Truth, Value

Assist
Help 64.0%
Me 6.0%
Assistant 4.0%
2.0% Aid, Blind, Broth, Desist, First, Football, Give, Hinder, In, Police, Shop, Support, Together

Assistance
Help 81.0%
* 4.8%
Aid 4.8%
2.4% AA, Assistant, Life-Belt, Shop

Astonish
Surprise 23.0%
Amaze 18.8%
* 8.3%
Astound 8.3%
Me 6.3%
Shock 6.3%
Gasp 4.2%
2.1% Amazed, Amazement, Awe, Cry, Gollywog, Gosh, Meant, No-One, Stare, Them, Why, Wonder

At
There 27.1%
On 8.3%
Home 6.3%
* 6.2%
Hat 4.2%
In 4.2%
It 4.2%
Noon 4.2%
To 4.2%
When 4.2%
Where 4.2%
You 4.2%
2.1% Bat, Easy, Last, Peace, Place, Position, Stare, That, The

Athlete+
Runner 25.0%
Foot 16.7%
Run 11.9%
Fit 6.0%
Track 6.0%
Sport 4.8%
Fast 3.6%
Running 3.6%
Feet 2.4%
Games 2.4%
Gymnast 2.4%
Hurdles 2.4%
Speed 2.4%
Sprinter 2.4%
Strength 2.4%
1.2% Black, Circuit, Leggings, Medal, Olympic, Sweat, Training

Atlas+
Map(s) 59.6%
World 21.4%
Book 9.5%
2.4% *, Heavy, Intelligent, Mountain

Atrocious
Bad 26.2%
Awful 21.4%
Terrible 16.7%
Appalling 9.5%
Disgusting 4.8%
2.4% Book, Dreadful, Everton, Fantastic, Feat, Horrid, Mistake, Nasty, Person

Attach+
Join 14.4%
Stick 13.3%
Tie 6.7%
Fix 5.6%
* 4.4%
Detach 3.3%
Link 3.3%
Pin 3.3%
Staple 3.3%
Close 2.2%
Connect 2.2%
Hold 2.2%
Together 2.2%
1.1% Add, Adhere, Append, Appendage, Bag, Belt, Bind, Bowlby, Button, Cling, Constraint, Drop, Friend, Get, Glue, Group, Hand, Importance, Jeep, Latch, Let, Limpet, Love, Meant, Mother, Sew, Snail, Stamp, Stuck, Weld

Attack+
Defend 26.2%
Fight 21.4%
Defence 9.5%
Kill 4.8%
Violence 4.8%
2.4% Aggression, Armed, Beat, Castle, Dark, Destroy, Fire, Force, Hit, Rape, Strike, Strong, Sword, War

Attempt
Try 58.0%
Not 4.0%
Suicide 4.0%
To 4.0%
2.0% *, ?, Do, Effort, Essay, Fail, Failure, First, Go, Good, Help, It, Murder, Succeed, Tempt

Attic
Loft 35.7%
House 11.9%
Top 11.9%
Roof 7.1%
Room 7.1%
2.4% Bedroom, Ceiling, Dark, Garret, Poky, Secrets, Skylight,

Stairs, Upstairs, Vase, Window

Auction+
Sell 40.5%
Sale 23.8%
Antique(s) 4.8%
Buy 4.8%
Lot(s) 4.8%
2.4% Bargain, Cattle, Furniture, Hammer, Horse, Market, Money, Pot, Room

Audition+
Act 9.5%
Play 7.1%
Sing 7.1%
Stage 7.1%
Trial 7.1%
Nervous 4.8%
Test 4.8%
Theatre 4.8%
Try-Out 4.8%
* 4.5%
2.4% Actor, Concert, Exam, Guess, Hell, Interview, Music II, Part, RADA, Rehearsal, Show, Singing, Song, Try, Trying

Auditor+
Accountant 14.3%
Accounts 14.3%
* 11.4%
Computer 4.8%
Listen 4.8%
Money 4.8%
Tax(es) 4.8%
2.4% Banker, Bills, Books, Boring, Calculate, Cash, Finance, Git, Listener, Office, See, Shout, Snoop, Test, Toilet, Trouble, Valuer

Aunt
Uncle 61.4%
Relative 9.1%
Cousin 4.6%
Family 4.6%
2.3% *, Female, Me, Music, Painting, Taff

Authentic
Real 40.0%
Genuine 20.0%
True 8.9%
Old 4.4%
2.2% Antique, Article, Authentic, Bridge, Cooking, Fake, Object, Original, Reliable, Rug, Style

Author
Book(s) 47.6%
Writer 26.2%
Write 7.1%
Pen 4.8%
2.4% *, Artist, Creation, Novel, Penguin, Venus

Authority+
Government 11.9%
Power 7.1%
Strong 7.1%
* 4.8%
Army 4.8%
Bureaucracy 4.8%
King 4.8%
Law 4.8%
2.4% Boss, Complex, Father, In, Local, Military, Minor, Morons, Mother, Over, Person, Police, Powerful, Ruler, Scare, Stern, Strict, Teacher, Top, Uniform, Version

Automobile
Car 78.6%
Roads 4.8%
2.4% America, Association, Crash, Factory, Motorbike, Pollution, Rolls-Royce

Avalanche+
Snow 85.7%
2.4% Danger, Fall, Helicopter, Mountain, Rock, Tintin

Avid
Keen 28.0%
Reader 18.0%
Fan 12.0%
* 4.0%
Enthusiastic 4.0%
Follower 4.0%
Livid 4.0%
2.0% Admire, Admirer, Animated, Bright, Captivated, David, Eager, Greedy, Lazy, Listener, Response, Rigid, TV

Await+
* 19.0%
Asleep 7.1%
Time 7.1%
Alive 4.8%
Attend 4.8%
For 4.8%
Wait 4.8%
2.4% Anticipate, Aware, Bide, Boring, Call, Dawn, Delay, Dolphin, Expect, Ody, Patience, Patient, Return, Sit, Sleep, Slumberous, Spin, Stay, Ton, Train

Awake+
Asleep 31.0%
Sleep 23.8%
Wide 11.9%
Alive 4.8%
Up 4.8%
2.4% Alert, Arise, Bed, Conscious, Dawn, Dose, Sleepy, Waken, Yawn

Award+
Prize 38.1%
Give 16.7%
Medal 7.1%
Present 4.8%
2.4% *, Bravery, Degree, Fee, Gift, Note, Payment, Penalty, Presentation, Receive, School, Star, Trophy, Winner

Awkward
Clumsy 31.1%
Difficult 6.7%
Shy 4.4%
Silence 4.4%
Uncomfortable 4.4%
2.2% *, Attitude, Bad, Confident, Coy, Customer, Easy, Funny, Gawky, Lean, Lout, Manner, Mess, Movement, Nice, Pest, Position, Spastic, Strange, Stuffy, Tricky

Axe+
Chop 14.3%
Cut 9.5%
Grind 9.5%
Wood 7.1%
Hammer 4.8%
Hatchet 4.8%
Pick 4.8%
Saw 4.8%
2.4% Chopper, Death, Eugene, Fall, Grinder, Head, Job, Killer, Knife, Man, Spade, Tax, Tool, Tree, Wield, Wielder

Baby
Face 11.9%
Boy 9.5%
Cot 7.1%
Cry 7.1%
Girl 7.1%
Child 4.8%
Sitter 4.8%
Smile 4.8%
2.4% Blues, Cake, Crying, Dead, Food, Infant, Kid, Mother, Pensioner, Person, Pink, Pram, Sister, Sleep, Stork, Tiny, Tot, Year

Back
Front 16.7%
Ache 9.5%
Forward 7.1%
Side 7.1%
Pain 4.8%
Spine 4.8%
2.4% *, Behind, Biter, Bone, Bored, Break, Brush, Date, Down, Forth, Garden, Hurt, Roots, Rude, Scrub, Shoulders, Sore, Strong, To-Back, Turn, Where

Backbite
* 25.0%
Bitch 14.6%
Hurt 8.3%
Attack 4.2%
Sharp 4.2%
Sound 4.2%
Stab 4.2%
2.1% Answer, Bass, Bee, Bitchy, Bite, Bite back, Cheek, Dog, Flea, Helm, Newspapers, Office, Retort, Snipe, Talkback, Technical, Teeth

Backbone
Spine 48.1%
Fish 7.7%
Body 5.7%
Strength 5.7%
* 3.8%
Strong 3.8%
Vertebrae 3.8%
1.9% Ache, Back, Biology, Column, Front bone, Grit, Man, Pillar, Skeleton, Stiff, Whalebone

Background
Foreground 21.3%
Noise 8.5%
Scenery 8.5%
* 6.4%
Black 4.3%
History 4.3%
Information 4.3%
Music 4.3%
Painting 4.3%
2.1% Ahead, Cloth, Curtain, Drop, Figure, Front, Home, Material, Near, Play, Research, Setting, Shape, Sky, Space, Trees

Bacteria
Germ(s) 38.1%
Mould 7.1%
Microbe(s) 4.8%
2.4% *, Bacterium, Biology, Cell, Dettox Dirt, Disease, Dish, DNA, Fungi, Gum, Illness, Insect, Laboratory, Microscope, Protozoa, Rat, Scum Slide, Spoken, Virus

Bad
Good 40.5%
Boy 7.1%
Breath 7.1%
Girl 4.8%
Taste 4.8%
Weather 4.8%
2.4% *, Apple, Habit, Impression, Maybe, Memory, Naughty, Nice, Rotten, Times, Timing, Unhappy, Vibe

Badminton+
Racket 21.4%
Tennis 14.3%
Game 11.9%
Shuttlecock 11.9%
Sport 9.5%
Squash 9.5%
Ball 4.8%
Net 4.8%
2.4% Cock, Court, Games, Shuttle, Soccer

Bag+
Sack 12.5%
Shopping 10.4%
Carry 6.2%
Hand 6.2%
Case 4.2%
Full 4.2%
Old 4.2%
2.1% Bottles, Carrier, Cat, Catch, Close, Gold, Handle, Hold, Holdall, Leather, Nails, Of-Beans, Paper, Plastic, Pouch, Rubbish, Sac, School, Search, Shoulder, Store, Suitcase, Take, Whale, Woman

Bake
Cake 55.3%
Oven 14.9%
Bread 12.8%
Cook 4.3%
Pie 4.3%
2.1% *, Bun, Leaf

Balance
Scale(s) 16.7%
Weight(s) 16.7%
Act 4.2%
Equal 4.2%
Equilibrium 4.2%
Swing 4.2%
Tightrope 4.2%
Trapeze 4.2%
Weigh 4.2%
2.1% Account, Act, Beam, Debt, Equation, Giddy, Head, Hearing, Libra, New, Nike, Par, Plank, Power, Proportion, Sheet, Trapeze-Act, Well

Balcony
Veranda 13.3%
* 8.7%
Porch 6.7%
Scene 6.7%
Terrace 4.4%
2.2% Alcove, Balustrade, Bedroom, Danger, Death, Edge, Flowers, Genet, Holiday, Hotel, House, Iron, Italy, Juliet, Outside, Overlooking, Romeo, Sea, Spire, Street, Sun, Top, Tree, View, Wave, White, Window

Ball
Bat 13.3%
Bounce 11.1%
Game 8.9%
Foot 6.7%
Kick 6.7%
Chain 4.4%
Throw 4.4%
2.2% *, Beach, Bearing, Bouncing, Boy, Catch, Dance, Grass, Hoop, Juggle, Park, Pitch, Play, Point, Red, Score, Socket, Volleyball, Wall, Wind

Ballad+
Song 73.8%
Poem 4.8%
2.4% *, Accepted, Lay, Pass, Poetical, Singing, Story, Tale, Tomato

Ballet
Dance 31.0%
Shoe(s) 21.4%
Dancer 19.0%
2.4% Childhood, Classical, Dancing, Grace, Jazz, Opera, Poem, Ribbons, School, Slipper, Theatre, Thin

Balloon+
Air 14.6%
Float 10.4%
Red 10.4%
Pop 8.3%
Ball 4.2%
Bubble 4.2%
Hot 4.2%
Sky 4.2%
Up 4.2%
2.1% Ascend, Barge, Blow, Burst, Coloured, Crossing, First, Fly, Mad, Moon, Party, Pooh, Ride, Rising, Sail, Swell, Yellow

Ballot+
Vote 42.9%
Box 23.8%
Election 11.9%
2.4% Auction, Con, Democratic, Lottery, Paper, Politics, Poll, Question, Sell

Ban
Banish 16.7%
* 12.5%
Stop 10.5%
Bar 4.2%
Bomb 4.2%
Car(s) 4.2%
2.1% -D-Aid, Abolish, All, Allows, Banner, Censor, Drive, Driving, Exclude, From, Government, Hate, It, March, Marched, Music, Obstruct, Prevent, Pub, Record, Smoking, Sport, Tree

Band
Elastic 9.5%
Music 9.5%
Brass 7.1%
Stand 7.1%
Drums 4.8%
Hair 4.8%
Rock 4.8%
2.4% *, Banal, Bandstand, Box, Brain, Brothers, Cream, Jazz, Mettalica, Military, Orchestra, Plays-On, Practice, Radio, Ring, Rubber, Show, Singer, Song, Tape, Trumpet, Wagon

Bandage+
Wound 26.2%
Cut 16.7%
Plaster 9.5%
Help 4.8%
Hurt 4.8%
Injury 4.8%
Wrap 4.8%
2.4% Arm, Blood, Cast, Head, Heal, Illness, Injured, Leg, Levels, Lint, Nurse, Pain

Bandit+
Gun 7.1%
Outlaw 7.1%
Pirate 7.1%
Chocolate 4.8%
Gangster 4.8%
One-Armed 4.8%

Robber 4.8%
Thief 4.8%
2.4% *, American, Arse, Brigand, Cowboy, Criminal, Crook, Deer, Desert, Highwayman, Hold-up, Hooded, Mexico, Moustache, Rascal, Rob, Rogue, Scarf, Spanish, Suzuki, Take, Time, Western

Bane+
* 23.9%
Life 13.0%
Bad 8.7%
Wolf('s) 6.5%
Mirror 4.3%
Trouble 4.3%
2.2% Albatross, Annoyance, Arrogant, Bath, Curse, Fire, Grass, Harelip, Hay, Joe, Looks, Marie, Pain, Proud, Swim, Tiresome, Wash, Watch, Woe

Banish
Ban 16.0%
Away 14.0%
Rid 6.0%
* 4.0%
Exclude 4.0%
Exile 4.0%
From 4.0%
Send-Away 4.0%
2.0% Bar, Evict, Expel, Go, Hamlet, Kingdom, Leave, Ostracise, Out, Out, Outlaw, Outside, Point, Power, Prison, Quick, Send-Forth, Stop, Traffic, Vanish, Vanquish, Welcome

Banquet
Feast 48.8%
Food 19.5%
Dinner 9.8%
2.4% Ball, Eat, Grandeur, King, Meal, Party, Sumptuous, Tomatoes, Trestle, Wine

Baptise+
Christen 21.4%
Christian 14.3%
Church 11.9%
Water 11.9%
Christianity 4.8%
Religion 4.8%
Wet 4.8%
2.4% *, Anoint, Baby, Batman, Communion, Confirmation, Font, God, God-Daughter, Name, Profound

Barbara
Streisand 36.7%
Cartland 26.5%
* 10.6%
Jackson 4.1%
Windsor 4.1%
2.0% Hairdresser, Lennon, Name, Pekinese, Roberts, Rogers, Stanwyck, Taylor, Thompson

Bare
Naked 31.2%
All 10.4%
Bottom 6.3%
Feet 6.3%
Nude 6.3%
Skin 6.3%
Back 4.2%
2.1% *, Boards, Bum, Buttocks, Care, Chest, Dressed, Essentials, Fact, Ground, Hare, Legs, Mountain, Neck

Bargain+
Sale 16.7%
Buy 11.9%
Cheap 9.5%
Market 7.1%
Shop 7.1%
Basement 4.8%
Hunt 4.8%
Price 4.8%
2.4% Break, Bucket, Cost, Good, Haggle, Hunter, Obtain, Rubbish, Sales, Sell, Snip, Store, Street, Value

Barge+
Canal 35.4%
Pole 18.8%
Boat 16.7%
Push 8.3%
River 8.3%
2.1% Flat, Heavy, Sail, Sainsburys, Ship, Trade, Water

Bark+
Dog 54.2%
Tree 31.2%
Bite 4.2%
2.1% Beethoven, Birch, Papyrus, Silver, Wood

Barn+
Owl(s) 27.1%
Farm 12.5%
Dance 10.4%
Yard 10.4%
Door 6.3%
Hay 6.3%
House 4.2%
Red 4.2%
2.1% Barge, Cow, Grain, Heaney, Hill, Sheep, Side, Wind, Wood

Baron+
Knight 9.5%
Land 9.5%
Beef 7.1%
Empty 7.1%
Infertile 7.1%
Lord 7.1%
Bare 4.8%
Desert 4.8%
Dry 4.8%
2.4% Castle, Childless, Conceive, Cunt, Dead, Deserted, Earl, Field, Heathland, Moor, Stark, Villain, Von-Munhause, Waste, Wasteland, Womb

Barrack+
Army 28.6%
Soldier 26.2%
Room(s) 7.1%
Block 4.8%
2.4% *, -Cade, Abuse, Attack, Cape, Fight, Guard, Hate, Naval, Road, Shout, Sleep, Soldiers, Spoil

Barrel+
Beer 41.7%
Oil 6.2%
Roll 6.2%
Gun 4.2%
Laughs 4.2%
Rum 4.2%
2.1% Ale, Apples, Cooper, Escape, Fun, House, Keg, Laugh, Of-Beer, Onions, Organ, Over, Pub, Round, Shotgun, Tar

Bars
Prison 28.9%
Drink(s) 11.1%
Cell 6.7%
Chocolate 6.7%
Jail(s) 6.7%
Fire 4.4%
Gold 4.4%
Mars 4.4%
Window 4.4%
2.2% Beer, Broken, Cage, Drinking, End, Hands, Parallel, Stars, Stripes, Wall

Basement+
Flat 27.5%
Cellar 25.0%
Ground 7.5%
House 7.5%
Dank 5.0%
2.5% *, Bottom, Cave, Cold, Damp, Deep, Flooding, Floor, Low, Scary, Stairs

Basic+
Simple 31.0%
Language 19.0%
Computer(s) 14.3%
Easy 7.1%
2.4% Cheap, Crude, Elementary, Level, Low, Necessary, Necessity, OK, Pascal, Prolog, Skill, Solid

Basin+
Sink 35.7%
Bowl 21.4%
Wash 9.5%
Water 9.5%
2.4% Bath, Haircut, Hairwash, Ouse, Oval, Pitcher, Pudding, Sediment, Tap, White

Basket
Case 44.4%
Weave 8.9%
Wicker 8.9%
Fruit 6.7%
Cat 4.4%
Rubbish 4.4%
2.2% Ball, Bin, Bread, Clothes, Currency, Eggs, Food, Linen, Mushroom, Shopping

Bastard+
* 14.3%
Child 11.9%
Illegitimate 9.6%
Man 7.1%
Son 7.1%
Bitch 4.8%
Hate 4.8%
2.4% Bad, Birth, Brother, Cunt, Evil, Father, Fool, Fuck, Horrid, Men, Mother, Pug, Slang, Sod, Sur, Thatcher, What

Bat+
Ball 27.1%
Cricket 10.4%
Hell 10.4%
Belfry 6.2%
Wing 6.2%
Bird 4.2%
2.1% Animal, Arno, Barn, Dark, Darkness, Flitter, Hit, Mad, Man, Night, Play, Squeak, Table, This, Vampire, Wind, Winged

Batch+
Lot 20.8%
Bread 8.3%
Group 6.2%
Cake(s) 4.2%
Eggs 4.2%
Set 4.2%
2.1% Assignment, Box, Buns, Catch, Coke, Consignment, Cottage, Header, Hen, Home, Job, Large, Loaf, Loaves, Lump, Maggie, Number, Of-Hens, Papers, Process, Roof, Sample, Sequence, Weight

Bath+
Water 35.4%

Tub 14.6%
Shower 8.3%
Soak 4.2%
Soap 4.2%
Time 4.2%
Wet 4.2%
2.1% Clean, Hot, Mat, Plug, Pub, Relax, Tin, Together, Tone, Towel, Wallow, Wash

Bathroom+
Bath 13.0%
Scales 8.7%
Toilet 8.7%
Wash 8.7%
Cabinet 6.5%
Mat 6.5%
Shower 6.5%
Suite 4.3%
Water 4.3%
2.2% Chair, Cleanliness, Lavatory, Loo, Mirror, Pink, Robe, Sink, Soap, Steam, Towel, Tub, Wall, Wipe, Zone

Bathtub
Water 26.9%
Soap 15.4%
Ring 5.7%
Bath 3.8%
Bubbles 3.8%
Shower 3.8%
Wet 3.8%
1.9% Black, Brush, Bubble-Bath, Foam, Full, Hot, Matey, Rug, Scum, Soak, Swim, Taps, Warm, Wash, Washbasin, Waves, White, Zinc

Batter+
Fish 18.8%
Hit 14.6%
Beat 10.4%
Pancake 10.4%
Wife 10.4%
Ram 6.2%
2.1% Baby, Child, Cod, Fritter, Fry, Heart, Mothers, Parent, Punch, Sea, Smash, Thump, Torn, Wives

Battle
War 35.6%
Ground 11.1%
Fight 6.7%
Ship 6.7%
Gun(s) 4.4%
2.2% Abbey, Armour, Bighorn, Britain, Bulge, Charge, Cry, Hardened, Hastings, Heated, Hum, Sea, Shield, That, Trafalgar, Zone

Bayonet+
Gun 21.4%
Rifle 9.5%
War 9.5%
Kill 7.1%
Stab 7.1%
Knife 4.8%
Sword 4.8%
2.4% *, Arrow, Battle, Charge, Fight, Hairnet, Napoleon, Practice, Soldier, Spear, Spike, Strike, Truncheon, Violent, Weapon

Beach+
Sand 27.8%
Sea 12.2%
Ball 7.8%
Sun 5.6%
-Comber 2.2%
Bum 2.2%
Echo 2.2%
Party 2.2%
Swim 2.2%
1.1% Australia, Baker, Berwick, Bikini, Bleach, Boys, Burn, Comb, Gaza, House, Mat, Peace, Pebbles, Playa, Quiet, Sandy, Seaside, Shingle, Stone, Strand, Sunbathe, Sunblock, Sunny, Swimmers, Towel, Umbrella, Vast, Venice, Warm, Waves, Whale, Wood

Beak+
Bird 52.1%
Bill 20.8%
Duck 6.2%
Gull 4.2%
2.1% Birdy, Bite, Claw, Eagle, Judge, Pointed, Seagull, Sharp

Bear
Hug 18.6%
Teddy 9.3%
Animal 7.0%
Brown 4.7%
Carry 4.7%
Down 4.7%
Grudge 4.7%
Polar 4.7%
2.3% Anxiety, Away, Brain, C?, Cave, Cub, Danger, Dog, Forest, Humphrey, Jungle, Necessity, Paw, Rug, Sleep, Up, Vicious

Beat
Drum 23.4%
Hit 12.8%
Egg(s) 10.6%
It 4.3%
Rhythm 4.3%
Up 4.3%
2.1% Bang, Banter, Basketball, Blow, Brush, Copper, Down, Drug, Generation, Group, Hard, Hurt, Music, Pole, Police, Skin, Stick, Strap, Surrender

Become
Change 14.0%
* 7.0%
Be 7.0%
Arrive 4.7%
Transform 4.7%
Turn 4.7%
2.3% Able, Actress, Begin, Being, Butterfly, Chrysalis, Come, Develop, Evolve, Famous, Friend, Get, Grow, Know, Leader, Learn, Life, Make, Old, One, Priest, Realise, Rich, Someone, You

Bee
Sting 24.0%
Honey 22.0%
Bumble 12.0%
Hive 8.0%
Buzz 4.0%
Keeper 4.0%
2.0% Bee, Bee's-Knees, Bonnet, Buzzy, Farm, Fly, Knee, Lady, Light, String, Summer, Wasp, Yellow

Beehive
Honey 27.1%
Hair 14.6%
Sting 8.3%
Hair-Do 6.3%
Bee(s) 4.2%
Buzz 4.2%
Hairspray 4.2%
Swarm 4.2%
2.1% *, Apiary, Behave, Earwig, Hairstyle, House, Light, Nest, Queen, Sixties, Tree, Wasp, Yellow

Beer
Glass 23.8%
Ale 19.0%
Drink 11.9%
Belly 4.8%
Spirit(s) 4.8%
2.4% *, Alcohol, Bitter, Drinker, Drunk, Fosters, Froth, Garden, Jug, Lager, Mat, Paunch, Please, Skittles, Smell

Beg+
Borrow 23.4%
Poor 17.0%
Ask 4.3%
For 4.3%
Homeless 4.3%
Money 4.3%
More 4.3%
Please 4.3%
Steal 4.3%
Tramp 4.3%
2.1% Beggar, Crawl, For-More, Hand, Howl, Knees, London, Need, Poverty, Question, Take, Tubes

Begin
Start 48.9%
End 19.1%
Again 12.8%
* 4.3%
With 4.3%
2.1% Finish, Life, Perform, Romance, Story

Beginner
Starter 20.5%
Start 18.2%
Novice 13.6%
* 6.8%
New 6.8%
Absolute 4.5%
Complete 4.5%
2.3% Begin, Chess, Exam, Expert, Learner, Newcomer, Novelty, Proficiency, Swimmer, Tyro, Veteran

Beginning
End 45.2%
Start 38.1%
2.4% Bible, Christmas, Ending, First, Genesis, In-The, Term

Belief
Religion 22.2%
Faith 13.3%
God 8.9%
Creed 4.4%
None 4.4%
System 4.4%
2.2% Believed, Chant, Church, Culture, Disbelief, Firm, Hope, Idea, Inner, Knowledge, Lie, My, Real, Reason, Religious, Tenet, Thought, Vow, Wish

Believe
Know 16.3%
* 9.3%
Dream(s) 9.3%
Faith 9.3%
Truth 9.3%
In 7.0%
Me 4.7%
2.3% Accept, Agree, Belief, Bible, Follow, God, Hate, Hope, Hymn, Idea, Like, See, Sincere, Story, Trust

Bell
Ring 57.8%
Church 6.7%
Door 6.7%
2.2% *, Alarm, Andy, Bike, Bottoms, Boy, Clang, Dong, Fire, Food, Gold, Pull, Ringer

Belt+
Trousers 22.9%
Buckle 8.3%
Leather 8.3%
Up 8.3%
Braces 6.2%
Waist 6.2%
Girdle 4.2%
Hit 4.2%
Tight 4.2%
2.1% Below, Cloth, Dog, Door, Flash, Hard, Hold, Lace, Lassoo, Pull, Safety, Strap, Turntable

Benefit
Dole 17.1%
* 12.2%
Good 9.8%
Housing 7.3%
Agency 4.9%
Charity 4.9%
Help 4.9%
Unemployment 4.9%
Welfare 4.9%
2.4% Aim, Asset, Bonus, Detriment, DSS, Gain, Money, Mutual, Office, Sickness, State, Supplement, Wealth

Bent
Crooked 9.5%
Over 9.5%
Straight 9.5%
Double 7.1%
Shape 7.1%
* 4.8%
Curve 4.8%
Stick 4.8%
2.4% Angle, Broken, Cop, Damage, Down, Elbow, Fork, Head, Hell, Junior, Metal, Nail, Narrow, Play, Queer, Round, Safety-Pin, Twig

Beseech+
Plead 21.4%
Ask 14.3%
Beg 14.3%
Implore 9.5%
2.4% *, Appeal, Barrister, Beggar, Berserk, Besiege, Castle, Hate, Loo, Plea, Please, Prayer, Pry, Request, Search, Stuck, Talk

Besiege+
Castle 21.4%
Attack 9.5%
City 9.5%
Fight 9.5%
* 4.8%
Surround 4.8%
Town(s) 4.8%
War 4.8%
2.4% Battle, Dead, Defend, Engulf, Fort, Fortress, Inundate, Invade, Paris, Siege, Starve, Surrounded, Wall

Best
Worst 35.7%
Fit 16.7%
George 7.1%
Good 7.1%
Top 4.8%
2.4% Ability, Better, Choice, Clothes, Days, Favourite, Friend, Greatest, Man, Most, Right, Time

Bet+
Horse(s) 22.9%
Money 14.6%
Wager 10.4%
Gamble 6.2%
Shop 6.2%
Lose 4.2%
Race 4.2%
Win 4.2%
2.1% Bookie, Break, Call, Cash, Lay, Pay, Poker, Racecourse, Sly, Stream, Track, Uncertain, Wage

Beverage
Drink 51.0%
Tea 12.2%
Beer 10.2%
2.0% *, Alcohol, Bacardi, Brew, Coffee, Food, Fosters, Letter, Pub, Tizer, Vodka, Whisky, Wine

Bias+
Binding 12.5%
Unfair 8.3%
Prejudice 6.3%
Against 4.2%
Favour 4.2%
Lean 4.2%
One-Sided 4.2%
Referee 4.2%
Sway 4.2%
2.1% Attitude, Bent, Cheat, Coin, Correct, Envy, Fair, Leaning, Mean, Mislead, One, Opinion, Police, Sun, Swing, Tape, Towards, Transistor, Twist, Uneven, Weight, Wheel, Wrong

Bib+
Baby 62.5%
Tucker 18.8%
Dribble 4.2%
2.1% *, Bottle, Lie, Mess, Nappy, Overalls, Protect

Bicycle+
Pump 19.0%
Wheel 16.7%
Chain 9.5%
Car 4.8%
Lock 4.8%
Ride 4.8%
2.4% Frame, Guilt, Lamp, Lights, Peddle, Rack, Red, Rothar, Stolen, Struggle, Tandem, Tired, Transport, Tricycle, Two, Tyre, Wheels

Big+
Small 35.4%
Large 25.0%
Huge 8.3%
Fat 4.2%
Little 4.2%
2.1% Beak, Ben, Body, Enormous, Giant, Grand, Great, House, Little, Man, Mountain

Bigamy
Marriage 21.3%
Wives 12.8%
Man/Men 10.6%
* 4.3%
Incest 4.3%
Two 4.3%
2.1% Aah, America, Bellamy, Creep, Dwell, Falsehood, Good-Luck, Lies, Lots, Monogamy, Polygamy, Sin, Sinful, Treachery, Twosome, Unfair, Unlawful, Woman, Wrong

Bike+
Cycle 20.8%
Car 14.6%
Ride 12.5%
Cambridge 8.3%
Wheel(s) 6.3%
Motor 4.2%
2.1% *, Chain, Chew, College, Fall, Handlebar, Lock, Pedal, Racer, Rad, Shed, Spoke, Thief, Tricycle, Tyre, Yard

Billiard+
Ball 42.9%
Table 38.1%
Cue 4.8%
Snooker 4.8%
2.4% Bar, Game, Hall, Pool

Billion+
Million 26.2%
Dollar(s) 14.3%
Lots 14.3%
Money 9.5%
Gold 7.1%
* 4.8%
Loads 4.8%
Pounds 4.8%
2.4% A-Lot, Man, Many, Thousand, Who, Zillion

Billow+
Wind 31.2%
Cloud 12.5%
Sail 12.5%
Wave 6.2%
Fire 4.2%
Out 4.2%
Sheets 4.2%
Smoke 4.2%
2.1% Belch, Fly, Gale, Pillow, Plume, Puff, Rush, Sleep, Washing, Windy

Billy
The-Kid 14.0%
Bragg 8.2%
Goat 8.2%
Idol 8.2%
Joel 8.2%
* 6.1%
Connolly 6.1%
Liar 6.1%
Wilder 6.1%
Boy 4.1%
Graham 4.1%
Kid 4.1%
2.0% Bear, Fury, Grey, Howe, Muffin, Preston, Silly, The-Fish

Bin+
Rubbish 33.3%
Liner 22.2%
Dust 6.7%
Empty 3.3%
Litter 3.3%
Waste 3.3%
Chuck 2.2%
Dustbin 2.2%
File 2.2%
Food 2.2%
1.1% Clean, Computer, Dump, Dustman, Dustmen, Fat, Finish, Garbage, Horrible, Out, Paper, Pedal, Plastic, Refuse, Reject, Throw, Trash

Bind
Rope 12.8%
Tie(s) 12.8%
Book 8.5%
Weed 6.4%
Cover 4.3%
Feet 4.3%
Together 4.3%
2.1% *, Bandage, Boots, Chains, Chore, Date, Find, Gauze, Glue, Het-Up, Paper, Problem, See, Sew, String, Tape, Tight, Unbind, Up, Wind, Wood, Wrap

Bingo+
Hall 19.0%
Card 14.3%
Game 14.3%
House 9.5%
Win 7.1%
Money 4.8%
Number 4.8%

2.4% Caller, Finish, Fuel, Fun, Jolly, Lotto, Millions, Prize, Snap, Spot-On, Yes

Biology
Chemistry 19.0%
Science 11.9%
Body 4.8%
Cell(s) 4.8%
Exam 4.8%
Lesson 4.8%
Physics 4.8%
School 4.8%
Teacher 4.8%
2.4% *, A-Levels, Electra, Experiment, Frog, Geology, Lab, Make-Up, Plants, Practice, Reproduction, Species, Test, Theory, Zoology

Birch+
Tree 56.2%
Silver 10.4%
Twig 8.3%
Wood 8.3%
Whip 4.2%
2.1% Alder, Bark, Beat, Burke, Cane, Switch

Birdcage
Bird(s) 18.0%
Budgie 10.0%
Canary 6.0%
Parrot 6.0%
* 4.0%
Bars 4.0%
Prison 4.0%
Song 4.0%
Trapped 4.0%
Walk 4.0%
2.0% Birdie, Bird-Dog, Budgerigar, Capture, Escape, Gilded, Green, Hanging, Herman, Messy, Metal, Nightingale, Pigeon, Sawdust, Sing, Trap, Tweetybird, White

Birth
Baby 24.4%
Death 24.4%
Day 13.3%
Rate 4.4%
2.2% Beginning, Blood, Bloom, Born, Cage, Control, Date, Dead, Life, Marriage, New, Night, Red, Right, Wonder

Birthday+
Party 34.8%
Cake 10.9%
Present(s) 8.7%
Happy 6.5%
* 4.3%
Card 4.3%
Christmas 4.3%
2.2% ?, Age, April, Candle, Day, February, God, Me, Mine, Sixty, Time

Biscuit+
Tea 14.3%
Tin 14.3%
Chocolate 8.3%
Barrel 7.1%
Crumb(s) 7.1%
Cake 4.8%
Digestive 4.8%
Food 3.6%
Break 2.4%
Cookie 2.4%
Cracker 2.4%
Sweet 2.4%
Wafer 2.4%
1.2% *, Bourbon, Bread, Butter, Cereal, Cheese, Coffee, Cream, Crunch, Crunchy, Dog, Eat, Eater, Hunger, Lettuce, Milk, Pastry, Snack, Take

Bishop+
Priest 14.6%
Mitre 10.4%
Pawn 8.3%
Chess 6.2%
Knight 6.2%
Pope 6.2%
Durham 4.2%
King 4.2%
Rich 4.2%
Robe(s) 4.2%
2.1% Actress, Arch, Archbishop, Cardinal, Castle, Cathedral, Catholic, Church, Deacon, Diocese, Hat, Prince, Python, Rook, Sack

Bit+
Piece 28.6%
Byte 16.7%
Horse 16.7%
Bite 4.8%
Computer 4.8%
Part 4.8%
Small 4.8%
2.4% Block, Bridle, Champ, Drill, Fragment, Middle, Side, Teeth

Bite
Tooth/Teeth 34.0%
Dog 14.9%
Eat 10.6%
Hard 6.4%
Apple 4.3%
Back 4.3%
Into 4.3%
2.1% *, Big, Blood, Gnat, Hole, Mouth, Pie, Savage, Shark

Bitter
Sweet 50.0%
Beer 11.9%
Taste 9.5%
Lemon 4.8%
Twisted 4.8%
2.4% *, Acid, Angry, Attack, Bit, Experience, Lager, Wind

Black
White 76.2%
Bird 7.1%
Night 7.1%
2.4% Blue, Cat, Dark, Green

Blackboard
Chalk 54.8%
Rubber 11.9%
School 7.1%
Black 4.8%
Jungle 4.8%
2.4% Board, Class, Classroom, Eraser, Slab, White, Whiteboard

Blame
* 19.5%
Fault 9.8%
Guilt 9.8%
Culpability 4.9%
Guilty 4.9%
2.4% Accuse, Anger, Argument, Aspersion, Attribute, Game, Hall, Innocent, Me, People, Point, Punish, Responsibility, Shadow, Slander, Smear, Someone, Trouble, Unfair, Worthy, Wound, You

Bland
Boring 22.2%
Tasteless 13.3%
Taste 8.9%
2.2% *, Beige, Blank, Bobby, Bold, Coffee, Dry, Dull, Exciting, Flavour, Grey, Hamilton, Insipid, Jean, Lard, Limpid, Nothing, Paper, Perfume, Plain, Spicy, Striking, Tasty, White

Blank+
Space 16.7%
Empty 14.6%
Face 8.3%
Cheque 6.2%
White 6.2%
Cartridge 4.2%
Expression 4.2%
Mind 4.2%
Page 4.2%
Sheet 4.2%
2.1% Ammunition, Clear, Crossword, Nothing, Paper, Scrabble, Slate, Stare, Terry, Vacant, Wall, Wogan, Word

Blatant
Obvious 30.0%
Lie(s) 22.0%
Loud 4.0%
Rude 4.0%
2.0% Bare, Blast, Clear, Coldness, Cry, Evident, Foul, Mischievous, Mistake, Noise, Push, Refusal, Regard, Rough, Stop, Straight-Up, Stupid, Subtle, Transgression, Unconcerned

Bleat
Sheep 63.8%
Lamb 25.5%
2.1% Baba, Bzz, Goat, Note, Whine

Bleed+
Blood 29.8%
Cut 17.0%
Death 8.5%
Wound 8.5%
2.1% *, Accident, Artery, Bloody, Die, Dry, Finger, Injury, Into, Leak, Nose, Party, Profound, Profuse, Red, Scar, Vein

Blend
Mix 40.0%
Coffee 28.0%
Blender 6.0%
Together 6.0%
2.0% Colour, Gold, It, Liquidiser, Mixer, Mixture, Seven, Tea, Type, Whisk

Bless+
Priest 12.5%
Church 10.4%
House 10.4%
Curse 8.3%
God 6.2%
You 6.2%
Child 4.2%
2.1% Approve, Benediction, Blame, Disguise, Grieve, Guide, Happy, Holy, Honour, Love, Luck, Pope, Praise, Pray, Promise, Religious, Saint, Soul, Worship

Blind
See 19.0%
Sight 16.7%
Man 7.1%
Window 7.1%
* 4.8%
Eye(s) 4.8%
Fold 4.8%
Person 4.8%
Sighted 4.8%
2.4% Alley, Bat, Curtain, Day, Deaf, Dog, Mice, Open, Side, Stick, Unsighted

Blitz+
War 41.7%

Bomb(s) 14.6%
Fire 8.3%
German(s) 6.2%
Krieg 6.2%
2.1% Bomber, Bombing, Damage, Destroy, Fall, Germany, Lightning, River, Shooting, Warfare, Wart

Blizzard
Snow 69.8%
Storm 7.0%
Cold 4.7%
2.3% *, Damage, Gale, Sun, White, Wind, Windy, Winter

Blond+
Hair 29.2%
Girl 20.8%
Brunette 8.3%
Woman 6.2%
Dark 4.2%
2.1% Blass, Fair, Handsome, Head, Light, Mistake, Mix, Mixer, Mother, Nice, Pretty, Sexy, White, Wig, Yellow

Blood+
Gore 18.8%
Red 18.8%
Cut 8.3%
Wound 8.3%
Pool 6.2%
Stain 6.2%
Guts 4.2%
Hurt 4.2%
2.1% Bleed, Charm, Cover, Death, Donate, Haemorrhage, Money, Over, Roof, Scab, Vein, Wet

Blossom+
Flower 47.9%
Cherry 14.6%
Tree(s) 10.4%
Peach 4.2%
Spring 4.2%
Time 4.2%
2.1% Bleed, Bloom, Fruit, Grow, Love, May, Shoot

Blot+
Ink 35.4%
Landscape 16.7%
Mark 4.2%
Paper 4.2%
Spot 4.2%
2.1% *, Blob, Chip, Copy, Dab, Mistake, Moist, Out, Smear, Smudge, Southern, Spill, Stain, Stands, Tasch, Test, Wood

Blow
Dry 12.8%
Wind 12.8%
Job 10.6%
Bubble 8.5%
Hit 6.4%
Mind 4.3%
Nose 4.3%
Out 4.3%
Suck 4.3%
2.1% *, Account, Away, Back, Blow, Bomb, Candle, Caress, Hair, Joint, Know, Lips, Puff, Up, Weather

Blue
Sky 24.0%
Green 14.0%
Bird 10.0%
Colour 6.0%
Sea 6.0%
Moon 4.0%
Red 4.0%
2.0% Aeroplanes, Aids, Azure, Baby, Calm, Chelsea, Electric, Heaven, Light, Navy, Nose, Paint, Sunshine, Tangled-Up-In, Velvet, Yellow

Blueprint
Plan 22.9%
* 10.4%
Paper 8.3%
Copy 6.3%
Architect 4.2%
Map 4.2%
Original 4.2%
2.1% Acre, Architecture, Blue-Peter, Book, Building, Copyright, Data, Design, Document, Draft, Film, Fingerprint, Letter, Magazine, Penis, Signature, Silver-Print, Snort, Template

Blunder+
Mistake 60.4%
Buss 6.2%
Error 4.2%
Fault 4.2%
Trip 4.2%
2.1% Blame, Bust, Door, Err, Fall, Lighthouse, Lost, Oops, Police, Slip

Blunt+
Instrument 25.6%
Knife 23.3%
Sharp 22.2%
Edge 5.6%
Pencil 3.3%
Dull 2.2%
Frank 2.2%
Weapon 2.2%
1.1% Force, Hard, Harsh, Metal, Object, Point, Rude, Sarcastic, Scissors, Spy, Start, Straight

Blush+
Red 35.4%
Cheek(s) 12.5%
Embarrass 8.3%
Pink 6.2%
2.1% Blue, Bride, Embarrassed, Enjoy, Fade, Fear, Hair, Love, Maid, Make-Up, Pluck, Redden, Roots, Rouge, Scarlet, Shame, Shy, Spare

Board
Black- 23.1%
Wood 7.7%
Blackboard 5.7%
Bread 5.7%
Game 5.7%
* 3.8%
Flat 3.8%
Iron 3.8%
Walk 3.8%
1.9% Bed, Chalk, Chess, Director, Fed-Up, Get-On, Hard, Head, Ironing, Lodging, Meeting, Nothing, Notice, Peg, Room, Rubber, Shelf, Ship, Wall

Boast+
Brag 27.2%
* 7.6%
Proud 4.3%
Arrogant 3.3%
Ego 3.3%
Pride 3.3%
-Ful 2.2%
Lie 2.2%
Loud 2.2%
Show-Off 2.2%
1.1% Age, Annoying, Arrogance, Ask, Better, Big, Bighead, Claim, Crow, Dad, False, Full, Glee, Glory, Hollow, House, Humble, Impress, Lift, Man, Manager, Men, Nigel, Obnoxious, Pig, Prat, Proclaim, Raise, Rich, Say, Shout, Showy, Spirit, Talk, Tell, Town, Twit, Vaunt, Wanton

Boat+
Ship 22.9%
Sail 14.6%
Water 12.5%
House 10.4%
Sea 8.3%
Yacht 4.2%
2.1% Boatie, Craft, Dock, Float, Island, Keel, Lake, People, Quay, River, Sink, Tide, Yard

Body
* 17.6%
Soul 17.6%
Shop 4.4%
Beautiful 3.3%
Legs 3.3%
Count 2.2%
Dead 2.2%
Guard 2.2%
Heat 2.2%
Skin 2.2%
Stocking 2.2%
Stomach 2.2%
1.1% Anatomy, Arm, Armour, Builder, Clothes, Conscious, Control, Corpse, Curves, Exercise, Figure, Fit, Fitness, Flesh, Fluid, Gorgeous, Grave, Group, Hunt, Image, Language, Lotion, Mass, Mind, Motion, Naked, Nap, Odour, Parts, Sex, Shape, Suit, Trunk, Woman, Women

Bog+
Peat 14.6%
Cat 8.3%
Marsh 8.3%
Toilet 6.2%
Water 6.2%
Off 4.2%
2.1% Bark, Bodmin, Damp, Dip, Dog, Down, Fen, Ireland, Irish, Mire, Moor, Mud, People, Person, Pete, Pool, Quagmire, Sewage, Shed, Slime, Smell, Stuck, Swamp, Sword, Weave

Boil+
Water 10.4%
Cook 6.2%
* 4.2%
Bubble 4.2%
Kettle 4.2%
Law 4.2%
Simmer 4.2%
Soup 4.2%
2.1% Anger, Bat, Blind, Blister, Blood, Broth, Bruise, Bump, Burn, Burst, Centigrade, Doctor, Dry, Egg, Head, Heat, Hot, Lance, Milk, Oil, Over, Pan, Pinch, Pot, Rabbit, Skin, Sore, Spot

Bomb
Blast 28.6%
Explosion 14.3%
Shell 7.1%
Explode 4.8%
Nuclear 4.8%
Time 4.8%
War 4.8%
2.4% Atom, Atomic, Black, Bounce, Death, Fire, Flash, Hit, Job, London, Scare, Shelter, Terrorist

Bond+
James 12.2%
Premium 6.7%
Link 5.6%
Love 4.4%
Tie 4.4%

* 3.3%
Friendship 3.3%
Glue 3.3%
Marriage 3.3%
Attachment 2.2%
Bind 2.2%
Brooke 2.2%
Hold 2.2%
Money 2.2%
1.1% Bail, Band, Basildon, Bear, Binding, Chain, Chemistry, Covalent, Deal, Deposit, Emotional, Father, Friend, Friendly, Happy, Income, Life, Male, Man, Nice, Oath, Obligation, Of, Parent, Promise, Spy, Stick, Strain, Strength, Strong, Stuck, Tea, Tied, Tight, Together, Unite, Walk, Word

Bone+
Marrow 18.8%
Dog 10.4%
Dry 8.3%
Leg 6.3%
Skeleton 6.3%
Knee 4.2%
Skin 4.2%
2.1% *, Age, Archaeology, Back, Calcium, Cancer, China, Dead, Disease, Hard, Idle, Meal, People, Splint, Tiding, Twinge, White, Wish, Yard

Bonnet+
Hat 29.2%
Car 22.9%
Easter 6.2%
Hood 6.2%
Baby 4.2%
Boot 4.2%
2.1% Best, Blue, Bow, Cap, Cape, Graham, Hair, Lace, Lady, Singer, Straw, Strings, Summer

Bony+
Thin 18.8%
Fish 14.6%
Skinny 14.6%
Skeleton 10.4%
* 4.2%
Napoleon 4.2%
2.1% Elbow, Fine, Fingers, Hand, Hard, Knee, Lax, Leg, M, Marrow, Nobbly, Part, Sharp, Slim, Thigh, Tough

Boo+
* 41.3%
Hiss 10.9%
Ghost 8.7%
Baby 4.3%
Betty 4.3%
Fright 4.3%
2.2% Boot, Hi, Hoo, Mistake, Phone, Photograph, Shock, Shoo, Surprise, Telephone, Yah

Book+
Read 22.9%
Bible 8.3%
Page 8.3%
Library 6.2%
Shelf 6.2%
Words 6.2%
Worm 6.2%
Learn 4.2%
Mark 4.2%
Novel 4.2%
2.1% Bought, Burn, Cow, Escape, Info, Open, Review, Story, Title, Token, Writing

Boomerang+
Return 19.0%
Australia 16.7%
Back 14.3%
Throw 7.1%
Kangaroo 4.8%
Stick 4.8%
Aborigine 3.6%
Australian 3.6%
Aussie 2.4%
Retrieve 2.4%
Turn 2.4%
1.2% *, Aboriginal, Again, Before, Come-Back, Gun, Henry, Outback, Person, Returns, Round, Thing, Under, Weapon

Boot
Shoe 30.0%
Car 10.0%
Black 8.0%
Boy 6.0%
Foot 6.0%
Sale 6.0%
Big 4.0%
Kick 4.0%
Lace(s) 4.0%
Leg 4.0%
2.0% ?, Car-Boot, Dr-Marten, Mud, Polish, Soccer, String, Tack, Wellington

Bootleg
Tape 25.0%
Whisky 16.7%
Record(s) 8.3%
* 6.3%
Illegal 6.3%
Album 4.2%
Gin 4.2%
Pirate 4.2%
2.1% Bob-Dylan, Boots, Catalyst, Copy, Deal, Fake, Feather, Illicit, Moonshine, Old-Man, Rum, Smuggler

Boredom
* 7.1%
Dull 7.1%
Dullness 4.8%
Tired 4.8%
Yawn 4.8%
2.4% Blank, Boredom, Bread, Chair, Crime, Dark, Depressed, Dilapidated, Dole, Dreary, Empty, Ennui, Factor, Freedom, Home, Interest, Lack-Lustre, Mindless, School, Slow, Snooze, Stare, Stimulation, Studying, Tedious, Tedium, This, Time, TV, Work

Boris
Becker 34.7%
Karloff 20.8%
Yeltsin 20.4%
* 6.1%
2.0% Beekoff, Bold, Dead, Godunov, Man, Newton, Pasternak, Spy, Tennis

Born
Baby 21.2%
Died 9.6%
Free 9.6%
Birth 7.7%
Life 7.7%
Again 5.7%
* 3.8%
Child 3.8%
Live 3.8%
Nee 3.8%
1.9% Alive, Blood, Bred, Conceived, Die, Late, Me, Mother, Star, Water, Wild, Young

Boss
Manager 22.0%
Man 14.6%
Work 12.2%
* 7.3%
Head 7.3%
Employer 4.9%
2.4% Ashtray, Authority, Chief, Colleague, Decisions, Dominate, Fat, Jerk, Nova, Old, Patron, Suit, Superior, Top

Both
Two 38.0%
Together 18.0%
Each 6.0%
Neither 4.0%
Of 4.0%
2.0% Couple, Duo, Each, Ears, Men, One, Pair, People, Sex, Sides, Times, Too, Twins, Us, Ways

Bother
Trouble 17.1%
Hassle 12.2%
Annoy 9.8%
* 7.3%
Fuss 7.3%
Sister 4.9%
Try 4.9%
2.4% Boots, Botheration, Brother, Drat, Family, Harass, Hot, Irritation, Lot, Pain, Ruddy, Shrug, Sister, With, Worry

Bottom
Top 40.0%
* 6.7%
Line 6.7%
Deep 4.4%
Head 4.4%
Up 4.4%
2.2% Bum, Cheeks, Drop, End, Floor, Her, Pit, Rock, Sex, Sink, Step, Trousers, Under, Underwear, Well

Bough
Tree 53.7%
Branch 19.5%
* 14.6%
Break 4.9%
2.4% Council, Dough, Stem, Trunk

Boulder
Rock 35.7%
Stone 19.0%
Colorado 7.2%
* 4.8%
Building 4.8%
Mountain 4.8%
2.4% Block, Building-Site, California, Climbing, Dash, Grey, Heavy, Hill, Over, Store

Bounce+
Ball 44.7%
Castle 10.6%
Back 6.4%
Dog 4.3%
2.1% *, Baby, Cheque, Clean, Dryer, Free-Play, Happy, High, Jump, Jumper, Over, Spring, Tigger, Trampoline, Washing

Bowl
Fruit 11.9%
Fish 9.5%
Cereal 7.1%
Soup 7.1%
Spoon 7.1%
Cricket 4.8%
Cup 4.8%
Sugar 4.8%
2.4% Baker, Ball, Breakfast, Cherries, Cornflakes, Custard, Dog, Doggy, Muesli, Noodles, Of-Fruit, Over, Plate, Porridge, Rice, Round, Wood, Yoghurt

Bowler+
Hat 81.3%
Cricket 6.3%
* 6.3%
2.1% Batsman, Snow, Steel

Box
* 8.9%
(Of)-Tricks 6.7%
Lid 6.7%
Chocolate(s) 4.4%
Hat 4.4%
Toys 4.4%
2.2% Bag, Brownie, Browning, Car, Cardboard, Carry, Carton, Close, Closed, Compact, Contents, Cube, Fight, Full, In, Inside, Jack, Jewellery, Letter, Match, Nails, Pandora, Plant, Shaker, Square, Suit, Sweets, Tin, Top

Boy
Girl 73.8%
Son 7.1%
Friend 4.8%
Shorts 4.8%
2.4% Child, Cub, Man, Wonder

Boyfriend
Girlfriend 42.0%
Girl 6.0%
Lover 6.0%
Man 6.0%
* 4.0%
Fiance 4.0%
Partner 4.0%
2.0% Beau, Cherry, Dark, Dawn, Drag, Freckle, Friend, Kiss, Lisa, Love, Pain, Relationship, Sex, Who

Branch
Tree 61.9%
Bank 16.7%
2.4% Break, Crossroads, Leaf, Link, Loop, Olive, Root, Twig, Wood

Brave
Indian 14.6%
Man 12.5%
Strong 10.4%
Boy 6.3%
Valiant 6.3%
* 6.2%
Coward 4.2%
2.1% Bizarre, Bold, Bravado, Courage, Courageous, Effort, Fearless, Few, Fit, Gallant, Good, Hard, Hero, Lion, New, Timid, Warrior, Way, World

Brawl
Fight 52.1%
* 8.3%
Catch 6.3%
Bat 4.2%
2.1% Bar, Beat, Brag, Clobber, Court, Eye, Football, Fruit, Game, Noise, Racket, Tavern, Trick, Tussle

Bread
Butter 45.8%
Board 8.3%
Water 8.3%
Knife 4.2%
Milk 4.2%
Roll 4.2%
2.1% *, Bin, Brown, Butler, Circuses, Food, Head, Hole, Loaf, No, Sandwich, Yeast

Break
Snap 23.1%
Kit-Kat 7.7%
Mend 7.7%
Crack 5.7%
Fast 5.7%
* 3.8%
Crash 3.8%
Damage 3.8%
Down 3.8%
Glass 3.8%
1.9% Broke, Broken, Coffee, Heart, Hurt, In, Neck, Open, Out, Relax, Shatter, Short, Smash, Stop, Time, Wind

Breathalyser
Drink 22.9%
Police 20.8%
Alcohol 16.7%
Drunk 12.5%
Test 4.2%
2.1% Analyse, Asthma, Beer, Blow, Breath, Car, Chemical, Stink

Breathe
Air 40.4%
* 6.4%
Chest 6.4%
Lung(s) 6.4%
Respire 4.3%
2.1% Alive, Breast, Deep, Deeply, Easy, Fast, Fresh, Hard, In, Inhale, Last, Mist, Nose, Out, Oxygen, Relax

Breed
Dog(s) 21.3%
Rabbit(s) 12.8%
Animal(s) 8.5%
* 6.4%
Children 6.4%
Multiply 4.3%
Type 4.3%
2.1% Ape, Bees, Cats, Ducks, Growth, Half, Horses, Kid, People, Pig, Pups, Rare, Sex, Snakes, Sort, Straw, Well

Breeze
Wind 50.0%
Cool 4.2%
Draught 4.2%
2.1% *, Air, Andrew, Blocks, Blow, Breath, Chill, Daffodil, Fair, Flutter, Fresh, Hive, Light, Rain, Sea, Storm, Summer, Trees, Window, Zephyr

Brew
Tea 36.0%
Beer 18.0%
Up 6.0%
Boil 4.0%
Drink 4.0%
Make 4.0%
2.0% *, Boddingtons, Coffee, Crater, Hops, It, Kit, Malt, Mix, Quick, Special, Stewed, Witch, Yeast

Bride+
Groom 66.7%
Wedding 10.4%
Husband 4.2%
2.1% Hope, White, Church, God, Wife, Broad, Frankenstein, Wealth, Marriage

Bridge
River 31.3%
Water 14.6%
Sighs 10.4%
Cards 4.2%
Cross 4.2%
Over 4.2%
2.1% *, Far, Game, Join, Kwai, Match, River-Kwai, Sigh, Street, Swollen, Toll, Troubled, Troubles, View, Waters

Brief
Short 40.0%
Case 11.1%
Quick 8.9%
Encounter 4.4%
Small 4.4%
2.2% *, Affair, Clipped, Description, Essay, Event, Lesson, Letter, Long, Pelican, Solicitor, Story, Trousers, Underpants

Briefcase
Paper(s) 12.0%
Black 10.0%
Leather 6.0%
Office 6.0%
Work 6.0%
Brown 4.0%
Business 4.0%
Suitcase 4.0%
2.0% Attache, Bank, Bowler, Briefcase, Businessman, Case, Designer, Document, Full, Glasses, Hard, Large-Case, Lock, Money, Office-Worker, Official, Plastic, Sandwiches, Satchel, Suit, Travel, Umbrella, Underwear, Valise

Bright
Light 21.5%
Sun 11.1%
* 4.4%
Breezy 4.4%
Dark 4.4%
Shiny 4.4%
Day(s) 3.7%
Sunny 3.7%
Colour(s) 3.0%
Dull 3.0%
Beautiful 2.2%
Cheerful 2.2%
Eyes 2.2%
Bulb 1.5%
Early 1.5%
Happy 1.5%
Intelligent 1.5%
Sky 1.5%
Spark 1.5%
Star 1.5%
Yellow 1.5%
0.7% Articulate, Blue, Boy, Button, Cloudy, Dim, Eyed, Future, Jewel, Jolly, Jovial, Jumper, Lamp, Like, Lively, Lovely, Ray, Ring, Sharp, Shining, Stare, Tiger, Warm, Young

Brigitte
Bardot 49.0%
Nielson 30.6%
* 10.4%
2.0% Fonda, Mum, Roll, Save, Witch

Brisk
Walk 29.2%
Fast 25.0%
Quick 20.8%
Speedy 4.2%
Swift 4.2%
2.1% Abrupt, Bracing, Breeze, Down, Rapid, Sharp, Smart, Stroll

Brittle
Bone(s) 18.8%
Break 14.6%
Snap 12.5%
Fragile 8.4%
Peanut 6.3%
Glass 4.2%
Ice 4.2%

Toffee 4.2%
2.1% *, Brush, Delicate, Fit, Frail, Hair, Hard, Iron, Little, Metal, Stone, Tiny, Weak

Broad+
Bean(s) 25.0%
Wide 14.6%
Sword 8.3%
* 4.2%
Long 4.2%
Minded 4.2%
Shoulders 4.2%
Side 4.2%
2.1% Acre, Belt, Bent, Big, Cater, Daylight, Dim, Girl, Knife, Lady, Narrow, River, Sheet, Street, Woman

Broadcast
News 36.5%
Radio 9.6%
Television 7.7%
TV 7.7%
* 3.8%
Emit 3.8%
Sound 3.8%
1.9% BBC, Bring, Ell, House, Issue, Microphone, Old, Programme, Public, Reporter, See, Seed, Sheet, Video

Bronze+
Statue 16.7%
Age 12.5%
Gold 10.4%
Medal 10.4%
Silver 10.4%
Adonis 4.2%
Tan 4.2%
2.1% *, Brass, Find, Gleam, Iron, Medallion, Metal, Money, Ring, Shine, Steel, Sun, Suntan, Weapon, Yellow

Broom+
Handle 29.2%
Sweep 20.8%
Brush 8.3%
Cupboard 6.2%
Stick 6.2%
Witch 6.2%
Fish 4.2%
Flower 4.2%
2.1% Air, Alfred, Bang, Colour, Sonic, Town, Wilt

Broth+
Soup 62.5%
* 12.5%
Cook 4.2%
2.1% Bach, Brew, Gruel, Hot, Note, Rough, Scotch, Stew, Wait, Water

Brother+
Sister 77.1%
2.1% Apple, Argue, Big, Brown, Enemy, Friend, In-Law, Mother, Nick, Small, Son

Brown
White 16.3%
Black 8.2%
Colour 8.2%
Bottle 6.1%
Eyes 6.1%
Sugar 6.1%
* 4.1%
Bear 4.1%
Mud 4.1%
2.0% Beer, Blue, Bobby, Bread, Coat, Comfort, Dog, Drab, Dull, Green, Hair, Light, Pant, Porridge, Shit, Tan, Tree, Trousers

Brunch
Lunch 33.3%
Food 20.8%
Breakfast 8.3%
* 4.2%
2.1% American, Beans, Bourgeoisie, California, Coffee, Early-Lunch, Eat, Elevenses, Macdonalds, No, Pancakes, Punch, Sunday, Wimpy, Yoghurt

Brush
Hair 20.0%
Paint 15.6%
Stroke(s) 8.9%
Tooth 8.9%
Comb 6.7%
Off 4.4%
Teeth 4.4%
Up 4.4%
2.2% *, Aside, Bore, Bristle, Cart, Clean, Dirt, Dustpan, Floor, Scrub, Soft, Sweep

Bubble+
Burst 35.4%
Bath 16.7%
Soap 10.4%
Boy 8.3%
Boil 4.2%
Break 4.2%
2.1% Balloon, Blow, Blue, Broth, Car, Froth, Pop, Sea, Squeak, Toil

Bud
Flower 28.6%
Tree 16.3%
Rose 10.2%
Holly 8.2%
Leaf 8.2%
Weiser 4.1%
2.0% Acorn, Beer, Berry, Billy, Blossom, Darling, Guy, Name, Near, Nip, Sea, Sticky

Bug
Bear 12.0%
Beetle 12.0%
Bug 12.0%
Insect 10.0%
Annoy 6.0%
Bee 6.0%
* 4.0%
Ant 4.0%
2.0% ?, Black, Carpet, Eavesdrop, Flea, Jam, Lady, Microphone, Pest, Room, Small, Snug, Spider, Tail, Wall, Wasp

Build
Brick(s) 29.8%
House 23.4%
Construct 8.5%
Up 6.4%
Destroy 4.3%
2.1% Blocks, Building, Create, Demolish, Make, Shanty, Site, Size, Storey, Strong, Tall, Wall, Work

Building
Site 16.3%
Brick 14.3%
House 14.3%
* 8.2%
Blocks 8.2%
Architect 4.1%
Big 4.1%
2.0% Conditions, Edifice, Grey, Hat, High, Opaque, Shop, Society, Stone, Tower, Wall, White, Window, Worker

Bull+
Cow 29.2%
Fight 8.3%
Horn(s) 6.3%
Horse 4.2%
Round 4.2%
Shit 4.2%
2.1% *, Bat, Bear, Blood, Boar, Cage, Cattle, Field, Folly, Game, Headed, Idiot, Male, Mislead, Raging, Red, Soup, Stupid, Table, Tain, Taurus

Bullet+
Gun 71.4%
Weapon(s) 7.2%
Fire 4.8%
2.4% Fish, Golden, Missile, Proof, Silver, Tent, Wound

Bulletin+
News 59.5%
Board 16.7%
Newspaper 7.1%
2.4% Agenda, File, Journal, Magazine, Notice, Paper, Proof

Bully+
Boy 33.3%
Beef 6.2%
* 4.2%
Big 4.2%
Bother 4.2%
Hurt 4.2%
School 4.2%
Tease 4.2%
2.1% Beat, Burn, Can, Cheat, Creature, Dominate, Fight, For, Girl, Goat, Hard, Off, People, Pick, Provoke, Rival, Twit

Bump+
Head 12.5%
Hit 10.4%
Car(s) 8.3%
Fall 8.3%
Boat 4.2%
Crash 4.2%
Knock 4.2%
Lump 4.2%
Road 4.2%
Start 4.2%
2.1% Bang, Boil, Bruise, Bust, Hump, Hurt, Knob, Mound, Mr, Off, Over, Ride, Rowing, Run, Shove, Sore

Bun+
Oven 27.1%
Cake 14.6%
Currant 12.5%
Fight 8.3%
Bread 6.2%
Cream 6.2%
Sticky 6.2%
Hair 4.2%
2.1% Apple, Baker, Beefburger, Chelsea, Food, Fun, Plum

Bunch+
Flower(s) 35.4%
Grapes 25.0%
Group 6.2%
Hair 4.2%
2.1% *, Bluebells, Brady, Fools, Gather, Honey, Houses, Keys, Lot, Lots, Of-Grapes, People, Pick, Together

Buoyant+
Float(s) 34.8%
Floating 13.0%
Happy 10.9%
Water 8.7%
Afloat 6.5%
Sea 6.5%
* 4.3%
Buoy 4.3%
2.2% Bubble, Bubbly, Light, Ship, Uplifted

Burn
Fire 23.4%
Scald 6.4%

Up 6.4%
Wood 6.4%
Flame 4.3%
Hell 4.3%
Hurt 4.3%
Match 4.3%
2.1% Arson, Books, Bridge, Degree, Fever, Fingers, Ground, Hand, Heart, Heat, Hospital, Napalm, Oil, Out, Pain, Paper, Skin, Sum, Toast

Burst
Balloon 22.9%
Open 8.3%
Explode 6.3%
Out 6.3%
* 4.2%
Bubble 4.2%
Over 4.2%
Overflow 4.2%
Sun 4.2%
2.1% Applause, At, Bag, Bang, Big, Blow, Break, Cloud, Dam, Full, Laughter, Path, Pop, Spot, Stomach, Wet, Wide

Bus
Red 20.4%
Stop 20.4%
Coach 6.1%
Car 4.1%
Driver 4.1%
London 4.1%
Seventy-Three 4.1%
Timetable 4.1%
Train 4.1%
2.0% *, ?, Adventure, Cavern, Conductor, Double-Decker, Lane, No.Ten, Pan, Ride, Route, Taxi, Time

Bush+
Tree 45.8%
Shrub 6.2%
Australia 4.2%
Desert 4.2%
Green 4.2%
Hedge 4.2%
Man 4.2%
Plant 4.2%
2.1% *, Baby, Black, Fallow, Fire, George, Leaf, Moses, Rose, Thick, Weed

Business
Man 10.6%
Money 8.5%
Suit 8.5%
Deal 6.4%
Meeting 6.4%
Pleasure 6.4%
Busy 4.3%
Finance(s) 4.3%
Job 4.3%
Profit 4.3%
Work 4.3%
2.1% *, Associate, Card, Diploma, Duty, Like, Manager, Papers, Park, Partner, Place, Report, Studies, Study, Venture

But
* 15.4%
If 9.6%
Not 7.7%
For 5.7%
However 5.7%
Or 5.7%
And 3.8%
No 3.8%
1.9% Abut, Although, Arse, Bottom, Cigarette, Do, End, Hesitate, Hit, Maybe, Only, Out, Ram, Since, So, Sometime, Stammer, Stop, Then, Thought, What, While

Butcher+
Meat 41.7%
Baker 22.9%
Kill 8.3%
2.1% Blood, Carve, Cuts, Evil, Family, Fight, Gore, Hook, Knife, Painting, Pig, Pork, Slaughter

Butterfly
Wing(s) 14.0%
Moth 10.0%
Caterpillar 6.0%
Colour 6.0%
Fly 6.0%
Egg 4.0%
Flower(s) 4.0%
Net 4.0%
2.0% *, Animal, Colourful, Country, Crayon, Delicate, Fight, Garden, Grub, Insect, Larvae, Leaf, Life, Pink, Plant, Pretty, Red, Red-Admiral, Snake, Sun, The-Times, Wasp, Yellow

Buttermilk
Cow 12.5%
* 10.4%
Cream 8.3%
Yellow 8.3%
Cheese 6.3%
Drink 6.3%
Sweet 6.3%
Butter 4.2%
Fat 4.2%
Honey 4.2%
Milk 4.2%
2.1% Bucket, Churn, Creamy, Frost, Looking, Rich, Sick, Sour, Water, Watery, Yoghurt, Yuck

Button+
Hole 31.0%
Sew 9.5%
Thread 9.5%
Coat 4.8%
Hook 4.8%
Press 4.8%
Sewing 4.8%
2.4% *, Belle, Dress, Fasten, Jumper, Keyboard, Penny, Pin, Quick, Shirt, Stud, Up, Zip

Buy
Sell 23.4%
Spend 21.3%
Clothes 10.6%
Money 8.5%
Shop 6.4%
Present 4.3%
Purchase 4.3%
2.1% Acquire, Book, Bought, Buy, Food, House, It, Own, Parcel, Steal, Want

By
* 16.6%
Night 6.3%
Bye 4.2%
Near 4.2%
Then 4.2%
Way 4.2%
2.1% About, And, Book, Buy, By, Bye-Bye, Go, Gone, Good, His, Large, Leave, Leg, Line, Means, Next, Next-To, Now, River, Side, Stand, Stander, Them, The-By, Tile-By, Time, What, While, Word

Cabbage+
Patch 35.7%
Vegetable 11.9%
Lettuce 7.1%
Carrot 4.8%
Cauliflower 4.8%
Plant 4.8%
2.4% Bacon, Banana, Brassica, Chinese, Dinner, Garden, Greens, Sex, Smell, Soup, Water, White, You

Cabin+
Ship 17.9%
Crew 10.7%
Cruiser 10.7%
Log 10.7%
Boat 7.1%
Hut 6.0%
Boy 4.8%
Berth 2.4%
Block 2.4%
Bunk 2.4%
Hole 2.4%
House 2.4%
Room 2.4%
Yacht 2.4%
1.2% Aeroplane, Barge, Bed, Box, Deck, Ferry, Fisherman, Hutch, Navel, Shaft, Train, Trunk, Window, Wood

Cable+
Car 43.8%
Wire 18.8%
Wireless 10.4%
TV 6.2%
Telephone 4.2%
Television 4.2%
2.1% Lift, Network, Snap, Snow, Telecommunications, Undersea

Cafe
Coffee 39.0%
Restaurant 14.6%
Tea 9.8%
Bar 4.9%
Drink 4.9%
France 4.9%
2.4% Bistro, Crib, Dome, Music, Noir, Paris, Pinocchio, Station, Tables, Windows

Cage+
Bird 39.6%
Animal 10.4%
Lion 8.3%
Captive 6.3%
Trap 4.2%
Zoo 4.2%
2.1% Bars, Beast, Fire, Hope, Man, Miner, Monkey, Parrot, Pet, Prison, Stop, Tight, Wire

Cake
Bake 13.3%
Icing 13.3%
Eat 11.1%
Sweet 6.7%
Tea 6.7%
Birthday 4.4%
2.2% *, Biscuit, Coffee, Cooking, Crumbs, Cup, Current, Decoration, Eat, Fruit, Hole, Ice, Jam, Marie-Antoinette, Mix, Nice, Plate, Slice, Spoon, Table

Calculate+
Sum 13.3%
Add 11.9%
Number 11.9%
Maths 9.5%
Calculator 4.8%
Compute 4.8%
Figure 4.8%
2.4% *, Arithmetic, Ask, Assess, Cost, Count, Determine, Estimate, Machine, Multiply, One, Stop, Texas, Think, Work

Calf+
Cow 60.4%
Sleeve 8.3%
Leg 6.2%
Lamb 4.2%
Link 4.2%
2.1% Birth, Collar, Dinner, Heel, Length, Muscle, Thigh, Young

Call
Tele/Phone 32.6%
Out 10.9%
Shout 8.7%
Girl 4.3%
Yell 4.3%
2.2% Beckon, Doctor, Friend, Ghost, Hear, Help, Him, Holler, Loud, Mother, Name, Now, Ring, Scare, Sign, Sneer, Speak, Up

Calm
Water(s) 13.3%
Down 11.1%
Sea 11.1%
Stormy 6.7%
Peaceful 4.4%
Placid 4.4%
Quiet 4.4%
Weather 4.4%
2.2% Anxious, Bay, Cool, Day, Holy, Mellow, Ocean, Panic, Passive, Person, Relaxed, Ruffled, Serene, Soft, Steady, Warm, Wind, Worried

Calmness
Sea 11.9%
Tranquility 11.9%
* 9.5%
Peace 7.1%
Quiet 7.1%
Serene 7.1%
Serenity 4.8%
2.4% Beach, Bland, Blue, Calm, Cloud, Cool, Cross, Fatigue, Meditation, Passive, Placid, Placidity, Pleasant, Security, Soothe, Soothing, Together

Calorie+
Diet 22.9%
Food 14.6%
Fat 10.4%
Count 8.3%
Eat 6.2%
Joule 6.2%
Control 4.2%
Counter 4.2%
Weight 4.2%
2.1% Controlled, Counting, Energy, Fattening, Fuel, Intake, Newspaper, Scale, Watch

Camel+
Hump 37.5%
Desert 18.8%
Hair 10.4%
Cigarette(s) 8.4%
Back 6.2%
Dromedary 4.2%
2.1% Bump, Giraffe, Model, Ride, Sahara, Smell, Water

Camera+
Film 24.3%
Photo(s) 19.5%
Picture 9.8%
Flash 4.9%
Lens 4.9%
Photograph 4.9%
Shot 4.9%
Shutter 4.9%
2.4% Angle, Bag, Camera, Excellent, Holiday, Landscape, Light, Ray, Snap

Canal+
Barge 25.0%
Boat(s) 18.8%
River 8.3%
Bridge 4.2%
Ditch 4.2%
Panama 4.2%
Water 4.2%
2.1% *, Cutting, Grand, Holiday, Lock, Mars, Nile, Soft, Straight, Stream, Trip, Tunnel, Union, Venice, Wide

Cancel+
* 14.3%
End 9.5%
Postpone 7.1%
Stop 7.1%
Train(s) 7.1%
Off 4.8%
2.4% Annul, Bank, Blow, Cancer, Chance, Correct, Cross, Flat, Forget, Go, Knock, Lace, Local, Match, Negate, Put, Quit, Resign, Shot, Strike, Strike-Off

Cancer+
Death 29.2%
Lung 10.4%
Die 8.3%
Crab(s) 6.3%
* 4.2%
Research 4.2%
2.1% Breast, Capricorn, Cell, Cure, Dog, Growth, Illness, Kitten, Lungs, Mrc, Pancreas, Radiation, Scorpio, Statistic, Stomach, Throat, Victim, Worry

Candid
Camera 50.0%
Frank 6.0%
Honest 6.0%
Open 6.0%
Truthful 6.0%
2.0% Albicans, Candy, Date, Did, History, Orange, Peel, Pose, Revealing, Shy, Sordid, Student, Truth

Candle+
Light 26.8%
Wick 19.5%
Flame 12.1%
Wax 12.1%
Stick 4.9%
2.4% *, Dinner, Eliza, Fire, Flux, Hold, Kitchen, Lit, Match, Romantic

Cane+
Sugar 18.8%
Abel 16.7%
Whip 16.7%
Hit 12.5%
Stick 8.3%
2.1% Bamboo, Bean, Beat, Chair, Gang, Hard, Island, Lashes, Punish, School, Teach, Wicker, Wood

Canine+
Dog 66.7%
Feline 4.8%
Friend 4.8%
Tooth 4.8%
2.4% Asinine, Bitch, Canis, Distemper, Doglike, Knone, Teeth, Wolf

Canvas+
Tent 21.4%
Paint 16.7%
Painting 16.7%
Bag 4.8%

Election 4.8%
Painter 4.8%
2.4% *, Art, Batik, Bed, Frame, Full, Harrass, Party, Picture, Representative, Sail, Vote

Canyon
Grand 58.1%
Deep 11.6%
America 4.7%
Drop 4.7%
2.3% Alton-Towers, Cave, Geography, Great, Gully, Hall, River, Valley, Yellow

Cap+
Hat 45.6%
Top 5.6%
Fit 4.4%
Head 4.4%
Cloth 3.3%
Fits 3.3%
Contraceptive 2.2%
Hand 2.2%
1.1% *, Andy, Block, Cat, Cuticle, Diaphragm, Dutch, England, Feather, Flat, Guard, Gun, Headwear, In-Hand, Jock, Mat, Peak, Peaked, Pigeon, Play, School, Schoolboy, Stick, Uniform, Wear

Capability
Ability 18.6%
Able 18.6%
Brown 9.3%
* 4.7%
Capacity 4.7%
Do 4.7%
Good 4.7%
Skill 4.7%
2.3% Aim, Can, Competence, Dull, Ease, Expert, Extent, Great, Over, Performance, Succeed, Success

Cape+
Cloak 20.8%
Crusader 12.5%
Coat 6.2%
Hood 6.2%
Hope 6.2%
Batman 4.2%
Gown 4.2%
2.1% *, Bay, Clothing, Cod, Dark, Hone, Horn, Intruder, Manage, Mask, Mountain, Poncho, Rain, Riding, Robe, Shawl, Stalker, String, Superman

Capsize+
Sink 31.0%
Boat 21.4%
Overturn 21.4%
Ship 4.8%
Drowning 2.4%
Over 2.4%
Spill 2.4%
Storm 2.4%
Submerge 2.4%
Turn 2.4%
Turnover 2.4%
Water 2.4%
1.1% Canoe

Captain+
Ship 69.0%
Leader 4.8%
2.4% Boat, Captive, Chief, Field, General, Industry, Mate, Officer, Pilot, Pugwash, Skipper

Caption+
Cartoon 14.3%
Heading 11.9%
Word(s) 7.1%
Advert 4.8%
Newspaper 4.8%
Phrase 4.8%
Title 4.8%
2.4% *, Advertisement, Comic, Escape, Idea, Meaning, Motive, Notice, Photo, Piece, Point, Print, Say, Saying, Sentence, Sheet, Slogan, Story, Strip, Text

Captive+
Prisoner 34.5%
Hostage 9.5%
Held 7.1%
* 6.0%
Audience 6.0%
Cage 4.8%
Escape 2.4%
Kidnap 2.4%
Prison 2.4%
Slave 2.4%
1.2% Army, Bars, Caged, Captain, Captor, Caught, Imprison, In-Jail, Israel, Jailed, Member, Native, Romans, Rope, Tied, Victim, War, Warder, Whole

Car+
Drive 9.5%
Van 6.0%
Bike 4.8%
Crash 4.8%
Motor 4.8%
Vehicle 4.8%
Wheel(s) 4.8%
* 3.6%
Bicycle 2.4%
Drive 2.4%
Engine 2.4%
Fumes 2.4%
Pollution 2.4%
Road 2.4%
Truck 2.4%
Wash 2.4%
1.2% Aerial, Aston-Martin, Audi, Autobahn, Automobile, Bomb, Boot, Bus, Carriage, Crash, Escort, Fast, Fiat, Go, Good, Insurance, Key, Leather, Maintenance, Mercedes, Mobility, More, Noise, Petrol, Peugeot, Porsche, Red, Ride, Start, Steering, Transport, Travel, Tyres

Card+
Birthday 12.5%
Sharp 10.4%
Game 6.2%
Joker 6.2%
Pack 6.2%
Trick 6.2%
Christmas 4.2%
Paper 4.2%
Playing 4.2%
Table 4.2%
Visiting 4.2%
2.1% Bridge, Call, Calling, Criminal, Deal, File, Flat, Games, Hole, Jack, Play, Post, Send, Sender, Show

Cardboard+
Box 38.1%
Paper 16.7%
City 11.9%
Cut-Out 11.9%
House 4.8%
2.4% *, Deprivation, Notice, Pen, Poster, Tearing, Waterloo

Caretaker
Janitor 19.5%
* 12.2%
School 9.8%
Building 4.9%
Man 4.9%
Old-Man 4.9%
Pinter 4.9%
2.4% Broom, Cleaner, Creaky, Dungarees, Garden, Grey, Grey-Coat, Guard, Jobsworth, Keys, Mr-Foot-(Michael), Old, Pensioner, Porter, Security, Temporary, Undertaker

Cargo
Ship(s) 46.0%
Boat 10.0%
Hold 6.0%
Banana(s) 4.0%
Freight 4.0%
Plane 4.0%
2.0% ?, Barge, Carrier, Carry, Container, Customs, Deck, Heavy, Load, Luggage, Ocean-Liner, Packet, Shipment

Carl
* 27.3%
Lewis 16.3%
Perkins 6.1%
Jackson 4.1%
Jung 4.1%
Marx 4.1%
2.0% Bridgewater, Brown, Carvalho, Clayton, Cooper, Doris, German, Kosser, Lagerfield, Name, Naughty, Newton, Papenfus, Parsons, Rogers, Sagan, Watson, Will, Young

Carnation+
Flower 54.8%
Rose 14.3%
Milk 11.9%
Pink 4.8%
Wedding 4.8%
2.4% Cream, Crown, Death, Red

Carol+
Christmas 38.1%
Song 19.0%
Sing 10.7%
Singer(s) 10.7%
* 3.6%
Singing 3.6%
Hymn 2.4%
Xmas 2.4%
1.2% Card, Church, Concert, Day, Easter, Fire, Grey, Sell, Service

Carpenter+
Wood 31.0%
Jesus 9.5%
Joiner 4.8%
Joseph 4.8%
Table 4.8%
2.4% *, Chest, Craftsman, Creation, Door, Friend, Furniture, Hardin, John, Knife, Nail, Sailor, Singer, Walrus, Woodwork, Work, Worker, Workforce

Carpet
Rug 25.0%
Floor 11.5%
Wool 9.6%
Mat 5.7%
Beater 3.8%
Cleaner 3.8%
Furry 3.8%
Red 3.8%
Shagpile 3.8%
Soft 3.8%
1.9% Brush, Bug, Carpet-Sweeper, Cloth, Flying, Furniture, Green, Layer, Matting, New, School, Tacks, Tile

Carrot+
Stick 25.6%
Donkey 11.1%
Rabbit 10.0%
Orange 7.8%

Vegetable 7.8%
Cake 2.2%
Gold 2.2%
Onion 2.2%
1.1% *, Apple, Beetroot, Bugs-Bunny, Cabbage, Carrotine, Chunk, Crunch, Cruncher, Crunchy, Diamond, Dog, Eat, Egg, Food, Fruit, Green, Juice, Lettuce, Pony, Potato, Raw, Red, Soup, Top, Turnip, Vitamins, Yellow

Carry
Bag(s) 13.0%
On 13.0%
Hold 8.7%
Cash 6.5%
Heavy 6.5%
Load 6.5%
Bundle 4.3%
Lift 4.3%
Porter 4.3%
2.2% Baby, Back, Basket, Box, Burden, Case, Child, Goods, Lug, Out, Shopping, Stretcher, Support, Take, Truck, Water

Cart
Horse 59.6%
Wheel(s) 19.1%
Apples 4.3%
2.1% Barrow, Bullock, Donkey, Go, Load, Race, Wagon, Wooden

Carton
Milk 58.0%
Box 12.0%
Orange 6.0%
Cartoon 4.0%
2.0% Book, Card, Cardboard, Cigarette, Cottage-Cheese, Juice, Mouse, Pack, Packet, Yoghurt

Carve
Up 16.7%
Meat 14.6%
Cut 10.4%
Wood 8.3%
* 4.2%
Beef 4.2%
Chop 4.2%
Knife 4.2%
Sculpt 4.2%
2.1% Bone, Cave, Chicken, Crawl, Idol, In-Skin, Joint, Name, Niche, Off, Shape, Slice, Turkey, Write

Cary
Grant 67.3%
* 14.5%
Fisher 6.1%
Name 4.1%
2.0% Cooper, Roger, Twin, Twine

Case
Book 12.5%
* 10.4%
Bag 6.3%
Brief 6.3%
Box 4.2%
History 4.2%
Point 4.2%
Suit 4.2%
2.1% Answer, Bash, Briefcase, Brown, Clothes, Court, Drop, Enquiry, Joint, Judge, Law, Mental, Open, Report, Study, Tool, Travelling, Typeface, Violin, Wine, Winning, Witness, Work

Cash+
Money 52.1%
Hand 12.5%
Carry 6.2%
Cheque 6.2%
2.1% Bank, Box, Cage, Credit, Dosh, In, Market, Point, Sterling, Till

Castle+
Sand 15.2%
Air 6.5%
Keep 6.5%
Moat 6.5%
Fort 4.3%
Hill 4.3%
House 4.3%
King 4.3%
Knight 4.3%
Tower 4.3%
Turret 4.3%
2.2% Bouncy, Brick, Caernarvon, Chapel, Chepstow, Howard, Mansion, Old, Palace, Room, Ruin, Sky, Stones, Strong, Wall, Windsor

Casual
Clothes 21.4%
Dress 11.9%
Relaxed 11.9%
Sex 9.5%
* 7.1%
Acquaintance 7.1%
2.4% Affair, Cool, Easy, Formal, Informal, Loose, Neat, Planned, Serious, Slack, Smart, Trousers, Wear

Casually+
* 28.6%
Jeans 9.5%
Dressed 7.1%
Slowly 7.1%
2.4% Attack, Calmly, Clothes, Cool, Denim, Dress, Fling, Formal, Haphazard, Laid, Leisurely, Nearly, Relaxed, Slow, Steal, Suit, Untidy, Wear, Without

Casualty+
Accident 26.2%
Hospital 23.8%
Ward 11.9%
War 7.1%
Death 4.8%
Patient 4.8%
2.4% *, Broken, Crash, Doctor, Fatality, Hurt, Injure, Injury, Victim, Wounded

Cat+
Dog 66.7%
Mat 6.2%
Flap 4.2%
Mouse 4.2%
2.1% Animal, Bird, Black, Drake, Home, Kitten, Marmaduke, Mate, Splodge

Catch
Ball 24.0%
Fish 10.0%
Throw 8.0%
Cold 6.0%
Net 6.0%
Twenty-Two 6.0%
Hold 4.0%
Latch 4.0%
2.0% Back, Can, Caught, Disease, Drop, Fall, Hook, Me, Mouse, Rabbit, Rope, Salmon, Snare, Snatch, Trap, Twenty

Catchword
Phrase 50.0%
* 8.3%
Catchphrase 4.2%
Gameshow 4.2%
Slang 4.2%
2.1% Brace, Bruce, Buzz, Comedian, Forsyth, Fun, Game, Motto, Puzzle, Saying, Show, Speak, Stupid, Word

Cathedral+
Church 35.4%
Spire 25.0%
Choir 8.3%
City 8.3%
Tower(s) 4.2%
2.1% Bliss, Ely, Glory, Gothic, Green, Lichfield, Square, St-Pauls, Town

Cauldron+
Witch 35.7%
Pot 33.3%
Boil 4.8%
Fire 4.8%
2.4% *, Bubble, Bubbling, Burn, Hot, Kettle, Stir, Witches, With

Cause+
Effect 39.6%
Way 10.4%
Reason 8.3%
Event 4.2%
First 4.2%
Happen 4.2%
2.1% Affect, Blame, Death, Fall, Fool, Just, Make, Money, Occur, Result, Start, Strike, Yes

Cave
Man 20.9%
Dark 11.6%
Bat(s) 7.0%
Coves 7.0%
Hole 7.0%
In 4.7%
2.3% Bear, Canyon, Cavern, Cliffs, Deep, Dig, Diver, Dwelling, Fire, Geography, Grotto, Jump, Limestone, Nick, Painting, Rocks, Sea, Wet, Wulworth

Celery+
Vegetable 21.4%
Salad 9.5%
Stick 9.5%
Crunchy 7.1%
Bloody 4.8%
Water 4.8%
2.4% Carrot, Celery, Cheese, Crisp, Crunch, Eat, Food, Horrible, Leaf, Lettuce, Pay, Rhubarb, Salt, Seasoning, Soup, Stew, Vegetarian, Yuk

Cello
Violin 30.6%
Music 12.2%
Player 12.2%
Oboe 8.2%
* 4.1%
Bow 4.1%
Instrument 4.1%
Orchestra 4.1%
Play 4.1%
2.0% Camilla, Casals, Helen, Bass, Fiddle, Grandpa, String, Wood

Cellar+
Basement 21.4%
Wine 16.7%
Attic 7.1%
Dark 7.1%
Damp 4.8%
2.4% *, Bar, Beer, Bottom, Church, Cold, Door, Down, Dungeon, Food, House, Man, Room, Sales, Steps, Tradesman, Underneath, Vendeuse

Cement+
Mixer 25.0%
Concrete 9.1%
Bricks 5.7%
Building 5.7%
Sand 4.5%
Mix 3.4%
Rock 3.4%
Builder 2.3%
Dry 2.3%
Fix 2.3%
Hard 2.3%
Mortar 2.3%
Shoes 2.3%
Solid 2.3%
Stick 2.3%
Works 2.3%
1.1% Bag, Block, Bond, Boots, Boulder, Builds, Clay, Fire, Garden, Glue, Grey, Ground, Plaster, Pleat, Shed, Soil, Straw, Workman

Century+
Hundred 23.3%
Year(s) 19.8%
Time 8.1%
Old 7.0%
* 4.7%
Cricket 4.7%
History 3.5%
100 2.3%
Age 2.3%
Decade 2.3%
Era 2.3%
Guard 2.3%
Twentieth 2.3%
1.2% Ago, Annum, Army, Centurion, Future, Guild, Long, Nineteen, One, Siecle, Singer, This, Turn

Ceramic+
Pottery 31.0%
Tile 16.7%
Pot 14.3%
Hob 7.1%
Clay 4.8%
Dish 4.8%
Porcelain 4.8%
2.4% Blue, Enamel, Glass, Paint, Potters, Vase, Wool

Cereal+
Breakfast 54.8%
Packet 7.1%
Wheat 7.1%
2.4% Appliance, Bowl, Branflakes, Corn, Many, Morning, Novel, Number, Parallel, Programme, Sequential, Toast, Weetabix

Chagrin+
* 39.1%
Sad 8.7%
Annoyed 4.3%
2.2% Anxiety, Disgust, Dismay, Embarrassment, Gnash, Green, Grin, Hurt, Luck, Morbid, Pique, Red, Regret, Sadness, Shame, Shark, Smile, Tedious, Unhappy, Unlucky, Upset, Wry

Chain+
Mail 14.3%
Link 11.9%
Ball 4.8%
Bicycle 4.8%
Bike 4.8%
Letter 4.8%
Lock 4.8%
Metal 4.8%
Slavery 4.8%
2.4% *, Chainsaw, Event, Gang, Gold, Iron, Jewellery, Locked, Medal, Music, Necklace, Rain, Reaction, Saw, Tie, Whip

Chalk+
Cheese 54.3%
Blackboard 19.6%
Board 8.7%
Cliff 4.3%
Dover 4.3%
2.2% Colour, Crayon, Lime, White

Challenge
Anneka 18.8%
* 10.4%
Dare 4.2%
Fight 4.2%
Race 4.2%
Test 4.2%
Them 4.2%
Try 4.2%
2.1% Attack, Bet, Bold, Change, Compete, Competition, Compute, Defy, Difficult, Dual, Everything, Gamble, Game, Good, Him, Match, Money, Offer, Quiz, Stronger, University, Work

Chance
Luck 21.4%
Dice 9.5%
* 7.1%
Lucky 7.1%
Risk 7.1%
Take 7.1%
2.4% Arrival, Card, Coin, Encounter, Evens, Game, Get, Lost, Million, Monopoly, Offer, One, One-In-A-Million, Opportunity, Second, Tennis, Throw

Change+
Alter 19.6%
Money 17.4%
* 10.9%
Clothes 4.3%
Times 4.3%
2.2% All, Alternation, Chain, Circle, Correct, Different, Dynamic, Edge, Green, Hair, Help, Mutate, Over, Revolution, Roundabout, Switch, Swop, Transform, Trousers, Weather

Chaos
* 9.5%
Order 9.5%
Theory 9.5%
Mess 7.1%
Confusion 4.8%
Crazy 4.8%
2.4% Anarchy, Biscuit, Butterfly, Calm, Disorder, Eternity, Fun, Hectic, Hurricane, Mayhem, Natural, Noise, People, Pictures, Riot, Room, Rubbish, Science, Start, Trouble, Wild, World, Wreck

Chaotic+
Mad 14.3%
Mess 9.5%
Messy 7.1%
* 4.8%
Chaos 4.8%
Disorganised 4.8%
Motion 4.8%
Numbers 4.8%
2.4% Crisis, Difficult, Disorder, Evil, Fool, Fractal, Frantic, Hell, Lab, Life, Madcap, Madness, Maths, Neutral, Order, Rubbish, Strange, Theory, Trouble

Chase
Run 12.8%
Hunt 10.6%
Car 6.4%
Dog 6.4%
* 4.3%
After 4.3%
Away 4.3%
Fox 4.3%
Game 4.3%
Hare 4.3%
Over 4.3%
Rabbit 4.3%
Woman 4.3%
2.1% Catch, Deer, Horse, Man, Me, Paper, People, Police, Race, Rat, Victim

Chat
Talk 44.0%
Up 8.0%
Chatter 4.0%
Phone 4.0%
2.0% *, About, Back, Box, Bus, Casually, Chatty, Chit, Crowd, Friends, Gossip, Hat, Line, Mouth, Natter, Show, Tea, Telephone, Tom, With

Cheerfulness
Happy 21.3%
Smile 21.3%
Happiness 19.1%
Friendly 4.3%
Gay 4.3%
2.1% Abounds, Bouncy, Buoyancy, Cheerfulness, Daffodil, Glee, Glow, Good, Humour, Jolly, Laugh, Life, Sadness, Smiling

Chef
Cook 65.9%
Food 17.1%
2.4% De-Patie, Garden, Hat, Knife, Onions, Restaurant, Salad, Sauce

Cherry
Pie 42.2%
Tree 15.6%
Cake 6.7%
Red 6.7%
Orchard 4.4%
Stone 4.4%
2.2% -Ade, Apple, Brandy, Drop, Flavour, Fruit, Pip, Stalk, Strawberry

Chest
* 28.6%
Drawers 6.1%
Size 6.1%
Breast 4.1%
Hairy 4.1%
Large 4.1%
Of-Drawers 4.1%
Pain 4.1%
2.0% Big, Blanket, Body, Box, Bust, Cuddly, Draws, Expansion, Hair, Head, High, Infection, Lock, Nut, Thorax, Top, Torso, Trunk, Wood, X-Ray

Chew
Eat 14.6%
Gum 14.6%
Food 12.5%
Munch 10.4%
Tobacco 6.3%
* 6.2%
Cud 4.2%
Fat 4.2%
Masticate 4.2%
Teeth 4.2%
2.1% Amble, Bit, Bubble, Cheese, End, Hard, It, Mumble, Through

Chief
Indian(s) 42.9%
Tribe 7.1%
* 4.8%
Boss 4.8%

Head 4.8%
2.4% Big, Cordon-Bleu, Fire-Brigade, Hat, In-Charge, King, Leader, Master, Native, Police, Red-Indian, Staff, Top, Vauxhall, Whip

Child
Mother 9.2%
Baby 8.0%
Kid 6.9%
Small 5.7%
* 4.6%
Minder 4.6%
Young 4.6%
Girl 3.4%
Play 3.4%
Adult 2.3%
Boy 2.3%
Games 2.3%
Infant 2.3%
Toddler 2.3%
Toy(s) 2.3%
1.1% -Hood, Abuse, Bairn, Beater, Benefit, Bother, Care, Clever, Cot, Crossing, Dead, Dog, Education, Help, Hope, Innocent, Like, Line, Meek, Mine, Molest, Molester, Naughty, Noisy, Prodigy, Smash, Teenager, Time, Tot, White

Childbirth
Pain 32.0%
Baby 14.0%
Hospital 6.0%
Woman 6.0%
Labour 4.0%
Mother 4.0%
2.0% *, Agony, Birth, Childcare, Christian, Contract, Cot, Cry, Curse, Early, Natal, Nativity, Nurse, Underwater, Vagina, Whole, Yuk

China
Cup 19.0%
Doll 14.3%
Plate(s) 11.9%
Clay 9.5%
Bone 4.8%
Crockery 4.8%
Red 4.8%
2.4% Bowl, Communist, India, Japan, Pot, Sea, Service, Shop, Tea, Tea-Cup, Tea-Set, Tray, Vase

Chisel+
Hammer 26.1%
Tool 17.4%
Wood 6.5%
Face 4.3%
Saw 4.3%
Statue 4.3%
2.2% Carpentry, Carve, Carving, Chip, Cold, Cut, File, Giaiometti, Hack Make, Nail, Screwdriver, Sculpture, Sharp, Snip, Spanner

Chocaholic
Chocolate 27.1%
Far 14.6%
Alcoholic 6.3%
Addict 4.2%
Eat 4.2%
2.1% Belgian, Cadbury's, Mars Bar, Addicted, Anonymous, Bar, Bowl, Catholic, Choca Mocha, Chocolater, Dark, Food, Girlfriend, Good, Greedy, Muncher, Myself, Obese, Sweet, Sweet Tooth

Chocolate
Brown 11.9%
Sweet 11.9%
Bar 9.5%
Egg 7.1%
Milk 7.1%
Wrapper 7.1%
2.4% Box, Cake, Calories, Cigar, Course, Dark, Delicious, Diet, Drink, Easter, Eat, Eclair, Heaven, Mars, Mousse, Satisfaction, Sticky, White-Chocolate, White-Milky-Bar

Choice
Decision 11.9%
Option(s) 11.9%
Cut 4.8%
Elect 4.8%
Make 4.8%
Select 4.8%
Selection 4.8%
2.4% *, Array, Chocolates, Choose, Either, Exact, Few, Food, Forced, Freedom, Hard, Mine, Multiple, No, Open, Opt, Pardon, Pick, Prime, Shift, Sweets, Voice

Choir+
Sing 31.2%
Boy(s) 14.6%
Angels 10.4%
Singing 8.3%
Church 4.2%
Song 4.2%
Stall(s) 4.2%
2.1% Angelic, B, Cathedral, Chancel, God, Heaven, Heavenly, Kings, Practise, Quire, Singers

Choose
Pick 14.9%
Select 12.8%
* 10.6%
Choice 10.6%
Decide 10.6%
2.1% Button, Dress, Fussy, Goods, Grab, Item, Many, Me, More, Nuts, Options, Own, Selection, Sweets, Take, Target, Want, Women, Words

Chop
Suey 12.5%
Up 8.4%
Meat 8.3%
Cut 6.3%
* 6.2%
Chip 4.2%
Mix 4.2%
Pork 4.2%
Slice 4.2%
Steak 4.2%
2.1% All, Board, Change, Cleaver, Cook, Fat, Food, Hash, Knife, Lamb, Mend, Parsley, Shop, Snap, That, This, Veg, Wood

Chuckle
Laugh 72.9%
2.1% *, Cackle, Charly, Cry, Giggle, Happy, Hound, Laughed, Loud, Mouth, Much, Nukkle, Smile

Christmas
Day 23.0%
Tree 15.0%
Card 10.3%
Eve 5.1%
Present 5.1%
Pudding 5.1%
Time 5.1%
2.6% Cake, Carol, Cracker, Dark, Decorations, Father, Noel, Ribbon, Santa, Stocking, Tide, Uncle

Chunnel
Tunnel 43.8%
France 12.5%
Channel 6.2%
* 4.2%
Dig 4.2%
Train 4.2%
2.1% Asphyxiate, Channel-Tunnel, Cheese, Chimney, Dis, Fairy, Hole, Irritating, Mole, Rats, Slow, Turret

Church+
Steeple 23.9%
Chapel 8.7%
Cross 8.7%
Spire 8.7%
Pray 6.5%
God 4.3%
Religion 4.3%
Service 4.3%
Tower 4.3%
2.2% Altar, Bells, Cathedral, Catholic, Christ, Congregation, Hall, Mass, Mouse, People, Reason, Vicar

Cigar
Smoke 57.8%
Smell 8.9%
Ash 4.4%
Pipe 4.4%
2.2% Box, Chew, Chomp, Cigarette, Cigar-Band, Fag, Fox, Hamlet, Holder, Leaves, Rich

Cinema+
Film 41.3%
Picture 8.7%
Screen 8.7%
Seat 6.5%
Fun 4.3%
Movie(s) 4.3%
2.2% *, Cinnamon, Cloves, Goer, Odeon, People, Scope, Show, Theatre, Ticket, Usher, Vision

Circus+
Animal(s) 21.4%
Clown 16.7%
Ring 14.3%
Elephant 7.1%
Fun 7.1%
Circle 4.8%
Freak(s) 4.8%
2.4% *, Act, Horse, Performer, Piccadilly, Smarts', Theatre, Train, Trapeze

Cistern+
Toilet 33.3%
* 14.3%
Tank 11.9%
Water 7.1%
Pump 4.8%
2.4% Analysis, Bog, Bubble, Commuter, Engine, Function, Geyser, Movement, Pipe, Pot, Way, Window

Citizen+
Person 19.0%
* 9.5%
Country 9.5%
City 7.1%
Good 4.8%
Kane 4.8%
Member 4.8%
Smith 4.8%
2.4% Advice, Arrest, Bourgeois, Cane, Denizen, Friend, Me, Object, Peoples, Populace, Right, Sleep, State, Upright, Voter

City
London 24.4%
Centre 7.3%
Lights 7.3%

Town 7.3%
Metropolis 4.9%
Urban 4.9%
2.4% Bomb, Businessmen, Car, Dirt, Dweller, Gent, House, Limits, Mess, New-York, Office, Pavement, Pollution, Smoke, State, Time, Towers, Traffic, Westminster

Claim
Insurance 13.3%
Money 10.0%
* 6.7%
Form 6.7%
Ask 5.6%
Stake 5.6%
Benefit 3.3%
Tax 3.3%
Demand 2.2%
False 2.2%
Fame 2.2%
Right(s) 2.2%
Say 2.2%
Suggest 2.2%
Think 2.2%
1.1% Accuse, Acknowledge, Aim, Allege, Ask-For, Baggage, Bonus, Buy, Charge, Declare, Find, For, Gold, Gold-Mine, It, Land, Mine, Nothing, Own, Payment, Pretend, Prize, Propose, Rebate, Response, State, Take, Wage

Clamour+
Noise 22.9%
Shout 12.5%
Climb 4.2%
Crowd 4.2%
Fight 4.2%
2.1% *, Ask, Beg, Bustle, Call, Chorus, Clammy, Cry, Din, Distress, Enjoyment, Franz, Halloo, Look, Mate, More, Race, Shouting, Stammer, Sweat, Try, Tug, Want, Words, Yell

Clap
Hand(s) 61.0%
* 4.9%
Applause 4.9%
VD 4.9%
2.4% Act, Applaud, Appreciate, Concert, Loud, Music, Scab, STD, Thunder, TV-Show, Upon

Clarinet+
* 13.2%
Oboe 13.2%
Flute 10.0%
Instrument 10.0%
Music 10.0%
Horn 4.4%
Play 3.3%
Player 3.3%
Reed 3.3%
Wood 3.3%
Bassoon 2.2%
Orchestra 2.2%
Wind 2.2%
1.1% Black, Blow, Chord, Concerto, Concerts, Environ, Jazz, Kerry, Sax, Saxophone, Sell, Symphony, Trombone, Weather, Woodwind

Clasp
Hold 16.0%
Hand(s) 14.0%
Grasp 10.0%
Grab 8.0%
Grip 8.0%
Catch 4.0%
Chain 4.0%
Coat 4.0%
Together 4.0%
2.0% Brooch, Clench, Clutch, Fasten, Gold, Hair, Holder, It, Locket, Loose, Purse, Saved, Tight, To

Class+
School 35.4%
Room 14.6%
Teacher 6.2%
War 6.2%
Form 4.2%
Pupil(s) 4.2%
2.1% Blackboard, Category, Conflict, Desk, Group, Learn, Mark, Middle, People, Status, Struggle, System, Teach, Work

Classical
Music 78.6%
Modern 7.1%
2.4% Fine, Greek, Piano, Plato, Prose, Romantic

Classroom
Desk(s) 17.3%
School 17.3%
Teacher 11.5%
Blackboard 9.6%
Chalk 3.8%
1.9% *, Back, Big, Bully, Capers, Child, Class, Destroy, Empty, Full, Girl, Help, Kids, Light, Noisy, Old, People, Rowdy, Smell, Square, Windows

Claw
Bird 7.1%
Cat 7.1%
Eagle 7.1%
Hook 7.1%
Paw 7.1%
Talon 7.1%
Animal 4.8%
Blood 4.8%
Tiger 4.8%
Tooth 4.8%
2.4% *, Bear, Claw, Fist, Flesh, Foot, Hammer, Hand, Hen, Hooded, Monster, Pigeon, Rake, Red, Scratch, Sharp

Clean+
Dirty 25.0%
Polish 6.2%
Shine 6.2%
Teeth 6.2%
Tidy 4.2%
Wash 4.2%
Window(s) 4.2%
2.1% *, Bedder, Clear, Cleavage, Fast, Floor, Friend, Glass, Neat, Paper, Preen, Rag, Sheets, Shining, Shiny, Smart, Spring, Squeaky, Streets, Sweep, White

Cleanse
Clean 20.0%
Soap 13.3%
Wash 11.1%
Face 4.4%
2.2% Baptise, Cleaner, Cloth, Cosmetics, Cotton, Cream, Deeply, Dirt, Dirty, Domestic, Ethnic, Liquid, Lotion, Purify, Rinse, Scrub, Skin, Squeeze, The, Vim, Water, Wipe

Clever
Intelligent 14.3%
Stupid 11.9%
Bright 9.5%
Clogs 7.1%
* 4.8%
Boy 4.8%
Smart 4.8%
Sod 4.8%
2.4% Bastard, Cat, Cunning, Daft, Dick, Dum, Intricate, Know, Me, Person, Professor, Silly, Think, Trevor, Wise, Words

Cliff+
Hanger 47.9%
Hang 8.3%
Dover 6.2%
Fall 6.2%
Face 4.2%
Sea 4.2%
2.1% Cloud, Coast, High, Ocean, Overhang, Richard, Rope, Seagull, Statistics, Top, White

Climate+
Weather 41.7%
Hot 10.4%
Warm 8.3%
Humid 4.2%
Temperate 4.2%
Tropical 4.2%
Warmth 4.2%
2.1% Cold, Earth, Height, Meteorology, National, Opinion, Planet, Rain, Sun, Tropics, Wet

Climb+
Mountain 35.4%
Fall 10.4%
Hill 10.4%
Frame 8.3%
Ladder 4.2%
Rope 4.2%
Up 4.2%
2.1% *, Ascend, Cliff, Mount, Mountains, Plant, Rock, Stretch, Surmount, Top, Tree

Cling
Film 28.3%
On 13.0%
To 13.0%
Baby 4.3%
Hold 4.3%
Monkey 4.3%
Tight 4.3%
2.2% Arms, Back, Chimp, Clasp, Emotional, Fright, Grip, Hang, Hold-Tight, Hug, Infant, Mother, Satin

Clog+
Shoe 41.7%
Dance 10.4%
Dutch 8.3%
Holland 8.3%
Block 4.2%
Drain 4.2%
Foot 4.2%
Wooden 4.2%
2.1% Dutchman, Fill, Ice, Plug, Sink, Stop, Wheel

Clone+
Same 16.7%
Gene 9.5%
Genetic(s) 9.5%
Alien 4.8%
Double 4.8%
Type 4.8%
2.4% Bee, Biology, Copy, Copycat, Cyclone, DNA, Doctor, Exact, Fiction, Friend, Future, Human, Identical, Mate, One, Pair, Research, Robot, Sibling, Sister, Zombie

Closed
Open 46.7%
Door(s) 17.8%
Shop 8.9%
Shut 6.7%
2.2% Book, Box, Castle, Circuit, End, Eyes, Full, No-Entry, Stop

Clothes-peg
Line 40.0%
Washing 13.3%
Clothes 6.7%
Clothes line 6.7%
Hang 6.7%
Coat 4.4%
Nose 4.4%
2.2% Air, Cloakroom, Hook, Stool, Wash, Washing Line, Wind, Wood

Clothing
Fashion 7.1%
* 4.8%
Dress 4.8%
Jacket 4.8%
Naked 4.8%
Shirt 4.8%
Shop 4.8%
2.4% Apparel, Basque, Clothes, Colourful, Cotton, Covered, Jeans, Jumper, Manufacturer, Material, Money, Peg, People, Protective, Rags, Rail, Red, Shoes, Shopping, Stall, Stylish, Suit, Tie, Togs, Trousers, Underwear, Wear

Cloud+
Sky 37.5%
Nine 14.6%
Rain 10.4%
Lining 4.2%
White 4.2%
2.1% Cuckoo, Darkness, Earth, Field, Fluff, Furrowed, Glory, Horizon, Mind, Over, Overhead, Rainy, Silver, Snow

Clown+
Circus 47.9%
Nose 6.2%
Fool 4.2%
Fun 4.2%
Funny 4.2%
Laugh 4.2%
Smile 4.2%
2.1% Acrobat, Actor, Around, Dance, Face, Harlequin, Juggler, Mess, Nose-Red, Sad, Tears, Tree

Cluck+
Hen 33.3%
Chicken 20.8%
Time 14.6%
Tick 8.3%
Duck 4.2%
2.1% Bird, Chick, Clock, Face, Feather, Fowl, Hand, Ring, Whistle

Clue+
Detective 12.5%
Idea 10.4%
Game 8.3%
Hint 6.2%
Crime 4.2%
Crossword 4.2%
Guess 4.2%
Mystery 4.2%
2.1% *, Answer, Case, Clouseau, Cluedo, Detect, Evidence, Find, Give, Giveaway, Glue, Homes, Hunt, Inspector, Less, Lost, Message, Puzzle, Quiz, Sleuth, Solve, Test

Clumsy
Awkward 8.9%
Oaf 6.7%
* 4.4%
Break 4.4%
Careless 4.4%
Drop 4.4%
Gauche 4.4%
Person 4.4%
Stupid 4.4%
2.2% Agile, Alert, Bear, Big, Cack-Handed, Clod, Clot, Clown, Fall, Fat, Fool, Foot, Gawky, Girlfriend, Hands, Inelegant, Inept, Klutz, Live, PMT, Sarah, Slow, Unbalanced, Walk

Coach
Horse(s) 20.9%
Bus 16.3%
Football 9.3%
Car 7.0%
Train 7.0%
Driver 4.7%
Journey 4.7%
Load 4.7%
Ride 4.7%
2.3% Crash, Down, Hire, National-Express, Ranch, Station, Teach, Trainer, Trip

Coal+
Fire 37.5%
Black 8.3%
Scuttle 8.3%
Mine 6.2%
Burn 4.2%
Hole 4.2%
Miner(s) 4.2%
Newcastle 4.2%
2.1% *, Bunker, Flame, Fuel, Heat, Hod, House, Mountain, Oil, Shute, Soot

Coarse
Rough 33.3%
Fine 9.5%
Bread 4.8%
Grass 4.8%
Hair 4.8%
Rude 4.8%
2.4% Beard, Board Broad, Crude, Direction, Dry, Fish, Fishing, Grain, Humour, Language, Nasty, Pate, Smooth, Vulgar, Words

Coast+
Sea 27.1%
Beach 14.6%
Clear 10.4%
Line 8.3%
Guard 6.2%
Shore 4.2%
2.1% Box, Cliff, Coast, Drift, East, Edge, Gears, Process, Road, Rock, Roll, Sand, Ship, Strip

Coat+
Hanger 18.8%
Hat 12.5%
Jacket 12.5%
Button 4.2%
Dress 4.2%
Hook 4.2%
Scarf 4.2%
2.1% *, Arms, Black, Cloak, Clothing, Cold, Cover, Draw, Dry, Fur, Gown, Long, Mac, Paint, Rack, Rain, Stand, Tails, Warm

Cob
Corn 64.0%
Bread 6.0%
Horse 6.0%
2.0% ?, Born, Cab, Fish, Meal, Mood, Nob, Nut, Pony, Roll, Web, Yellow

Cobweb
Spider 79.2%
2.1% Clinging, Corner, Dew, Dust, Fine, Grey, Maize, Pretty, Shiny, Web

Cock
Hen 25.0%
-Roach 9.6%
Bird 9.6%
Bull 7.7%
Farm 5.7%
Sure 5.7%
Chicken 3.8%
Fight 3.8%
Robin 3.8%
Rooster 3.8%
1.9% Cockerel, Crow, Cunt, Dick, Feathers, Hat, Penis, Sick, Tail, Up, Willy

Cockerel
Hen 26.2%
Chicken 11.9%
Crow 11.9%
Cock 9.5%
Bird 7.1%
2.4% *, Animal, Birdie, Coop, Dawn, Eggs, Farm, Farmyard, Fowl, Luck, Mussel, Rooster, Spurs, Tottenham

Cocktail
Drink 36.0%
Stick 10.0%
Party 8.0%
Cabinet 6.0%
Dress 6.0%
Alcohol 4.0%
Glass 4.0%
Waitress 4.0%
2.0% Bar, Blue, Bomb, Cherry, Laughter, Margarita, Pineapple, Prawn, Red, Rusty-Nail, Waiter

Coconut+
Milk 19.0%
Shy 16.7%
Palm 14.3%
Tree 14.3%
Oil 4.8%
Tropical 4.8%
2.4% Abroad, Banana, Fair, Fairground, Foliage, Fruit, Ice, Juice, Monkey, Shell, Stall

Cod+
Fish 54.2%
Fillet 6.2%
Haddock 6.2%
Piece 6.2%
Chips 4.2%
Liver 4.2%
Roe 4.2%
War 4.2%
2.1% Iceland, Mackerel, Plaice, Taste, Trawl

Coin+
Money 25.0%
Toss 14.6%
Realm 10.4%
Penny 8.3%
King 6.2%
Cash 4.2%
Dollar 4.2%
2.1% *, Antoinnette, Gleam, Head, Pence, Phrase, Pound, Queen, Round, Shilling, Shine, Spin, Stamp

Cola
Coke 49.0%
Drink 12.2%
Can 6.1%
Bear 4.1%
Bottle 4.1%
Pepsi 4.1%
2.0% America, Boy, Cake, Coca, Cube, Fizz, Glass, Nut, Pop

Cold+
Hot 29.2%
Ice 14.6%
Winter 10.4%
Wet 8.3%
Freeze 4.2%
Sneeze 4.2%
Warm 4.2%

2.1% *, Caught, Coat, Feet, Heart, Icy, Kitchen, Night, Nose, Snow, Sore, Weather

Collar+
Shirt 23.8%
Tie 21.4%
Neck 11.9%
Cuff 4.8%
Sleeve 4.8%
Stiff 4.8%
2.4% Blouse, Blue, Button, Church, Colour, Dog, Felt, Red, Sits, Sweaty, White

College+
School 25.6%
Work 12.1%
Student(s) 9.8%
Education 7.3%
* 6.1%
Building 2.4%
Scarf 2.4%
1.2% Accommodation, Bar, Birkbeck, Block, Class, Collage, College, Course, Doctor, Don, Friends, Graduate, Grass, Hall, Here, Ivory-Tower, Learning, Lecture, Life, London, Oxford, Physics, Room, Social, Southgate, Studies, Study, Yuck

Collide
Crash 29.2%
Hit 27.1%
Smash 8.3%
Bump 6.3%
Car 6.3%
Bang 4.2%
With 4.2%
2.1% Ball, Clash, Impinge, Jump, Meet, Rush, Trucks

Comb+
Hair 41.3%
Brush 28.3%
Traffic 6.5%
2.2% *, Beach, Cloth, Crew, Hairbrush, Ice-Cream, Pen, Teeth, Thread, Trees

Come
Go 21.3%
Here 14.9%
Home 10.6%
Dancing 8.5%
* 6.4%
Again 4.3%
Hither 4.3%
To 4.3%
2.1% Arms, Arrive, Back, Beckon, Bring, In, Live, On, Over, Up, Visit, With

Comedian+
Funny 35.5%
Laugh 11.8%
* 6.5%
Comic 6.5%
Humour 4.3%
Joke 4.3%
Ben 3.2%
Bob 2.2%
Dave 2.2%
1.1% Actor, Alternative, Book, Boring, Clown, Clumsy, Cockles, Fun, Grin, Jimmy, Joker, Ken, Laughing, Laughter, Lenny, Liam, Lover, Rib, Sad, Stand, Tarbuck, Tommy, Wall

Comet+
Halleys 21.4%
Star(s) 16.7%
Halley 14.3%
Sky 9.5%
Space 7.1%
Tail 4.8%
Universe 4.8%
2.4% Fir, Fire, Furniture, Meteor, Planet, Rock, Shop, Strip, Trail

Comic+
Strip 31.0%
Book 23.8%
Relief 9.5%
Magazine 7.1%
Story 4.8%
2.4% *, Cartoon, Fun, Laugh, Laughter, Paper, Read, Stand, Type, Viz

Commence+
Start 54.8%
Begin 38.1%
2.4% End, Initiate, Now

Commend+
Recommend 16.7%
Good 11.9%
Praise 11.9%
* 9.5%
Highly 9.5%
Award 7.1%
2.4% Acclaim, Action, Admire, Approve, Congratulate, Deed, Hope, Like, Medal, Reward, Thank, Welcome, Well-Done, You

Commerce
Business 34.0%
Money 17.0%
* 6.4%
Sale(s) 6.4%
Sell 4.3%
Trade 4.3%
2.1% Advert, Banks, Began, Book, City, Coin, Industry, Material, N.H.S., Port, School, Shops, Traffic

Common
Land 14.6%
* 6.3%
Ground 6.3%
Law 6.3%
Grass 4.2%
Park 4.2%
Place 4.2%
Usual 4.2%
Wealth 4.2%
Word 4.2%
2.1% Cause, Cheap, Clapham, Graze, Green, Idiot, Knowledge, Language, Make, Muck, Name, People, Plain, Plenty, Popular, Rare, Room, Sense, Vulgar, Wandsworth

Commonwealth
Queen 13.5%
Country 11.5%
Nation(s) 11.5%
Empire 9.6%
* 7.7%
Countries 7.7%
Britain 3.8%
Institute 3.8%
1.9% ?, Africa, Australia, Black, Colonial, Community, EEC, Flag, History, Kensington, Leaders, Of-Nations, Realm, State, Together

Commute+
Travel 42.7%
Train 23.8%
London 4.8%
2.4% *, Associate, Box, Bus, Daily, Live, Move, Railway, Sentence, Tube, Underground, Work

Competence
Ability 35.7%
Good 11.9%
Able 9.5%
Incompetence 7.1%
* 4.8%
Capable 4.8%
Stupid 4.8%
2.4% Learning, Manage, Robot, Sentence, Sixpence, Straight, Talent, Vulnerability, Well

Complex
Difficult 15.6%
Simple 13.3%
Easy 11.1%
Hard 6.7%
Puzzle 6.7%
Complicated 4.4%
2.2% *, Account, Algebra, Corridors, Detail, Herb, Mate, Molecules, Negotiation, Number, Personality, Phenomena, Phenomenon, Problem, Scene, Shopping, Think, Weird, Wiry

Computer+
Machine 15.2%
Screen 13.0%
Game(s) 6.5%
Aid 4.3%
Keyboard 4.3%
Programme 4.3%
Terminal 4.3%
Word 4.3%
2.2% Algorithm, Boring, Calculator, Complicated, Desk, Detest, Difficult, Hard, Help, Key, Lap, Logic, Manual, Skill, Software, Technical, Technology, Tedious, VDU, Whizz, Words

Conceal+
Hide 92.9%
2.4% Hidden, Pretend, Show

Concede+
Give 38.1%
Give-In 9.5%
* 7.1%
Defeat 7.1%
Give-Up 7.1%
Let 4.8%
Lose 4.8%
2.4% Admit, Allow, Give-Way, Retreat, Submissive, Submit, Surrender, Tennis, Yield

Conceit+
Pride 19.0%
Vanity 13.3%
* 9.5%
Arrogance 7.1%
Lie 7.1%
Arrogant 4.8%
2.4% Bighead, Bitch, Damage, Deception, Destroy, Exaggeration, Face, Haughty, Him, Horrible, Nasty, Pompous, Proud, Shame, Snob, Spite

Conceive+
Idea 14.3%
Pregnant 14.3%
Baby 9.5%
* 7.1%
Birth 7.1%
Think 7.1%
Create 4.8%
2.4% Bear, Believe, Conceit, Develop, Egg, Fertilize, Gather, Give, Impregnate, Invent, Make,

Produce, Sex, Start, Think-Of

Concept
Idea 50.0%
* 7.1%
Art 4.8%
2.4% Album, Artistic, Categorisation, Category, Concepts, Immaculate, Installation, Late, Mind, Notion, Object, Philosophy, Physics, Plea, Prudence, Understanding

Concern
Worry 27.7%
Care 25.5%
Age 8.5%
* 4.3%
Matter 4.3%
Worried 4.3%
2.1% Business, Charity, Child, Dwell, For, Frown, Lack, Mine, Mother, Pity, Show, Though

Conclusion
End 66.7%
Final 7.1%
Decision 4.8%
2.4% A-Book, Dissertation, Ending, Essay, Experiment, Finish, Result, Summary, Thinking

Concrete
Cement 19.5%
Hard 9.8%
Block 7.3%
Building 7.3%
Solid 7.3%
Jungle 4.9%
Mixer 4.9%
Slab 4.9%
2.4% Bags, Corner, Evidence, Foundations, Garden, Grey, Mix, Path, Pavement, Paving, Ragga, Road, Stone, Tarmac, Wire

Confess
Priest 18.8%
Admit 14.6%
Tell 12.5%
Truth 6.3%
Give 4.2%
Lie 4.2%
Say 4.2%
To 4.2%
2.1% *, Abhor, Absolution, Catholic, Deny, Give-In, Guilt, Humble, I, Loudly, Obey, Own, Secret, Torture, Trial

Confetti+
Wedding 72.9%
Marriage 6.2%
2.1% Bride, Buy, Camera, Floor, Love, Mess, Paper, Party, Recycle, Throw

Confide+
Tell 35.7%
Secret 19.0%
Trust 14.3%
Friend 4.8%
2.4% *, Divulge, Entrust, Exchange, Helpful, Listen, Promise, Secrets, Share, To, Whisper

Confidential
Secret 45.2%
Private 33.3%
Document 4.8%
2.4% Information, Interesting, Letter, Papers, School, Secrecy

Confine
Imprison 9.5%
Prison 9.5%
Restrict 9.5%
Enclose 7.1%
Hold 7.1%
Shut 7.1%
Hide 4.8%
Keep 4.8%
Limit 4.8%
Stop 4.8%
Trap 4.8%
2.4% Bed, Cage, Captive, Cell, Confide, Interr, Lock, Reduce, Secure, Shackle, Space

Connect
Link 16.0%
Join 14.0%
Four 8.0%
Together 6.0%
Wire 6.0%
With 6.0%
* 4.0%
Attach 4.0%
Disconnect 4.0%
Plug 4.0%
2.0% 4, Add, Agree, Card, Change, Contact, Couple, Five, It, Make, Plug-In, Them, Tube, Up

Consent
Allow 18.0%
Age 10.0%
Agree 8.0%
Give 8.0%
Adult 6.0%
Permission 4.0%
Refuse 4.0%
2.0% Accept, Acquiesce, Age-Of, Agreement, Always, Authority, Form, Lack, Licence, Marginal, Marriage, Mutual, Of, Participate, Permit, Quick, Rape, Sex, To, Withdrawn

Consequence
Result 28.6%
* 14.3%
Action(s) 4.8%
End 4.8%
Fault 4.8%
Game(s) 4.8%
2.4% After, Book, Chances, Ending, Happening, Jail, No, Nothing, Outcome, Product-Of, Realise, Reason, Sequence, Trouble, Truth, Ultimate

Consume
Eat 60.4%
Food 10.4%
* 6.2%
2.1% All, Everything, Fire, Passion, Shop, Soup, Take, Time, Use, Vomit, Wealth

Contend+
Fight 14.3%
Compete 9.5%
Argue 4.8%
2.4% *, Attempt, Battle, Believe, Challenge, Claim, Combat, Confine, Confound, Content, Cope, Deal, Enter, Fiercely, Fighter, Happy, Hold, Maintain, Meet, Play, Please, Repeat, Suffer, Throne, Title, Try, Vie, Win, With, Yield

Content
Happy 52.0%
Detail(s) 4.0%
Full 4.0%
2.0% *, -Ment, Belly, Box, Cat, Chocolate, Discontent, Empty, Fire, Form, Fulfilment, Hold, Inside, Item, Lap, Satisfied, Satisfy, Serene, Smug, With

Converse+
Talk 66.7%
Speak 14.3%
Chat 7.1%
2.4% Communicate, Convert, Convex, Discuss, How

Convert+
Change 35.7%
Christian 14.3%
Religion 11.9%
2.4% Beetle, Calter, Canoe, Catholicize, Change-Around, Christianity, Church, Code, Exchange, Implement, Kick, Manson, Physics, Reach, Talk, Type

Cook+
Food 20.0%
Broth 14.4%
Book 8.9%
Chef 8.9%
Kitchen 8.9%
Clean 6.7%
Bake 2.2%
Thief 2.2%
Woman 2.2%
1.1% *, Ability, Apron, Cake, Captain, Chef's, Chop, Cleaner, Cradle, Cuisine, Curry, Feed, Hat, Lover, Mother, Oven, Pan, Pot, Recipe, Serve, Spoiling, Toast, Washerwoman

Cooked
Food 21.4%
Raw 21.4%
Meal 19.0%
Ham 4.8%
2.4% *, Apple, Bacon, Baked, Biscuit, Breakfast, Burnt, Eat, Goose, Heated, Hot, Over, Rice, Uncooked

Cooker
Gas 25.0%
Stove 12.5%
Food 10.4%
Oven 10.4%
Cook 8.3%
Kitchen 8.3%
* 4.2%
Hob 4.2%
2.1% Ceramics, Eat, Fire, Hood, Hot, Kettle, Pressure, Utensil

Cookie
Biscuit 52.4%
Chocolate 9.5%
Chip 7.1%
Jar 7.1%
Monster 4.8%
2.4% America, Biccy, Butter, Cake, Crumble, Crumbs, Sweet, Tablet

Cool
Cold 11.1%
Hot 8.9%
Warm 8.9%
Blue 6.7%
Breeze 6.7%
Cucumber 4.4%
Place 4.4%
Shade 4.4%
Spot 4.4%
2.2% Aid, Cat, Chill, Clean, Control, Customer, Dude, Headed, Light, Paddle, Reception, Refrigerator, Sea, Snow, Tan, Touch, View, Water

Cope
With 20.0%
Manage 18.0%
* 6.0%
Able 6.0%
Julian 6.0%
Can't 4.0%
Do 4.0%
Survive 4.0%
2.0% Ability, Able, Can, Care, Coppice, Dope, Follow, Good, Housewife, Life, Mother, Stress, Together, Well, Which, Worry

Copy
Cat 16.7%
Photo 10.4%
Book 8.3%
Paper 8.3%
* 4.2%
Machine 4.2%
Mine 4.2%
Print 4.2%
Shop 4.2%
Type 4.2%
2.1% Another, Ape, Change, Cheat, Colour, Mimic, Out, Page, Photocopy, Real, Reproduce, This, Where, Write, Xerox

Core+
Apple 54.2%
Centre 14.6%
Shout 6.2%
Wow 4.2%
2.1% Carve, Crow, Earth, Esprit, Hard, Middle, Reactor, Rich, Root, Speak

Correct
Right 33.3%
Wrong 20.0%
Mark(s) 4.4%
Politically 4.4%
2.2% Answer, Attitude, Correction, Description, Exam, Example, Good, Incorrect, Language, Method, Political, Procedure, Slip, Spelling, Tick, Why, Work

Cosmetic+
Make-Up 21.4%
Surgery 21.4%
Lipstick 7.1%
Perfume 7.1%
Animals 4.8%
Face 4.8%
False 4.8%
2.4% Cruelty, Fake, Lips, Looks, Lotion, Make, Nothing, Pretty, Sex, Superficial, Surgeon, Women

Cost+
Price 27.1%
Money 20.8%
Effective 6.2%
Expense 6.2%
Centre 4.2%
Expensive 4.2%
Living 4.2%
Pay 4.2%
2.1% Amount, Benefit, Count, Counting, Gold, High, Packet, Pounds, Shop, Spend, Wage

Costume+
Dress 25.6%
Clothes 14.4%
Play 7.8%
Party 5.6%
Drama 3.3%
Show 3.3%
* 2.2%
Clown 2.2%
Design 2.2%
Designer 2.2%
Fancy 2.2%
Jewellery 2.2%
Swimming 2.2%
Theatre 2.2%
Wear 2.2%
1.1% Acting, Actor, Australian, Ball, Bathing, Change, Cloak, Department, Kleid, Make-Up, Outfit, Parade, Stage, Tradition, Uniform, Waiting, Wig

Cosy
Warm 33.3%
Fire 8.3%
House 6.3%
* 6.2%
Bed 4.2%
Comfy 4.2%
Snug 4.2%
2.1% Cat, Chair, Close, Corner, Cushion, Fine, Flat, Light, Raw, Relationship, Relax, Room, Rug, Slippers, Sofa, Soft

Cot+
Baby 64.3%
Death 26.2%
9.5% Bed

Cotton
Wool 29.2%
Shirt 8.3%
Bud 6.3%
T-Shirt 6.3%
* 4.2%
Field(s) 4.2%
Linen 4.2%
Mill(s) 4.2%
Thread 4.2%
2.1% Ball, Blouse, Cloth, Clothes, Cool, India, Jeans, Nylon, Pickers, Rug, Silk, Skirt, Smock, White

Cotton reel
Thread 24.4%
Sew 22.2%
* 11.1%
Needle 6.7%
Cotton 4.4%
Sewing 4.4%
Spin 4.4%
2.2% American, Cloth, Deuce, Fed, Pulley, Roll, Round, String, Tank, Wool, Yarn

Couch
Potato 26.7%
Cushion 8.9%
Sofa 8.9%
Bed 6.7%
Lie 4.4%
Lounge 4.4%
Settee 4.4%
Sit 4.4%
2.2% Blanket, Cover, Curl, Green, Lips, Lying-Down, Psychiatrist, Psychologist, Relax, Seat, Sleep, Soft, Test, TV

Could
Would 16.7%
You 16.7%
Can 10.4%
Should 8.3%
Able 6.3%
Will 6.3%
* 6.2%
Be 4.2%
Might 4.2%
Not 4.2%
We 4.2%
2.1% Ask, Cold, Come, Couldn't, Door, Maybe

Country
Origin 19.0%
England 11.9%
Side 9.5%
Green 4.8%
Home 4.8%
Manor 4.8%
2.4% Boy, Bumpkin, City, Countryside, Fair, Field, File, Foreign, France, House, King, Land, Landscape, State, This, Trees, Turkey, Western, Wide

Couple
Pair 19.0%
Two 14.3%
Single 11.9%
* 4.8%
Marriage 4.8%
Married 4.8%
Partner 4.8%
2.4% Chain, Children, Days, Friend, His, Hitch, House, Joint, Link, Man-&-Woman, Of, One, Twin, Twosome, Up

Courage+
Brave 19.6%
Bravery 19.6%
Bitter 8.7%
Beer 6.5%
Fear 4.3%
Lion 4.3%
Strength 4.3%
2.2% Ale, Badge, Battle, Bear, Dutch, Endurance, Food, Fortitude, Knight, Latitude, Lust, Mother, Risk, Truth, Valiant

Courtship
Love 19.0%
Romance 16.7%
Marriage 14.3%
Couple 7.1%
Ritual 7.1%
* 4.8%
2.4% Boyfriend, Dance, Date, Dress, Flirt, Friends, Hard, Lovers, Mating, Medieval, Missing, Quiet, Woo

Cousin+
Aunt 16.7%
Relative 16.7%
Uncle 8.3%
Relation 7.1%
Brother 6.0%
Friend 6.0%
Sister 6.0%
Family 4.8%
* 3.6%
Kissing 2.4%
Nephew 2.4%
Perfect 2.4%
1.2% Alison, Boy, Country, Daughter, Filial, Janna, Major, Marry, My, Niece, Person, Rachel, Relate, Richard, Second

Cove
Bay 21.7%
Cave 21.7%
Sea 10.9%
Sand 6.5%
Beach 6.5%
2.2% Bag, Broken, Camp, Cliffs, Coast, Covet, Headland, Inlet, Lulworth, Rabbit, Safe, Smuggle, Stoney, Water, Wentworth

Cover
Up 25.0%
Over 14.6%
* 10.4%
Blanket 4.2%
Cloth 4.2%
Hide 4.2%

2.1% All, Bed, Book, Coat, Comprehensive, Covert, Duck, Lid, Manhole, Open, Protect, Roof, Shelter, Shot, Sleep, Story, Tunnel, Waterfront

Crack
Break 10.4%
Open 10.4%
Cocaine 8.3%
Up 8.3%
Wall 8.3%
Drug 6.3%
* 4.2%
Smack 4.2%
2.1% Broken, Chip, Craze, Creak, Down, Fault, Hole, Ice, It, Joke, Line, Not, Pavement, Plank, Service, Solve, Upon, Vase, Window

Craft+
Art 12.5%
Boat 12.5%
Ship 12.5%
Skill 8.3%
Fair 4.2%
Make 4.2%
Trade 4.2%
Wood 4.2%
Work 4.2%
Workshop 4.2%
2.1% Artisan, Basket, Design, Fare, Handmade, Handwork, Maker, Man, Pot, Rope, Shape, Spin, Technology, Woodwork

Cram+
Baby 12.5%
Exam 10.4%
Stuff 8.3%
Fit 6.2%
In 6.2%
Exams 4.2%
Fill 4.2%
Push 4.2%
Shove 4.2%
Tight 4.2%
2.1% *, Crowd, Eat, Everything, Food, Full, Geese, Handle, Into, Mouth, Pack, Press, School, Split, Squeeze, Steve, Words

Crane+
Bird 27.1%
Lift 16.7%
Building 6.2%
Neck 6.2%
Stork 6.2%
Build 4.2%
Lever 4.2%
2.1% Bill, Driver, Heron, High, Load, Long, Long-Legs, Metal, One-Leg, Pond, Site, Stream, Swing, Tower

Cranny+
Nook 85.4%
Crook 4.2%
2.1% Crag, Crevice, Peak, Rock, Wainscot

Crash+
Car 35.4%
Bang 20.8%
Hit 8.3%
Accident 4.2%
Barrier 4.2%
Cars 4.2%
2.1% Aircraft, Bike Collide, Course, Die, Drive, Fall, Helmet, Market, Smash, Splat

Crater+
Moon 52.1%
Volcano 8.3%
Hole 6.2%
Face 4.2%
Mass 4.2%
Meteorite 4.2%
Pit 4.2%
2.1% Cave, Dip, God, Impact, Laser, Lunar Maker, Shell

Cravat+
Tie 73.8%
Necktie 7.1%
Neck 4.8%
2.4% Gentleman, Homosexual, Ian, Illustrious, Poseur, Scarf

Crave+
Want 20.8%
Desire 18.8%
Food 8.3%
Lust 6.2%
Need 6.2%
Yearn 6.2%
Chocolate 4.2%
Hunger 4.2%
Long 4.2%
2.1% After, Cradle, Drink, Greed, Hanker, Heroin, Longing, Madness, Sex, Urge

Crawl
Baby 25.0%
Walk 16.7%
Knees 6.3%
Swim 6.3%
Beg 4.2%
Creep 4.2%
2.1% Ant, Australian, Cave, Crawler, Die, Floor, Four, Front, Insect, Kneel, Legs, Lobster, Sand, Slide, Slither, Squirm, Stop, Under

Craze+
Mad 20.8%
Fad 8.3%
Skateboard 6.2%
Fashion 4.2%
Golf 4.2%
Paving 4.2%
Trend 4.2%
2.1% Congratulate, Crack, Crave, Cult, Daft, Desire, Diamond, Drug, Flares, Folle, Hippy, Horse, Madness, Man, Maze, Pavement, Rage, Shatter, Silly, Top, Whim, Wild, Yoyo

Cream+
Milk 33.3%
Cake 10.4%
Crop 6.2%
Cheese 4.2%
Sugar 4.2%
Tea 4.2%
Whip 4.2%
2.1% Bun, Cat, Egg, Face, Flow, Honey, Jelly, Lick, Mushrooms, Of, Pop, Puff, Salve, Scum, Top, Tube

Crease+
Trousers 24.4%
Iron 18.9%
Fold 15.6%
Press 5.6%
Clothes 3.3%
Wrinkle 3.3%
* 2.2%
Dress 2.2%
Line 2.2%
Shirt 2.2%
Trouser 2.2%
Up 2.2%
1.1% Bat, Bend, Buttock, Cricket, Crinkle, Crisp, Crumple, Cut, Material, Paper, Pleat, Rumple, Sheet, Stubborn, Untidy

Create
Make 32.0%
Art 8.0%
God 8.0%
Invent 6.0%
Destroy 4.0%
Birth 4.0%
Painting 4.0%
2.0% *, Artist, Beer, Build, Carry, Creation, Disturbance, Document, Grow, Idea, Me, Mould, Pan, Story, Waste, Whole-New, World

Creation
God 34.0%
* 8.5%
Genesis 6.4%
Make 6.4%
World 6.4%
Destroy 4.3%
Earth 4.3%
Life 4.3%
2.1% Begin, Begot, Bible, Dream, Eden, Game, Garden, Generate, Got, Myth, New, Nuclear

Creature
Comfort(s) 26.2%
Animal 19.0%
Bug 7.1%
* 4.8%
Beast 4.8%
Dog 4.8%
2.4% Bird, Dangerous, Dinosaur, Feature, Forest, Graze, Green, Insect, Lagoon, Mermaid, Small, Snake, Swamp, Toad

Creed+
Belief 39.6%
Colour 16.7%
Bible 14.6%
2.1% Athanasian, Believe, Black, Breed, Brethren, Calling, Church, Faith, God, Kind, King, Preach, Religion, Sing

Creek
Water 21.3%
River 19.1%
Paddle 6.4%
* 4.3%
Australia 4.3%
Jacobs 4.3%
2.1% Abbey, American, Boat, Dangerous, Door, Floor-Boards, Groan, Gully, Hole, Moan, Mountain, Noise, Rock, Shit, Smell, Spring, Squeal, Stag, Stream

Creep
Crawl 36.2%
Spider 6.4%
Man 4.3%
Slowly 4.3%
Swot 4.3%
2.1% *, Alley, Bully, Caterpillar, Crawly, Fall, Hate, Insect, Ivy, Mail, Monster, Night, Person, Quiet, Show, Sleep, Slimey, Slither, Spider's-Web, Squelch, Up

Cremate+
Burn 58.7%
Bury 10.9%
Death 10.9%
Dead 4.3%
2.2% *, Body, Fire, Funeral, Incinerate, Nan

Cricket+
Bat 20.8%
Ball 14.6%
Match 14.6%
Not 6.2%
Grasshopper 4.2%

Sport 4.2%
White 4.2%
2.1% Boring, Bowl, Evening, Football, Green, Locust, Play, Rugger, Score, Stump, Sunday, Umpire, Village, Whites, Wicket

Crime+
Punishment 31.2%
Commit 6.2%
Murder 6.2%
Criminal 4.2%
Police 4.2%
Punish 4.2%
Robbery 4.2%
Wave 4.2%
2.1% Anger, Burglar, Caught, Evil, Kill, Money, Paid, Passion, People, Prison, Rob, Robber, Sin, Skill, Steal, Thief, Wrong

Crimson
Red 47.9%
Clover 6.3%
Colour 6.3%
Blush 4.2%
Purple 4.2%
Scarlet 4.2%
* 4.1%
2.1% Bat, Bright, Gold, Lake, Leaf, Lips, Pirate, Robe, Scar, Take, Violet

Crisis
Drama 7.1%
* 4.8%
Christmas 4.8%
Disaster 4.8%
Emergency 4.8%
Help 4.8%
Management 4.8%
Problem 4.8%
War 4.8%
What 4.8%
2.4% Airplane, At-Christmas, Bad, Breakdown, Chaos, China, Comic, Danger, Distress, East, Government, Hope, International, Life, Loan, Mid-Life, News, Pain, Shelter, Trouble, Worry

Croak
Frog 67.4%
Die 15.2%
Throat 6.5%
Toad 6.5%
2.2% Hoarse, Noise, Sore

Crooked
Bent 32.0%
Man 8.0%
Stick 6.0%
Straight 6.0%
Mile 4.0%
Nose 4.0%
Teeth 4.0%
2.0% ?, Awkward, Billet, Bumpy, Bun, Cop, Dodgy, Finger, Hag, Houser, Old-Woman, Pole, Road, Round, Staff, Thief, Twisted, Wavy

Cross+
Church 15.2%
Angry 13.0%
Tick 6.5%
* 4.3%
Jesus 4.3%
Religion 4.3%
Road 4.3%
2.2% Bear, Blades, Burning, Chain, Christ, Christian, Crescent, Crux, Fire, Grave, Inverted, Mad, Nought, Path, Rectangle, Reference, Road, Stone, Traverse, Upset, Whip, Wood

Crow
Bird 35.4%
Black 18.8%
Raven 6.3%
Fly 4.2%
Road 4.2%
2.1% *, Aloud, Blackbird, Boast, Caw, Crap, Duck, Fact, Gossip, Nest, Over, Rook, Scare, Stalk, Witch

Crowd+
People 47.9%
Control 4.2%
Many 4.2%
Mass 4.2%
2.1% Bustle, Busy, Concert, Crab, Face, Flowing, Football, Full, Gathering, Heart, Lost, Lots, Multitude, Noise, Pull, Push, Suffocate, Throng, Trouble

Crown+
King 27.1%
Jewel(s) 14.5%
Glory 10.4%
Thorns 10.4%
Head 8.3%
Prince 6.2%
Queen 4.2%
2.1% Castle, Ether, Hit, Knight, Royal, Ruler, Sceptre, State, Wear

Cruel+
Kind 18.8%
Nasty 10.4%
Mean 8.3%
Evil 6.2%
Wicked 6.2%
Hard 4.2%
Harsh 4.2%
Horrible 4.2%
Master 4.2%
Unkind 4.2%
2.1% Animal, Arms, Beat, Enemy, Fast, Fate, Feather, Hurt, Hurtful, Leader, Sad, Terrible, Tyrant, Vicious

Crumble+
Apple 33.3%
Fall 8.3%
Pudding 8.3%
Cake 4.2%
Custard 4.2%
Rhubarb 4.2%
2.1% Apricot, Biscuit, Bread, Break, Collapse, Cookie, Decay, Desert, Disintegrate, Dry, Empires, Flake, Food, Gooseberry, Grains, Life, Pastry, Pie

Crush
Orange 14.0%
Squash 14.0%
Smash 12.0%
Squeeze 8.0%
* 6.0%
Can 6.0%
Ice 6.0%
2.0% Apple, Bar, Destroy, Down, Drink, Flatten, Girl, Hard, Juice, Kill, Mush, Pen, Ribs, Rush, Stretch, Tin, Up

Crust+
Bread 73.4%
Earth 4.3%
Pie 4.3%
Cake 2.1%
Hard 2.1%
1.1% *, Coat, Crab, Crystal, Ducks, Friend, Greed, Mantle, Outside, Tart, Upper

Cry
Tear(s) 18.6%
Weep 13.9%
Sad 11.6%
Baby 9.3%
Out 6.9%
Aloud 4.7%
Shout 4.7%
2.3% *, Blub, Freedom, Hate, Laugh, Loud, Off, Please, Salt, Shame, Sleep, Snivel, Upset, Wolf

Cryptic
Clue 27.1%
Crossword 22.9%
Message 8.3%
* 6.2%
Difficult 4.2%
Puzzle 4.2%
2.1% Answer, Church, Code, Encoded, Eye, Factor, Hard, Hidden, Letter, Mountain, Old, Tank, Unknown

Cuddle
Hug 28.0%
Embrace 6.0%
Teddy 6.0%
Warm 6.0%
Warmth 6.0%
Mum 4.0%
Soft 4.0%
Toy 4.0%
Up 4.0%
2.0% Babies, Bare, Bunny, Caress, Child, Cosy, Drunk, Enclose, Fold, Girlfriend, Hold, Kiss, Me, Muddle, Together, With

Cup+
Saucer 51.1%
Tea 8.9%
Mug 6.7%
Win 4.4%
Full 2.2%
Winner 2.2%
1.1% Ale, Award, Blessing, Cater, Chalice, Coffee, Drink, Egg, Flow, Glass, Hold, Hotspur, Kitchen, Liverpool, Overflow, Paper, Plate, Sugar, Take, Trophy, Water

Cupboard
Bare 12.0%
Cup 8.0%
Kitchen 8.0%
Love 6.0%
Plate(s) 6.0%
Shelf 6.0%
Dog 4.0%
Full 4.0%
Store(s) 4.0%
2.0% Closed, Dashboard, Desk, Door, Dust, Empty, Floor, Hall, Handle, Hanger, Heart, Hook, Keep, Larder, Pots, Room, Shelves, Stanley, Storage, Teacup, Tins

Cur
* 41.7%
Dog 20.8%
Curfew 4.2%
2.1% Bad, Bar, Beast, Car, Coward, Cur, Curd, Curse, Fur, Man, Mongrel, Scum, Try, Victorian, What, -Tain

Curfew+
Night 35.7%
Late 9.5%
Dark 7.1%
Time 4.8%
War 4.8%
2.4% Africa, Contain, Coup, Curtail, Darkness, Daybreak, Death, Dusk, Early, East, Hour, Inside, Law, Military, Poland, Pub

Curly
Hair 49.5%
Straight 13.0%
* 3.2%
Perm 2.2%
Sue 2.2%
Watts 2.2%
Wavy 2.2%
Wurly 2.2%
1.2% Blonde, Brown, Crisps, Cute, Dark, Fat, Frizzy, Head, Iron, Locks, Lofty, Ringlet, Round, Soft, Tail, Tight, Wave, Waves, Wind

Currant
Bun 46.2%
Raisin 17.3%
Sultana 7.7%
* 3.8%
Fruit 3.8%
Jam 3.8%
1.9% Cake, Electric, Electricity, Jelly, Nice, Pan, Pie, Raspberries, Sweet

Current
Bun 8.9%
Now 8.9%
Water 8.9%
Past 6.7%
Affairs 4.4%
Electricity 4.4%
Event 4.4%
Present 4.4%
River 4.4%
Stream 4.4%
Voltage 4.4%
Wave 4.4%
2.2% Account, Electric, Electrical, Fast, Issue, New, News, Ninety-Three, Occasion, Previous, Recent, Soon, Strike, Sultana

Curse+
Swear 37.5%
Witch 8.3%
Money 6.2%
Damn 4.2%
Spell 4.2%
String 4.2%
Werewolf 4.2%
2.1% *, Agony, Bewitch, Blame, Bless, Fall, Hex, Oath, Pocket, Terror, Toil, Traveller, Wallet, Word

Cushion
Pillow 16.7%
Soft 10.4%
Sit 8.3%
Felt 6.2%
Sofa 6.2%
Cover 4.2%
Seat 4.2%
Settee 4.2%
2.1% *, Bed, Blow, Buttocks, Chair, Comfort, Comfy, Couch, Lush Orange, Padded, Pamper, Peter, Pin, Soften, Throw, Velour, Velvet, Whoopee

Custard+
Yellow 21.4%
Pie 11.9%
Banana(s) 7.2%
Powder 7.2%
Cream 4.8%
Milk 4.8%
Pudding 4.8%
Rhubarb 4.8%
Tart 4.8%
2.4% *, Apple, Crumble, Eggs, Elephant, Indian, Jelly, Loose, Nice, Prunes, Sauce, School

Custom+
Excise 21.4%
Tradition 14.3%
Culture 4.8%
Rite(s) 4.8%
2.4% Belong, Boat, Cap, Cow, Custard, Customer, Duty, Habit, Handshake, History, Local, Made, Men, Money, More, Mores, Officer, Official, Peace, Port, Ritual, Special, Way

Cut+
Knife 11.4%
Bleed 7.1%
Hair 7.1%
Blood 5.7%
Scissors 5.7%
Finger 4.3%
Out 3.6%
Snip 3.6%
Throat 3.6%
Up 3.6%
Wound 3.6%
Glass 2.9%
Graze 2.9%
Bruise 2.1%
Hurt 2.1%
Off 2.1%
Tear 2.1%
* 1.4%
Chop 1.4%
Sever 1.4%
Slice 1.4%
0.7% Above, Arm, Blow-Dry, Cruel, Cut, Deep, Down, Dried, Gold, Golf, Grass, Hand, Hobble, Lose, Meat, Paper, Pay, Plaster, Razor, Rip, Scrape, Scratch, Separate, Sharp, Sore, The-Crap, Thin, Through, Thrust

Cute
Sweet 14.3%
Baby 10.2%
Cuddly 10.2%
Doll 6.1%
* 4.1%
Pretty 4.1%
Toy 4.1%
2.0% Animal, Boy, Cat, Chicken, Coy, Dishy, Face, Fluffy, Girl, Kitten, Little, Love, Nice, Pale, Pet, Petite, Pink, Rabbit, Small, Twee, Ugly, Weary

Cutlass+
Sword 45.2%
Pirate 14.3%
Knife 11.9%
Coward 4.8%
2.4% *, Blade, Crystal, Cutable, Fiend, Hand, Hook, Meat, Sabre, Sailor

Cutlet+
Lamb 23.8%
Meat 19.0%
Nut 16.7%
Chop 4.8%
Food 4.8%
Knife 4.8%
Pork 4.8%
Veal 4.8%
2.4% *, Beef, Blade, Eat, Fish, Rump, Steak

Cycle
Bike 32.0%
Wheel(s) 12.0%
Ride 6.0%
Round 6.0%
Motor 4.0%
Pedal 4.0%
Track 4.0%
2.0% Bicycle, Chain, Circle, Events, Life, Loop, Menstruation, Monthly, Motorcycle, Period, Rhythm, Saddle, Spokes, Tri-, Tricycle, Tyre

Cyclone+
Wind 52.4%
Hurricane 19.0%
Storm 4.8%
Weather 4.8%
Windy 4.8%
2.4% Annie, Anticyclone, Tornado, Turmoil, Typhoon, Whirlwind

Daffodil+
Flower 28.6%
Spring 14.3%
Yellow 14.3%
Bulb 4.8%
Rose 4.8%
Tulip 4.8%
2.4% Daisy, Eat, Green, Leek, Marigold, Narcissus, Painting, School, Violet, Wales, Welsh, Wordsworth

Dairy+
Milk 25.0%
* 20.8%
Cow 10.4%
Produce 6.3%
Farm 4.2%
Product 4.2%
What 4.2%
2.1% Alter, Bright, Brilliant, Butter, Death, Differ, Herd, Milky, Queen, Tree, Vulgar, Wide

Dam
Water 31.3%
Buster 14.6%
Beaver 6.3%
River 6.3%
Burst 4.2%
2.1% Amsterdam, Awful, Bridge, Dental, Drain, Drat, Draw, Dyke, Hans, Lie, Me, Mother, Nation, Sew, Swear, Swine, Wall, Waterfall

Damage
Hurt 17.3%
Break 7.7%
* 5.7%
Broken 3.8%
Car 3.8%
Done 3.8%
Film 3.8%
Hit 3.8%
Wreck 3.8%
1.9% Accident, Beak, Beaters, Bust, Cost, Costly, Destroy, Destruction, Fire, Glass, Harm, Holes, Inc, Litigation, Loud, Maim, Pain, Person, Prevention, Ruin, Smash, Suf, Window, Wood

Damp
Wet 43.8%
Dry 6.3%
Wall(s) 6.3%
* 4.2%
Cold 4.2%
Grass 4.2%
Moist 4.2%
2.1% Bathroom, Cave, Cloth, Course, House, Letter, Lettuce, Mouse, Patch, Patches, Sponge, Thing, Towel

Dance
Music 13.0%
Around 8.7%
Disco 8.7%
Floor 6.5%
Crazy 4.3%
Step(s) 4.3%
2.2% Ballroom, Bee, Club, Crazily, Dinner, Dizzy, Fast, Fire, Float, Fun, Happy, Jig, Jive, Mad, More, Move, Naked, Prance, Sing, Skip, Song, Square, Sweat, Tango, Trance, Wolf

Dangle+
Hang 35.4%
String 8.3%
Dingle 6.3%
Angle 4.2%
Down 4.2%
Drop 4.2%
Fish 4.2%
Wave 4.2%
2.1% Bead, Bell, Carrot, Christmas, Drift, Drip, Entice, Hand, Hold, Jewel, Maggot, Swing, Thread, Twisted

Dare
Dan 10.4%
Devil 10.4%
Me 10.4%
* 8.3%
To 8.3%
You 8.3%
Truth 4.2%
Win 4.2%
2.1% Afraid, Attempt, Bet, Care, Chicken, Danger, Dangerous, Defy, Do, Double, Game, Good, Of, Speak, Stare, Threaten, Try

Dark
Light 33.3%
Night 20.0%
Side 4.4%
Skin 4.4%
2.2% Absence, Black, Bright, Brow, Cavern, Corner, Matter, Ness, Out, Passage, Secret, Seedy, Shadow, Stars, Times, Twilight, Wood

Dart+
Board 25.0%
Arrow 6.3%
Pub 6.3%
Run 6.3%
Throw 6.3%
Flight 4.2%
Games 4.2%
Light 4.2%
2.1% Amazon, Beer, Black, Bristow, Bullseye, Cold, Dagger, Dim, Dress, Driven, Fish, Flash, Fool, Loki, Mouth, Night, Ribbon, Sharp

Dash+
Run 18.8%
* 8.3%
Across 4.2%
Fast 4.2%
Off 4.2%
Quick 4.2%
Rush 4.2%
Sauce 4.2%
2.1% -Ing, About, Around, Brave, Clothes, Colon, Comma, Cut, Dabble, Dart, Dish, Goal, Hopes, Loo, Race, Slash, Smash, Sprint, Spurt, Three-Minute, Throw, Tube, Wish

Dashboard
Car 60.0%
Drive 6.0%
Desk 4.0%
Speedo 4.0%
2.0% Black, Clock, Crash, Dials, Distance, Dust, Flashpan, Furry, Indicator, Plastic, Speed, Walnut, Wooden

Date+
Time 10.9%
* 6.5%
Calendar 6.5%
Apple 4.3%
Birthday 4.3%
Fig 4.3%
Fruit 4.3%
Man/Men 4.3%
Stone 4.3%
Today 4.3%
Year 4.3%
2.2% Birth, Blind, Boyfriend, Data-phone, Day, Death, Line, Love, Mark, Now, Old, Out, Palm, Party, Plum, Prune, Romantic, Taste, Tree

Day
Night 41.7%
Break 8.3%
Time 8.3%
Long 6.3%
School 6.3%
Light 4.2%
Sun 4.2%
2.1% *, Care, Dream, Gay, Journey, Might, Month, News, Sunday, Sunlight

Daylight
Sun 23.1%
Hours 13.5%
Night 9.6%
Day 7.7%
Sunshine 5.7%
Bright 3.8%
Dark 3.8%
Light 3.8%
Morning 3.8%
Night-Time 3.8%
1.9% *, Blue, Bulb, Darkness, Dawn, Evening, Fall, Midnight, Savings, Time, Window

Dazzle+
Bright 20.8%
Glare 12.5%
Light 10.4%
Star 6.3%
Daze 4.2%
Dip 4.2%
Razzle 4.2%
Ships 4.2%
Sparkle 4.2%
2.1% Blaze, Blind, Deceive, Devil, Dry, Eyes, Fool, Gleam, Glister, Glitter, Headlights, Lights, Shine, Starlight

Dead
Alive 28.6%
Loss 9.5%
End 7.1%
Gone 4.8%
Head 4.8%
2.4% Age, Buried, Coffin, Dead, Deceased, Die, Friend, Good, Gravestone, Heavy, Mother, Mourn, Old, Quiet, Relative, Ringer, Sad, Sleep, Still

Deal
Card(s) 63.8%
2.1% *, Bad, Bridge, Business, City, Dodgy, Good, Kent, Money, Out, Pact, Poker, Share, Strike, With, Wood, Wool

Decker
Double 57.8%
Bus 24.4%
* 8.9%
Black 4.4%
2.2% Cards, Chair

Death+
Grave 12.5%
Life 10.4%
Despair 4.2%
Destruction 4.2%
Die 4.2%
Dumb 4.2%
Funeral 4.2%
Sorrow 4.2%
2.1% Bury, Coffin, Cold, Corpse, Darkness, Dawn, Dead, Drake, Empty, Graveyard, Grief, Hear, House, Loss, Morbid, Resurrection, Row, Sadness, Silent, Squander,

Still, Sting, Venice, Wish, Yesterday

Decade
Year(s) 40.9%
Ten 23.8%
* 6.8%
2.3% Ten Years, Twenty Years, Age, Century, Dance, Long Time, Past, Seventies, Time

Declare
State 12.6%
Customs 12.5%
Say 12.5%
* 8.3%
Announce 4.2%
Cricket 4.2%
Love 4.2%
Speak 4.2%
2.1% All, Amazement, Exclaim, Give-In, Give-Up, Hide, Independence, Interest, Note, Nothing, Post, Show, Speech, Statement, Tell, To, VAT, Want

Decoration
Medal(s) 21.4%
Christmas 19.0%
Cake 11.9%
Paint 11.9%
Flowers 4.8%
2.4% *, Balloons, House, Icing, Lights, Military, New, Ornate, Painter, Paper, Parading, Plant, Wall

Defence
Attack 11.9%
Army 9.5%
Gun(s) 7.1%
Ministry 7.1%
Self 7.1%
Missile(s) 4.8%
Nuclear 4.8%
Offence 4.8%
War 4.8%
2.4% Alternative, Defeat, Fight, Fleet, Hit, Look-After, Mechanism, Military, Minister, Passive, Police, Posture, Realm, System, Verdict, Waste

Deft+
Skillful 10.4%
Adept 8.3%
Agile 8.3%
Swift 8.3%
Neat 6.3%
Skilled 6.3%
Able 4.2%
Adroit 4.2%
Clever 4.2%
Good 4.2%
* 4.2%
2.1% Accurate, Careful, Charm, Clumsy, Competent, Dexterity, Dumb, Efficient, Fast, Handy, Light, Nimble, Nimble Fingered, Oaf, Quick

Delicate
Fragile 14.3%
Flower 8.2%
Gentle 6.1%
Soft 6.1%
Touch 6.1%
* 4.1%
China 4.1%
Lace 4.1%
Light 4.1%
Strong 4.1%
Thin 4.1%
2.0% OK, Balance, Bird, Dainty, Ease, Fine, Flavour, Glass, Heavy, Lily, Membrane, Precise, Pretty, Subject, Taste, Tiny, Young

Delicatessen
Food 26.2%
Shop 16.7%
Meat(s) 9.5%
Sausage 7.1%
Eat 4.8%
Pastrami 4.8%
2.4% Cake, Cafe, Cold Meats, Counter, Grocer, Houmous, Italian, Salami, Smell, Strawberries, Sweets, Yum

Delirium
Fever 27.9%
Tremens 11.6%
Mad 9.3%
* 7.0%
Ill 7.0%
Illness 7.0%
Ecstatic 4.7%
2.3% Anxiety, Chaos, Delusion, Fit, Happy, Madness, Priest, Sleep, Stupor, Trance, Unwell

Demand
Ask 41.7%
Want 12.5%
Bill 8.3%
* 4.2%
Angry 4.2%
Order 4.2%
2.1% Act, Argue, Bank, Find, It, Money, Payment, Rights, Supply, Try, Urgency, Withdraw

Den
Lion(s) 24.0%
Hide 6.0%
Lair 6.0%
Play 6.0%
* 4.0%
Bear 4.0%
Children 4.0%
Hideaway 4.0%
Iniquity 4.0%
Tree-House 4.0%
2.0% Alcove, Cave, Dent, Dirty, Dog, Fire, Fox, Foxes, Hell, How, Leaves, Live, Mess, Millwall, Otter, Room, Secret, Study

Dennis
Menace 26.5%
Waterman 12.2%
* 8.5%
Thatcher 8.2%
Healey 6.1%
Hopper 6.1%
Nielson 6.1%
Taylor 6.1%
Brown 4.1%
Norris 4.1%
2.0% Gnasher, Law, Name, Norden, Quaid, The-Menace

Dense
Thick 48.0%
Forest 8.0%
Cloud(s) 4.0%
Heavy 4.0%
Stupid 4.0%
Wood 4.0%
2.0% *, Bastard, Brush, Dent, Hole, Jungle, Liquid, Matter, Murky, Person, Population, Smug, Solid, Thin

Dent
Car 32.0%
Mark 8.0%
Bend 6.0%
Hole 6.0%
* 4.0%
Arthur 4.0%
Bash 4.0%
Bump 4.0%
Tooth(Teeth) 4.0%
2.0% Bang, Bonnet, Bruise, Crash, Damage, Dent, Dint, Flat, Floss, Metal, Pride, Scrap, Small-Village-In-Westmoreland, Wing

Depose+
King(s) 23.9%
Dictator 8.7%
Usurp 8.7%
* 4.3%
Leader 4.3%
2.2% Napoleon, Country, Coup, Crown, Deposit, Dethrone, End, Fall, Kill, Knock, Lose, Monarch, Oust, Out, Push, Put Down, Regime, Remove, Resign, Rid, Sack, Stop, Unseat

Depression
Sad 17.0%
Anxiety 6.4%
Sadness 6.4%
Anger 4.3%
Down 4.3%
Low 4.3%
2.1% Blackness, Boredom, Clinical, Disaster, End, Fed-Up, Gloom, Great, Grey, Guilt, Help, Hole, Lull, Misery, Mood, Mother, Resentment, Sorrow, Suicide, Sulk, Thirty, Trance, Unhappiness, Upset, Void, Weather, Worry

Depth
Water 14.6%
Deep 12.5%
Charge 10.4%
Sea 8.3%
Dark 6.3%
Feeling 4.2%
Height 4.2%
Meaningful 4.2%
Pool 4.2%
Width 4.2%
2.1% *, Breadth, Darkness, Depression, Forest, Gauge, Measurement, Murky, Ocean, Out, Sentient, Swimming, Understand

Desert
Sand 19.6%
Dry 13.0%
Island 10.9%
Hot 6.5%
Orchid 4.3%
Sky 4.3%
2.2% *, Arid, Arizona, Cake, Camel, Chocolate, Disc, Fathers, Flower, Heat, Lose, Oasis, Peach, Pudding, Rat, Rock, Storm, Sweet, Water

Desk+
Work 16.7%
Top 14.6%
Chair 12.5%
Table 10.4%
Lamp 8.3%
Write 8.3%
School 6.3%
Bureau 4.2%
Writing 4.2%
2.1% Class, Light, Office, Pencil, Space, Teacher, White

Destitute
Poor 30.0%
Homeless 14.0%
Beggar 6.0%
Alone 4.0%
Broke 4.0%

Tramp 4.0%
2.0% *, Down, Down-And-Out, Grey, House, Lowly, Moan, Money, Moneyless, Old, Once, Out, Pauper, Poverty, Prostitute, Rich, Skint, Streets, Weak

Destruction
Building(s) 12.8%
Bomb 10.6%
Destroy 10.6%
War 6.4%
Construction 4.3%
Ruin 4.3%
2.1% Blown-Up, Blow-Up, Build, Bulldozer, Demolish, Demolition, Eve, Explosion, Extinction, Fight, Free, God, Hazard, Horrid, Horror, IRA, Needless, Nigh, Property, Rain-Forest, Rubble, Site, Swipe, Test, Weapons

Detective
Police 16.7%
Morse 9.5%
Novel 7.1%
Sherlock-Holmes 7.1%
Spy 7.1%
* 4.8%
Story 4.8%
2.4% Ace, Cluedo, Criminal, Dick, Friend, Game, Guns, Inspector, In-Charge, Magnifying-Glass, Private-Eye, Private-Investigator, Search, Singing, Snoop, Spy, TV, Watching

Devil
Worship 20.8%
Evil 12.5%
Angel 8.3%
Care 6.3%
Demon 6.3%
God 6.3%
Bad 4.2%
Satan 4.2%
2.1% *, Cares, Catch, Disguise, Drake, Dyke, Goat, Hell, Imp, Incarnate, Tail, Watcher, Worshipper

Devise
Plan 19.0%
Invent 16.7%
Think 11.9%
* 4.8%
Idea(s) 4.8%
Make 4.8%
2.4% Compile, Control, Create, Destroy, Develop, Divine, Engineer, Game, Make-Up, Originate, Plot, Scheme, Strategy, Think-Up, Try, Work

Dew
Drop(s) 33.3%
Morning 18.8%
Grass 10.4%
Rain 6.3%
Wet 6.3%
2.1% Attach, Clover, Cow, Damp, Dawn, Fresh, Frost, Green, Jew, Milk, Point, Water

Dial
Telephone 31.2%
Phone 14.6%
Murder 10.4%
Number 8.3%
Ring 6.2%
Knob 4.2%
Sun 4.2%
2.1% *, Date, Disc, Drug, Help, In, Letters, Lim, M, Watch

Diamond
Jewel(s) 9.5%
Ring 9.5%
Cut 7.1%
Gold 7.1%
Carbon 4.8%
Forever 4.8%
Stone 4.8%
2.4% *, ?, Ashes, Back, Bright, Clear, Colour, Crystal, Expensive, Geezer, Hard, Jewellery, Light, Like, Mine, Pearl, Precious, Ruby, Shape, Sparkle, Wealth

Did
Not 40.4%
Done 19.2%
* 15.4%
Do 7.7%
Don't 3.8%
1.9% Act, Dare, Didn't, Past, Was, Went, What

Die
Death 20.9%
Hard 14.0%
Live 11.6%
End 4.7%
Grave 4.7%
2.3% *, Asleep, Cemetery, Coffin, Cure, Dead, Deceased, Dog, Fade, Fall, Humiliation, Kill, Live, Sad, Shrivel, Soon, Sorry, What, White

Diesel
Engine 39.6%
Fuel 29.2%
Oil 10.4%
Train 8.3%
Fume(s) 6.3%
2.1% Lorry, Motor, Sun

Diet
Food 28.6%
Slim 11.9%
Weight 11.9%
Thin 7.1%
* 4.8%
Pill 4.8%
2.4% Abstain, Anorexia, Coke, Eat, Fad, Fat, Healthy, Hunger, Measure, Plan, Regime, Women

Difficult
Hard 53.1%
Easy 12.2%
2.0% Blank, Case, Child, Idea, Life, Pleasant, Problem, Soon, Sums, Tall, Test, Times, Tricky, Woman, Work, Working, Writing

Dig
Hole 29.2%
Grave 10.4%
Bury 8.3%
Garden 6.2%
Spade 6.2%
Delve 4.2%
Down 4.2%
Dug 4.2%
Find 4.2%
Soil 4.2%
2.1% Dump, Earth, Gold, Jab, Mine, Shovel, Trench, Trowel, Up

Din
Noise 79.2%
Loud 4.2%
Racket 4.2%
2.1% Headache, Horrible, Lid, Noisy, Plug, Shout

Dingy
Boat 25.5%
Dark 14.9%
Dirty 6.4%
Grey 4.3%
Room 4.3%
2.1% Base, Damp, Dank, Dirt, Dreary, Dull, Grotty, House, Lousy, Low, Park, Plastic, Sad, Sail, Sailboat, Scrappy, Seedy, Small, Smelly, Water

Dip
Sheep 14.6%
Stick 14.6%
Down 4.2%
Hollow 4.2%
Swim 4.2%
2.1% *, Big, Chocolate, Deep, Dick, Dig, Dipper, Dive, Drop, Duck, Dunk, Fair, Fall, Fondue, Ladle, Lights, Lucky, Pen, Pond, Salad, Silly, Sky, Slip, Slope, Spoon, Sway, Tip, Water

Diplomat
Foreign 10.7%
* 7.1%
Ambassador 6.0%
Politician 6.0%
Embassy 4.8%
Bag 3.6%
Government 3.6%
Abroad 2.4%
Briefcase 2.4%
Country 2.4%
Immune 2.4%
Immunity 2.4%
Politics 2.4%
Service 2.4%
1.2% Amnesty, Away, Bastard, Black-Shoes, Boss, Britain, Career, Careful, Consul, Cream, Dad, Dinner-Suit, Envoy, Exempt, Honour, Important, International, Liar, Man, Office, Official, Orange, Posh, Reason, Representative, Servant, Speak, Statesman, Suit, Tactful, Talks, Uniform, Yellow

Dirty
Clean 26.7%
Washing 8.9%
Water 8.9%
Laundry 6.7%
2.2% Bastard, Clothes, Dancing, Devil, Dirt, Ink, Kitchen, Leaves, Linen, Messy, Mind, Old, Pig, Rotten, Shirt, Smell, Smelly, Soiled, Trick, Unclean, Untidy, Word

Disagree
Argue 59.5%
Agree 7.1%
Argument 4.8%
Object 4.8%
Row 4.8%
2.4% Accord, Again, Conflict, Disaccord, Disrespect, Fight, No, Stomach

Disappear
Vanish 47.6%
Find 9.5%
Go 9.5%
Gone 4.8%
2.4% Appear, Away, Bilbo, Evaporate, Hide, Improve, Invisible, Lose, Magic, Mystery, Reappear, Remove

Disarray
Mess 23.9%

* 10.9%
Chaos 8.7%
Array 6.5%
Untidy 6.5%
Dishevelled 4.3%
2.2% Anarchy, Awry, Confusion, Crime, Dishevel, Disorder, Disorganisation, Disorganised, Hair, Knives, Messy, Muddle, Orderly, Panic, Pencils, Rearrange, Things, Untidiness

Disclose
Reveal 28.6%
Tell 16.7%
Secret 11.9%
Open 9.5%
Show 7.1%
2.4% *, Discover, Discredit, Inform, Information, Letter, Source, Tablet, Take, Uncover, Unveil

Discord
* 7.1%
Argue 7.1%
Harmony 7.1%
Music 7.1%
Accord 4.8%
Concord 4.8%
Noise 4.8%
2.4% Angst, Antagonists, Apart, Argument, Bad, Chaotic, Confusion, Disagree, Disco, Discourse, Disharmony, Enchant, Hate, Jar, Joint, Mess, Note, Orchestra, Sound, Strife, Tune, Union, Unity, Unrest

Discount
Cheap 9.5%
Bargain 7.1%
Offer 7.1%
Price 7.1%
Shop 7.1%
Store 7.1%
Money 4.8%
Sale 4.8%
Save 4.8%
2.4% Automatic, Budget, Cheaper, Co-Op, Con, Cut, Discount, Exclude, Free, Odd, Off, Payment, Purchase, Reduce, Sell, Voucher, Warehouse

Discourse
Talk 20.2%
Conversation 11.9%
Speech 9.5%
* 5.9%
Discussion 4.8%
Chat 3.6%
Analysis 2.4%
Argument 2.4%
Converse 2.4%
Deviant 2.4%
Dialectic 2.4%
Discuss 2.4%
Harmony 2.4%
Language 2.4%
Lecture 2.4%
Rhyme 2.4%
Wrong 2.4%
1.2% Anger, Boring, Current, Disco, Disunity, Golf, Intercourse, Miscourse, Narrative Rhetoric, River, Sad, Socrates, Speak, Tennis

Discover
Find 66.7%
Treasure 4.8%
Unearth 4.8%
2.4% America, Country, Create, Gold, Ideas, Learn, Research, Reveal, Secret, Voyage

Disease
Illness 26.2%
Ill 23.8%
Death 9.5%
Cure 4.8%
2.4% Cholera, Decay, Disorder, Distant, Distemper, Germ, Head, House, Leprosy, Rare, Ridden, Scum, Scurvy, Sick, World

Disgrace
* 19.6%
Shame 17.4%
Bad 10.9%
Terrible 6.5%
Sad 4.3%
2.2% Blame, Disgust, Drunk, Embarrass, Faeces, Grace, Honour, Humiliation, Life, Luck, Misbehave, Naked, Poor, Punishment, School, Sin, Trouble, Woe, Wrong

Dish
Plate 28.6%
Bowl 11.9%
Pie 9.5%
Kitchen 4.8%
Meal 4.8%
2.4% Carrot, China, Container, Course, Eat, Food, Forth, Full, Glass, Gravy, Kiss, Meat, Pan, Satellite, Serve, Soup, Washer

Disk
Record 25.0%
Drive 16.7%
Computer 14.6%
Compact 10.4%
Floppy 8.3%
Round 4.2%
Soup 4.2%
2.1% Baby, Black, Bright, Flat, Jockey, Slipped, Spine, Throw

Dismount
Horse 57.1%
Off 7.1%
* 4.8%
Get 4.8%
Leave 4.8%
2.4% Disjoin, Disk, Dismember, Down, Gate, Pull, Ride, Take, Undo

Disobey
Naughty 19.0%
Order(s) 19.0%
* 7.1%
Disobedient 4.8%
Obey 4.8%
Rebel 4.8%
Rule(s) 4.8%
Wrong 4.8%
2.4% Aliens, Annoy, Bad, Child, Command, Deceive, Evil, Flout, Good, Ignore, Problem, Tantrum, Unruly

Disorder
Chaos 54.8%
Order 7.1%
Mess 4.8%
2.4% Array, Disarray, Discord, Disease, Dismay, Disorganize, Ill, Lost, Messy, Muddle, Riot, Unrest, Untidy, Wrong

Dispatch
Send 54.8%
Rider 11.9%
Letter 7.1%
Away 4.8%
Kill 4.8%
Post 4.8%
2.4% Messenger, Port, Release, Rid, Send-Off

Distant
Far 45.0%
Near 6.8%
Cousin(s) 4.5%
Relative 4.5%
2.3% *, Evasive, Faraway, Fog, Here, Hills, Horizon, Land, Life, Lives, Long, Memory, Past, Person, Place, Star, Travel

Distemper
Dog 38.1%
Disease 9.5%
Illness 7.1%
Paint 7.1%
Animal 4.8%
Die 4.8%
2.4% Canine, Fever, Guts, Horse, Ill, Indigestion, Pain, Rabid, Sick, Style, Vet, Virus

Distress
Cry 7.1%
Damsel 7.1%
Help 7.1%
Sorrow 7.1%
* 4.8%
Confusion 4.8%
Fear 4.8%
Flare 4.8%
Sad 4.8%
Upset 4.8%
2.4% Anger, Anguish, Anxiety, Attack, Dismay, Emotion, Fraught, Love, Maiden, Message, Pain, Sea, Signal, Stress, Tears, Tragic, Trouble, Worry

Distrust
* 32.6%
Hate 8.7%
Fear 6.5%
Dislike 4.3%
Liar 4.3%
Lie 4.3%
Wary 4.3%
2.2% Askance, Beard, Cynical, Dealer, Destroy, False, Government, Infidel, Lose, Lost, Police, Sly, Stupid, Suspicion, Trust, Unfaithful

Divide
Multiply 21.4%
Separate 14.3%
Split 14.3%
Subtract 11.9%
Conquer 4.8%
Halve 4.8%
Rule 4.8%
2.4% Add, Country, Cut, Egg, Half, Mathematics, Part, Ruler, Share, Sums

Divine
God 28.6%
Godly 11.9%
Holy 9.5%
Heavenly 7.1%
Good 4.8%
Regal 4.8%
2.4% Beauty, Celestial, Draw, Godlike, Great, Heaven, Intervention, Mercy, Mortal, Music, Nirvana, Pleasant, Rule, Wonderful

Do
Make 16.3%
Don't 14.0%
* 7.0%
Act 7.0%
Done 7.0%
Die 4.7%
Lot 4.7%

Nothing 4.7%
Right 4.7%
Something 4.7%
Work 4.7%
2.3% Achieve, Action, Complete, Go, It, Not, Say, What

Document
Paper(s) 59.5%
Article 4.8%
Bill 4.8%
2.4% Book, Briefcase, Deed, Doctor, Folder, Law, Legal, Passport, Rule, Secret, Sheet, Text, Type

Dodge
Avoid 12.5%
Car 8.3%
Escape 8.3%
Miss 8.3%
Swerve 6.2%
* 4.2%
Artful 4.2%
Duck 4.2%
Hit 4.2%
Rain 4.2%
2.1% Agile, Blow, Bound, Dart, Dickens, Evade, Fair, Hide, Netball, Raindrops, Roger, Run, Sideways, Sway, Traffic, Truck, Weave

Dog
Cat 51.1%
Bark 8.9%
Lead 6.7%
2.2% Animal, Bite, Bone, Days, Dog, Flea, Fog, Horse, Hound, House, Hunt, Life, Shit, Tired, Woolly

Dogcart
* 29.2%
Race 12.5%
Go-Cart 8.3%
Horse 6.3%
Children 4.2%
Dog 4.2%
Wheel 4.2%
2.1% Beauty, Cat, Catnap, Film, Kennel, Mane, Racing, Rag-And-Bone, Ride, Sleigh, Small, Tinker, Truck, Wood

Dogwood
* 30.8%
Tree 21.2%
Rose 15.4%
Flower(s) 5.7%
Brown 3.8%
1.9% Blossom, Cat, Dog-Rose, Herb, Island, Plant, Red, Shit, Song, Timber, Wedgewood, Wood

Doll
House 33.3%
Toy 12.5%
Play 8.3%
Dress 6.2%
Child 4.2%
Girl 4.2%
2.1% Baby, Barbie, Bread, Bright, Car, Game, Grey, Mannequin, Plate, Plaything, Pram, Puppet, Rag, Sindy, Woman

Dolphin
Whale 19.0%
Fish 16.7%
Sea 14.3%
Mammal 11.9%
Friend 4.8%
2.4% Beauty, Fin, Flipper, Friendly, Grey, Intelligence, Nice, Ocean, Porpoise, Regicide, Sea-Lion, Squeak, Swimming, Water

Domain
Kingdom 23.9%
Home 17.4%
Area 8.7%
Realm 8.7%
Range 4.3%
Territory 4.3%
2.2% Above, Castle, Ground, Ideas, Jungle, King, Knot, Lair, Mine, Now, Over, Power, Protein, Region, Sydney

Dominion
Kingdom 17.4%
Land(s) 10.9%
King 8.7%
* 6.5%
Theatre 6.5%
Empire 4.3%
Republic 4.3%
State 4.3%
2.2% Authority, Carolingions, Castle, Concert, Dominate, Dominican, Great, Home, Lord, Power, Powerful, Realm, Rule, Sisters, Status, World

Don
Johnson 20.4%
* 12.9%
Maclean 10.2%
Juan 6.1%
Brennan 4.1%
Duck 4.1%
Giovanni 4.1%
Quixote 4.1%
Thomson 4.1%
2.0% Corleone, Cortes, Dad, Fardon, Godfather, Henderson, Idiot, Ivy, Milligan, Name, Oxford, Ragga, Reagan, Spencer, Uncle

Donate
Give 39.6%
Money 29.2%
Blood 8.3%
Charity 4.2%
2.1% *, All, Doughnut, Green, Kidney, Liver, Nothing, Pledge, Some

Donkey
Ride 18.8%
Ass 12.5%
Horse 12.5%
Mule 10.4%
Carrot 6.2%
Cart 6.2%
Years 6.2%
Ears 4.2%
2.1% Bray, Jesus, Kong, Mare, Patient, Pin, Pony, Sands, Spanish, Stick, Transport

Door
Handle 20.8%
Open 14.6%
Knob 6.2%
Shut 6.2%
Stop 6.2%
Entrance 4.2%
Frame 4.2%
Wall 4.2%
2.1% Boring, Bovine, Closed, Closing, Drab, Glad, House, Key, Opening, Paint, Room, Sad, Unsmiling, Way, Way-Out, Window

Doorbell
Ring(s) 66.7%
Knocker 6.3%
Ding-Dong 4.2%
2.1% Bell, Buzzer, Coat, Ding, House, Noise, Press, Right, Sound, Step, Wire

Doorknob
Handle 25.0%
Brass 13.5%
Door 13.5%
Key 7.7%
Open 7.7%
* 3.8%
Bell 3.8%
Gold 3.8%
Knocker 3.8%
1.9% Front-Door, Hand, Hold, Knob, Knock, Switch, Tray, Turn, Yellow

Doss
* 31.2%
Sleep 16.7%
Tramp 8.3%
Rest 6.2%
Lazy 4.2%
Work 4.2%
2.1% Bad, Cats, Disk, Drop, Dross, Easy, Gold, House, Laze, Lie, Nothing, Rat, Stick, What

Double
Two 11.9%
Single 7.1%
Take 7.1%
Trouble 7.1%
Cream 4.8%
Identity 4.8%
Life 4.8%
Vision 4.8%
2.4% *, Body, Bogey, Entendre, Glasses, Indemnity, Loss, Nothing, Pair, Quick, Rule, Sight, Time, Top, Treble, Twice, Twin, Up, Whammy, Win

Doubt
* 12.5%
Wonder 8.3%
Fear 6.3%
Question 6.3%
Worry 6.3%
Full 4.2%
Sure 4.2%
Thomas 4.2%
2.1% Beard, Believe, Change, Deceive, Doubtful, Faith, Guess, In, It, Mistrust, Mumble, No, Reserved, Self, Shady, Shame, Suspicion, Trust, Truth, Uncertainty, Vague, Whether, Worried

Dove
Peace 29.2%
Bird 20.8%
Cote 16.7%
White 6.2%
Pigeon 4.2%
Tail 4.2%
2.1% Ark, Devil, Hawk, Love, Olive, Pal, Spring, Turtle, Wing

Down
Up 40.5%
And-Out 4.8%
Out 4.8%
Ward 4.8%
2.4% *, Below, Bottom, Depressed, Fall, Falling, Grade, Hard, Hill, Kent, Lift, Market, Mouth, Side, Sledge, Slide, Spiral, Stream, Syndrome

Downtown
City 14.0%
Uptown 12.0%
Manhattan 8.0%
New-York 8.0%
Shops 4.0%
Sleazy 4.0%

2.0% Area, Billy-Joel, Brandreth, Busy, Car, Chicago, China, Club, Detroit, Dionne, Down, Fun, Ghetto, Girl, Going, Lights, Litter, Road, Shopping, Slum, Suburb, Taxi, Town, Traffic, Vancouver

Downward
Upward(s) 31.0%
Motion 7.1%
Slope 7.1%
Spiral 4.8%
Stairs 4.8%
Trend 4.8%
Up 4.8%
2.4% Aaagghhh, Below, Cascade, Drop, Fall, Force, Forwards, Go, Hill, Ho, Mobility, Process, Slide, Stream, Wind

Drab+
Dull 29.2%
Boring 20.8%
Dreary 12.5%
Grey 8.3%
Plain 4.2%
2.1% Bare, Blue, Brown, Clothes, Colour, Dingy, Drip, Nasty, Paint, Shabby, Streets, Wall

Draft+
Wind 20.8%
* 6.3%
Air 4.2%
Breeze 4.2%
Chess 4.2%
Cold 4.2%
Plan 4.2%
Windy 4.2%
Write 4.2%
2.1% Beer, Blow, Board, Choice, Cold-Wind, Contract, Cool, Deep, Draw, Dregs, Dry, Gap, Letter, Mode, Out, Pint, Rough, Soldier, Will, Window, Write-Up

Drag+
Pull 33.3%
Bore 8.3%
Carry 8.3%
Net 6.2%
Cigarette 4.2%
Race 4.2%
2.1% *, Ball, Bus, Chair, Dirt, Fag, Fall, Foot, Long, Party, Queen, Rope, Slow, Smoke, Sniff, Transvestite, Woman

Dragon+
Fly 20.8%
Fire 14.6%
Slay 8.3%
George 6.2%
Knight 6.2%
Old 6.2%
2.1% Breath, Dungeon, Feet, Fiery, Fight, Flames, Frail, Girlfriend, Horror, Kill, Matron, Monster Princess, Puff, Story, Wales, Witch, Wonderful

Dragonfly
Insect 17.3%
Pond 15.4%
Wings 11.5%
* 3.8%
Blue 3.8%
Buzz 3.8%
1.9% Bees, Bluefly, Butterfly, Colourful, Country, Eyes, Fairy, Flit, Flutter, Fly, Free, Green, Horrid, Larva, Purple, Short, Speed, Spider, Summer, Sweden, Vibrate, Water

Drain+
Pipe 14.6%
Sewer 12.5%
Gutter 8.3%
Water 8.3%
Ditch 6.2%
Down 6.2%
Smell 6.2%
* 4.2%
Hole 4.2%
2.1% Cover, D, Dry, Empty, Exhaust, Joist, Mend, Rain, Sewage, Sink, Street, Suck, Tyre, Well

Dram+
Whisky 41.7%
Drink 10.4%
* 6.3%
Scotch 6.3%
Wee 6.3%
Weight 4.2%
2.1% -Buie, Beauty, Beer, Dreary, Drop, Glamorous, Gram, Measure, Ounce, Pump, Rock, Tot

Draw
Picture(s) 26.2%
Pen 7.1%
Art 4.8%
Design 4.8%
Paper 4.8%
Pencil 4.8%
2.4% *, Artist, Back, Cartoon, Doodle, Gun, It, Line, Lottery, Luck, Man, Money, Paint, Pleasure, Poker, Prize, Resources, Scribble, Smoke, Straw

Dread+
Fear 56.3%
Hate 6.3%
Judge 6.3%
Lock 4.2%
Nought 4.2%
Worry 4.2%
2.1% Anguish, Awful, Bore, Drear, Help, Locks, Loss, No, Scared

Dream
Sleep 31.9%
Nightmare 8.5%
Fantasy 6.4%
Clouds 4.3%
Night 4.3%
On 4.3%
State 4.3%
2.1% *, Bad, Boat, Down, Escape, Hazy, Hope, Interpretation, Man, Pleasant, Sequence, Sheep, Sky, Sleepiness, Time, Vacant, Wish

Dredge+
Mud 10.4%
River 10.4%
Drawl 10.4%
Canal 4.2%
Clear 4.2%
Lake 4.2%
Sift 4.2%
Silt 4.2%
Sludge 4.2%
2.1% Boat, Bottom, Depths, Dig, Differ, Ditch, Down, Drag, Drain, Electricity, Net, Rake, Scoop, Sea, Seabed, Search, Ship, Sieve, Sugar, Sunk, Water

Drench+
Wet 32.0%
Soak 24.0%
Rain 18.0%
Soaked 4.0%
2.0% *, Blood, Coat, Dry, Her, Judy, Skin, Soaking, Sweat, Tired, Water

Dress+
Clothes 14.6%
Skirt 12.5%
Up 10.4%
Church 4.2%
Gown 4.2%
Robe 4.2%
Shirt 4.2%
2.1% Fine, Frilly, Frock, Girl, Headgear, Length, Material, Nice, Nicely, Occasion, Preach, Pretty, Sense, Sew, Silk, Smart, Smartly, Style, Suit, Wear, Well, Woman

Dresser
Table 17.8%
* 6.7%
Clothes 6.7%
Wardrobe 6.7%
Bedroom 4.4%
Coat 4.4%
Furniture 4.4%
2.2% Antique, Big, Cabinet, Chest-Of-Drawers, Cupboard, Draw, Drawers, Dress, Dressing, Film, Fuel, Kitchen, Mirror, Oak, Pine, Plates, Rail, Read, Up, Wear, Welsh, Wooden

Drift+
Wood 18.0%
Away 16.0%
Snow 16.0%
Wander 8.0%
* 4.0%
Off 4.0%
Sail 4.0%
2.0% About, By, Down, Drive, Flake, Flow, Inn, Log, Net, Over, River, Sea, Sway, Wave, White

Drill+
Hole 13.0%
Bit 10.9%
* 6.5%
Army 6.5%
Hammer 6.5%
Fire 4.3%
Sergeant 4.3%
Tool 4.3%
2.2% Bad, Core, Chisel, Concrete, Dagger, Dentist, Differ, Easy, Electric, Mechanical, Plastic, Pneumatic, Regular, Safe, Saw, Scared, Sound, Wary, Workmen

Drone
Bee(s) 47.9%
Noise 8.3%
Bore 4.2%
Boring 4.2%
Wasp 4.2%
2.1% *, Blah-Blah, Carry-On, Ceaseless, Fish, Fly, Groan, Hum, Lecture, Moan, Nasal, On, Queen, Radio, Whinge

Drool+
Dribble 14.6%
Slobber 12.5%
* 10.4%
Spit 6.3%
Food 4.2%
2.1% Book, Dog, Drill, Drip, Greed, Hunger, Letch, Look, Love, Lust, Old Men, Paint, Painted, Pen, Pencil, Picture, Saliva, Scene, Slaver, Slime, Slurp, Stick, Taste, Wet, Yum

Drop
Fall 16.3%
Dead 14.0%
Ocean 11.6%
Down 7.0%
2.3% Ball, Break, Darn, Dead-Donkey, Dew, Discard, Floor, Glass, High, Large, Nineteens, Off, Oil, Out, Pen, Run, Scone, Shot, Small, Table, Tilt, Water

Drought+
Dry 22.9%
Famine 16.7%
Water 14.6%
Rain 12.5%
Ethiopia 8.3%
Desert 4.2%
2.1% Africa, Fair, Fish, Heat, Lack, Neglect, Storm, Sun, Thirst, Waterless

Drown
Water 34.0%
Die 10.6%
Death 8.5%
Swim 6.4%
Float 4.3%
Rat 4.3%
2.1% *, Cats, Clown, Dead, Dive, Down, Hand, Horrible, Out, Pond, Pool, Sea, Sink, Submerge, Suffocate

Drug
Dope 8.3%
Needle(s) 8.3%
Addict 6.3%
Heroin 6.3%
Poison 6.3%
High 4.2%
Inject 4.2%
Medicine 4.2%
Pusher 4.2%
Sleep 4.2%
Take 4.2%
2.1% Amphetamine, Aspirin, Case, Chemical, Cold, Dangerous, Destroy, Doctor, Heal, Hospital, Ill, Incense, Injection, Love, Opium, Pain, Pill, Problem, Sedate

Drunk
Alcohol 18.8%
Beer 8.3%
Pissed 6.3%
Win 6.3%
Bottle 4.2%
Disorderly 4.2%
Drink 4.2%
Man 4.2%
Pub 4.2%
Punch 4.2%
2.1% Alcoholic, Booze, Cambridge, Charge, Crash, Drive, Fall, Head, Ill, Influence, Lord, Often, Pisshead, Sick, Stupor, Tramp, Water

Drunken
Stupor 38.1%
Man 11.9%
Sober 9.5%
Beer 4.8%
Drink 4.8%
State 4.8%
2.4% Alcohol, Disarray, Disgusting, Fall, Fool, Interlude, Merry, Problem, Slob, Unwell, Walk

Dry
Wet 34.0%
Hair 14.9%
Desert 8.5%
Arid 4.3%
Bone 4.3%
Clean 4.3%
Cold 4.3%
Rot 4.3%
Skin 4.3%
2.1% *, Riser, Suit, Sun, Warm, Washing, Weather, Wine

Dual
Two 22.9%
* 8.3%
Carriage-Way 6.3%
Fight 6.3%
Action 4.2%
Both 4.2%
Control 4.2%
Nature 4.2%
Single 4.2%
2.1% Bullet, Deck, Die, Duality, Duet, Engine, Guns, Identity, Lane, Lives, Loading, Personality, Purpose, Role, Route, Twice, Twin

Duck
Pond 29.2%
Drake 8.3%
Swan 6.3%
Bird 4.2%
Goose 4.2%
Out 4.2%
Platypus 4.2%
Quack 4.2%
2.1% Board, Bob, Bottoms-Up, Chick, Dodge, Down, Duckling, Hen, River, Squat, Stoop, Swims, Swing, Thames, Water, Weed, Wet

Duke+
Duchess 37.5%
Earl 25.0%
Lord 8.3%
King 4.2%
2.1% Crown, Edinburgh, Hazzard, Knight, Prince, Queen, Royalty, Wayne, Westminster, White, Windsor

Dull
Boring 27.1%
Toy 8.3%
Cloudy 6.3%
House 6.3%
Play 6.3%
Dark 4.2%
Dim 4.2%
Overcast 4.2%
2.1% Black, Bright, Clear, Cloud, Crystals, Dawn, Day, Dirty, Dream, Dreary, Dry, Hot, Light, Misty, Night, Plain

Dullness
Boring 15.2%
Boredom 8.7%
Grey 8.7%
Dreary 6.5%
Bore 4.3%
Dim 4.3%
Relax 4.3%
2.2% A?, Ability, Ache, Bored, Bright, Brightness, Colour, Dark, Deadness, Deed, Dinginess, Drab, Headache, Light, Monotony, Pain, Rain, Shine, Stupidity, Thick, Work

Dummy
Baby 16.7%
Run 10.4%
Idiot 6.3%
Dead 4.2%
Dumb 4.2%
Me 4.2%
Puppet 4.2%
Shop 4.2%
Stupid 4.2%
Suck 4.2%
Tailor(s) 4.2%
2.1% Chance, Clothes, Declarer, Doll, Fool, Mannequin, Model, Mouth, Pretend, Shop-Window, Silly, Useless, Variable, Window, Wooden, Word

Dung
Cow 31.3%
Beetle 8.3%
Manure 8.3%
Shit 8.3%
Smell 8.3%
* 4.2%
Heap 4.2%
Horse 4.2%
Mess 4.2%
2.1% Animal, Country, Cows, Crap, Gap, Midden, Muck, Stables, Steam

Dusk+
Dawn 33.3%
Night 22.9%
Sunset 10.4%
Dark 8.3%
Twilight 6.3%
Evening 4.2%
2.1% Branches, Dust, Eve, Mist, Moon, Nightfall, Sun

Dust
Dirt 22.9%
Ashes 12.5%
Ash 6.3%
Dry 6.3%
Cobweb 4.2%
Dawn 4.2%
Death 4.2%
Heat 4.2%
2.1% Ball, Bowl, Cough, Dusk, Dust, Eyes, Falls, Filthy, Fine, Hidden, Mirror, Moat, Settle, Sneeze, Sunset, Sweep, Wipe

Duster+
Dust 19.6%
Clean 13.0%
Cloth 10.9%
Feather 8.7%
* 6.5%
Hoover 4.3%
Polish 4.3%
Yellow 4.3%
2.2% Bin, Blackboard, Board, Brush, China, Cleaning, Fluff, Housework, Hustle, Load, Paper, Pledge, Sweep

Dwarf
Small 18.8%
Elf 10.4%
Gnome 10.4%
Midget 8.3%
Short 8.3%
Snow-White 8.3%
Giant 6.3%
Goblin 4.2%
Little 4.2%
Troll 4.2%
2.1% Boots, Circus, Dragon, Head, Mine, Poisoned, Porg, Snow

Dwell
Live 31.9%
House 27.7%
Home 6.4%
Linger 6.4%
Think 4.3%
2.1% Abode, Cave, Dither, Dwelling, Hang-Around, Inhabit, Island, Like, Living, Nigh, Stay

Each
Every 34.0%
One 22.0%
Other 6.0%
Both 4.0%
Of 4.0%
Own 4.0%
Way 4.0%
2.0% All, Equal, Ever, Individual, More, Peach, Person, Price, Separate, Time, Way-Bet

Eager
Beaver 37.5%
Keen 16.7%
Please 10.4%
* 6.2%
Want 4.2%
2.1% Able, Anxious, Enthusiastic, Get-On, Good, Help, Hunger, Now, Quick, Smart, To, Willing

Ear
Ring 12.8%
Hear 10.6%
Lobe 8.5%
Nose 8.5%
Ache 6.4%
Wax 6.4%
Earring 4.3%
Hearing 4.3%
2.1% Drum, Eye, Face, Flesh, Hair, Head, Hole, Mark, Mouth, Nibble, Noise, Piece, Pierce, Piercing, Plug, Shoot, Sting, Wig

Early
Late 38.1%
Morning 21.4%
Bird 7.1%
Day(s) 4.8%
Rise 4.8%
2.4% Bed, Born, Children, Closing, Here, Learning, Seven-O'Clock, Sun, Warning, Young

Earn
Money 51.1%
Work 8.5%
Job 6.4%
2.1% A-Lot, Cash, Deserve, Greek, Have, Keep, Living, More, Much, Pay, Penny, Salary, Self, Spend, Wage, Worth

Eastern
Western 38.1%
Promise 11.9%
Oriental 7.1%
Bloc 4.8%
Europe 4.8%
Front 4.8%
Japan 4.8%
2.4% Ancient, Desert, Eye, India, Shore, West, Wind, Wing, World, Wrong

Easy
Hard 23.1%
Simple 13.0%
* 3.7%
Chair 3.7%
Difficult 3.7%
Rider 3.5%
2.2% Bad, Calm, Facile, Fun, Going, Just, Lay, Meat, Morning, Not, Peasy, Quick, Try

Eat
Food 57.4%
Drink 6.4%
Up 4.3%
2.1% Cake, Consume Delicious, Dinner, Egg, Feed, Full, Hair, Hunger, Meal, Morsel, Mouth, Nice, Sleep, Sweet

Ecstasy
Drug(s) 27.7%
Joy 17.0%
Happy 8.5%
Agony 6.4%
Love 6.4%
Delight 4.3%
Happiness 4.3%
Rave 4.3%
Tablet 4.3%
2.1% *, E, Good, Nightclub, Orgasmic, Pleasure, Wonderful, Wow

Educate
Teach 23.8%
Learn 21.4%
School 19.0%
* 4.8%
Learning 4.8%
2.4% Certificate, Children, Class, Doctrine, Facilitate, Glass, Indoctrinate, Instruct Live, People, Rita

Education
School 42.9%
Learn 7.1%
* 4.8%
Book(s) 4.8%
Learning 4.8%
System 4.8%
2.4% Building, Expensive, Full-Time, GCE, Grant, Health, Management, Need, Pin, Student, Team, Thick, University

Edwina
Curry 91.8%
2.0% Carroll, Hanlan, Rice, Sox

Effluent
Waste 19.0%
* 11.9%
Sewage 11.9%
Rich 7.1%
Flowing 4.8%
River 4.8%
Rubbish 4.8%
Shit 4.8%
Water 4.8%
2.4% Environment, Exhaust, Flow, Fluent, Fluid, Nasty, Pipe, Pollution, Sewer, Sewerage, Smelly

Egg
Yolk 16.7%
Shell 14.3%
Boiled 9.5%
Chicken 7.1%
Hen 7.1%
White 7.1%
* 4.8%
Custard 4.8%
Embryo 4.8%
Nog 4.8%
2.4% Bad, Boil, Delicate, Easter, Hard, Hard-Boiled, Round, Timer

Eggplant
Aubergine 46.0%
* 4.0%
Cheese 4.0%
Egg 4.0%
Food 4.0%
2.0% America, Australia, Breadfruit, Breakfast, Casserole, Cheeseplant, Cook, Cress, Delicious, Flower, Fried, Leaves, Nice, Plant, Purple, Squash, Tomato, Vegetarian, Web

Eight
Nine 46.8%
Number 10.6%
O'Clock 6.4%
Piece(s) 6.4%
After 4.3%
Seven 4.3%
Spider 4.3%
2.1% Ball, Figure, Fold, Gate, Less, Six, Ten

Elastic+
Band 54.8%
Stretch 21.4%
Knicker(s) 4.8%
Rubber 4.8%
2.4% Firm, Game, Plaster, Plastic, Pliable, Snap

Elbow+
Grease 28.6%
Arm 26.2%
Knee 14.3%
Joint 11.9%
Room 7.1%
2.4% Angle, Arse, Bone, Give, Point

Electrocute
Kill 20.8%
Die 10.4%
Electric 6.3%
Electricity 6.3%
Shock 6.3%
Chair 4.2%
Death 4.2%
Pain 4.2%
2.1% *, AC, ES Treatment, Careful, Current, Dead, Electric Chair, Electrify, Energy, Execute, Flash, Fry, Plug, Prisoner, Sizzle, Toaster, Wealthy, Wire

Elegant
Dress 12.5%
Lady 8.3%
* 6.2%
Fine 4.2%
Grace 4.2%
Graceful 4.2%
Person 4.2%
2.1% Ball, Beautiful, Black, Chic, Clothes, Expensive, Fashion, Flash, Fragile, Gay, Girl, Glove, High, Jewellery, Legs, Neck, Palace, Posh, Pretty, Smart, Splendid, Suit, Swan, Sweet, Trim, Ugly, Watch

Elephant
Trunk 28.9%
Grey 13.3%
Mouse 6.7%
Zoo 6.7%
* 4.4%
Big 4.4%
2.2% Africa, Animal, Beer, Boly, Circus, Clumsy, Donkey, Ears, Hat, Heavy, Jungle, Life, Mice, Remember, Trap, Tusk

Elizabeth
Taylor 32.7%
* 24.8%
Queen 10.2%
Second 10.2%
Arden 4.1%
First 4.1%
Jones 4.1%
2.0% Aunt, Bowen, Mary, Stuart, Tudor

Elvis
Presley 85.7%
Costello 6.1%
Rock 4.1%
2.0% King, Music

Emerald+
Green 38.1%
Isle 19.0%
Jewel 7.1%
Stone 7.1%
Diamond 4.8%
Gem 4.8%
2.4% *, City, Crystal, Gold, Jewellery, Necklace, Wealth

Emergency
Ambulance 9.8%
* 7.3%
Accident 7.3%
999 4.9%
Crisis 4.9%
Danger 4.9%
Exit 4.9%
Help 4.9%
Rush 4.9%
Service(s) 4.9%
Ward 4.9%
2.4% Code, Doctor, Fire-Engine, Hospital, Hurry, Life, Noise, Number, Power, Problem, Quick, Red, Serious, Stop, Sudden, Tragedy

Emotion
Cry 21.4%
Love 14.3%
Tears 14.3%
Happy 7.1%
Sad 7.1%
Fear 4.8%
Feeling(s) 4.8%
2.4% *, Guilty, Laughter, Life, Loss, Open, Pain, Petrol, Pity, Red, Stress

Empty
Full 33.3%
House 14.3%
Vacant 7.1%
Vessel(s) 7.1%
Box 4.8%
Cup 4.8%
2.4% *, Bottle, Crate, Glass, Head, Hollow, Pocket, Stack, Street, Vase, Void, Words

Encrust+
Bread 13.0%
* 10.9%
Cake 6.5%
Cover 6.5%
Earth 4.3%
Hard 4.3%
Jewels 4.3%
Scab 4.3%
Stone(s) 4.3%
2.2% Agate, Bury, Close, Coat, Copious, Coral, Crystal, Diamonds, Form, Fossil, Grimy, Hidden, Mouldy, Old, Snow, Tart, Toast, Top, Volcano

End
Finish 26.8%
Beginning 14.6%
Start 9.8%
Begin 4.9%
Book 4.9%
Final 4.9%
Over 4.9%
Road 4.9%
Stop 4.9%
2.4% Bend, Black, Blank, Drop, Fire, Game, Peace, The, The-Cul-Desac-Sign

Endanger+
Species 10.9%
* 8.7%
Animal 4.3%
Cliff 4.3%
Fear 4.3%
Harm 4.3%
Hurt 4.3%
Red 4.3%
Risk 4.3%
2.2% Accident, Alarm, Danger, Dangerous, Escape, Help, Kill, Lives, Of, Peril, Persecute, Ruin, Scared, Sign, Start, Threaten, Trouble, Unsafe, Warn, Watch, Water, Whole, Wildlife

Enfold+
* 15.2%
Cover 8.7%
Fold 8.7%
Hug 6.5%
Wrap 6.5%
Envelope 4.3%
2.2% Blanket, Catch, Collapse, Crease, Embrace, Enclose, Entwine, False, Inside, Napkin, Pages, Pancake, Paper, Pleat, Robe, Shut, Surround, Tear, Tell, Time, Trap, Turn, Wood

Engine
Car 26.2%
Train 16.7%
Motor 7.1%
Oil 7.1%
Steam 7.1%
* 4.8%
Fire 4.8%
Machine 4.8%
Room 4.8%
2.4% Driver, Going, Hot, Piston, Power, Red, Thomas

English+
Language 28.6%
French 11.9%
Bad 4.8%
Irish 4.8%
Scottish 4.8%
2.4% *, Bastard, Envy, Gentlemen, Great, House, Me, Mustard, Polish, Rose, Saxon, Scots, Servant, Speech, Stiff, Student, Welsh, Xenophobia

Engrave+
Carve 9.5%
Etch 9.5%
Stone 9.5%
Cut 7.1%
Glass 4.8%
Jewel 4.8%
Mark 4.8%
Name 4.8%
Type 4.8%
2.4% Design, Emboss, Enjoin, Gold, Grave, Indell, Insight, Medal, Metal, Personalise, Plate, Scar, Scratch, Silver, Tombstone, Write, Writing

Enlist+
Army 26.1%
Join 19.6%
Sign 13.0%
* 4.3%
Enrol 4.3%
List 4.3%
Soldier 4.3%
2.2% Conscription, Enjoin, Gulf, Help, Look, Pressgang, Scared, Services, Take, Ticket, Volunteer

Enormous+
Huge 54.8%
Big 21.4%
Large 9.5%
2.4% Elephant, Giant, Massive, Monstrous, Pylon, Space

Enterprise
Business 20.9%
Starship 20.9%
Star-Trek 9.3%
Initiative 7.0%
Business 4.7%
Company 4.7%
Good 4.7%
Star 4.7%
Start 4.7%
USS 4.7%
2.3% Adventure, Allowance, Forum, Free, Spok, Unit, Will

Enthusiastic
Keen 20.0%
Happy 14.0%
Eager 10.0%
* 8.0%
Energy 4.0%
Loud 4.0%
2.0% Bright, Cheerful, Deadbeat, Dog, Euthanasia, Excited, Fan, Forward, Good, Great, Hip, Interested, Joy, Person, Schoolgirl, Shout, Support, Swimmer, Test, Total

Entwine+
Twist 15.2%
String 10.9%
* 6.5%
Embrace 6.5%
Rope 6.5%
Tangle 6.5%
Tie 6.5%
Wrap 4.3%
2.2% Catch, Cord, Cuddle, Draw, Enfold, Ivy, Link, Lips, Lock, Love, Lovers, Rip, Trap, Twine, Twisted, Us, Wind

Envelope+
Letter 66.7%
Paper 11.9%
Seal 4.8%
2.4% Amplitude, Boss, Brown, Parcel, Post, Postal, Stamp

Envious
Jealous 48.9%
Green 20.0%
Envy 4.4%
Jealousy 4.4%
2.2% *, Behaviour, Fear, Girlfriend, Hate, Idol, Love, Sibling, Weary

Envy
Green 36.2%
Jealousy 21.3%
Greed 6.4%
Jealous 6.4%
Red 4.3%
2.1% *, Bad, Deny, Desire, Fear, Gloat, Me, Need, Penis, Spoil, Success

Enzyme
Biology 23.3%
Catalyst 7.0%
* 4.7%
Chemical 4.7%
Protein 4.7%
Science 4.7%
Small 4.7%
Spit 4.7%
2.3% Acid, Amino, Bacteria, Bio-Zed, Biochemical, Blood, Chemistry, Co-Enzyme, Complex, Damage, Energy, Food, Isolate, Paste, Peptin, Pituitary, Reaction, Yeast

Equal
Same 14.6%
Equality 6.3%
Opportunity(s) 6.3%
Plus 6.3%
Women 6.3%
Level 4.2%

Measure(s) 4.2%
2.1% *, Alike, Chance, Division, Equanimity, Equivalent, Even, Fair, Life, Not, Opposite, Par, Partners, Parts, Pay, Peer, Rights, Scales, Sex, Subtract, Terms, Tie, Times, To, Unequal

Error
Mistake 54.0%
Wrong 12.0%
Correct 6.0%
Fault 4.0%
2.0% *, Calculator, Car, Fool, Happens, Minus, Of, Sin, Slip, Space, Tippex, Ways

Estate+
House 19.6%
Agent(s) 17.4%
Housing 10.9%
Land 10.9%
Management 8.7%
* 6.5%
Car 6.5%
2.2% Farm, Field, Grounds, Large, Manage, Park, Property, Real, Wealth

Estimate
Guess 43.7%
* 10.4%
Time 6.3%
2.1% About, Add, Amount, Approximate, Arrival, Assess, Builder, Expense, Give, House, Number, Quantify, Rough, Sum, Try, Under, Why, Work, Worth

Estuary
River 57.4%
Water 17.0%
Birds 4.3%
2.1% *, Dee, Large, Outlet, Pond, Sea, Sluggish, Southend, Thames

Europe
Continent 14.3%
* 7.0%
Currency 6.1%
EC 6.1%
France 6.1%
Map 6.1%
Big 4.1%
Country 4.1%
Land 4.1%
Spain 4.1%
2.0% America, Asia, Brussels, Channel, City, Community, Crap, Far, Flag, French, Holiday, Inner, Inter-Rail, Italy, Large, Place, Tunnel, Westernised, World

Eurosceptic
* 16.7%
MP(s) 8.3%
Tory 8.3%
Europe 6.3%
Politics 6.3%
Maastricht 4.2%
Conservative 4.2%
2.1% Brussels, France, Heat, Major, Ridley, UK, Cynic, Cynical, Economist, Euphemism, Fear, For Healing, Indecisive, Nationalistic, Parliament, Politician, Septic, Socialist, Stupid, Treaty, Tubes, Weird

Evade
Avoid 20.9%
Miss 10.4%
* 8.3%
Hide 8.3%
Question 6.3%
Capture 4.2%
Escape 4.2%
Kick 4.2%
2.1% Break, Dodge, Fares, Ignore, It, Join, Point, Say, Skirt-Around, Slip, Soldier, Spoil, Tine, Trespass, Try, Twist

Even
Odd(s) 33.3%
Steven(s) 7.1%
Keel 4.8%
More 4.8%
Rough 4.8%
Uneven 4.8%
2.4% *, Balance, Break, Equal, Flat, Ground, Handed, If, Level, Now, Out, Quits, Score, Smooth, Steady, Stephen, Tone

Every
Day 25.0%
One 22.9%
Each 12.5%
Where 8.3%
Time 6.3%
* 4.2%
Now 4.2%
2.1% All, Book, Boy, People, Person, Smell, True, Way

Eventfully
* 23.8
Happening(s) 11.9%
Event 7.1%
Busy 4.8%
Full 4.8%
Happen 4.8%
2.4% Active, At Last, Blurb, Boredom, Complete, Day, Evening, Exciting, Going On, Good, Horse, Important, Journey, Manifold, Moment, Productive, Uneventful

Evidence
Proof 16.7%
Court 14.3%
Body 11.9%
Crime 7.1%
* 4.8%
Police 4.8%
2.4% Aliens, Body-Of-Evidence, Clue, Court, Document, Envelope, Example, Exhibit, Facts, Fingerprints, Incriminating, Jury, Lies, Reflection, Skull, Trial, Why

Evil
Bad 14.6%
Devil 14.6%
Good 12.5%
* 10.4%
Witch 6.3%
Demon(s) 4.2%
Spirit 4.2%
Wicked 4.2%
2.1% Cruel, Deed, Hate, Head, Kneevil, Malevolent, Man, Men, Nasty, Non-Existent, People, Satan, Schmeerel, Seas

Examine
Test 37.5%
Look 10.4%
* 8.3%
Doctor 8.3%
See 4.2%
2.1% Airport, Examination, Experiment, Fear, Glance, Inspect, Medical, Observe, Paper, Patient, Probe, Stare, Thoroughly, Year, You

Excel+
Good 19.0%
Brilliant 11.9%
Achieve 4.8%
Best 4.8%
Exceed 4.8%
Win 4.8%
2.4% Better, Correct, Elite, Excess, Fast, Great, Height, High, Lotus, Lower, Over, Perform, Prize, Shine, Star, Stupendous, Succeed, Superlative, Surpass, Tops, Well

Excess+
Much 11.9%
Extra 7.1%
Fat 7.1%
More 7.1%
Over 7.1%
Overflow 4.8%
Too-Much 4.8%
2.4% *, Airport, Alcohol, Baggage, Consumption, Enough, Extortionate, Food, Greed, Increase, Indulgent, Overeat, Overmuch, Overweight, Quantity, Stuff, Superabundance, Surfeit, Too, Waste

Exchange+
Swop(s)(swap) 21.7%
Rate 19.6%
Money 15.2%
Mart 10.9%
Change 4.3%
2.2% Barter, Coins, Currency, Extreme, Foreign, Give, Market, Mix, Names, Penfriend, Promise, Stocks, Student, Value

Excise+
Cut 23.8%
Remove 14.3%
Customs 11.9%
Duty 11.9%
* 7.1%
2.4% Cleave, Cut-Out, Eradicate, Erase, Exorcist, Extricate, Fit, Ghost, Power, Rid, Rip-Out, Show, Withdraw

Excitement
Fun 9.8%
Happy 7.3%
Joy 7.3%
Thrill 7.3%
* 4.9%
Happiness 4.9%
Love 4.9%
Party 4.9%
Passion 4.8%
2.4% Adrenalin, Child, Coffee, Crowd, Dull, Elation, Elation, Engender, Enthused, Excrement, Fatigue, Feelings, Fulfilment, Health, Horror, Keenness, Roar, Scream, Sex

Exclaim+
Shout 50.0%
Surprise 7.1%
* 4.8%
Cry 4.8%
Mark 4.8%
Shock 4.8%
2.4% Exclude, Exhale, Loud, Question, Rejoice, Remark, Say, Speak, Startle, State

Excuse
Me 19.0%

Reason 14.3%
* 9.5%
Sorry 9.5%
Apology 4.8%
Pardon 4.8%
2.4% Allow, Answer, Dismiss, Forgive, Go, Let-Off, Lie, Meaningless, Mind, None, Note, Please, Problem, Remedy, Trouble, Wrong

Exile+
Away 9.5%
Refugee 9.5%
Country 7.1%
Hide 4.8%
Leave 4.8%
2.4% *, Abroad, Alone, Ban, Banished, Captive, Castaway, Communist, Flee, Foreigner, Fugitive, Go, Good, Govern, Island, Land, Leader, Lost, Out, Political, Prisoner, Remove, Shah, State, Throw, Victim, Withdraw

Expansion
Growth 9.5%
Big 7.1%
* 4.8%
Contraction 4.8%
Detraction 4.8%
Open 4.8%
Widen 4.8%
2.4% Arrows, Balloon, Board, Build, Enlarge, Expand, Expanse, Explosion, Fieldwork, Gasses, Grow, Growing, Hot, Imperialism, Increase, Larger, Lead, Metal, Mind, Policy, Size, Tank, Telescope, Under-Funding, Width

Expensive
* 22.4%
Dear 18.4%
Money 10.2%
Cheap 8.2%
Watch 6.1%
Clothes 4.1%
Cost 4.1%
2.0% Brown, Car, Cheque, Dress, Fur, Jacket, Jewelry, Nothing, Perfume, Place, Rich, Steep

Explain
* 27.1%
Why 10.4%
Talk 6.3%
Teach 4.2%
2.1% Away, Carefully, Client, Clue, Demonstrate, Difficult, Discuss, Elucidate, Explanation, Explicate, Fist, Help, Lecture, Make-Clear, Meaning, Problem, Question, Reason, Say, State, Talking, Tell, Think, This, Well

Explore
Find 14.6%
Look 8.3%
Search 8.3%
Adventure 6.3%
Investigate 4.2%
See 4.2%
2.1% Arctic, Beach, Caves, Depths, Die, Discover, Go, Green, Grope, Hunt, Ice, It, Journey, Jungle, Land, Livingstone, Look-For, North-Pole, Pith-Helmet, Seek, Sex, Touch, Travel, Where, Wild

Explosive
Bomb 59.5%
Bang 9.5%
Gun 7.1%
Dynamite 4.8%
2.4% Bag, Blast, Bullet, Fire, Flash, Material, Sound, Sudden

Exposure
Cold 17.0%
Film 10.6%
Camera 8.5%
Sun 8.5%
Photo 6.4%
Open 4.3%
Vulnerable 4.3%
2.1% Bare, Exhibition, Fear, Flasher, Hike, Hole, Lens, Light, Mountain, Naked, Newspaper, Outside, Quick, Raincoat, Rocks, Time, Toxin, White

Express+
Train 21.4%
Say 14.3%
Speak 9.5%
Delivery 7.1%
Fast 7.1%
Coffee 4.8%
Show 4.8%
Tell 4.8%
2.4% Articulate, Desire, Infer, Language, Out, Paper, Sell, Speed, State, These, Yourself

Exquisite+
Beautiful 16.7%
Wonderful 11.9%
Delicate 7.1%
Fine 7.1%
Lovely 7.1%
Marvellous 4.8%
Perfect 4.8%
Superb 4.8%
Taste 4.8%
2.4% Beauty, Delightful, Flower, Formed, Intricate, Legs, Magnificent, Nice, Pain, Petite, Rare, Small, Unique

Extend+
Lengthen 13.6%
* 9.5%
Line 7.1%
Stretch 7.1%
Long 4.8%
2.4% Beyond, Continue, Elongate, Erect, Extreme, Hair, House, Improve, Increase, Ladder, Length, Link, Make-Long, Nails, Prolong, Pull-Out, Reach, Reach-Out, Ruler, Spread, Telescope, Tend, Time

Extra
More 25.0%
Time 16.7%
* 8.3%
Help 4.2%
Plus 4.2%
Special 4.2%
2.1% Big, Bold, Care, Cash, Coffee, Double, Dry, Excess, Film, Hard, Helping, Ice-Cream, Less, Long, Other, Plenty, Sample, Things

Extreme
* 8.3%
Cold 6.3%
End(s) 6.3%
Far 6.3%
Noise 6.3%
Hot 4.2%
Violence 4.2%
Weather 4.2%
2.1% Average, Care, Case, Circumstance, Close-Up, Conviction, Different, Emotion, Fascist, Hit, Large, Me, Outer, Outrageous, Outright, Position, Poverty, Power, Small, Strong, Stupidity, Temperature, Test, Unction, View, Wide

Eye
Ball 15.6%
Glasses 6.7%
Lash(es) 6.7%
Lid 6.7%
See 6.7%
Ear 4.4%
Needle 4.4%
Sight 4.4%
Socket 4.4%
Witness 4.4%
2.2% *, Black, Brow, Burn, Drops, Face, Glass, Lens, Level, Look, Mouth, Pie, Sore, Test, Water, Wink

Fabric+
Cloth 33.3%
Material 26.2%
Cotton 9.5%
Conditioner 7.1%
Clothes 3.6%
Dress 3.6%
Soft 3.6%
1.1% Cleaner, Curtains, Denim, India, Pattern, Patterned, Raven, Skirt, Society, Space, Texture

Fabulous+
Great 28.6%
Wonderful 9.5%
Marvellous 7.1%
Amazing 4.8%
Myth 4.8%
Wondrous 4.8%
2.4% Ace, Beyond, Bright, Brilliant, Castle, Excellent, Fabric, Fantastic, Good, Incredible, Magnificent, Ok, Perfume, Splendid, Stupendous, Train, Travel

Facetious+
* 9.5%
Obnoxious 7.1%
Sarcastic 7.1%
Facile 4.8%
Funny 4.8%
Picky 4.8%
Silly 4.8%
2.4% Awful, Awkward, Bastard, Cheeky, Childish, Conceited, Crazy, Dictionary, Finicky, Ignorant, Mean, Nasty, Obnoxious, Odd, Pig, Rabbit, Rat, Remark, Rude, Sardonic, Scathing, Slime, Smart, Wicked

Fade
Away 41.7%
Grey 10.4%
* 6.3%
Colour 6.3%
Distant 4.2%
Loose 4.2%
2.1% Black, Decay, Disappear, Glow, Ink, Jeans, Out, Shade, Shine, Suntan, Vanish, White, Wipe

Failure
Success 20.0%
Exam 11.1%
Pass 6.7%
Loss 4.4%
2.2% *, Brakes, Break, Crisis, Degree, Drop-Out, Electricity, Fall, Fast, Fault, Flop, Hopeless, Inadequate, Incompetence, Learn, Lose, Loser, Me, Miss, Nothing, Past, Power, Reward, Sad, Strength, Unsuccessful

Faint
Fall 14.6%
Heart 12.5%
Weak 8.4%
Hearted 8.3%
Away 6.3%
* 4.2%
Collapse 4.2%
2.1% Black-Out, Church, Colour, Conscious, Die, Dizzy, Faint, Fall-Over, Fault, Fish, Ill, Law, Light, Line, Over, Sleepy, Smell, Swoon, Transparent, Unconscious

Faith
God 20.8%
Religion 14.6%
Hope 12.5%
Belief 8.3%
* 6.2%
Blind 4.2%
Trust 4.2%
2.1% Christian, Church, Dean, Faithful, Floor, George-Michael, Heal, Healer, Heretical, In-Person, Nothing, No-More, True, True-Love

Falcon
Bird 54.0%
Crest 14.0%
Eagle 12.0%
Hawk 4.0%
2.0% Breast, Bridge, Fierce, Glove, Keeper, Peregrine, Prey, Pub

Fall
Down 22.9%
Autumn 10.4%
Hurt 10.4%
Leaves 6.3%
* 4.2%
Cut 4.2%
Rise 4.2%
2.1% Asleep, Band, Bandage, Break, Bruise, Descend, Drop, Grace, Lark, London, Mountain, Nero, Over, Plummet, Thing, Water, Wind, Wood

Fallible+
* 15.2%
Infallible 10.9%
Human 8.7%
Wrong 6.5%
Error 4.3%
Fault 4.3%
Gullible 4.3%
Mistake(s) 4.3%
Normal 4.3%
Pope 4.3%
2.2% Believe, Ease, Fail, Faulty, God, Joke, Liar, Naive, Phallic, Point, Sex, Stupid, Truth, Weak

Fallout
Nuclear 40.4%
Bomb 9.6%
Radiation 9.6%
* 7.7%
Shelter 5.7%
Fight 3.8%
1.9% ?, Aftermath, Airplane, Argument, Bed, Descent, Die, Dusk, Nuclear-Bomb, Parachute, Plane, War, Zone

False
True 23.8%
Lie 14.3%
Teeth 7.1%
Hood 4.8%
Impression(s) 4.8%
Moustache 4.8%
2.4% Alarm, Friend, Hearted, Hollow, Hopes, Humour, Identity, Liar, Nose, Real, Rumour, Start, Statement, Truth, Unreal, Word, Wrong

Falsehood
Lie(s) 64.3%
Truth 11.6%
* 7.1%
2.4% Deceit, Fake, Guilt, Priest, Untrue, Untruth, Wig

Famish
Hungry 22.2%
Starve(d) 20.0%
Hunger 17.8%
Eat 8.9%
* 4.4%
Famine 4.4%
Food 4.4%
Starving 4.4%
2.2% Africa, Full, Horse, Lungs, McDonald's

Famous+
Well-Known 9.5%
* 7.1%
Celebrity 7.1%
Infamous 7.1%
Person 7.1%
Star 7.1%
Celebrated 4.8%
Grand 4.8%
Known 4.8%
Renowned 4.8%
Rich 4.8%
2.4% Actor, Fashion, Groups, Hero, Integrate, Name, Notorious, People, Polite, Popular, Queen, Reagan, Strong

Fancy+
Like 33.3%
Free 14.3%
* 11.9%
Man 9.5%
Cake 7.1%
Love 4.8%
2.4% Complex, Frill, Girl, Glamour, Hat, Hotel, Ice, Women

Fantasy
Dream 27.3%
World 9.1%
Castle 6.8%
Island 4.5%
Reality 4.5%
Story 4.5%
2.3% Adventure, Cyberpunk, Desire, Dragon, Fairy, Far, Figure, Game, Image, Land, Like, Science, Science-Fiction, Sex, Sexual, Surreal, Unreal, Writer, Writing

Far
Away 40.0%
Near 31.1%
2.2% *, Aeroplane, Canada, Cry, Distance, Distant, Fetched, Horizon, Out, Removed, Seen, Shore, Travel

Farm+
Animal(s) 43.5%
Cow(s) 17.4%
Yard 6.5%
Farmer 4.3%
House 4.3%
Pig 4.3%
2.2% *, Corn, Country, Countryside, Green, Hen, Mud, Sheep, Straw

Farmhouse
Bread 10.4%
Cheese 8.3%
Country 8.3%
Cheddar 4.2%
Chicken(s) 4.2%
Cottage 4.2%
Cow(s) 4.2%
Stone 4.2%
Tree 4.2%
2.1% *, Animals, B&B, Bank, Butter, Dog, Duck, Farm, Farmer, Hens, Holiday, Horse, Kitchen, Lane, Milk, Mouse, Mud, Picture, Rustic, Sheep, Village, Yard

Farmland
Field(s) 9.6%
Animals 7.7%
Cow(s) 7.7%
Green 7.7%
Arable 5.7%

* 3.8%
Furrow 3.8%
Grass 3.8%
House 3.8%
Sheep 3.8%
1.9% Acre, Agriculture, City, Country, Countryside, Earth, Farmer, Grassy, Grazing-Land, Grey, Heathland, Home, Oak, Pig, Ploughed, Problems, Ranch, Red, Smell, Soil, Space, Tractor

Fashion
Clothes 19.5%
Parade 7.3%
Show 7.3%
Victim 7.3%
Chic 4.9%
Trend 4.9%
2.4% Accessories, Catwalk, Change, Clothing, Core, Custom, Design, Designer, Fad, Grunge, Guru, Industry, Item, Mag, Model, Paris, Photographer, Scene, Shops, Star, Style

Fast
Quick 32.0%
Slow 14.0%
Car 8.0%
Animal 4.0%
Lane 4.0%
Speed 4.0%
Speedy 4.0%
2.0% Colin-Jackson, Eddy, Fast, Furious, Leg, Mover, Rapid, Run, Shake, Slow, Stuck, Swift, Talker, Train, Write

Fat
Thin 33.3%
Obese 11.1%
* 4.4%
Bacon 4.4%
Cat 4.4%
2.2% Arms, Beef, Big, Chops, Greedy, Lard, Large, Lean, Obesity, Overweight, People, Person, Reduction, Roll, Round, Sarah, Small, Tallow

Father+
Mother 47.6%
Son 19.0%
* 7.1%
Dad 7.1%
Figure 7.1%
Man 4.8%
2.4% Bald, Parent, Sire

Fathom+
Deep 28.6%
Sea 21.4%
Depth 11.9%
Out 4.8%
Water 4.8%
2.4% Deduce, Distance, Fall, Figure, Find, Full, Hut, League, Six, Swim, Think, Understand

Fault
Crack 11.9%
Blame 9.5%
Error 9.5%
Line(s) 9.5%
* 7.1%
Mistake 7.1%
Wrong 7.1%
Electric 4.8%
Foot 4.8%
2.4% Blame, Earthquake, Electrical, Faults, Finder, Help, Liability, Own, Strata, Tolerant, Vault, Zone

Feast
Food 28.6%
Banquet 14.3%
Chicken 9.5%
Famine 4.8%
Ice-Cream 4.8%
Meal 4.8%
2.4% *, Babette, Bar, Belhazer's, Chocolate, Christmas, Day, Father, Fun, Meat, Medieval, Orgy, Party, Service

Feed
Food 26.1%
Fish 13.0%
Birds 6.5%
Duck(s) 6.5%
Eat 4.3%
Poor 4.3%
Sheep 4.3%
Water 4.3%
2.2% *, Carrion, Cat, Cattle, Chicken, Cows, Dog, Give, Horse, Me, Mice, Mouth, Nourish, Rabbit

Feedback
* 10.4%
Response 8.3%
Answer 6.3%
Amplifier 4.2%
Guitar 4.2%
Information 4.2%
Loop 4.2%
Talk 4.2%
2.1% Allow, Bang, Bio, Computer, Criticism, Eat, Enough, Fightback, Info, Inform, Life, Office, Positive, Radio, Reaction, Respond, Revert, Sense, Sound, Squall, System, Tape, Teacher, Trend, Tutorial, Work

Feel
Touch 18.8%
* 8.3%
Emotion 6.3%
Good 6.3%
Hurt 6.3%
Pain 6.3%
Love 4.2%
Well 4.2%
2.1% Angry, Body, Desire, Easy, Empathise, Ill, Massage, Me, Nice, Push, Secure, Sensation, Sense, Sensual, Sentiment, Strongly, Unhappy, Up, Yuk

Feeling
Emotion 26.2%
Good 9.5%
* 7.1%
Touch 7.1%
Happy 4.8%
Ill 4.8%
Sense(s) 4.8%
2.4% Arm, Belief, Compassion, Desire, Felt, Good, Grumpy, Health, Hurt, Love, Loving, Sensation, Sick, Strength, Well

Feline+
Cat(s) 78.6%
Catlike 4.8%
Lion 4.8%
2.4% Catty, Panther, Sexy, Smooth, Tiger

Fence
Garden 13.3%
Post 13.3%
Wood 6.7%
Barrier 4.4%
Climb 4.4%
Gate 4.4%
Paint 4.4%
Wire 4.4%
2.2% Boundary, Bush, Danger, Fight, Gran, Hedge, High, In, Jump, Money, On, Path, Picket, Rail, Round, Sheet, Slat, Sport, Sword, Wash

Ferment
Brew 25.0%
Beer 22.9%
* 6.3%
Wine 6.3%
Drink 4.2%
2.1% Boat, Brewery, Bubble, Cheese, Hope, Juice, Make, More, Overnight, Rot, Stir, Tighten, Volcano, War, Wisp, Yeast

Fertile+
Soil 21.4%
Egg 9.5%
Land 7.1%
Baby 4.8%
Fecund 4.8%
Ground 4.8%
Seed 4.8%
Sterile 4.8%
2.4% *, Again, Birth, Crescent, Delta, Field, Garden, Green, Growth, Imagination, Life, Lush, Plain, Rich, Woman, Women

Fervent
* 10.0%
Fever 8.0%
Avid 6.0%
Desire 6.0%
Hope 6.0%
Keen 6.0%
Admirer 4.0%
Believer 4.0%
Eager 4.0%
Frenzy 4.0%
2.0% Beer, Belief, Committed, Drink, Energy, Fan, Ferment, Fervour, Follower, Go, Gripped, Lie, Love, Politician, Rabid, Shining, Stream, Strong, Supporter, Tempest, Wish

Fetch
Carry 40.0%
Bring 16.0%
Get 16.0%
Dog 12.0%
2.0% And, Ball, Errand, Execute, More, Quick, Stick, Wood

Few+
Many 26.2%
Little 14.3%
Poor 4.8%
Rare 4.8%
See 4.8%
Seldom 4.8%
Window 4.8%
2.4% *, Chosen, Far, Hardly, Less, Lots, Minimal, Not, One, Plenty, Room, Sea, Sight, Uncommon, Word

Fiddle
Violin 33.3%
Instrument 8.3%
Music 8.3%
Play 8.3%
Player 4.2%
2.1% About, Annoy, Books, Chain, Cheat, Crook, Doodle, Fart, Fiddler, Fuss, Knee, Nero, Roof, Steal, Sticks, Take, Tweak, UB40

Fidget
Move 18.8%
* 10.4%

Hand(s) 8.3%
Finger(s) 6.3%
Fumble 6.3%
Midget 4.2%
Shake 4.2%
Still 4.2%
Twitch 4.2%
2.1% Bum, Church, Cinema, Feet, Fiddle, Gadget, Hop, Kid, Lazy, Movement, Nervous, Play, Restless, Sit, Squirm, Tamper, Wander

Field
Grass 17.3%
Green 15.4%
Farm 5.7%
* 3.8%
Corn 3.8%
Dream 3.8%
1.9% Apple, Area, Batman, Bread, Copse, Cow, Crop, Crow, Expedition, Farmer, Flowers, Furrow, Ground, Grow, Ireland, Land, Left, Mouse, Play, Poppy, Share, Space, Sports, Strawberries, Wheat, Work

Fierce
Lion 12.2%
Angry 6.1%
Dog 6.1%
Fire 6.1%
Strong 6.1%
Wild 6.1%
Bad 4.1%
Fighter 4.1%
Violent 4.1%
Wind 4.1%
2.0% *, Animal, Attack, Battle, Dangerous, Debate, Ferocious, Fiery, Fury, Growl, Mean, Rabbit, Rage, Rash, Rat, Storm, Teeth, Temper, Tiger, War, Writing

Fight
Fist(s) 12.5%
Box 8.3%
Boxing 6.3%
Hit 6.3%
Battle 4.2%
Boxer 4.2%
Good 4.2%
War 4.2%
Win 4.2%
2.1% *, Bar, Bash, Brawl, Cut, Dog, For, Game, Hard, Hate, Match, Pub, Punch, Ring, Scrap, Shy, Smash, Stick, Strength, Struggle, Tussle, With

Fill
Up 20.9%
Cup 7.0%
Full 7.0%
Glass 7.0%
Bottle 4.7%
Empty 4.7%
2.3% *, Belly, Bowl, Cement, Complete, Drop, Fill, Flow, Food, Gap, Jug, Merge, Out, Over-Flowing, Petrol, Pitcher, Sand, Teapot, Top-Up, Water

Filling
Dentist 19.0%
Teeth 14.3%
Tooth 14.3%
Cabinet 11.9%
* 4.8%
Cream 4.8%
Station 4.8%
2.4% Cake, Cavity, Cherry, Desk, Empty, In, Jam, Metal, Office, Pudding, Top

Film
Cinema 19.0%
Camera 11.9%
Movie(s) 9.5%
Star 7.1%
Cling 4.8%
Noir 4.8%
2.4% Act, Book, Buff, Celluloid, Director, Edit, Kodak, Picture, Processing, Reel, Sequence, Set, Showing, Skin, Society, Technicolour, TV, Works

Fine
Weather 11.1%
Good 8.9%
Thin 6.7%
Bright 4.4%
Clear 4.4%
Line(s) 4.4%
Okay 4.4%
Wine 4.4%
2.2% Bad, Cash, Day, Dust, Gold, Great, Happy, Love, Money, Nice, Person, Police, Sharp, She, Sheer, Speeding, Style, Sunny, Sunshine, Tooth, Well, Wispy

Finger
Thumb 18.8%
Hand 12.5%
Ring 12.5%
Nail 10.4%
Touch 8.3%
* 4.2%
Digit 4.2%
Point 4.2%
Puppet 4.2%
2.1% Chocolate, Cut, Glove, Hole, Index, Knee, Paint, Painting, Tips, Trigger

Fire
Ball 24.0%
Hot 10.0%
Flame 8.0%
Escape 6.0%
Heat 4.0%
Sack 4.0%
Smoke 4.0%
Water 4.0%
2.0% Alarm, Bird, Burning, Caveman, Coal, Dame, Eater, Gun, Hazard, Hell, Hit, House, Island, Light, Lit, Sea, Shoot, Spit

Firebomb
IRA 14.6%
Blast 6.3%
Explode 6.3%
Explosion 4.2%
House 4.2%
Terrorist 4.2%
2.1% *, Ambulance, Army, Arson, Attack, Bang, Bomb, Bottle, Burn, City, Crash, Damage, Dangerous, Dead, Fly, Grenade, Incendiary, Ireland, London, Malcolm-X, Milk-Bottle, Rectangular, Smart, Squad, Terror, Terrorise, Throw, Underground, War

Fireman
Fire 19.2%
Sam 9.6%
Helmet 7.7%
Engine 5.7%
Fire-Engine 5.7%
* 3.8%
Hat 3.8%
1.9% Ambulance, Dangerous, Hose, Hunting, Jim, Job, Ladder, Lift, Officer, Person, Pole, Policeman, Pump, Red, Safety, Siren, Toby, TV, Uniform, Water, Woman, Yellow, Yellow-Hat

First
Last 33.3%
Second 15.6%
One 4.4%
Time 4.4%
2.2% 2nd, Account, Assignment, Come, Day, Eager, Equal, Initial, Out, Past, Payment, Person, Post, Premier, Prime, Scale, Shot, Thing, Try

Fish
Sea 10.2%
Chips 8.2%
Wanda 8.2%
Swim 6.1%
* 4.1%
And-Chips 4.1%
Finger 4.1%
Paste 4.1%
Smelly 4.1%
Tank 4.1%
2.0% Bowl, Drink, Eel, Farmer, Flat, Food, Fry, Meat, Orange, Out, Pie, River, Scales, Shark, Silver, Silvery-Thing, Smell, Spoon, Water, Wet, White

Fishcake
Chips 14.0%
Food 10.0%
Eat 8.0%
Batter 4.0%
Breadcrumbs 4.0%
Fry 4.0%
Potato 4.0%
2.0% *, Beans, Birdseye, China, Chip-Shop, Delicious, Disgusting, Fake, Fingers, Fishwife, Fishy, Horrible, Lake, Mush, Mushy, Neck, Oatcake, Orange, Packet, Salmon, School, Smells, Smelly, Synagogue, Yuk, Yummy

Fishpond
Fish 18.8%
Water 8.3%
Garden 6.3%
Weed(s) 6.3%
* 4.2%
Lillies 4.2%
Swim 4.2%
2.1% Algae, Atlantic, Brasenose, Breed, Bubble, Dirty, Fling, Frog, Grandparents, Lily, Lizard, Mill, Rod, Skin, Small, Smell, Spawn, Stagnant, Stream, Tank, Toad, Trout, Village

Fit
Healthy 16.7%
Unfit 11.9%
Tight 9.5%
In 7.1%
Sport(s) 7.1%
Clothes 4.8%
Size 4.8%
2.4% *, Aerobics, Fiddle, First, Loose, Man, Move, Muscle, Screw, Shoe, Slob, Smooth, Thin, Type, Well

Five
Alive 19.1%
Six 10.6%
Famous 6.4%
Fingers 6.4%
Four 6.4%
Ten 6.4%
Hand 4.3%
Hours 4.3%
Number 4.3%
O'Clock 4.3%

2.1% *, Child, Dime, Feet, Fourteen, Guys, Hundred, Integer, Million, More, O, Toes

Fix
Mend 40.9%
It 9.1%
Jim 6.8%
Repair 6.8%
Break 4.5%
2.3% Arrange, Correct, Drink, Glue, Heroin, High, Junky, Needle, Set, Something, Stick, Syringe, Up, Work

Flag
Ship 11.1%
Country 8.9%
Fly 8.9%
Pole 8.9%
Wave 8.9%
* 4.4%
2.2% Blue, British, Burn, Convenience, Danish, Dial, Down, Flagpole, Flog, Nation, Nation-State, Pavement, Post, Race, Raise, Red, Shit, Signal, Union-Jack, USA, Wind

Flagrant+
* 14.3%
Obvious 11.9%
Abuse 4.8%
Disregard 4.8%
Flavour 4.8%
Overt 4.8%
Smell 4.8%
Violation 4.8%
2.4% Abandon, Blank, Blatant, Blaze, Burning, Denial, Disobey, Exotic, Flamboyant, Flout, Hussey, Loud, Mean, Obsession, Open, Outrageous, Robust, Thoughtless, Uncaring

Flannel+
Towel 28.3%
Wash 17.4%
* 8.7%
Cloth 8.7%
Face 6.5%
Flower 4.3%
2.2% Baby, Bathroom, Jacket, Rose, Soap, Sponge, Trousers, Waffle, Washing, Water, Wet

Flash
Light 18.0%
Bulb 10.0%
Gordon 10.0%
Camera 8.0%
Harry 6.0%
Lightning 4.0%
2.0% Back, Bang, Black, Blind, Bright, Burn, Card, Dance, Floor, Gun, Liquid, Orange, Point, Quick, Red, Reporter, Sex, Soap, Spark, Wanker, White, Zip

Flashback
Memory 27.1%
* 6.3%
Light 6.3%
Back 4.2%
Drugs 4.2%
Film 4.2%
Time 4.2%
2.1% Abuse, Acid, Agony, Amnesia, Bright, Bulb, Dance, Drama, Experience, Flashdance, Gordon, Lightning, Mind, Past, Quick, Screen, See, Sequence, Thunder, Trip, TV

Flat
* 26.5%
Chest 8.2%
House 8.2%
Plain 8.2%
Chested 4.1%
Holland 4.1%
Smooth 4.1%
2.0% Cold, Curly, Expanse, Garden, Head, Line, Mine, Pancake, Plane, Round, Sheet, So, Square, Steppe, Studio, Tall, Tina, Wood

Flawless
Perfect 42.2%
Diamond 11.1%
Beauty 4.4%
Complexion 4.4%
2.2% *, Clear, Court, Crystal, Cut, Dip, Fault, Gem, Good, Jewel, Mess, Performance, Pure, Skin, Smooth, Soiled, Untarnish

Fling
Affair 21.3%
Throw 21.3%
Highland 8.5%
* 6.4%
Away 4.3%
Brief 4.3%
Chuck 4.3%
Party 4.3%
2.1% Casual, Drink, Fair, Flem, Hurl, Out, Round, Sex, Sorry, Stone, Wide, Woman

Float
Swim 17.0%
Water 17.0%
Sink 12.8%
Boat 8.5%
Fishing 4.3%
2.1% *, About, Air, Buoy, Chamber, Cork, Crawl, Drift, Drown, Fish, High, Ice-Cream, Penguin, Quickly, Sky, Tank, Towel, Up

Flood
Water 44.4%
Ark 6.7%
Gate(s) 6.7%
Rain 6.7%
River 4.4%
2.2% Awash, Cost, Deluge, Drought, Dry, Gutter, Land, Noah, The, Torrent, Underground, Wales, Wet

Flower
Petal 26.2%
Bloom 9.5%
Bud 9.5%
Vase 9.5%
Power 7.1%
Bed 4.8%
2.4% *, Bird, Bright, Carnation, Daisy, Head, Heart, Leaf, Leaves, Man, Pollen, Pot, Rose, Stem

Fluid
Liquid 33.3%
Water 31.2%
Beer 4.2%
Drink 4.2%
Wet 4.2%
2.1% *, Glass, Gravity, Milk, Mobile, Motion, Ounces, Seminal, Syringe, Urine, Warm

Fluoride+
Toothpaste 42.9%
Teeth 11.9%
Water 9.5%
Chemical 4.8%
Chlorine 4.8%
Tooth 4.8%
2.4% Carbon, Chemist, Element, Margarine, Paste, Pills, Tablet, Toothbrush, Work

Fly
Aero/Plane 17.0%
Wall 12.8%
Insect 8.5%
Out 6.4%
Away 4.3%
Bird 4.3%
Buzz 4.3%
Jump 4.3%
Swat 4.3%
2.1% *, Air, Annoyance, Ball, Clouds, Dream, Fish, Flee, Fruit, Paper, Sky, Spray, To, Up, Wasp, Wings

Foggy
Misty 24.4%
Mist 13.3%
Day 8.9%
Dew 6.7%
London 4.4%
Night 4.4%
Pea 4.4%
Smog 4.4%
2.2% Autumnal, Blinding, Clear, Damp, Fear, Grey, Haze, Outside, Thick, Unclear, Weather, Wet

Fold+
Crease 23.9%
Paper 15.9%
Bend 6.8%
Cloth 5.7%
Up 4.5%
Clothes 3.4%
Sheet(s) 3.4%
* 2.3%
Sheep 2.3%
Tear 2.3%
1.1% Away, Bedsheets, Blanket, Crumple, Cusp, Cut, Envelope, Faults, Field, Fold, Garment, Iron, Linen, Logical, Manifold, Material, Mountain, Origami, Over, Pleat, Protein, Spindle, Tidy, Tie, Unfold

Folk
Music 22.2%
Song(s) 22.2%
Lore 15.6%
People 13.3%
Dance 4.4%
2.2% A-Gathering, Cat, Costume, Hero, Home, Simple, Stone, Tale, Tune, Yolk

Follow+
Leader 28.6%
Lead 21.4%
Behind 4.8%
Sheep 4.8%
2.4% Back, Dog, Ensue, Follow, Go, Guide, Home, Man, Me, On, Path, Seek, Suit, Tame, Track, Trail, You

Fondant
Sweet(s) 16.0%
Cream 14.0%
Icing 10.0%
* 6.0%
Chocolate 6.0%
Cheese 4.0%
Fancy 4.0%
Ice 4.0%
Melt 4.0%
2.0% ?, Chewy, Church, Creamy, Creme, Desert-Creams, Eat, Fruit, Icing-Sugar, Nothing, Soft, Sweetie, Swiss, Tart, Wish, With

Food
Eat 21.4%
Drink 16.7%
* 9.5%
Hungry 7.1%
Plate 7.1%
2.4% Apple, Comfort, Dinner, Essential, Grub, Japanese, Life, Liquid, Meals, Parcel, Processor, Sandwich, Stuff, Tasty, Thought, Wine

Foot
Shoe 19.1%
Ball 17.0%
Mouth 12.8%
Toe(s) 8.5%
Bath 4.3%
Feet 4.3%
Rot 4.3%
Smell 4.3%
Sock 4.3%
Sore 4.3%
2.1% Cliff, Hand, Hard, Head, Limp, Odour, Wall, White

Football
Player 20.4%
Game 16.3%
Match 10.2%
Soccer 6.1%
* 4.1%
Mud 4.1%
Sport 4.1%
Pitch 3.1%
2.0% Ball, Boredom, Boring, Club, Diego, Fan, Goal, Hooligan, Lads, Lineker, Liverpool, Mania, Netball, Rand, Territory

For
Against 40.0%
* 10.0%
Ever 10.0%
You 10.0%
Give 4.0%
What 4.0%
2.0% After, And, Fortune, Her, Long, Me, Number, Person, Self, The, To

Forbid
* 8.3%
Allow 8.3%
Ban 6.3%
Fruit 6.3%
No 6.3%
Prevent 6.3%
Deny 4.2%
Disallow 4.2%
Me 4.2%
Stop 4.2%
2.1% Arm, Bar, Can't, Defy, Door, Father, Forbade, God, Have, Not, Not-Allowed, Planet, Preacher, Preclude, Refuse, Stern, Strict, Told, Wrong, You

Force
Field 14.3%
Power 9.5%
Army 7.1%
Gale 7.1%
* 4.8%
Energy 4.8%
Hard 4.8%
Newton 4.8%
2.4% Air, Array, Attack, Big, Blow, Brutal, Equal, Insist, Majestic, Nuclear, Pressure, Pull, Punch, Push, Strength, Tension, Violence, Work

Foreign+
Abroad 11.9%
Strange 11.9%
Alien 9.5%
Stranger 9.5%
Country 7.1%
French 7.1%
Africa 4.8%
Different 4.8%
Overseas 4.8%
2.4% *, Abroad, Aid, Desert, Europe, Food, Friend, Land, Oriental, Student, Word, Xenophobia

Forest
Tree(s) 35.6%
Wood(s) 17.8%
Fire 11.1%
Green 11.1%
Dark 4.4%
Dense 4.4%
2.2% Camping, Deep, Gateau, Mountain, Pine, Primeval, River

Forget
Remember 25.0%
Memory 12.5%
* 8.3%
Me-Not 6.3%
Flower 4.2%
Forgetful 4.2%
Lose 4.2%
2.1% About, Disremember, Drop, Exam, Full, Idea, Key(s), Know, Meeting, Memory, Never, Not, Past, Problem, Something, Sorry

Forgive
Forget 31.9%
Me 6.4%
Sin 6.4%
Catholic 4.3%
Sad 4.3%
2.1% Boy, Church, Curse, Free, Good, Guilt, Him, Humour, Hurt, Love, Mercy, Mistake, Pardon, Peace, Pity, Plead, Pray, Religion, Sorry, Sympathy, Upset, Wrong

Fork+
Knife 44.3%
Spoon 22.7%
Eat 5.7%
Lift 3.4%
* 2.3%
Road 2.3%
1.1% Bat, Bend, Bird, Boy, Cork, Devil, Garden, Lift-Truck, Lightning, Plate, Prong, Split, Tine, Truck, Tuning, Up

Form+
Shape 21.7%
* 8.7%
Paper 8.7%
Class 6.5%
Colour 4.3%
2.2% Application, Body, Cast, Clay, Coat, Create, Deer, Details, Fawn, Fill, Filling, Hurt, Letter, Line, Matter, Order, Register, Rise, Side, Teacher, UB40, Word, Write

Formal+
Dress 23.0%
Informal 12.5%
Wear 8.3%
* 4.2%
Occasion 4.2%
Smart 4.2%
2.1% Abstracts, Art, Attire, Conduct, Dance, Dull, Education, Format, Grand, Important, Introduction, Letter, Night, Opinion, Past, Polite, Question, Rule, Shape, Strict, Suit

Formation+
Dancing 21.4%
* 4.8%
Aircraft 4.8%
Dance 4.8%
Flying 4.8%
Form 4.8%
Make 4.8%
Rock 4.8%
2.4% Army, Brick, Circle, Cloud, Construct, Destruction, Division, Earth, Fight, Group, Grouping, Line, Made, Military, Phalanx, Plan, Set, Shape, Swimming

Former
Before 12.6%
Latter 10.4%
Previous 8.3%
* 6.2%
Ex 4.2%
Farmer 4.2%
Last 4.2%
Later 4.2%
Lover 4.2%
Old 4.2%
Pupil 4.2%
2.1% After, Boss, Client, Days, Door, Earlier, First, Glory, Letter, Life, Model, Oil, Past, Self, State, Was

Fortune+
Money 26.1%
Teller 17.4%
Luck 15.2%
Rich 6.5%
* 4.3%
2.2% 100, Ball, Chance, Diamonds, Gold, Good, Made, Make, Millionaire, Misfortune, None, Tablet, Wealth, Win

Found
Lost 75.6%
Out 4.4%
2.2% *, Appear, Ball, Discovered, Find, Happy, Object, Something, Watch

Four
Five 30.6%
* 14.3%
Number 4.1%
Pack 4.1%
Quart 4.1%
Square 4.1%
Tops 4.1%
2.0% Fifteen, Foot, Gang, Legs, Nuclear, Of, Of-A-Kind, Of-Us, Quads, Quartet, Same, Seasons, Sisters, Three, Times, Twenty, Two

Fragile
Break 16.0%
Glass 14.0%
Delicate 12.0%
Weak 10.0%
Breakable 8.0%
2.0% Agile, Balance, Box, Broken, Care, Careful, China, Cup, Earth, Frail, Gentle, Heart, Ornament, Sensitive, Soft, Strong, Thing, Touch, Tough, Vase

Fragrance
Smell 62.2%
Perfume 20.0%
2.2% Aroma, Chanel, Flower, Fortune, Girlfriend, Stale, Taste

Frail
Old 24.0%
Weak 18.0%
Fragile 16.0%
Elderly 6.0%

Break 4.0%
Lady 4.0%
2.0% Bones, Decrepit, Delicate, Fail, Frigid, Granny, Grey, Horse, Meek, Old-Age, Old-Lady, Quail, Tremble, Woman

Fragrant
Smell 28.0%
Perfume 21.0%
Roses 12.8%
Flower(s) 7.7%
Scent 5.1%
2.6% After shave, Aroma, Blossom, Body, Fragrant, Jasmine, Mist, Odour, Room

Frailty
Old 22.7%
Weakness 18.2%
Fragile 11.4%
Weak 9.1%
Age 6.8%
Delicate 4.5%
Strength 4.5%
2.3% Baby, Bones, Brittle, Faint, Grandmother, Harm, Shatter, Snap, Thin, Unit

Franchise+
Shop 21.4%
Money 9.5%
* 7.1%
Sell 7.1%
Business 4.8%
Vote 4.8%
2.4% Allies, Beefburger, Buy, Car, City, Deeds, Department, Foreign, Free, Joint, Kentucky, London, Merchandise, Operation, Purchase, Sales, Stamp, Together, Treaty

Franglais
French 25.0%
* 12.5%
(Miles)-Kington 6.2%
France 6.2%
Language(s) 6.2%
Bilingual 4.2%
English 4.2%
2.1% Comedy, Espanglish, Glass, Joanne, Laziness, Melange, Mixture, Newspaper, Nonsense, Outside, Painting, Pidgin, Private-Eye, Slang, Speech, Wine-Glass, Yoghurt

Frank
Sinatra 53.1%
Bruno 8.2%
* 6.5%
Spencer 6.1%
Bough 6.1%
2.0% Bell, Carson, Frankly, Glad, Howard, Ifield, Lee, Skunk, Uncle, Who

Free
Easy 8.0%
Liberty 8.0%
Wind 6.0%
Air 4.0%
Life 4.0%
Nelson-Mandela 4.0%
Prison 4.0%
2.0% *, Allow, As, Bird, Born, Constrained, Cost, Costly, Fall, Falling, Form, Gift, Happy, Let, Liberation, Lie, Music, Myself, Not, Nothing, Open, Phone, Release, Ride, Single, Slave, Trapped, Travel, Wild, Willy, Zone

Freedom
Liberty 13.3%
Fighter 11.1%
Movement 8.9%
Prison 8.9%
* 6.7%
Fight 4.4%
Free 4.4%
2.2% At, Autocracy, Biko, Choice, Cry, Escape, Exile, Expression, From, Love, Now, Of, Open, Oppression, Relative, Room, Run, Spirit

Freeze
Cold 38.3%
Ice 27.7%
Dried 4.3%
Fridge 4.3%
Snow 4.3%
2.1% Cool, Food, Frame, Hot, Ice-Cream, Pond, Thaw, Thermometer, Time, Water

French horn
Music 13.3%
Orchestra 13.3%
Blow 8.9%
Brass 8.9%
Instrument 4.4%
Noise 4.4%
Play 4.4%
Trumpet 4.4%
* 4.4%
2.2% Band, Blast, Cats, Cream, Deep, Friend, Frog, Loud, Mountains, Mozart, Musician, Note, Opera, Radio 3, Sound

Fridge+
Cold 33.3%
Freezer 28.6%
Food 11.9%
Door 4.8%
White 4.8%
2.4% Beer, Box, Close, Cool, Furniture, Icebox

Friend
Foe 23.8%
Enemy 9.5%
Companion 4.8%
Hand(s) 4.8%
Love 4.8%
Mate 4.8%
Pal 4.8%
Sarah 4.8%
2.4% Best, Confidante, Forever, Friendly, Friendship, Fun, Girl, Girlfriend, Job, Life, Man, My, Neighbour, Ship, Smile, Talk

Frighten
Scare 30.4%
Children 6.5%
Ghost 6.5%
Fear 4.3%
Terrify 4.3%
2.2% *, Bully, Cat, Child, Dark, Dog, Dracula, Her, Me, Off, Scared, Scary, Scream, Sneer, Soon, Spiders, Spook, Stiff, Tear, Threaten, Wolf

Frivolous+
Fun 9.5%
Gay 7.1%
Happy 7.1%
Jolly 4.8%
Playful 4.8%
Silly 4.8%
Stupid 4.8%
Trivial 4.8%
Waste 4.8%
2.4% *, Capricious, Extravagant, Foolhardy, Frolic, Frothy, Joyful, Laugh, Laughing, Luxury, Nothing, Ostena, Party, Petty, Pursuits, Ribbon, Superficial, Uncaring, Wacky, Young

Fro
To 71.4%
From 6.3%
To-And 6.3%
Back 4.2%
2.1% *, Away, Frog, Joan, Swings, Too

Frock
Dress 60.4%
Clothing 6.2%
Skirt 6.2%
Smock 4.2%
2.1% *, Checkered, Coat, Evening, Good-Life, Lace, Party, Posh, Sock, Transvestite, Wear

Frog
Jump 20.0%
Leap 15.6%
Pond 11.1%
Toad 11.1%
Prince 8.9%
Green 6.7%
Hop 6.7%
2.2% Bounce, Chorus, Crossing, Dog, Legs, Newt, Tadpole, Throat, Water-Lily

Frolic+
Play 19.0%
Playful 7.2%
Dance 7.1%
Sex 7.1%
Spring 7.1%
Field 4.8%
Fun 4.8%
Joyous 4.8%
Jump 4.8%
Lamb(s) 4.8%
2.4% *, Antic, Frolicsome, Gamble, Gambol, Gay, Jacuzzi, Joy, Mess, Naked, Romp, Wood

From
To 27.1%
Where 10.4%
Here 8.3%
* 6.2%
Russia 4.2%
There 4.2%
2.1% Country, For, Fromage, Help, Homeland, Letter, Love, Me, Now, Nowhere, Out, Place, Present, Station, The-Station, Wales, What, When, Whom

Front
Back 48.9%
Row 22.2%
Door 6.7%
2.2% Car, Desk, End, Face, Facing, House, Line, Page, Shore, Trench

Frontal+
Full 17.1%
* 12.2%
Attack 12.2%
Back 9.8%
Lobe 9.8%
Face 4.9%
Nude 4.9%
2.4% Abuse, Assault, Behind, Brain, Brutal, Exposed, Facade, Lobotomy, Love, Rear, View, Weather

Frontier+
Border 26.8%
Boundary 9.8%
Battle 4.9%
Country 4.9%
Horse 4.9%
2.4% *, America,

American, Background, Barrier, Custom-Post, Edge, Final, Forward, Front-Line, Lost, Man, Mountain, Next, Pioneer, Post, Prairie, Towards, Wild, Wild-West

Frustrate+
Annoy 23.8%
* 7.1%
Stop 7.1%
Thwart 7.1%
Anger 4.8%
Irritate 4.8%
2.4% Angry, Annoyed, Annoying, Awful, Confuse, Deny, Difficult, Hard, Help, Hurt, Inhibit, Loathe, Look, Nothing, People, Prevent, Unable, Weird, Work

Fry
Egg(s) 23.4%
Cook 14.9%
Chips 10.6%
Fish 10.6%
Fat 6.4%
Pan 6.4%
Bacon 4.3%
Oil 4.3%
2.1% Aubergine, Breakfast, Burn, Chocolate, Food, Potatoes, Sausage, Smell, Up

Frying-pan
Fat 22.7%
Fry 13.3%
Cook 11.1%
Egg(s) 11.1%
Fire 11.1%
Bacon 4.4%
2.2% Burn, Cooker, Cooking, Eggs-And-Bacon, Feet, Food, Hard, Hot, Kitchen, Oil, Sausage, Sizzle, Spit

Fugitive+
Run 26.2%
Escape 9.5%
Prisoner 7.1%
Refugee 7.1%
Runaway 7.1%
Flee 4.8%
Hiding 4.8%
Justice 4.8%
2.4% *, Alarmed, Capture, China, Fig, Hide, Outlaw, Prison, Rascal, Runner, Running, Victim

Full
Empty 42.2%
Bodied 4.4%
House 4.4%
Lips 4.4%
Pint 4.4%
Speed 4.4%
2.2% Big, Box, Brimming, Complete, Cream, Dose, Face, Food, Force, Load, Petrol-Tank, Sack, Small, Steam, Top, Toss

Fur
Coat 28.0%
Animal(s) 16.0%
Cat 10.0%
Ball 4.0%
Collar 4.0%
Fluff 4.0%
2.0% Bear, Blood, Cupboard, Ermine, Feather, Fox, Hair, Man, Pelt, Seal, Soft, Stoat, Stole, Trade, Warm, Wet, Wrap

Furlong+
Horse 35.4%
* 12.5%
Mile 10.4%
Race 8.3%
Acre 4.2%
Final 4.2%
Racecourse 4.2%
2.1% Athlete, Chain, Fox, Heat, Lane, Length, Long, Run, Science, Short

Furnace+
Fire 45.2%
Hot 26.2%
Heat 7.1%
Burn 4.8%
2.4% Blast, Boiler, Fiery, Inferno, Iron, Steel, Volcano

Furnish+
House 23.8%
Room 19.0%
Chairs 7.1%
Decorate 7.1%
Furniture 7.1%
Apartment 4.8%
Chair 4.8%
Sofa 4.8%
2.4% Add, Decorative, Dwelling, Flat, Flooring, Fully, Nice, Polish, Provide

Further
Away 27.1%
More 16.7%
On 8.3%
* 6.3%
Afield 4.2%
Distant 4.2%
Far 4.2%
Than 4.2%
2.1% Afar, Again, Ahead, Continue, Dim, Farther, Flung, Long, Nearer, Over, To, Up

Fuse
Plug 33.3%
Wire 18.8%
Electricity 6.2%
Join 4.2%
Mend 4.2%
2.1% *, Amp, Blow, Blown, Blow-Up, Box, Breaker, Cylinder, Electric, Electrocute, Go, Light, Melt, Newspaper, Refuse, Thirteen-Amp

Future
Past 31.1%
Generations 4.4%
Life 4.4%
Present 4.4%
Tense 4.4%
Time 4.4%
2.2% 2050, Ahead, Ambition, Bleak, Clock, Engagements, Event, Expect, Fun, Mile, New, Old, Our, Prospects, Science, See, Space, Taste, Tomorrow, Virtual-Reality, When

Gable+
House 25.0%
End 16.7%
Roof 14.6%
Clark 10.4%
Green 8.3%
Window 6.2%
Great 4.2%
2.1% Cable, Dormitory, Eaves, Hansel, Old, Story, Thatch

Gag+
Joke 16.7%
Tie 14.6%
Mouth 12.5%
Bind 8.3%
Heave 4.2%
Retch 4.2%
Stop 4.2%
2.1% Baby, Blindfold, Bound, Close, Crime, Fun, Gasp, Hostage, Material, Reflex, Rob, Sick, Sickness, Spew, Talk, Throat, Try

Gain+
Win 27.1%
Lose 14.6%
Loss 12.5%
* 10.4%
Blood 4.2%
Earn 4.2%
Profit 4.2%
2.1% Advance, Artery, Endeavour, Got, Loose, Money, More, Play, Preen, Trick, Yard

Galaxy+
Stars 27.1%
Chocolate 22.9%
Star 14.6%
Universe 8.3%
Bar 4.2%
Mars 4.2%
Space 4.2%
2.1% Cosmos, Edge, Guide, Infinite, Milky, Milky-Way, Sky

Gale+
Wind 37.8%
Force 10.0%
Storm 6.7%
Hill 5.6%
Blow 4.4%
Yorkshire 4.4%
Windy 3.3%
* 2.2%
1.1% Agree, Calm, Fell, Fen, Free, Gate, Hay, Honey, Howl, Hurricane, Intense, Lake, Mistral, Prison, Rain, Restaurant, Roof, Split, Tree, Try, Valley, Warning, Wild

Gallant
Knight 22.0%
Brave 16.0%
Hero 14.0%
Soldier 6.0%
Bold 4.0%
Gent 4.0%
2.0% ?, Arthur, Big, Car, Courageous, Courteous, Galahad, Gentle, Gentleman, Gentlemanly, Horse, Kind, Noble, Rough, Strong, Tall, Woman

Gallery+
Art 33.3%
Painting(s) 27.1%
Picture(s) 14.6%
2.1% Audience, Commons, Galleon, Heartbeat, High, Long, Minstrel, Museum, Playing, Space, Theatre, Upper

Gallon+
Petrol 25.6%
Water 18.9%
Pint(s) 17.8%
Hat 8.9%
Oil 5.6%
Milk 3.3%
Volume 2.2%
1.1% *, America, At, Beer, Bucket, By, Car, Drink, Drum, Jar, Jug, Liquid, Litre, Measure, Pail, Tank, Whiskey, Wine

Gallop+
Horse(s) 42.9%
Canter 14.3%
Trot 14.3%
Fast 4.8%
Run 4.8%
2.4% French, Ghent, Hop, In, Newmarket, Poll, Rose, Trots

Gamble+
Bet 27.1%
Money 16.7%
Risk 12.5%
Lose 4.2%
Win 4.2%
2.1% BT, Cards, Casino, Chance, Clive, Debt, Gain, Game, Gold, Leap, Loss, No, Procter, Proctor, Roulette, Stake, Waste

Gap+
Hole 25.0%
Teeth 20.8%
Space 14.6%
Tooth 10.4%
Watford 6.2%
2.1% Air, Break, Crevice, Edge, Gulf, Hedge, Miss, Missing, Mouth, Through, Tube

Gape+
Open 16.7%
* 12.5%
Hole 10.4%
Stare 10.4%
Mouth 8.3%
Drug 6.2%
Look 4.2%
Wide 4.2%
2.1% Awe, Big, Cake, Date, Dig, Eye, Fence, Low, Make, Pool, Shallow, Wound, Yellow

Garment
Clothes 26.8%
Clothing 19.5%
Dress 12.2%
Cloth 9.8%
2.4% Bra, Clobber, Coat, Drape, Dress-Shop, Hang, Hanger, Item, Lipstick, Old-Clothes, Shoes, Skirt, Towel, Trouser

Garret+
Hostel 12.5%
Attic 10.4%
Room 6.2%
* 4.2%
Fitzgerald 4.2%
Hang 4.2%
House 4.2%
Loft 4.2%
Tower 4.2%
2.1% Army, Artist, Castle, Dark, Flat, Food, Garrison, Hangman, High, Hovel, Jewels, Name, Paris, Roof, Stable, Starving, Stick, Stir, Strangle, Student, Turret, War

Gary
Glitter 30.6%
Lineker 18.4%
* 12.9%
Powers 4.1%
2.0% Bornack, Boy, Cooper, Davies, Eyes, Football, Gillespie, Harris, Holland, Horrible, Lawer, Moore, Numan, Player, Summers, Thompson, Watson

Gas
Fire 9.6%
Smell(s) 9.6%
Leak 7.7%
Board 5.7%
Cooker 5.7%
Belsen 3.8%
Burn 3.8%
Heating 3.8%
Stove 3.8%
1.9% -Eous, Air, Burner, Camping, Cloud, Danger, Dangerous, Death, Electric, Explosion, Hob, Hot, Invisible, Laugh, Light, Main, Mark, Mask, Meter, Neon, Oxygen, Petrol, Sag

Gasp+
Breath 33.3%
Air 10.4%
Shock 10.4%
Breathe 8.3%
Amazement 6.2%
Cough 6.2%
Horror 6.2%
2.1% Aghast, Agog, Fear, Fish, Gosh, Last, Oh, Pant, Sigh

Gate+
Fence 11.9%
Way 7.1%
Field 4.8%
Garden 4.8%
Lock 4.8%
Open 4.8%
Path 4.8%
Walk 4.8%
2.4% Bar, Barrier, Bull, China, Close, Door, Electric, Head, Heaven, Hell, Hinge, In, Iron, Latch, Obstruction, Port, Post, Shop, Skull, Vault, Wall, Wicket

Gauge+
Measure 18.8%
* 10.4%
Railway 8.3%
Judge 6.2%
Assess 4.2%
2.1% Brown, Distance, Don't, Estimate, Fine, Game, Guess, Jam, Level, Lock, Meter, Narrow, Old, Pressure, Small, Sorry, Steam, Temperature, Time, Track, Tyre, Vacuum, Warrant, Water, Worth

Gauze+
Bandage 8.3%
Cut 8.3%
Muslin 8.3%
Fine 6.2%
Bunsen 4.2%
Lint 4.2%
Swab 4.2%
Tripod 4.2%
Veil 4.2%
Wire 4.2%
2.1% Airy, Asbestos, Bush, Cloth, Davey, Felt, Flame, Gossamer, Hospital, Mesh, Moors, Muslim, Net, Sieve, Sterile, Strip, Tape, Thin, Veiling, Window, Wound

Gaze+
Look 28.1%
Stare 14.6%

See 9.4%
Eyes 4.2%
Watch 3.1%
Dream 2.1%
Long 2.1%
1.0% *, Afar, Away, Awe, Blind, Casually, Concentrate, Desire, Distant, Emptiness, Far, Gazette, Glance, Hard, Hidden, Hound, Longingly, Love, Lovingly, Memory, Nights, Precious, Regard, Scenery, Shock, Star, Stone, Up, Upon, View, Watch, Weeks, Wistful, Wonder, Wonderingly

Generator+
Electricity 31.0%
Electric 9.5%
Power 9.5%
Engine 7.1%
Heater 4.8%
Light 4.8%
Motor 4.8%
2.4% *, Big, Boat, Boiler, Breakdown, Energy, Line, Producer, Provider, Turbine, Van

Gentle
Giant 12.0%
Soft 12.0%
Kind 10.0%
Caring 6.0%
Lamb 6.0%
Man 6.0%
Ben 4.0%
Mild 4.0%
Quiet 4.0%
Smooth 4.0%
Stroke 4.0%
Touch 4.0%
2.0% Guy, Hard, Lady, Meek, Music, Rough, Soothe, Strong, Swift, Tough, Warm, Weak

Gentleman
Lady 30.0%
Man 14.0%
Woman 10.0%
Blonde(s) 4.0%
Ladies 4.0%
Polite 4.0%
Suit 4.0%
Top-Hat 4.0%
2.0% Black, Bowler-Hat, Caller, Class, Club, Gentleman, Handkerchief, Hat, Monsieur, Snob, Style, Top-Hat-And-Tails, Umbrella

Genuine
Real 51.1%
Article 13.3%
Fake 11.1%
True 6.7%
2.2% Amazement, Award, Counterfeit, False, Feelings, Honest, Sincere

George
Michael 20.4%
Harrison 16.3%
* 11.1%
Bush 8.2%
Boy 6.1%
Best 4.1%
2.0% Barker, Benson, Blake, Bungle, Dragon, Formby, Harris, Helen, Herbert, King, Mall, Me, Name, Parker, Show, Third, Zippy

Germ
Disease 17.1%
Bacteria 9.8%
Ill 9.8%
Bleach 4.9%
Cell 4.9%
Illness 4.9%
Infect 4.9%
Wheat 4.9%
2.4% *, Amoeba, Breed, Cold, Dead, Dettol, Dirt, Green, Kill, Kitchen, Life, Molecule, Sick, Truth, Violent, Virus, Warfare

Germanic+
* 13.0%
German 10.9%
Language(s) 10.9%
Teutonic 10.9%
Adolf 4.3%
Aryan 4.3%
Deutsch 4.3%
Hitler 4.3%
2.2% Aerobics, Anglo-Saxon, Black, Blond, Country, Foreign, French, Gaul, Helga, Hispanic, Holiday, Hun, Kraut, National, People, Plant, Race, Script

Gestation+
Period 21.7%
Birth 19.6%
Pregnant 13.0%
* 8.7%
Baby/ies 6.5%
Pregnancy 6.5%
Egg 4.3%
Elephant 4.3%
2.2% Aliens, Cut, Dance, Fallow, Fertilization, Gesture, Sex

Get
Have 10.9%
Take 6.5%
Up 6.5%
Away 4.3%
Give 4.3%
Go 4.3%
In 4.3%
Obtain 4.3%
2.2% *, About, Achieve, Ahead, Carter, Down, Fetch, Find, Girl, Got, Hold, Job, Knotted, Lost, Morning, Now, Out, Own, Ready, Rid-Of, Smart, Stuffed, Sum, That, Together, Want

Ghost+
Ghoul 14.6%
Dream 6.2%
House 6.2%
Phantom 6.2%
Spectre 6.2%
* 4.2%
Dead 4.2%
Fright 4.2%
Haunt 4.2%
Spirit 4.2%
Spook 4.2%
White 4.2%
2.1% Buster, Creepy, Dark, Hamlet, Haunted, Horror, Machine, Night, Proud, Shadow, Shirt, Spooky, Star, Town, Watcher

Gift+
Present 52.1%
Give 4.2%
God 4.2%
Token 4.2%
Wrap 4.2%
2.1% Birthday, Chance, Day, Free, Gab, Greek, Life, Paper, Parcel, Prize, Sister, Wedding, Wrapped, Wrapping

Giggle+
Laugh 68.8%
* 8.3%
Girls 4.2%
Smirk 4.2%
2.1% Ache, Chuckle, Fun, Guffaw, Happy, Mirth, School

Gin
Tonic 36.5%
Drink 9.6%
Whisky 5.7%
Alcohol 3.8%
And-Tonic 3.8%
Lemon 3.8%
Sloe 3.8%
1.9% &T, *, Beefeater, Booze, Bottle, Ginger, Ginseng, Gordon's, Hot, Nig, Palace, Rum, Rummy, Sin, Sling, Vice, Vodka

Ginormous
Big 29.2%
Huge 27.1%
Enormous 8.3%
Large 8.3%
Massive 8.3%
2.1% *, Enormous-Gin, Gigantic, House, Schoolgirl, Small, Tonic, Very-Big, Very-Large

Giraffe
Neck 42.2%
Tall 28.9%
Africa 4.4%
Long 4.4%
2.2% *, Animal, Eyes, Heat, Penguin, Spots, Tree, Unicycle, Zoo

Give+
Take 31.2%
Present 13.5%
Receive 9.4%
Up 6.3%
Donate 4.2%
Away 3.1%
Hand 3.1%
Generous 2.1%
Gift 2.1%
Love 2.1%
Money 2.1%
Prize 2.1%
To 2.1%
1.0% Back, Concede, Confiscate, Free, Gain, Gave, Hand-Over, Happy, Lend, Me, Over, Pain, Please, Reap, Take-Away, Want

Glad
Happy 47.7%
Smile 6.8%
Pleased 4.5%
Rags 4.5%
Relieved 4.5%
2.3% *, All, Displeased, Emotion, Gay, Good, Great, Hand, Nest, Pleasure, Sad, Tidings, To-Be, To-Be-Gay

Glamour+
Fashion 10.4%
Girl 10.4%
Model 10.4%
Puss 8.3%
Glitter 6.2%
Chic 4.2%
Star 4.2%
2.1% *, Beauty, Fade, Fame, Girls, Glitz, Glory, Gloss, Grammar, Hollywood, Lipstick, Looks, Magazine, Nice, Photography, Power, Splendour, Stage, Style, The, Thin, Wealth

Glance+
Look 30.2%
See 12.5%
Glimpse 7.3%
Blow 4.2%
At 3.1%

Eye(s) 3.1%
Around 2.1%
Chance 2.1%
Peer 2.1%
Sidelong 2.1%
Sideways 2.1%
Strike 2.1%
Up 2.1%
1.0% *, Askance, Backwards, Bounce, Cricket, Cursory, Daffodils, Down, Fear, Glasses, Harvey, Look-At, Notice, Peer, Quick, Seek, Seen, Shoulder, Snatch, Spot, Stare, Upwards, Watch

Glass+
Drink 14.6%
Wine 14.6%
Cup 12.5%
Window 8.3%
House(s) 4.2%
Jar 4.2%
Shatter 4.2%
Water 4.2%
2.1% *, Beer, Bottomed, Break, Breaking, Clear, Cut, Full, Glasses, Mirror, Oath, Pane, See-Through, Smash, Test, Ware

Glasses
Eyes 13.3%
See 11.1%
Drink(s) 6.7%
Spectacles 6.7%
Sun 4.4%
Vision 4.4%
2.2% *, Bald, Beer, Blind, Break, Clever, Contact-Lenses, Crack, Egg, Glass, Horn-Rimmed, Lenses, Nose, Ray, Rim, Short-Sighted, Sight, Smear, Specs, Table, Ugly, Wash, Wear

Gleam+
Shine 56.2%
Glitter 6.2%
Eye 4.2%
Shiny 4.2%
Sparkle 4.2%
2.1% Brightly, Dark, Eyes, Following, Glimmer, Glow, Idea, Information, Jewel, Teeth, Twinkle, Wisp

Glenda
Jackson 87.8%
* 4.2%
2.0% Actrice, Davies, Fox, Upstairs

Glimpse+
See 45.8%
Eye(s) 10.4%
Sight 7.3%
* 3.1%
Glance 3.1%
Peek 3.1%
Look 2.1%
1.0% Brief, Catch, Curtain, Fleeting, Flight, Future, Gleam, Glimmer, Hope, Knife, Leaves, Moon, Notice, Of, Peep, Perceive, Recce, Seek, Seen, Spot, Spy, Through, Veil, Watch, Window

Globe+
World 56.2%
Earth 10.4%
Round 6.2%
Trot 4.2%
Trotter 4.2%
2.1% Awareness, Low, Map, Orbit, Sphere, Splay, Spool, Style, Third

Glory+
Hope 18.8%
Honour 10.4%
Be 8.3%
Boys 6.2%
God 6.2%
Power 6.2%
Hallelujah 4.2%
War 4.2%
2.1% *, Boy, Christ, Crown, Days, Death, Fame, Heaven, Joy, Kingdom, Lord, Praise, Shine, Sticky, Sun, Vain, Win

Gloss+
Paint 37.5%
Shine 27.1%
Over 8.3%
Matt 4.2%
2.1% Coat, Cover-Up, Easy, Finish, Lip, Magazine, Shimmer, Shiny, Sticky, Text, Wall

Glove+
Hand(s) 73.0%
Fit 6.2%
Puppet 4.2%
2.1% Challenge, Close, Compartment, Finger, Hand-In, Mitten, Shoe, Velvet

Glow
Worm(s) 37.5%
Dark 12.5%
Bright 10.4%
Shine 8.3%
Fire 4.2%
Hot 4.2%
Lamp 4.2%
Light 4.2%
2.1% *, Flow, Grate, Luminous, Radiate, Row, Snow

Glue+
Sniff 27.1%
Stick 20.8%
Sniffer 6.2%
Green 4.2%
Paper 4.2%
Red 4.2%
Sniffing 4.2%
Sticky 4.2%
2.1% Girl, Gloom, Gum, Horses, Paste, Sky, Smell, Stuck, Thick, Tight, Together, Uhu

Go+
Stop 21.4%
Away 19.0%
Leave 9.5%
Start 9.5%
Come 7.1%
Now 4.8%
Out 4.8%
2.4% Between, Buck, Flour, Girl, Gone, Move, Red, There, To, Visit

Goal+
Football 27.1%
Score 20.8%
Aim 10.4%
Post 10.4%
Ball 6.2%
Own 6.2%
Shoot 6.2%
Silver 4.2%
2.1% Fall, Mine, Mouth, Net

Goat+
Kid 10.4%
Billy 8.3%
Cheese 8.3%
Milk 8.3%
Nanny 6.2%
Sheep 6.2%
Beard 4.2%
Eat 4.2%
Head 4.2%
Herd 4.2%
2.1% Cheese, Cow, Eats, Farm, Horn, Horse, Idolize, Long, Love, Mascot, Old, Pen, Ram, Sacrifice, Separate, Skin, Want

God+
Heaven 6.2%
Jesus 6.2%
Worship 6.2%
Angel 4.2%
Belief 4.2%
Devil 4.2%
Head 4.2%
Love 4.2%
One 4.2%
2.1% *, Almighty, Bible, Christ, Deity, Eden, Faithful, Give, Great, Idea, Joke, King, Machine, Maelstrom, Maker, Man, Me, Mercy, Nonsense, Nothing, Nun, Religion, Sky, Soul, Sunbeam, Theology, Universe

Gold+
Silver 45.8%
Dust 8.3%
Mine 6.2%
Coin 4.2%
Digger 4.2%
Rush 4.2%
2.1% *, Bullion, Dig, Expensive, Find, Glitter, Glitters, Hand, Medal, Money, Myrrh, Prospector, Rich

Good
Bad 62.1%
Boy 8.0%
Evil 3.4%
Girl 2.3%
Times 2.3%
Wines 2.3%
1.1% *, Ace, Clean, Clever, Dog, God, Gold, Great, Health, Humour, Kind, Lollipop, Lord, News, Plato, Shag, Very, Vibrations, Work

Goon+
* 28.3%
Show 17.4%
Comic 4.3%
Fool 4.3%
Funny 4.3%
Harry 4.3%
Idiot 4.3%
Joke 4.3%
Python 4.3%
2.2% Baboon, Bob, Goof, Goose, Mug, Purple, Radio, Silly, Spike, Spook, Yacht

Gore+
Blood 52.1%
Horn 10.4%
* 6.2%
Bull 6.2%
Cut 4.2%
2.1% Bad, Belgium, Boar, Guts, Horror, Kensington, Muck, Skirt, Spear, Stab

Gorilla
Ape 20.0%
Mist 13.3%
Monkey 13.3%
Hair(y) 8.9%
* 4.4%
Fury 4.4%
Zoo 4.4%
2.2% Big, Black, Cage, Chimp, Chimpanzee, Flotilla, Forest, Godzilla, Heart, In-The-Mist, Muck, Suit, Ugly, War

Gossip+
Talk 20.0%
Column 11.1%
Chatter 8.9%
Chat 7.8%
-Monger 4.4%
Scandal 4.4%
Slander 4.4%
People 3.3%
Women 3.3%
Fence 2.2%
Hot 2.2%
Rumour 2.2%
Tattle 2.2%
Words 2.2%
1.1% Bad, Bitch, Chit-Chat, Columnist, Converse, Dot, Girl, Idle, Lady, Lie, Malicious, Mean, Natter, Spite, Tell, Whisper, Wit, Woman, Work

Grab
Hold 19.1%
Take 12.8%
Grasp 8.5%
Crane 6.4%
Hand 6.4%
Snatch 6.4%
* 4.3%
2.1% All, Anger, Bag, Clasp, Dutch, Get, Give, Handbag, Handle, Hard, Kidnap, Purse, Run, Scare, Seize, Shoot, You

Grace+
God 11.7%
Kelly 8.5%
Favour 7.4%
Prayer 4.3%
Fall 3.2%
Jones 3.2%
* 2.1%
Beauty 2.1%
Dancer 2.1%
Darling 2.1%
Elegance 2.1%
Finesse 2.1%
Meal(s) 2.1%
Mercy 2.1%
Poise 2.1%
1.1% Abounding, Amain*, Archbishop, Ballet, Charm, Church, Curtsey, Dance, Danger, Delicate, Dignity, Dinner, Dress, Duty, Full, Gentle, Hexagram, Lady, Land, Love, Mannerly, Manners, Mealtime, Monday, Name, Of-God, Plate, Posture, Pressure, Princess, Race, Religion, Royal, Royalty, Seven, Smooth, Splendour, Table, Teeth, Trust

Grade+
A 13.0%
Mark 13.0%
Exam(s) 8.7%
First 6.5%
* 4.3%
Degree 4.3%
Pass 4.3%
2.2% Alpha, Average, Best, Cheese, Class, Eight, Fail, Grey, Higher, List, Low, Plait, Plan, Primary, Sample, Scale, School, Score, Sort, Standard, Test

Gradual+
Slowly 26.2%
Slow 11.9%
Change 7.1%
* 4.8%
Decline 4.8%
Eventual 4.8%
Nearly 4.8%
2.4% Almost, Bit, Correct, Graduate, Hourly, Increase, Increments, Insipid, Little, Rate, Recession, Slight, Slope, Steady

Graduate+
Student 33.3%
University 11.9%
Degree 9.5%
Me 7.1%
Undergraduate 4.8%
2.4% Cap, Career, College, Course, Dustin, Hoffman, Mrs, Museum, Pass, School, Success, Technology, Yes

Graft+
Work 31.2%
Skin 22.9%
Tree 10.4%
* 4.2%
Plant 4.2%
Sew 4.2%
2.1% Centre, Get, Green, Grip, Grow, Hard, Heavy, Leg, Letter, Sapling, Stick

Grain+
Sand 27.1%
Wheat 14.6%
Corn 10.4%
Rice 4.2%
Seed 4.2%
Wood 4.2%
2.1% *, Barley, Bin, Clever, Dust, Embargo, Flour, Food, Grape, Green, Horse, Kong, Salt, Smooth, Sun, Tree, Trigo

Gram+
Ounce 31.2%
Weight 31.2%
Weigh 10.4%
Kilo 4.2%
2.1% -Mer, After, Cracker, Litre, Mass, Phone, Pound, Record, Small, Speed, Tiny

Grand+
Piano 29.2%
Big 8.3%
Fine 6.2%
Duke 4.2%
Great 4.2%
Hall 4.2%
Hotel 4.2%
Mother 4.2%
Thousand 4.2%
2.1% Baroque, Castle, Clock, Duchess, Father, Good, House, Large, Magnificent, Majestic, Mansion, Money, Old, Stand, Wonderful

Granny+
Old 22.9%
Smith 18.8%
Grandpa 12.5%
Age 4.2%
Aunt 4.2%
Flat 4.2%
Grandad 4.2%
2.1% *, Aged, Annex, Apple, Basher, Bond, Chair, Cloak, Dead, Grandma, Knot, Mother, Nanny, Uncle

Grant+
Money 25.0%
Give 14.6%
Student 10.4%
Cheque 8.3%
Allow 4.2%
Pig 4.2%
2.1% Agree, Bull, Education, Enable, Enough, Gift, Government, Live, Low, Pay, Prayer, Request, Royalty, School, Sir, Wish

Grape
Fruit 26.5%
Juice 22.4%
Vine 14.3%
Wine 10.2%
Green 8.2%
Orange 4.1%
2.0% Apple, Beautiful, Black, Nut, Raisin, Rape, Squish

Grapefruit
Juice 14.0%
Sour 12.0%
Breakfast 10.0%
Fruit 8.0%
Yellow 8.0%
Bitter 6.0%
Orange 6.0%
Citrus 4.0%
Lemon 4.0%
Sweet 4.0%
2.0% ?, Bruise, Eat, Green, Horrible, Pineapple, Salad, Spoon, Sugar, Suit, Taste, Vine

Grasp+
Hold 47.9%
Clutch 10.4%
Grab 8.3%
Grip 8.3%
Seize 4.2%
Take 4.2%
2.1% Catch, Clasp, Clench, Cling, Fist, Hand, Rose, Snatch

Grass+
Green 52.1%
Lawn 10.4%
Cow 6.2%
Drugs 4.2%
Snake 4.2%
Tree(s) 4.2%
2.1% Field, Flesh, Garden, Grow, Grows, Herb, Pot, Sheep, Weed

Grasshopper
Green 17.8%
Cricket 15.6%
Grass 15.6%
Insect 8.9%
Jump 8.9%
Hop 6.7%
2.2% Ant, Crunch, Feast, Frog, Lawn, Leaf, Leap, Monkey, Newt, Rabbit, Tea, Tree

Grater+
Cheese 56.2%
Larger 10.4%
Lesser 8.3%
Smaller 6.2%
Less 4.2%
2.1% Apple, Carrot, God, Greatest, Nutmeg, Than, Weaker

Grave+
Digger 16.7%
Death 14.4%
Dig 12.2%
Dead 8.9%
Stone 7.8%
Yard 5.6%
Serious 4.4%
Tomb 4.4%
Churchyard 2.2%
1.1% Bad, Bury, Dark, Deep, Error, Flowers, Hearse, Heavy, Hole, Mausoleum, Mound, Mourn, Night, Rain, Robber, Sad, Side, Soil, Solemn, Trees, Undertaker, Victory

Gravel+
Pit 39.6%
Path 16.7%
Stone(s) 10.4%
Drive 6.2%
Sand 6.2%
Pebble(s) 6.2%

2.1% Grate, Ground, Lake, Rocks, Seabed, Stony

Gravy+
Meat 20.8%
Train 16.7%
Boat 12.5%
Sauce 6.2%
Thick 6.2%
Beef 4.2%
Brown 4.2%
Stain 4.2%
2.1% Browning, Food, Green, Jug, Juice, Ladle, Menu, Pastry, Pour, Pudding, Spoon, Steak

Graze+
Cow(s) 32.0%
Grass 20.0%
Eat 10.0%
Cut 4.0%
Hurt 4.0%
Knee 4.0%
Sheep 4.0%
2.0% *, Animal, Cattle, Disinfectant, Feed, Films, Goat, Grind, Horse, Look, Pull

Grease+
Film 10.4%
Lightning 10.4%
Oil 10.4%
Hot 8.3%
Slime 6.2%
Dirty 4.2%
Fat 4.2%
Grime 4.2%
Movie 4.2%
2.1% Athens, Block, Briest, Chips, Drip, Engine, Filth, Gun, Heat, Oily, Olivia, Short, Slimy, Smooth, Spot, Stain, Travolta, Turkey

Great
* 16.0%
Weak 16.0%
Enormous 10.0%
Smart 6.0%
Big 4.0%
Good 4.0%
Heavens 4.0%
Lion 4.0%
2.0% Beast, Emperor, Escape, Football, God, Grand, Immense, Joy, Majestic, Men, Mighty, News, Scott, Small, Strong, Super, Tiny, Wonderful

Greed+
Hunger 16.7%
Avarice 14.6%
Money 12.5%
Envy 10.4%
Lust 6.2%
Pig 4.2%
Want 4.2%
Wealth 4.2%
2.1% Anger, Fat, Food, Gluttony, Green, Guilt, Gut, Hungry, More, Obese, Plenty, Rich, Scrooge

Greek+
Latin 9.5%
Island 7.1%
Language 7.1%
Athens 4.8%
Cypriot 4.8%
God 4.8%
2.4% Abroad, All, Ancient, Black, Column, Costas, Dutch, Field, Illyrian, Isle, Kebab, Mediterranean, Odysseus, Olives, Play, Prose, Salad, Skirt, Slimy, Statue, Sun, Taverna, Topol, Tragedy, Yoghurt

Green+
Grass 35.4%
Yellow 10.4%
Field(s) 6.2%
House 6.2%
Blue 4.2%
Envy 4.2%
2.1% Eyes, Gleam, Gold, Grey, Leaf, Maths, Money, Park, Party, Peace, Purple, Red, Rotten, Summer, Valley, Young

Greenhouse
Effect 28.8%
Plant(s) 19.2%
Glass 17.3%
Hot 9.6%
Tomato 7.7%
Gas 3.8%
1.9% Flowers, Light, Pollution, Sea, Vegetable, Warm, Windows

Grief+
Sadness 20.8%
Death 18.8%
Sad 14.6%
Sorrow 14.6%
Pain 8.3%
Cry 6.2%
2.1% Anger, Bad, Fear, Good, Tear, Weep, Weird, Wine

Grill+
Toast 35.4%
Fry 12.5%
Bacon 8.3%
Cook 8.3%
Pan 6.2%
Food 4.2%
Heat 4.2%
2.1% *, Bowl, Boy, Burn, Grate, Interrogate, Interview, Roast, Snake, Steak

Grim
* 8.5%
Sad 6.4%
Dirty 5.3%
Face 5.3%
Dull 4.3%
Reaper 4.3%
Bleak 3.2%
Grey 3.2%
Stern 3.2%
"Up-North" 2.1%
Awful 2.1%
Dirt 2.1%
Faced 2.1%
Happy 2.1%
Horrible 2.1%
Smile 2.1%
1.1% ?, Bad, Bah, Black, Brim, Brothers, Conditions, Consequence, Cross, Dark, Day, Depressing, Dickens, Dour, Dowdy, Dwarf, Eiger, Fairy, Fairytale, Fiendish, Fierce, Find, Gross, Grotty, Leak, Mean, Pale, Play, Pleasant, Prison, Promise, Response, Serious, Tale, Terrible, Tidings, Under, Unkind, Weather

Grime+
Dirt 66.7%
Soot 6.2%
Filth 4.2%
Slime 4.2%
2.1% Chimney, Clean, Dirty, Grit, Grot, Muck, Mud, Muddy, Stone

Grin+
Smile 45.7%
Teeth 8.7%
And 4.3%
Bad 4.3%
Bear 4.3%
2.2% Buy, Cheek, Cheerful, Edge, Grass, Happy, Hated, Miserable, Mouth, Reaper, Sad, Smirk, Snarl, Snow, Work

Grind
Teeth 23.3%
Coffee 9.3%
Axe 7.0%
Stone 7.0%
Corn 4.7%
Work 4.7%
2.3% Bonk, Cheese, Cook, Core, Down, Flour, Grain, Grope, Halt, Hard, Hips, Joy, Mill, Nail, Pepper, Rub, Sex, Tired, Up

Grip
Hold 22.9%
Handle 12.5%
Hand 10.4%
Vice 6.3%
Grab 4.2%
Grasp 4.2%
Me 4.2%
Tightly 4.2%
2.1% Bicycle, Camera, Case, Club, Fasten, Firm, Get, Hard, Iron, Power, Reality, Shifter, Strong, Tennis, Tight

Groan
Moan 58.0%
* 4.0%
2.0% Ache, Car, Deep, Diarrhoea, Dislike, Grunt, Hurt, Laugh, Noise, Oh, Pain, Sigh, Tired, Ugh, Upset, Wail, What, Whine, Whinge

Groin+
Strain 16.7%
Leg 12.5%
Crutch 8.3%
* 4.2%
Ache 4.2%
Body 4.2%
Injury 4.2%
Knee 4.2%
Loin 4.2%
2.1% Belly, Crotch, Dick, God, Grain, Hairs, Itch, Legs, Ligament, Pain, Painful, Sea, Seashore, Tendons, Thigh, Trousers, Waist, Warm

Grotesque+
Ugly 52.4%
Awful 4.8%
Gargoyle 4.8%
Horrible 4.8%
Obscene 4.8%
2.4% Bad, Deformed, Disfigured, Disgusting, Evil, Hideous, Horrid, Horror, Huge, Mask, Monstrous, Nasty

Group
People 22.0%
Leader 7.3%
Sex 7.3%
Band 6.0%
Many 4.9%
Together 4.9%
2.4% *, Crowd, Dolphin, Family, Gathering, Job, Learning, Led, Match, Mixture, Outing, Peer, Play, Ring, Session, Set, Sing, Spirit, Therapy

Growl+
Dog 29.2%
Roar 8.3%
Bark 6.2%
Bear 6.2%
Gruff 6.2%
Lion 6.2%
Grunt 4.2%

Noise 4.2%
Snarl 4.2%
2.1% *, Angry, Deep, Fear, Fierce, Groan, Hound, Hunger, Low, Mutter, Snort, Tiger

Growth
Plant(s) 9.8%
* 4.9%
Big 4.9%
Hormone 4.9%
Size 4.9%
Spurt 4.9%
Tall 4.9%
2.4% Age, Alive, Bend, Bit, Child, Childhood, Develop, Economic, Economy, Expansion, Go, Green, Grow, Height, Increase, Large, Life, Low, Rapid, Root, Seedling, Shoot, Shrub, Stunt, Tumour, Vigour

Grub+
Food 45.8%
Maggot 16.7%
Worm 10.4%
Insect 6.2%
Caterpillar 4.2%
2.1% Bug, Earth, Earthworms, Fly, Mite, Stake, Street, Up

Gruel+
Porridge 25.0%
Soup 16.7%
Food 12.5%
Oliver 8.3%
Cook 4.2%
Hard 4.2%
Slop(s) 4.2%
2.1% *, Bacon, Book, Broth, King, Mess, More, Orphans, Pan, Stew, Thin

Grumble+
Moan 47.9%
Complain 14.6%
Groan 6.2%
Weed 6.2%
2.1% *, Dwarf, Fish, Noise, Open, Thunder, Tummy, Weeds, Whine, Whinge, Words, Worry

Grunt+
Pig 50.0%
Groan 16.5%
Snort 8.3%
Moan 4.2%
Noise 4.2%
2.1% Growl, Loud, Oink, Scream, Sneeze, Soldier, Sty, Warthog

Guard+
Soldier 14.6%
Honour 12.5%
Palace 8.3%
Dog 6.2%
On 6.2%
Castle 4.2%
Protect 4.2%
Van 4.2%
Watch 4.2%
2.1% Change, Cherish, Conceal, Driver, Fire, Gun, Life, Look, Man, Mouth, Office, Save, Security, Stand, Treasure, Well, White

Guess
* 12.5%
Question 12.5%
Estimate 8.3%
What 6.3%
Which 6.3%
Answer 4.2%
Quiz 4.2%
Think 4.2%
Who 4.2%
2.1% Ascertain, Ask, Bewilder, Chance, Clue, Divine, Error, Fluke, Game, Guesstimate, Hazard, How, Know, Perhaps, Rest, Stab, Try, Win

Guesstimate
Estimate 22.9%
Guess 22.9%
* 14.6%
2.1% Amount, Ants, Approximate, Approximise, Dictionary, Error, Figures, Find, Guess Estimate, Guest, Inaccurate, Make Up, Office, Production, Quest, Try, Visitor, Word, Yuck

Guide+
Lead 12.5%
Girl 10.4%
Scout 10.4%
Show 10.4%
Blind 6.2%
Help 6.2%
Tour 6.2%
Brownie 4.2%
Dog 4.2%
Leader 4.2%
2.1% Book, Holiday, Light, Path, Redeemer, Sherpa, Shine, Steer, Teach, Tourist, Traveller, Way

Guilty
Innocent 40.0%
Court 4.4%
Feeling(s) 4.4%
Plea 4.4%
Prison 4.4%
Sin 4.4%
Wrong 4.4%
2.2% *, Accused, As-Hell, By-Suspicion, Conscience, Jail, Judge, Men, Pea, Plead, Red, Ridden, Secret, Smile, Stealing

Guitar+
String 31.0%
Music 11.9%
Player 11.9%
Instrument 9.5%
Strum 7.1%
Play 4.8%
2.4% Band, Banjo, Carp, Clapton, Guitarist, Mandolin, Sing, Solo, Song, Tune

Gull
Sea 38.8%
Bird 24.5%
Water 4.1%
2.0% *, Autism, Boat, Cliff, Cooper, Dare, Fly, Great, Nothing, Plane, Rook, Seagull, Soar, Wave, Wing

Gunshot
Wound 48.0%
Bullet(s) 10.0%
Fire 6.0%
Bang 4.0%
Loud 4.0%
Smoke 4.0%
2.0% *, Body, Buck, Dead, Death, Gun, Marriage, Murder, Riccochet, Rifle, Sling, Western

Gut+
Stomach 22.9%
Feeling 12.5%
Reaction 8.3%
Cat 6.2%
* 4.2%
Belly 4.2%
Innard(s) 4.2%
Intestine 4.2%
Pain 4.2%
2.1% Ache, Blood, Body, Death, Greed, Liver, Pig, Pond, Quantifier, Rot, Strong, Trench, Wet, What

Guy
Fawkes 29.0%
Gorilla 8.2%
Man 8.2%
Doll 6.1%
* 4.1%
Chadwick 4.1%
Girl 4.1%
Michelmore 4.1%
Mitchell 4.1%
2.0% Buddy, Burgess, Fireworks, Ford, Forget, Gay, Jones, Laroche, Nikki, Paul, Pierce, Rope, Sis's

Gymnast
Athlete 12.2%
Bars 12.2%
Sport 7.3%
Russian 4.9%
Vault 4.9%
2.4% *, Ability, Acrobat, Aerobic, Agility, Beam, Beauty, Dancer, Energy, Fantastic, Fast, Fit, Flexibility, Flexible, Flip, Girl, Gym, Health, Korbut, Olga, Olympics, School, Stretch, Supple, Trapeze

Habit+
Monk 11.9%
Nun 9.5%
Often 9.5%
Common 4.8%
Custom 4.8%
Forming 4.8%
Lifetime 4.8%
Smoking 4.8%
Usual 4.8%
2.4% *, Action, Bad, Creature, Dress, Formed, Habitat, Hard, Hobby, Manner, Normal, Repeat, Routine, Smoke, Trait, Wont, Wrong

Hair
Long 17.0%
Net 12.8%
* 6.4%
Wet 6.4%
Cut 4.3%
Gel 4.3%
Skin 4.3%
2.1% Band, Bear, Braid, Brown, Brush, Bun, Clip, Hairnet, Head, Neat, None, Piece, Pin, Spray, Straight, Style, Tail, Today, Towel, Wig, Wool

Hairbrush
Comb 36.5%
Hair 34.6%
Bristles 5.7%
1.9% *, Beat, Bold, Fluff, Head, Hit, Long, Red, Smack, Soft, Tangly, Toothbrush

Half
Whole 16.7%
Pint 7.1%
Apple 4.8%
Full 4.8%
Measure(s) 4.8%
Moon 4.8%
Semi 4.8%
Split 4.8%
Time 4.8%
2.4% *, And-Half, Bad, Baked, Bat, Coherent, Cut, Day, Hearted, Measurement, One, Orange, Past, Segment, Semi-Circle, Side, Sixpence, Two

Halt
Stop 86.0%
2.0% Barrier, Edge, Go, Now, Policeman, Sign, Stumble

Ham
Egg(s) 14.0%
Sandwich 10.0%
Cheese 8.0%
Pig 8.0%
Bone 6.0%
Fisted 6.0%
Pink 6.0%
Pork 6.0%
Beef 4.0%
Joint 4.0%
2.0% Actor, Eat, Fist, Harm, Horrible, Lovely, Pair, Parma, Roll, Rye, Spam, Supermarket, Unkosher, Water

Hamlet+
Shakespeare 45.3%
Play 19.1%
Village 7.1%
Prince 4.8%
Town 4.8%
2.4% Henry, Kings, Macbeth, Omelette, Orestes, Othello, Stratford, To-Be-Or-Not

Hammock+
Bed 35.7%
Sleep 26.2%
Sling 7.1%
Tree 4.8%
2.4% Bunk, Hammer, Lie, Pillow, Rest, Sailor, Sea, Ship, Summer, Sun, Swinging

Hamper+
Picnic 27.5%
Food 22.5%
Hinder 10.0%
Basket 7.5%
Christmas 7.5%
2.5% Aunty, Bag, Case, Delay, Fortnum's, Hold, Laundry, Restrict, Wicker, Xmas

Hamster+
Gerbil 16.7%
Cage 11.9%
Mouse 11.9%
Pet 7.1%
Rat 7.1%
Animal 4.8%
Rodent 4.8%
2.4% *, Brother, Cheeks, Creature, Dead, Frog, Fur, Furry, Guinea, Hutch, John, Rabbit, Sandwich, Smell

Hand
Glove 21.4%
Finger 9.5%
Foot 9.5%
Arm 4.8%
Hold 4.8%
Shake 4.8%
2.4% Bag, Book, Down, Eye, Heart, Held, In-Hand, Job, Left, Made, Mouth, Off, Palm, Ring, Small, Warm, Warmer, Wash, Write

Handbag
Purse 13.3%
Leather 8.9%
Woman 8.9%
* 6.7%
Money 6.7%
Bag 4.4%
Key(s) 4.4%
2.2% Black, Briefcase, Carry, Coax, Door, Full, Gloves, Granny, Handle, Horrible, Mirror, Queen, Safe, Sag, Satchel, Shoe, Shoulder, Snatcher, Stolen, Strap, Wallet

Handful+
Lot(s) 14.3%
Sand 14.3%
* 7.1%
Enough 7.1%
Palm 7.1%
Fist 4.8%
Money 4.8%
2.4% Beans, Brother, Child, Coins, Dust, Fingers, Grab, Grain, Grasp, Hand, Load, Massage, Much, Packed, Trouble, Wheat

Handicap+
Disability 16.7%
Wheelchair 14.3%
Mental 9.5%
* 4.8%
Disadvantage 4.8%
Problem 4.8%
2.4% Child, Difficult, Disable, Disablement, Disease, End, Fault, Golf, Helpless, Hold, Horse, Infirm, Lame, Mongrel, Person, Physical, Racing, Sister, Writer

Handle
Door 29.2%
Touch 18.8%
Bar 4.2%
Broom 4.2%
Case 4.2%
Cup 4.2%
Hold 4.2%
Jug 4.2%
Pot 4.2%
2.1% Care, Down, Feel, Grip, Holder, Hot, Mug, Pan, Play, Spoon, Well

Handsome+
Man 16.7%
Pretty 16.7%
Good-Looking 11.9%
Face 7.1%
* 4.8%
Attractive 4.8%
Devil 4.8%
Nice 4.8%
2.4% Beautiful, Error, Good, Grand, Kind, Looks, Me, Rich, Smart, Stranger, Ugly, Wicked

Hanger
Coat 20.0%
On 20.0%
Clothes 15.6%
Aircraft 8.9%
Plane 6.7%
Aeroplane 4.4%
Lane 4.4%
Wire 4.4%
2.2% 17, Cupboard, Flight, Hanging, Holster, Jacket, Party

Happiness
Joy 17.0%
Sadness 8.5%
Smile 6.4%
* 4.3%
Content 4.3%
Life 4.3%
Sad 4.3%
2.1% Beam, Beloved, Bliss, Cheerfulness, Cigar, Contentment, Friends, Glad, Glow, Health, Holiness, Humour, Idyll, Knus?, Laugh, Laughter, Now, Peace, Sea, Smiling, Sorrow, Travel, Warm, Yellow

Happy
Sad 38.0%
Smile 14.0%
Cheerful 4.0%
Hour 4.0%
Lucky 4.0%
People 4.0%
2.0% Birthday, Boy, Bright, Chappie, Clappy, Colour, Crane, Face, Girl, Go-Lucky, Lie, Man, Round, Sort, Swift, Witty

Hard
Soft 29.8%
Life 7.1%
Rock 6.0%
Tough 4.8%
Boiled 3.6%
Difficult 3.6%
Edge 3.6%
Board 2.4%
Knock(s) 2.4%
Line(s) 2.4%
Nut 2.4%
Times 2.4%
Work 2.4%
1.2% Black, Brick, Cheese, Club, Cruel, Easy, Floor, Grey, Head, Heavy, Man, Nail, Pavement, Sell, Shoulder, So, Solid,

Surface, Test, Toffee, Up, Wood

Hardship
Poor 19.1%
Fund(s) 10.6%
Money 8.5%
Poverty 6.4%
* 4.3%
Need 4.3%
Student 4.3%
Tough 4.3%
2.1% Beggar, Difficulty, Fellow, Fellowship, Food, Friendship, Grant, Loan, Me, Means, Now, Privation, Story, Strength, Suffering, Toil, Want, Worry

Hare
Rabbit 61.5%
Hound 5.7%
Lip 5.7%
Animal 3.8%
Coursing 3.8%
1.9% *, Bell, Ears, Fox, Hair, Jack, Kill, Scrape, Tortoise, Winter

Harm
Hurt 27.3%
Damage 9.1%
* 6.8%
Kill 6.8%
Pain 6.8%
Good 4.5%
Harmful 4.5%
Hit 4.5%
Injure 4.5%
Pest 4.5%
2.2% Bad, Bee, Danger, Injury, Protect, Providence, Someone, Spiteful, Wound

Harrison
Ford 69.4%
George 10.2%
Rex 6.1%
* 4.1%
2.0% Actor, Birtwhistle, Doctor, Rebecca, Smith

Hasten
Quick 24.0%
Hurry 16.0%
Fast 12.0%
Speed 10.0%
Quickly 6.0%
Run 6.0%
Rush 4.0%
To-Add 4.0%
2.0% Add, Downfall, Fasten, Late, Out, Quicken, Quicker, To-Tell, Work

Hat
Cap 12.5%
Coat 12.5%
* 10.4%
Stand 10.4%
Head 8.3%
Trick 6.3%
Box 4.2%
Feather 4.2%
Scarf 4.2%
2.1% Ascot, Band, Bowler, Cat, Computer, Cricket, Hair, Pin, Pink, Rack, Sombrero, Warm

Hatchet+
Axe 57.1%
Hammer 4.8%
Knife 4.8%
2.4% *, Beat, Blood, Bury, Cherry-Tree, Chop, Head, Job, London, Mallet, Man, Racket, Saw, Throw

Hatred
Love 13.5%
Anger 11.5%
Fear 11.5%
* 5.7%
Detest 5.7%
Dislike 3.8%
Hate 3.8%
Malice 3.8%
Violence 3.8%
1.9% Arabs, Bathing, Bitter, Envy, Evil, Filth, Fire, Horror, Hurt, Ire, Jealousy, Loath, Loathing, Loud, Murder, Person, Shit, Ugly, Venom

Have
Hold 29.8%
Not 17.0%
Own 12.8%
* 6.4%
Have-Not-(n't) 6.4%
Possess 4.3%
2.1% Belong, Earn, Get, Gong, Good-Time, Go, Have, Money, Nothing, Save, Want

Havoc
Chaos 51.2%
Wreak 14.6%
Mayhem 7.3%
* 4.9%
Mess 4.9%
2.4% Affray, Hoover, Panic, Play, President, Storm, Trouble, Wreck

Hawk+
Bird 31.0%
Eagle 19.0%
Wind 7.1%
Dove 4.8%
Falcon 4.8%
2.4% Chop, Eye, Eyed, Handsaw, Hunt, Kite, Owl, Peddle, Pie, Predator, Raven, Stirred, Watch, What

Hazard
Danger 36.6%
Risk 7.3%
Warning 7.3%
Guess 4.9%
Lights 4.9%
Problem 4.9%
Warning 4.9%
2.4% Beacon, Caution, Chemical, County, Dangerous, Fear, Fire, Flame, Flashing-Lights, Roadblock, Safety, Snow

Head
Ache 23.4%
Shoulder(s) 8.5%
* 6.4%
Hair 6.4%
Top 6.4%
Brain 4.3%
Case 4.3%
Foot 4.3%
Master 4.3%
Start 4.3%
Toes 4.3%
2.1% Bad, Face, Features, Find, Hat, Injury, Match, Mind, Rest, Rope, Teacher

Headlong
Rush 26.0%
* 8.0%
Crash 6.0%
Car 4.0%
Dive 4.0%
Falling 4.0%
First 4.0%
Jump 4.0%
Straight 4.0%
2.0% Battle, Butt, Cabin, Collision, Dash, Flight, Head-First, Heedless, Into, In-Love, Lead, Love, Parallel, Plunge, Race, Run, Speed, Strong

Headscarf
* 10.4%
Scarf 8.3%
Head 6.3%
Square 4.2%
Wool 4.2%
Wrap 4.2%
2.1% Air, Ann, Arab, Band, Belly-Dancing, Bugatti, Cape, Chiffon, Colour, Hair, Hat, Hermes, Islam, Lady, Mother, Mum, Muslim, Neck, Old, Pattern, Pike, Pin, Queen, Red, Skin, Sloane-Ranger, Tiara, Warm, Wellies, Woman

Heal
Wound 25.5%
Plaster 8.5%
Doctor 6.4%
Mend 6.4%
Burn 4.3%
God 4.3%
Skin 4.3%
2.1% Bandage, Better, Church, Cure, Faith, Finger, Fix, Help, Hope, Hospital, Me, Miracle, Nature, Pain, Powerful, Save, Scab, Touch, Up

Healthy
Fit 26.2%
* 4.8%
Body 4.8%
Ill 4.8%
Mind 4.8%
2.4% Alive, Athletic, Baby, Break, Child, Clean, Found, Fresh-Air, Glowing, Hair, Happiness, Happy, Illness, Legs, Life, Lifestyle, Option, Outlook, Skin, Slim, Tree, Well, Young

Hear
Ear(s) 30.2%
Listen 18.6%
Noise 9.3%
About 4.7%
Deaf 4.7%
Me 4.7%
Shout 4.7%
2.3% *, Aid, Heard, Music, See, Song, Sound, Speech, This, Voice

Heart
Beat 24.4%
Blood 11.1%
Lung 8.9%
Red 6.7%
Attack 4.4%
Gold 4.4%
Liver 4.4%
Organ 4.4%
Soul 4.4%
Pump 3.3%
2.2% Ache, Break, Cary, Fire, Life, Matter, Sleeve, Tap, Transplant, Valve

Heat
Hot 15.6%
Cold 13.3%
Fire 8.9%
Warm 8.9%
Warmth 6.7%
Radiator 4.4%
2.2% Burn, Chill, Cool, Energy, Exhaustion, Happiness, Hopelessness, Intense, Light, Source, Steam, Stench, Sun, Sweat, Thermograph, Treatment, Up, Wave

Heathen+
Pagan 21.4%
* 7.1%

Atheist 4.8%
God 4.8%
Godless 4.8%
Heaven 4.8%
Savage 4.8%
2.4% Bad, Bible, Cave, Celt, Celtic, Church, Devil, Field, Gross, Ignoramus, Indian, Moor, Muslim, Religious, Sceptic, Scottish, Smart, Unbeliever, Unchristian, Uncouth

Heaven
Hell 47.6%
Cloud(s) 11.9%
God 4.8%
Sent 4.8%
White 4.8%
2.4% Angels, Charing-Cross, Forgive, Gate, Gay, Light, Luxury, Peaceful, Seven, Skies, Sky

Heavy
Weight 23.8%
Light 21.4%
Duty 4.8%
Load 4.8%
Metal 4.8%
2.4% *, Bummer, Case, Fat, Furniture, Hard, Heart, Lead, Lorry, Luggage, Man, Oak, Object, Rock, Solid, Weapon, Weather

Hedgehog
Prickly 8.0%
Road 8.0%
Spine(s) 8.0%
Squash 8.0%
Spike 6.0%
Spiky 6.0%
Animal 4.0%
Bristle 4.0%
Bristly 4.0%
Crisps 4.0%
Flea(s) 4.0%
Prickle(s) 4.0%
2.0% *, Blood, Car, Country, Cute, Garden, Grass, Hedge, Hedgerow, Log, Milk, Pig, Shrew, Spiny, Squashed, The-Animal

Helen
* 24.5%
Mirren 8.2%
Of-Troy 8.2%
Girl 4.1%
Keller 4.1%
Reddy 4.1%
White 4.1%
2.0% Bettles, Bingham, Chinese, Davids, Dewer, George, Girlie, Kemp, Lederer, Matthews, Miller, Moss, Mum, Name, Richards, Richardson, Robbins, Saint, Slater, Smith, Terry

Helicopter
Fly 17.8%
Blades 9.0%
Noise 8.9%
Pilot 6.7%
Plane 6.7%
Chopper 4.4%
Pad 4.4%
Rotor 4.4%
* 4.4%
2.2% Docklands, High, Hum, Land, Launch, Propellor, Rescue, Ride, Scandal, Sky, Travel, Wheel, Whirly, Wizz, Whir, Zoom

Heliport
Helicopter 54.2%
Airport 10.4%
Plane 6.3%
* 4.2%
Copter 4.2%
2.1% Chopper, Circle, City, Flight, Gatwick, Land, Marshal, Maxwell, Pad, Scilly-Isles

Helmet
Hat 17.8%
Bike 11.1%
Head 6.7%
Crash 4.4%
Hard 4.4%
Motorcycle 4.4%
Soldier 4.4%
War 4.4%
2.2% Army, Crank, Cycle, Fireman, Helmut, Hood, Iron, Jacket, Metal, Miner, Motorbike, Newton, Ride, Safety, Shield, Speed, Station, Steel, Tin

Help
Aid 43.9%
* 4.9%
Assistance 4.9%
Cry 4.9%
No 4.9%
Shout 4.9%
2.4% Aged, Assist, Desk, Despair, Drown, Give, Helpless, Life, Me, Medicine, Need, Needy, Please, Red-Cross

Hem
Skirt 45.8%
Line 12.5%
Dress 10.4%
Sew 6.3%
* 4.2%
2.1% Down, Edge, Garment, Pleat, Seam, Sewing, Stem, Stitch, Train, -Lock

Hen
Chicken 46.5%
Egg 14.0%
Chick 9.3%
Cock 7.0%
Coop 4.7%
2.3% *, Cook, Dirt, Duck, Farm, House, Night, Party

Her
Him 46.0%
She 10.0%
His 6.0%
* 4.0%
Hair 4.0%
2.0% Bag, Body, Brother, Coat, Dog, Dress, Feminine, Girl, Hat, Heart, Hymn, Ladyship, Lie, Own, World

Here
Now 43.8%
There 37.5%
* 6.2%
2.1% And-Now, Ear, Here, New, Place, Take

Herring
Fish 47.9%
Red 20.8%
Bone 18.8%
2.1% Bend, Bird, Fisherman, Swim

Hesitate+
Wait 19.0%
Pause 11.9%
Stop 11.9%
* 7.1%
Stumble 4.8%
Think 4.8%
Unsure 4.8%
2.4% Confused, Doubt, Embarrassed, Err, Halt, Lost, Prevent, Refrain, Restrain, Shake, Slow, Stammer, Stamp, Waver, Wonder

Hesitation
Pause 19.0%
Stop 16.7%
* 14.3%
Indecisive 4.8%
Stall 4.8%
Stutter 4.8%
Wait 4.8%
2.4% Cost, Halt, Help, Lost, Not-Certain, Not-Sure, Panic, Question, Sentence, Slow, Thought, Thoughtful, Unsure

Hide
Seek 41.9%
* 4.7%
Away 4.7%
Bird 4.7%
Find 4.7%
Tree 4.7%
2.3% Carefully, Cat, Coat, Conceal, Crouch, Dark, Face, From, Game, Money, Scream, Shooting, Show, Skin, Stash

High
Low 52.4%
Mountain 4.8%
Sky 4.8%
2.4% Altitude, Brow, Chair, Far, Flyer, Flying, Hopes, Kite, Length, Mighty, Note, Rise, Rope, Superior, Tall, Tower

Hijack+
Plane 47.6%
Aeroplane 4.8%
Capture 4.8%
Kidnap 4.8%
Terrorist 4.8%
2.4% Airliner, Airplane, Ambulance, Balaclava, Bomb, Guns, Highwayman, Hostage, Murder, Overtake, Robbery, Steal, Stop, Takeover

Him
Her 88.0%
His 4.0%
2.0% -Self, Man, Steve, Strong

Hire
Car 35.4%
Rent 12.5%
Borrow 8.3%
Buy 6.3%
* 6.2%
Fire 4.2%
Lease 4.2%
Out 4.2%
2.1% Dress, Equipment, Lower, Reward, Shop, Suit, Time, Tyre, Van

Hiss
Snake 44.0%
Cat 14.0%
Boo 8.0%
Snarl 4.0%
Spit 4.0%
2.0% *, Forked-Tongue, Hoot, Hose, Leak, Lisp, Miss, Mother, Noise, S, Sid, Smile, Them

Historic+
Old 23.9%
Ancient 10.9%
Monument 10.9%
Castle 6.5%
Building 4.3%
2.2% *, Age, Aged,

Archive, Books, Cathedral, Detail, Fascinate, Heritage, History, Lesson, Long, Moment, Places, Queen, Site, Teacher, Television, Treaty

History
Book(s) 14.9%
Past 14.9%
* 8.0%
Lesson 7.0%
Story 7.0%
Geography 4.6%
School 3.4%
War(s) 3.4%
Man 2.3%
Old 2.3%
Unveils 2.3%
1.1% Ad, Age, Ancient, Art, Class, English, Europe, Exam, Histiography, Lecture, Legend, Life, Modern, Museum, My, Net, Over, Pattern, Photograph, Present, Relics, Repeated, Report, Table, Teach, Weapon

Hit
Hard 21.3%
Miss 10.6%
Bat 8.5%
Punch 6.4%
Ball 4.3%
Man 4.3%
Stick 4.3%
Strike 4.3%
2.1% Attack, Car, Cry, Drugs, Drum, Fist, Her, Him, Hurt, Jerk, Music, No, Run, Score, Smack, Thump, Wall

Hockey
Stick 57.1%
Ball 8.2%
Game 8.2%
Player 4.1%
2.0% Boot, Lacrosse, Match, Net, Shorts, Slapshot, Sport, Strap, Team, Tennis, Tim

Hog
Pig 34.0%
Hedge 12.0%
Road 8.0%
Wash 6.0%
Animal 4.0%
Hedgehog 4.0%
Hound 4.0%
2.0% ?, Bog, Bull, Day, Grab, Greedy, Selfish, Spit, Steal, Swine, Wallop, Wart, Whiskers, Yuk

Hold
Hand(s) 23.3%
Tight 9.3%
Grasp 7.0%
Onto 7.0%
Grip 4.7%
Me 4.7%
2.3% *, Baby, Back, Behold, Bind, Fight, Give, Have, Heal, Hug, Keep, On, Rail, Ring, Squeeze, Take, Tight, Tightly

Holland
Dutch 20.4%
Flat 14.3%
Amsterdam 8.2%
Country 6.1%
Park 6.1%
Tulips 6.1%
Netherlands 4.1%
Windmill 4.1%
2.0% Barrett, Belgium, Blue, Bulbs, Dope, Dozier, Drugs, Dyke, East, Fabric, Gog, Jools, On-Sea, Rat, Van-Gogh

Hollow
Tree 24.4%
Empty 17.8%
Solid 8.9%
Hole 6.7%
Log 4.4%
Men 4.4%
Out 4.4%
Rough 4.4%
2.2% Box, Egg, Enemy, Gut, Head, Man, Oak, Round, Shallow, Sound, Trunk

Home
House 21.4%
Away 19.0%
Alone 7.1%
Front 7.1%
Heart 4.8%
Life 4.8%
Work 4.8%
2.4% Baby, Bound, Car, Chimney, Comfort, Coming, Farm, Hearth, Holiday, Parents, Roof, Tension, Warm

Honesty
Truth 26.7%
* 6.7%
Lie 6.7%
Truthfulness 6.7%
Dishonesty 4.4%
Policy 4.4%
Real 4.4%
True 4.4%
2.2% Beg, Box, Deceit, Faith, Good, Innocent, Integrity, Love, Nowhere, Open, People, Plant, Telling, Untrustworthy, Virtue

Honey
Bee(s) 30.0%
Sweet 20.0%
Pot 14.0%
Money 8.0%
Jar 6.0%
Clear 4.0%
2.0% Boyfriend, Bunny, Dear, Pool, Runny, Spoon, Taste, Trickle, Yellow

Honeybee
Hive 16.7%
* 10.4%
Wasp 10.4%
Honey 8.3%
Sting 6.3%
Buzz 4.2%
Flower 4.2%
Toast 4.2%
2.1% Cone, Dew, Fluffy, Fly, Honeycomb, Hum, Lame, Me, Melon, Monster, Nest, Pollen, Queen, Sticky, Stripe, Sweet, Water, Yellow

Honeydew
Melon 59.6%
Flower 9.6%
* 7.7%
Mildew 3.8%
Sweet 3.8%
1.9% Drop, Flavour, Garden, Grass, Milk, Water, Wet, Yellow

Honour
Obey 11.9%
* 9.5%
Duty 7.1%
Knight(s) 7.1%
Medal 7.1%
Pride 4.8%
2.4% Award, Blood, Castle, Chivalry, Courage, Disgrace, Dishonour, Esteem, Flag, Friend, Gentleman, Glory, Labour, Lord, Love, Maid, Parents, Prizzis, Respect, System, Trust, Valour

Hook+
Line 30.4%
Captain 15.2%
Fish 6.5%
* 4.3%
Coat 4.3%
Cup 4.3%
Fishing 4.3%
Peg 4.3%
2.2% Bar, Catch, Claw, Clothes, Cover, Crook, Food, Hand, Nail, New-Order, Sharp, Sinker

Hooligan+
Football 28.6%
Yob 19.0%
Vandal 11.9%
Thug 9.5%
Lout 7.1%
Idiot 4.8%
2.4% Bastard, Fan, It, Rough, Soccer, Violence, Yellow, Youth

Hoot
Horn 31.9%
Owl 17.0%
Car 8.5%
Laugh 6.4%
Howl 4.3%
2.1% *, Annoy, Beep, Bird, Call, Honk, Laughter, Nanny, Noise, Nose, Punk, Shoot, Tonk, Tooter, Two

Hop
Skip 44.7%
Jump 23.4%
Scotch 8.5%
Beer 6.4%
2.1% Barley, Bird, Bunny, Pole, Rabbit, Run, Sip, Step

Hope
Despair 12.2%
Faith 9.8%
Glory 9.8%
* 7.3%
Joy 7.3%
Strength 4.9%
Want 4.9%
2.4% Anchor, Aspiration, Charity, Deferred, Desire, Fear, Flower, Good, Happiness, Inhibit, Inspiration, Joanna, Less, Light, Look, Love, Pride, Wait, Yearning

Horizon+
Sea 14.3%
Sun 14.3%
Distant 7.1%
Far 7.1%
Sky 7.1%
Sunset 7.1%
Programme 4.8%
2.4% Artificial, Broaden, Cloud, Clouds, Distance, Edge, End, Filed, Film, Flat, Fuzzy, Line, Look, Merging, Scope, World

Horn+
Blow 9.5%
Cow 9.5%
Plenty 9.5%
* 7.1%
Bull 7.1%
Cob 4.8%
French 4.8%
Noise 4.8%
Trumpet 4.8%
Unicorn 4.8%
2.4% Antler, Blower, Bone, Buffalo, Car, Corn, Fog, Horse, Instrument,

Music, Rhino, Sound, Wheat

Horrid+
Nasty 26.2%
Awful 14.3%
Terrible 7.1%
Bad 4.8%
Hateful 4.8%
2.4% Appalling, Difficult, Disgust, Fear, Frightening, Hate, Horrible, Horror, Man, Monster, Rushed, Soft, Uggghh, Ugly, Unpleasant, Wicked, Woman, You

Horseplay
Fun 12.0%
* 8.0%
Frolic(s) 8.0%
Children 6.0%
Games 6.0%
Fool 4.0%
2.0% Antics, Around, Cart, Donkey, Fair-Play, Fighting, Fooling, Fool-Around, Foreplay, Foul, Horses, Joke, Laugh, Manure, Marx, Play, Prank, Pretend, Rough, Rough-House, Rowdy, Saddle, Scrap, Silly, Stable, Trample, Whip

Hospital+
Bed(s) 21.7%
Illness 6.5%
Nurse 6.5%
Patient(s) 6.5%
Accident 4.3%
Ambulance 4.3%
Cross 4.3%
Sick 4.3%
2.2% *, Antiseptic, Care, Clinic, Dead, Fear, Geriatric, Good, Ill, Man, Pain, Porter, Sickness, Smell, Treatment, Waiting, Ward, White

Hot
Cold 33.3%
Water 8.3%
Dog 6.3%
Day 4.2%
Fire 4.2%
Sun 4.2%
2.1% Bottom, Burn, Chocolate, Coffee, Gossip, House, Humid, Kettle, Night, Plants, Potato, Red, Sauna, Spicy, Sticky, Sultry, Summer, Sweat, Touch

Hotbed
* 23.1%
? 3.8%
Activity 3.8%
Dissent 3.8%
Flower(s) 3.8%
Trouble 3.8%
Warm 3.8%
1.9% Agitation, Blanket, Cold, Cold-Chair, Communism, Controversy, Decision, Discontent, Flares, Gossip, Licentious, Lies, Lives, Lust, Of-Reaction, Radical, Rebellion, Red, Revolution, Sands, Sheets, Sleep, Soccer, Solarium, Sunbed, Tub, Water, Young

Hotel+
Room 17.4%
Guest(s) 6.5%
Manager 6.5%
Bar 4.3%
Bed 4.3%
Bedroom 4.3%
Holiday 4.3%
Lobby 4.3%
Owner 4.3%
2.2% *, Browns, California, Car, Chambermaid, Complex, Crowd, Door, Expensive, Foyer, Home, Hostel, Motel, Out, Purple, Reception, Reservation, Sex, Sign, Stay

Hound
Dog 71.4%
Baskerville(s) 9.5%
Basset 4.8%
Fox 4.8%
2.4% Animal, Dachshund, Hedge, Hell

House
Home 28.6%
Garden 9.5%
* 4.8%
Break 4.8%
Roof 4.8%
Window(s) 4.8%
2.4% Boat, Bricks, Bungalow, Burglary, Call, Car, Cleaner, Door, Fire, Flat, Hold, Husband, Live, Party, Semi-Detached, Street, Tree, Wall

Household
Chore(s) 8.0%
Family 8.0%
Name 6.0%
Waste 6.0%
* 4.0%
Domestic 4.0%
Home 4.0%
Items 4.0%
Keeper 4.0%
Kitchen 4.0%
2.0% Administration, Article, Bills, Budget, Car, Cleaner, Full, Happy, Head, Housewife, Jobs, Management, Mother, Newspaper, Object, Paper, People, Pet, Room, Semi-Detached, Share, Utensil, Yoga

How
Now 28.0%
Why 16.0%
* 6.0%
Do 6.0%
When 6.0%
About 4.0%
Ever 4.0%
2.0% Ability, And-Why, Beautiful, Do-They-Do-That, Have, It, Much, Not, Old, Question, Question-Mark, That, Then, Use, Way

Howl
Wolf 27.7%
Cry 14.9%
Scream 10.6%
Yell 10.6%
Dog 6.4%
Bark 4.3%
Loud 4.3%
Owl 4.3%
2.1% *, Child, Loudly, Moan, Ululate, Wail, Wind

Hug
Love 19.6%
Bear 15.2%
Kiss(es) 13.0%
Arm(s) 10.9%
Hold 10.9%
Cuddle 8.7%
Squeeze 4.3%
Warm 4.3%
2.2% Affection, Comfort, Hold, Hurt, Loving, Me

Huge
Large 35.6%
Big 17.8%
Small 8.9%
Ball 4.4%
Elephant 4.4%
Rock 4.4%
2.2% Building, Delicate, Enormous, Giant, Gigantic, House, Massive, So-What, Thing, Tiny, Wide

Hum
Tune 34.8%
Bee 8.7%
Sing 8.7%
Buzz 6.5%
* 4.3%
2.2% Bug, Bum, Ding, Dinger, Drum, Ho, Motor, Mumble, Muse, Noise, Smell, Softly, Song, Sound, Throat, Whistle

Humble
Pie 32.0%
Low 10.0%
Meagre 6.0%
Bee 4.0%
Man 4.0%
Meek 4.0%
Modest 4.0%
Poor 4.0%
Proud 4.0%
Shy 4.0%
2.0% Alms, Bow, Cottage, Crumble, Dickens, Gentle, Grand, Grumble, Heart, Lowering, Pray, Slow

Humbug
Sweet 34.6%
Mint 11.5%
Rubbish 11.5%
Bah 7.7%
Nonsense 3.8%
Scrooge 3.8%
1.9% *, Bullshit, Cant, Geriatric, Grouch, Hypocrisy, Hypocrite, Miser, Old-Man, Snub, Stripes, Stripy, Victorian, Worry

Humiliation
Embarrassment 17.0%
* 6.4%
Red 6.4%
Shame 6.4%
Hurt 4.3%
Pride 4.3%
Small 4.3%
2.1% Arrogance, Bullying, Contempt, Defeat, Despair, Die, Disgrace, Domination, Down, Embarrass, Embarrassed, Fear, Joy, Laughter, Misery, Mistake, Oppressed, Pain, Pity, Sad, Sadness, School, Total, Upset

Hunt
Fox(es) 40.9%
Horse 11.4%
Chase 9.1%
Dog(s) 6.8%
Down 4.5%
2.3% *, Food, Fowl, Goose, Gun, Job, Kill, Life, Man, Me, Red-Coat, Rifle

Hurdle
Jump 42.9%
Athletic(s) 9.5%
Run 7.1%
Leap 4.8%
Olympics 4.8%
Steeplechase 4.8%
2.4% 400-Metres, Athlete, Coach, Fall, Head, Horse, Leapfrog, Pen, Runner, Stripe, Throw, Track

Hurricane+
Wind 35.7%
Storm 14.3%
Higgins 7.1%
Thunder 4.8%
2.4% *, ?, Annie, Charlie, Damage, Destruction, Disaster, Fire, Force, Gale, Lightning, Monsoon, Noise, Weather, Whirlwind

Hurry
Rush 22.7%
Fast 13.6%
Up 13.6%
Quick 9.1%
Run 4.5%
Speed 4.5%
Walk 4.5%
2.3% *, Along, Dawdle, Forward, Haste, Hasten, Man, Panic, Quickly, Rush-Hour, Slow, White

Hurt
Pain 39.5%
Me 7.0%
Badly 4.7%
Fall 4.7%
2.3% *, Agony, Arm, Bandage, Break, Dead, Harm, Help, Hit, Injured, Inside, Knee, Maim, Not, Ouch, Pin-Prick, Pride, Sad, Wound

Husband+
Wife 81.0%
Spouse 4.8%
2.4% *, Comfort, Daughter, Family, Love, Marriage

Hygiene+
Clean 50.0%
Cleanliness 23.8%
2.4% Dirt, Dispenser, Feminine, Nurse, Oral, Safe, Teeth, Wash, Washing, Waste, Water

Hymn
Song 38.1%
Church 16.7%
Book 11.9%
Prayer 7.1%
Psalm 7.1%
Sing 4.8%
2.4% Carol, Church, Religion, Saviour, Songbook, Twang

Hypnotic+
Trance 23.8%
Sleep 7.1%
Watch 7.1%
Mesmerise 4.8%
2.4% *, Aphrodisiac, Awful, Beat, Caution, Clock, Coin, Difficult, Doctor, Dream, Drug, Effect, Enchanting, Glass, Hypnotise, Lulling, Mystifying, Person, Scientist, Snake, Song, Stage, Tease, Transfixed

Ice
Cold 24.4%
Water 15.6%
Cube 13.3%
Cream 11.1%
Bucket 4.4%
Cake 4.4%
Snow 4.4%
2.2% Baby, Berg, Cool, Fridge, Iceland, Maiden, Pick, Rink, Skate, Temperature

Idea
Thought 28.9%
Think 11.1%
* 4.4%
Bright 4.4%
Bulb 4.4%
Lightbulb 4.4%
Mind 4.4%
Notion 4.4%
2.2% Balloon, Conception, Ear, Empathy, Good, Head, Mental, New, Novel, Plan, Question, Thin, Time, Wonderful

Idle
Lazy 44.0%
Hand(s) 8.0%
Engine 6.0%
Eric 6.0%
Time 4.0%
2.0% *, Bone, Bugger, Car, Loiter, Nothing, Race, Relax, Slow, Stop, Sunday, Thought, Useless, Waste, Weak, Wistful

Ignition+
Car 21.4%
Key 19.0%
Light 16.7%
Fire 14.3%
2.4% Burn, Engine, Exhaust, Ignite, Lighter, On, Petrol, Rocket, Spark, Start, Takeoff, Timing

Ignore
* 14.6%
Me 8.3%
Blank 6.3%
Avoid 4.2%
Hate 4.2%
Him 4.2%
People 4.2%
2.1% Acknowledge, Alienate, Alone, Arrogant, Cruel, Deaf, Dismiss, Face, Fire, Fool, Forget, Go-Away, Groan, Grunt, Hide, It, Jackie, Overlook, Rude, Shun, Slight, Snub, Still, This, Toad, Unfeeling

Imagine
Think 20.8%
Dream 8.3%
John-Lennon 6.3%
People 6.3%
* 4.2%
All 4.2%
Dream 4.2%
Fantasy 4.2%
Idea 4.2%
Thought 4.2%
2.1% Blue, Clouds, Daydream, Envisage, Extraordinary, Fancy, Game, Guess, Imagination, Just, Look, Mind, Picture, Reverie, Sing

Immediate+
Now 61.9%
Quick 7.1%
Soon 4.8%
Straightaway 4.8%
2.4% Instant, Quickly, Refusal, Sensation, Straight, Sudden, Time, Urgency, Wait

Immoral+
Wrong 21.4%
Bad 11.9%
Act(s) 4.8%
Moral 4.8%
Naughty 4.8%
2.4% Abortion, Amoral, Anxious, Christian, Different, Earnings, G, Good, Illegal, Illicit, Impolite, Indecent, Misery, New, Sinful, Sleep, Son, Unethical, Unfair, Unscrupulous, Unsound, Wicked

Implement+
Tool 40.5%
Knife 7.1%
Farm 4.8%
Spoon 4.8%
Use 4.8%
2.4% *, Do, Enforce, Farming, Fork, Hoe, Kitchen, Knives, Object, Operation, Practice, Put, Software, Spade, Strategy, Sword

Importance
Earnest 29.8%
* 17.0%
Significance 6.4%
Greatness 4.3%
Necessary 4.3%
2.1% Asset, Book, Good, Gravity, High, Image, Law, Money, None, Notoriety, Play, Point, Pride, Private, Significant, Snob, Special, Vital

Impose+
Force 16.7%
Rule(s) 9.5%
Inflict 4.8%
Put 4.8%
Restrict 4.8%
Sanction 4.8%
2.4% *, Annoy, Arrive, Choice, Fuss, Hard, Ideas, Inculcate, Insist, Interrupt, Law, Might, Newsen, Place, Push, Rejoin, Stick, Stop, Tax, Trap, Unwilling, Upon, Wield

Impotence
Man 12.8%
* 8.5%
Male 8.5%
Penis 6.4%
Sex 6.4%
Barren 4.3%
Limp 4.3%
Sad 4.3%
2.1% Anger, Black, Chastity, Childless, Dick, Drink, Droop, Dry, Empty, Fail, Failure, Inability, Justice, No, Nothing, Power, Sterile, Unable, Useless, Weakness

In
Out 76.0%
2.0% *, -Door, At, Bed, Enclosed, External, House, It, On, Pond, Side, Touch

Inanimate+
Dead 30.4%
Object 15.2%
Still 13.0%
* 6.5%
Animate 6.5%
Rock 4.3%
Stone 4.3%
2.2% Cartoon, Enamel, Lifeless, Not, Plasticine, Solid, Stop, Thing, Unlively

Inch+
Mile 33.3%
Measure 7.1%
Yard 7.1%
* 4.8%
Centimetre(s) 4.8%
Length 4.8%
Worm 4.8%
2.4% Away, By, Diet, Foot, Give, Half, Ink, Measurement, Millimetre, Pin, Pinch, Ruler, Scratch, Small

Incite
View 16.7%
* 9.5%
Encourage 9.5%
See 7.1%
Visible 7.1%
Persuade 4.8%
2.4% Demand, Depth, Forethought, Horizon, Insect, Inspiration, Instill, Invoke, Lost, Make, Murder, Near, Riot, Seeing, Seen, Suggest, Thought, Vie, Violence

Incorrect+
Wrong 81.0%
Answer 7.1%
2.4% Assumption, Error, Lie, Not, Stupid

Increase+
More 19.0%
Decrease 11.9%
Enlarge 9.5%
Add 7.1%
Augment 4.8%
Bigger 4.8%
Develop 4.8%
Grow 4.8%
2.4% Abundant, Addition, Build, Ever, False, Growth, Improve, Larger, Limit, Multiply, Plenty, Soar, Turn, Up

Indifference
* 13.0%
Apathy 6.5%
Attitude 4.3%
Bored 4.3%
Boredom 4.3%
Care 4.3%
Not-Care 4.3%
Shrug 4.3%
2.2% Accord, Ambivalent, Blotto, Careless, Disgust, Hostility, Ignorance, Impartial, Lack-Lustre, La-Belle, Life, Never, Nonchalance, Nonsense, Nothing, Not-Bothered, Placid, Reaction, Rudeness, Sensitive, So, Spoil, Stoic, Time, To

Indigo
Blue 28.0%
Violet 16.0%
Colour 14.0%
Purple 14.0%
Rainbow 12.0%
* 4.0%
2.0% Brown, Dye, Gorgeous, Janes, Nice, Sky

Infallible+
* 15.2%
Pope 8.7%
Right 8.7%
Fallible 6.5%
Correct 4.3%
Fail 4.3%
Faultless 4.3%
God 4.3%
2.2% Divine, Error Free, Exact, Fall, Fire, Immortal, Judge, Liar, Me, No, No-one, Normal,

Not Broken, Perfect, Stone, Subject, Truth, Uneasy, Untrue, Wrong

Infant
Child 59.5%
Baby 18.9%
Small 3.3%
Young 2.2%
1.1% Babe, Boy, Children, Cute, Death, Fat, Feeding, Infantile, Jesus, Kid, Mewling, Mine, Mother, Pupil, School

Infantile+
Childish 47.6%
Stupid 9.5%
Baby 7.1%
Immature 4.8%
Puerile 4.8%
Young 4.8%
2.4% *, Activity, Behaviour, Boy, Child, Childlike, Small, Smile

Infantry+
Army 40.5%
Soldier(s) 28.6%
Cavalry 7.1%
War 4.8%
2.4% Batallion, Child, Death, Infantry, List, Officer, Regiment, Troupe

Infirm+
Old 21.4%
Elderly 19.0%
Ill 11.9%
Weak 9.5%
Aged 7.1%
Crippled 4.8%
Sick 4.8%
2.4% Breast, Diseased, Doddery, Furnace, Hard, Health, Invalid, Tell, Unsteady

Informal+
Casual 21.4%
Dress 9.5%
Loose 7.1%
* 4.8%
Chat 4.8%
Dinner 4.8%
Formal 4.8%
Gathering 4.8%
2.4% Brief, Discussion, Easy, Free, Friendly, Fun, Great, Lieu, Normal, Party, Pleasant, Relaxed, Scruffy, Special, Suit, Tie

Infringe
Encroach 11.9%
* 7.1%
Benefit 7.1%
Annoy 4.8%
Border 4.8%
Break 4.8%
Haircut 4.8%
Privacy 4.8%
Rights 4.8%
2.4% Boundary, Bully, Comment, Copyright, Disrupt, Fringe, Impair, Impose, In, Interfere, Intrude, Invade, Join, Law, Liberty, Push, Rules, Space, Upon

Inhabit+
Live 76.2%
House 4.8%
Live-In 4.8%
2.4% Dwell, Dwelling, Habit, Houses, Place, Population

Inhibit+
Stop 35.7%
Prevent 11.9%
* 9.5%
Repress 4.8%
Retard 4.8%
2.4% Deceive, Deter, Disallow, Fear, Freud, Frighten, Frightened, Habit, Inhibit, Ken, Restrict, Train, Waste, Withdrawn

Initial
First 32.0%
Letter(s) 20.0%
Start 6.0%
Beginning 4.0%
Surprise 4.0%
2.0% *, A, Birth, Capital, D, GB, Name, Reaction, Response, Shock, Sign, Signature, Sum, This, Time, Try, Word

Initiative
Idea 14.9%
Start 10.6%
Leader 8.5%
* 6.4%
Take 6.4%
First 4.3%
Own 4.3%
2.1% Build, Clever, Course, Dominant, Drive, Enterprise, Fun, Go, Help, Innovate, Lack, Leadership, Leads, Mind, Notice, On-Own, Project, Success, Thought, Well, Worth

Injustice+
Law 15.2%
Wrong 13.0%
* 10.9%
Court 8.7%
Bad 4.3%
Judge 4.3%
Justice 4.3%
2.2% Amnesty, Balance, British, Cold, Criminal, Fault, Hurt, Illegible, Jury, Just, Land, Nasty, Poverty, Trial, Unfair, War, Wig, Wrongdoing

Inn
Pub 37.5%
Hotel 16.7%
Drink(s) 10.4%
Tavern 4.2%
2.1% *, Barrel, Beer, C17, House, Joseph, Keeper, Landlord, Motel, Oak, Red, Room, Sleep, Traveller

Innate+
Inborn 21.4%
* 9.5%
Born 7.1%
Intrinsic 7.1%
Inept 4.8%
Useless 4.8%
2.4% Bulletin, Dead, General, Idea, Inane, Inherent, Inseven, Inside, In-Born, Movement, Nativism, Object, Part, Passive, Silly, Simple, Stupidity, Too, Total

Inner
Outer 35.7%
Ear 11.9%
Life 9.5%
Circle 7.1%
Self 7.1%
Space 7.1%
City 4.8%
Soul 4.8%
2.4% *, Mind, Stomach, Thoughts, Tube

Innocent
Guilty 23.8%
Child 14.3%
Man 9.5%
Bystander 7.1%
Naive 7.1%
Eyes 4.8%
Person 4.8%
Shy 4.8%
2.4% Baby, Blame, Corrupted, Danger, Hard, Sweet, Victim, White, Wide-Eyed, Young

Insane+
Mad 78.6%
2.4% Asylum, Crazy, Criminal, Find, Foucault, Fruitcake, Judge, Loony, Raving

Inside+
Outside 45.2%
Out 16.7%
Within 7.1%
2.4% *, Box, Contents, Guts, Information, Inner, Interior, Intestines, Jar, Open, Orange, Warm, Warmth

Insincere+
False 11.9%
Honest 4.8%
Lie 4.8%
Lying 4.8%
Sincere 4.8%
Sly 4.8%
Untrue 4.8%
2.4% Bastard, Cruel, Deceit, Empty, Gift, Indifferent, Liar, Lies, Meaning, People, Person, Politician, Poor, Sock, Sorry, Trite, True, Unfair, Unfaithful, Unmeaning, Unpleasant, Unreliable, Untruthful, Word, You

Insist
Demand 22.9%
* 16.7%
Ask 6.3%
Argue 4.2%
Firm 4.2%
Force 4.2%
Forceful 4.2%
On 4.2%
Push 4.2%
Upon 4.2%
Want 4.2%
2.1% Beg, Boss, Bully, Determination, I, Oblige, Pushy, Resist, Thrust, Urge

Install+
Fit 26.2%
* 9.5%
Place 7.1%
Put 7.1%
In 4.8%
2.4% Affix, Bring, Cooker, Create, Depose, Equip, Equipment, Furniture, Give, Heater, Heating, Impose, Insert, Machine, Order, Run, Set, Television, Word-Processor

Instigate+
Start 52.4%
Begin 9.5%
* 4.8%
Commence 4.8%
2.4% Control, Crime, Encourage, Evil, Fight, Implement, Input, Law, Look, Police, Policeman, Prompt

Intend+
Mean 40.5%
Want 9.5%
Do 7.1%
Hope 4.8%
2.4% *, Action, Expect, Give, Go, Hurt, Intent,

Like, Marriage, OK, Plan, Promise, Realise, Will, Willing, Yours

Intense+
Deep 11.9%
Heavy 11.9%
Strong 9.5%
Pressure 7.1%
Hard 4.8%
Heat 4.8%
2.4% Absolute, Campers, Concentrated, Concentration, Demanding, Emotion, Emotional, Her, Hot, Light, Nervous, Overpowering, Relations, Relationship, Serious, Stress, Studious, Thought, Thoughtful, Vivid, Wary

Interpol
Police 58.3%
* 10.3%
Spy(s) 6.2%
2.1% Agency, Band, Crime, Foreign, France, Government, Inspector-Clouseau, Interpolate, Investigation, Name, Relations, Speaker

Interview+
Job 23.8%
Question 9.5%
Candidate 4.8%
Conversation 4.8%
2.4% *, Ask, Challenge, Choose, Dread, Employee, Frightening, Help, Interviewer, Nerves, Ordeal, People, Personal, Personnel, Procedure, Radio, Restart, Room, See, Skills, Study, Suit, Talk, Technique

Invite
Party 44.7%
Ask 14.9%
* 4.3%
Come 4.3%
Guest 4.3%
Want 4.3%
2.1% Courteous, Dinner, Go, Help, Invitation, Meal, Pune?, Receive, Soon, Tea, Welcome

Invoice
Bill(s) 28.6%
Money 14.3%
Receipt 9.5%
* 4.8%
Office 4.8%
Payment 4.8%
2.4% Accounts, Blue, Credit, Envelope, Lists, Note, Paid, Paper, Paperwork, Pay, Plus, Reminder, Solicitors, Sums

Irate+
Angry 65.2%
Anger 8.7%
Mad 4.3%
Person 4.3%
Red-Faced 4.3%
2.2% Annoyed, Cross, Furious, Man, Passion, Woman

Iron
Steel 16.3%
Board 9.3%
Fist 7.0%
Clothes 4.7%
Hard 4.7%
Metal 4.7%
Press 4.7%
Shirt 4.7%
Steam 4.7%
2.3% Bridge, Cable, Clean, Filings, Flat, Grid, Hoof, Hot, Implement, Maiden, Mask, Ore, Pig, Plate, Rider, Ship, Will

Ironing board
Iron 17.8%
Clothes 15.6%
Shirt(s) 11.1%
Flat 8.9%
Ironing 6.7%
Press 6.7%
Smell 4.4%
2.2% Asbestos, Chore, Clean, Fold, Fresh, Hard, Housework, Long, Meal, Straighten, Tails, Washing

Irony
Sarcasm 14.0%
* 9.3%
Humour 7.0%
Laugh 7.0%
Wit 4.7%
2.3% Board, Clever, Cold, Conversation, Coppery, English, Fact, Funny, Humble, Joke, Lost, Low, Metal, Nothing, Parody, Piano, Postmodern, Press, Riddle, Speech, Strange, Strong, Truth, Wise

Irritation
Annoy 13.0%
Annoyance 13.0%
Rash 13.0%
* 8.7%
Anger 8.7%
Scratch 8.7%
Itch 4.3%
Skin 4.3%
2.2% Angry, Anxiety, Bad-Manners, Frustrated, Fury, Hurt, Irradiation, Pain, People, Thus, Worry

Isaac
Newton 61.2%
Hayes 10.2%
* 6.4%
Bible 6.1%
Abraham 4.1%
2.0% Asimov, Gregory, Jacob, Manda, Stern, Walton

Jack+
Car 14.3%
Jill 14.3%
Lad 11.9%
Trade 11.9%
Up 11.9%
Build 4.8%
Jump 4.8%
Ripper 4.8%
2.4% *, Beanstalk, Box, Knife, Machine, Rabbit, Spade, The, Trades

Jackpot
Money 28.0%
Bingo 10.0%
Win 10.0%
Pools 6.0%
Prize 6.0%
Fruit-Machine 4.0%
Gold 4.0%
Hit 4.0%
2.0% Acepot, Cash, Cherry, Coins, Gamble, Goal, Golden-Shot, Lotto, Slot-Machine, Stew, Target, Vegas, Winner, Winnings

Jail
Prison 35.7%
Bird 16.7%
Bars 14.3%
Bait 7.1%
Break 7.1%
2.4% Blue, Gates, Held-Captive, Imprison, Lock, Man, Prisoner, Sentence

James
* 27.1%
Joyce 16.3%
Dean 8.2%
Bond 4.1%
Fox 4.1%
Hunt 4.1%
Taylor 4.1%
2.0% Baker, Brown, Cagney, Cousin, Fifth, Hetfield, Hill, King, Last, Lisa, Mechan, Second, Sitdown, Stewart, Stuart, Whale

Janitor
Caretaker 26.2%
School 11.9%
* 9.5%
Bucket 4.8%
Clean 4.8%
Cleaner 4.8%
Hat 4.8%
Jailer 4.8%
2.4% America, Battle, Boiler, Broom, Cleaning, Flats, France, Keeper, Man, Mop, School-Keeper, Toilet

Jargon+
Slang 19.0%
Words 16.7%
Computer 7.1%
Talk 7.1%
Lingo 4.8%
2.4% *, Advert, Claptrap, Complex, Culture, Dayglo, Esoteric, Help, Jingo, Joke, Know, Language, Linguistic, Philosophy, Phrase, Rubbish, Science, Technology, Word

Jealous
Envious 28.9%
Green 13.3%
Envy 11.1%
Lover 8.9%
Mind(s) 8.9%
Husband 4.4%
2.2% Adult, Angry, Article, Closed, Fear, Friend, Guy, Hate, Hurt, Sister

Jealousy
Envy 37.2%
Green 23.3%
* 7.0%
Rage 4.7%
2.3% Bad, Charm, Emotion, Fear, Feeling, Greed, Hate, Love, Meek, Of, Sisters, Weak

Jeffrey
Archer 59.2%
* 10.5%
Rainbow 6.1%
Bernard 4.1%
Rogers 4.1%
2.0% Daniels, Doreen, Garland, Howe, Man, Name, Osbourne, Spence

Jockey
Horse(s) 64.3%
Disc 7.1%
Rider 7.1%
Club 4.8%
2.4% Colours, Grand-National, Lester, Races, Ride, Short, Sport

Jog
Run 56.2%
Exercise 4.2%
Trainers 4.2%
Walk 4.2%
2.1% *, Blue, Bounce, California, Field, Fit, Jive, Knee, Memory, Park, Shoes, Sport, Tracksuit, Training, Yuppy

Join
Together 16.3%
Club 9.8%
In 7.6%
Meet 7.6%
Forces 4.5%
Link 4.3%
Up 4.3%
* 3.3%
Group 3.3%
Mend 3.3%
Unite 3.3%
Fuse 2.2%
Glue 2.2%
Hands 2.2%
1.1% Affiliate, Bridge, Brigade, Broken, Carpenter, Concatenate, Encircle, Enlist, Fix, Friends, Game, Joint, Knot, Lamb, Merge, Part, Party, Sex, Solder, Stick, Team, The-Club, Tie, Union, With, Wood

Joker
Card(s) 31.2%
Pack 14.6%
Fool 6.2%
Clown 4.2%
Comedian 4.2%
Funny 4.2%
Jester 4.2%
2.1% Batman, Happy, Jack-The-Lad, Joke, Juggler, Laugh, Laughter, Man, Ned, Play, Practical, Prank, Red, TV, Wally

Journal
Magazine 23.5%
Diary 15.3%
Book 12.9%
Paper 10.5%
Newspaper 9.3%
* 3.5%
Read 3.5%
News 2.4%
Periodical 2.4%
1.2% Article, Binding, Dust, Economist, Library, Of-Medicine, Page, Pen, Psychology, Secret, Text, Train, Weekly, Woman's

Journey
Travel 20.9%
Train 14.0%
Trip 11.6%
Car 9.3%
Time 9.3%
* 7.0%
End 4.7%
2.3% Adventure, Bike, Holiday, Home, Hotel, Man, Onerous, Road, Trail, Travelling, Voyage

Jovial
Happy 37.8%
Fun 6.7%
Jolly 6.7%
Smile 6.7%
2.2% *, Amusing, Banter, Cheerful, Christmas, Company, Crew, Fat, Fellow, Friendly, Jehovah, Love, Manner, Mean, Merry, Mood, Red, Story, Unhappy

Joy
Happy 23.4%
Happiness 21.3%
Full 4.3%
Laughter 4.3%
Sad 4.3%
2.1% About, Behold, Book, Ecstasy, Enjoy, Girl, Help, High, Hurrah, Jouissance, Jump, Life, Love, Merry, Mother, Pain, Ride, Sadness, Sense, Sex

Judge
Jury 31.0%
Wig 16.7%
Law 14.3%
* 9.5%
Court 4.8%
2.4% Corrupt, Damned, Honour, Joke, Judgement, Old, Pickles, Trial, Unfair, Vicar

Jump
High 14.9%
Up 14.9%
Leap 10.6%
Parachute 8.5%
Hop 4.3%
Joy 4.3%
Skip 4.3%
Spring 4.3%
2.1% *, Brave, Building, Die, Fall, Feet, Fell, Frog, In, Jack, Kangaroo, Kriss-Kross, Over, Suit, Trampoline, Walk

Jumper+
Sweater 23.8%
Pullover 9.5%
Woolly 7.1%
Cardigan 4.8%
Dress 4.8%
Knit 4.8%
Red 4.8%
Wool 4.8%
Woollen 4.8%
2.4% Climber, Clothes, Clothing, Clown, Flea, Garment, Jersey, Jumps, Mohair, Shirt, Up, Warm

Jumpy+
Nervous 26.2%
* 11.9%
Active 4.8%
Bean 4.8%
Nervy 4.8%
2.4% Bounce, Bouncy, Damian, Edge, Excited, Fraught, Free, Hop, Insect, Jack, Jerky, Jittery, Kangaroo, Running,

Scared, Scatty, Spring, Stress, Unrelaxed, Uptight

Junior

Senior	20.0%
School	17.8%
Young	8.9%
Child	6.7%
Partner	6.7%
High	4.4%
Office	4.4%
Younger	4.4%

2.2% Bent, Boy, Common-Room, Delinquent, Doctor, Elder, Helper, Janitor, League, Minister, Practitioner, Prom

Justice+

Law	17.7%
Court(s)	13.3%
Judge	8.9%
*	6.7%
Right	6.7%
Fair	4.4%
Injustice	4.4%
Peace	4.4%
Wig	4.4%

2.2% Done, Equality, Fairness, Good, Lawyer, Libra, Lord, Lord-Chief, Miscarriage, Rough, Rule, Scales, Truth

Juvenile+

Delinquent	42.9%
Young	26.2%
Youth	11.9%
Delinquent(s)	4.8%
Immature	4.8%

2.4% Child, Crime, Idiot, Youngster

Kale+
* 16.7%
Cabbage 12.5%
Curly 8.3%
Crop 6.2%
Stone 6.2%
Food 4.2%
John 4.2%
Lettuce 4.2%
2.1% Beetroot, Ceilidh, Cress, Fodder, Green, Hake, Leafy, Lucerne, Maize, Pheasant, Sea, Seaweed, Turnip, Wales, What, Wheat, Wind, Yard

Kangaroo
Jump 26.7%
Australia 20.0%
Pouch 15.6%
Bounce 8.9%
Hop 8.9%
2.2% Animal, Bouncing, Court, Dean, Hopper, Joey, Leap, Pocket, Zoo

Keep
Hold 12.8%
Castle 10.6%
* 4.3%
Away 4.3%
Have 4.3%
Retain 4.3%
Sake 4.3%
Stay 4.3%
Take 4.3%
2.1% Apart, Borrow, Box, Canteen, Clean, Contain, Goal, Grass, Life, Lock, Locker, Look, Lose, Mine, Out, Possess, Right, Safe, Save, Store, Throw, Word

Kennel+
Dog 89.6%
2.1% Chain, Club, Hut, Puppy, Worth

Key
Lock 48.9%
Door 15.6%
Hole 8.9%
Ring 8.9%
2.2% *, Caps, Clue, Fit, Florida, Gold, Latch, Turn

Keyboard
Piano 42.3%
Music 9.6%
Player 9.6%
Computer 7.7%
1.9% *, Black, Black-And-White, Desk, English, Fingers, Instrument, Ivory, Keys, Mouse, Organ, Play, Skates, Tests, Type

Kick+
Football 18.8%
Ball 10.4%
Foot 6.2%
Punch 6.2%
Hurt 4.2%
Start 4.2%
Thrill 4.2%
Hit 3.1%
2.1% Back, Balls, Boot, Bruise, Bucket, Conspiracy, Donkey, Fight, Groin, Hard, Head, Inside, Lunge, Ouch, React, Scratch, Shoe, Shove, Temper

Kidnap
Child 14.6%
* 10.4%
Steal 10.4%
Boy 6.3%
Take 6.3%
Victim 4.2%
2.1% Attempt, Capture, Free, Girl, Hold, Hood, Hostage, Island, Moon, People, Pirate, Plane, Plot, Ransom, Sleep, Snap, Snatch, Son, Them, Time, Treasure-Island, Unsafe, Woman

Kill
Die 10.9%
Murder 10.9%
Bird(s) 8.7%
Dead 8.7%
Knife 8.7%
Maim 8.7%
Death 6.5%
Hurt 6.5%
2.2% Anger, Attack, Dagger, Destroy, Gun, Insects, Me, Obliterate, Resurrect, Someone, Spear, Speed, Stop, Threaten, Weapon

Kin
Kith 24.0%
Family 16.0%
Mother 8.0%
Brother 4.0%
Folk 4.0%
Next 4.0%
Parents 4.0%
Relation(s) 4.0%
2.0% *, And-Spirit, Aunt, Blood, Brotherhood, Children, Cousin, Friend, Kids, Kindred, Mum, Next-Of, Relative, Ship, Sister, Spirit

King+
Queen 62.5%
Kong 6.2%
Castle 4.2%
Ruler 4.2%
2.1% -Dom, Blind, College, Crown, England, Maker, Monarch, Order, Pong, Throne, William

Kingdom
Realm 14.3%
Come 9.5%
England 7.1%
God 7.1%
* 4.8%
Country 4.8%
Empire 4.8%
Monarchy 4.8%
World 4.8%
2.4% Animal, Britain, Burma, Castle, Crown, Domain, Fairytale, Horse, King, Mighty, Myth, Place, Royal, Serf, United, Valley

Kipper
Fish 54.2%
Smell 6.3%
* 4.2%
Herring 4.2%
2.1% Breakfast, Cod, Dipper, Find, Poor, Red, Salt, Skipper, Smelly, Smoke, Sole, Sound, Tasty, Tea, Tie

Kippers
Fish 44.9%
Breakfast 8.2%
Smell 6.1%
Tea 6.1%
* 4.1%
Smelly 4.1%
Smoked 4.1%
2.0% Burgers, Cold, Eat, Fried, Isle-Of-Man, Morning, Porridge, Salty, Sardines, Split, Toast

Kiss+
Lip(s) 22.9%
Love 14.6%
Girl 6.2%
Hug 4.2%
Mouth 4.2%
Romance 4.2%
2.1% *, Boyfriend, Caress, Cheek, Cuddle, Death, Hat, Hot, Kate, Leave, Lick, Man, Me, Osculate, Sex, Sing, Slips, Smile, Sweet, Tongue, Touch

Kit
Bag 16.7%
-Kat 14.6%
Car 8.3%
* 6.3%
Sport(s) 6.3%
Drum 4.2%
Equipment 4.2%
Out 4.2%
2.1% Bicycle, Boots, Camping, Chelsea, Dance, Football, Games, Kitchen, Kitten, Model, Nest, Outfit, PE, Play, Sew, Up

Kitchen+
Sink 19.6%
Cook 10.9%
Food 8.7%
Utensil(s) 8.7%
Table 6.5%
Cooker 4.3%
Cooking 4.3%
Knife 4.3%
2.2% Clean, Clock, Cupboard, Cutlery, Floor, Garden, Leeches, Shiny, Stove, Toilet, Towel, Unit, Ware, White, Woman

Kite+
Fly 52.1%
High 22.9%
Wind 6.2%
Sky 4.2%
2.1% Chile, Croak, Dragonfly, Falcon, Flying, Loose, Windy

Kitten
Cat 57.7%
Small 5.7%
Fluffy 3.8%
Sex 3.8%
1.9% *, Ball, Claws, Cut, Cute, Furry, Grey, Mitten, Pet, Play, Puppy, Puss, Soft, Teeth, Wool

Kneel
Down 36.2%
Pray 12.8%
Knee(s) 10.6%
Church 6.4%
* 4.3%
Bend 4.3%
Prayer 4.3%
2.1% Altar, Before, Cassock, Hard, Kneeler, Knighted, Knighthood, Mat, Over

Knit
Jumper 38.3%
Wool 21.3%
Needle(s) 10.6%
Sew 6.4%
Sweater 4.3%
Wear 4.3%
2.1% Bones, Click, Fast, Jump, Knot, Peal, Weave

Knock
Door 44.7%
Wood 10.6%
Down 8.5%
Hit 6.4%
2.1% Airport, Attack, Back, Bang, Bump, Fight, Hear, Kneed, Knuckles, Nail, Off, On, Tap, Up

Know

*	18.8%
Understand	8.3%
Nothing	6.3%
Think	6.3%
All	4.2%
Me	4.2%

2.1% About, Awareness, Better, Brain, Deny, Don't, Facts, Feel, How, If, Is, Knowledge, Patience, Recognise, Remember, Sure, Tell, That, Thing, What, Who, Why, Wisdom, Work, You

Knowledge

*	9.1%
Books	6.8%
Power	6.8%
Clever	4.5%
Ideas	4.5%
Know	4.5%
Lack	4.5%
Learn	4.5%
Study	4.5%
Wisdom	4.5%

2.3% Belief, Bound, Brains, Educate, Encyclopaedia, Experience, Formal, General, Head, Inquiry, Intelligence, Ken, List, Of, School, Science, Spiritual, Taxi, Thought, Vacant

Labour
Pain(s) 24.4%
Work 24.4%
Hard 8.9%
Love 6.7%
Party 6.7%
Baby 4.4%
Conservative 4.4%
2.2% Election, Force, Horse, Lost, Profit, Red, Swear, Toil, Value

Lack
Lustre 22.0%
Without 8.0%
* 6.0%
Loss 6.0%
Money 6.0%
Need 6.0%
None 4.0%
Nothing 4.0%
Of 4.0%
2.0% Bleak, Brain, Deficit, Esteem, Full, Have, Hunger, Less, Lick, Littler, Not, Or, Respect, Short, Space, Thinness, Want

Lacrosse+
Game 19.6%
Sport(s) 13.0%
Ball(s) 8.7%
Hockey 8.7%
Stick 8.7%
Tennis 8.7%
Girls 3.3%
2.2% *, Cross, Fire, Girlies, Goal, Indians, Lacquer, Mass, Net, Netball, Play, School

Lad
Boy 66.7%
Lass 11.9%
Likely 4.8%
2.4% Cap, Casual, Lady, Male, Outdoors, Young, Youth

Ladder
Climb 24.4%
Step(s) 15.6%
Rung(s) 8.9%
Window 8.9%
Up 6.7%
Paint 4.4%
Top 4.4%
2.2% Decorating, Exact, Ezekiel, House, Jacob, Luck, Painter, Rope, Snake, Stair, Tall, Tights

Lady
Bird 16.0%
Woman 12.0%
Man 10.0%
Gentleman 8.0%
* 6.0%
Killer 6.0%
Tramp 4.0%
2.0% Duke, Fingers, Fragile, Gent, Glove, Gracious, Hen, Jane, Ladybird, Land, Lord, Luck, Manor, Mother, Penelope, Pretty, Stockings, Waiting

Ladybird
Insect 20.8%
Spot(s) 12.5%
Fly 8.3%
Beetle 6.3%
Butterfly 6.3%
Red 6.3%
* 4.2%
Book 4.2%
2.1% Ant, Bay, Beer, Bird, Bug, Burn, Bush, Buttons, Collar, Hateful, Rare, Scarab, Stories, Tail, Text

Lagoon+
Lake 34.8%
Blue 23.9%
Water 10.9%
Atoll 4.3%
Swamp 4.3%
2.2% Barrier, Bay, Blue-Waters, Coral, Deep, Picture, South-Seas, Swim, Tropical, Underwater

Lake
Water 26.1%
Pond 6.5%
Blue 4.3%
Calm 4.3%
Hill 4.3%
Pool 4.3%
Sea 4.3%
Tranquil 4.3%
Windemere 4.3%
2.2% Cove, Crimson, Cruise, Dark, District, Eerie, Home, Lady, Lagoon, Mountain, Peaceful, River, Shalimar, Swan, Tepid, Titikaka, Trasimere, Warm

Lament+
Sad 21.7%
Cry 10.9%
* 6.5%
Grieve 4.3%
Mourn 4.3%
Regret 4.3%
Sadness 4.3%
Song 4.3%
Sorrow 4.3%
2.2% Bewail, Complain, Dirge, Flaunt, Keen, Lose, Love, Mental, Miss, Rue, Sing, Sob, Sorry, Unhappy, Weep, Woe

Land
Mark 33.3%
Sea 20.0%
Country 4.4%
Earth 4.4%
Lord 4.4%
2.2% Agent, Block, Coast, Fill, Home, Island, Love, Mass, Mountains, Owner, Rock, Shore, Sight, Sparrow, Sunset

Landscape
Green 19.0%
Hill(s) 9.5%
* 7.1%
Constable 4.8%
Country 4.8%
Garden 4.8%
Gardener 4.8%
Grass 4.8%
Painter 4.8%
Picture 4.8%
Scenery 4.8%
2.4% Countryside, Nature, Photography, Portrait, Scene, Sea, Sun, Trip, Vast, View, Walking

Lane
Road 34.1%
Country 12.2%
Street 7.3%
* 4.9%
2.4% Apples, Back, Bus, Bush, Car, Countryside, Fast, Foliage, Green, Hedge, Lois, Overgrown, Path, Penny, Stones, Stream, Trees, West-End

Language+
Speak 11.9%
Speech 11.9%
Barrier 7.1%
Foreign 4.8%
Lab 4.8%
Learn 4.8%
2.4% Ability, Bad, Cognitive, Dialect, English, Error, French, Grammar, Interaction, Land, Linguist, Logic, Love, Native, Natural, Question, School, Semantics, Spoken, Talk, Teacher, Tool, Type

Lantern
Light 59.5%
Yellow 9.5%
Bulb 4.8%
Paper 4.8%
Red 4.8%
2.4% *, Flicker, Glow, Glowworm, Lamp, Oil, Switch

Large
Small 31.1%
Big 22.2%
Person 11.1%
House 4.4%
Huge 4.4%
2.2% Cow, Empty, Fat, Life, Little, Pasty, Penis, Room, Round, Scale, Space, Tiny

Late+
Early 35.7%
Comer 7.1%
Tardy 7.1%
Again 4.8%
Arrival 4.8%
Hurry 4.8%
Time 4.8%
2.4% Bad, Bus, Delay, Detention, Evening, Gone, Home, Hour, Never, Night, Pathetic, Penalty, Rush

Latin+
Greek 45.2%
Language 9.5%
French 4.8%
2.4% *, America, American, Awful, Class, Dictionary, Grace, Italy, Man, Mass, Old, Pope, Roman, Scholar, School, Teacher, Verb

Laugh
Cry 38.3%
Joke 12.8%
Smile 10.6%
Happy 6.4%
Enjoy 4.3%
Giggle 4.3%
Humour 4.3%
Mouth 4.3%
2.1% Aloud, Chuckle, Friends, Ha-Ha, Light, Teeth, Tickle

Laundry
Clothes 16.7%
Washing 14.3%
Dirty 11.9%
Bag(s) 9.5%
Clean 7.1%
Basket 4.8%
Wash 4.8%
2.4% Boredom, Boring, Chinese, Dryer, Eastenders, Line, Linen, List, Person, Sheet, Shirt, Smelly, White

Law
Order 16.7%
Police 14.3%
Legal 7.1%
Barrister 4.8%
Court 4.8%
Judge 4.8%
Suit 4.8%
2.4% *, Army, Bobby, Book, Boring, Breakers, Degree, Disorder, Hands, International, Lawyer, Long, Lord, Prison, Rules, Student, Wig

Lawrence
Olivier 36.7%
* 32.8%
Arabia 14.3%
D.H. 4.1%
Hardy 4.1%
2.0% Chatterley, Cricket, Durrell, Name

Lay+
Egg(s) 15.2%
Down 13.0%
Sleep 10.9%
Bed 8.7%
Sex 6.5%
By 4.3%
Lie 4.3%
2.2% *, Clerical, Copulate, Flat, Guard, Lady, Leg, Line, Love, Peace, Person, Preacher, Priest, Put, Seed, Snow

Laziness
Sleep 10.9%
Apathy 8.7%
Tired 8.7%
Sloth 6.5%
Sunday 6.5%
Bed 4.3%
Dull 4.3%
Idle 4.3%
Tiredness 4.3%
2.2% Attitude, Bad, Boredom, Dyslexia, Empty, Everyday, Home, Idleness, Indifference, Lethargy, Lie, Lost, Lounge, Lying, Pig, Slow, Stagnate, TV, Untidy

Lazy
Day 10.4%
Idle 10.4%
Boy 8.3%
Dog 8.3%
Slow 8.3%
Bones 6.3%
Tired 6.3%
Bastard 4.2%
Cat 4.2%
Lout 4.2%
2.1% *, Active, Death, Git, Me, Old, People, Person, Relax, Slack, Slacker, Sleep, Sleepy, Sod

Lead
Pipe(s) 15.6%
Weight 13.3%
Pencil 11.1%
Dog 8.9%
Piping 8.9%
Follow 6.7%
Brick 4.4%
Iron 4.4%
Shot 4.4%
2.2% *, Ahead, Balloon, Behind, Bullet, Fellow, Gold, House, Molten, Television

Lead+
Dog 23.4%
Follow 14.9%
Pipe 10.6%
Pencil 8.5%
Take 8.5%
Metal 4.3%
Wait 4.3%
2.1% *, Along, Captain, Collar, Led, Line, On, Party, Pull, Road, Show, Weight

Leaflet
Paper 21.4%
Pamphlet 16.7%
Flyer 14.3%
Booklet 4.8%
2.4% Advert, Bill-Poster, Book, Brochure, Campaign, Canvasser, CND, Distribution, Distributor, Door, Fly, Folded, Note, Post, Propaganda, Publicity, Unemployment, Words

Lean
Meat 9.3%
Thin 9.3%
On 7.0%
Over 7.0%
Against 4.7%
Fat 4.7%
To 4.7%
Wall 4.7%
2.3% *, Bacon, Beef, Bend, Cliff, David, Elbow, Fall, Fit, Frog, Learn, Mate, Pisa, Post, Rest, Rump, Sausage, Slant, Slim, Tower, Verge

Leap
Jump 27.9%
Frog(s) 16.3%
Over 9.3%
About 4.7%
Dark 4.7%
Far 4.7%
2.3% Away, Distance, Faith, Fence, Gap, Hedge, High, Land, Look, Out, Pool, Quantum, Run, Salmon, Up

Learn
School 14.9%
Teach 12.8%
Book(s) 8.5%
Read 6.4%
Education 4.3%
Lesson 4.3%
Word(s) 4.3%
2.1% *, Again, Blackboard, Class, Educate, Fast, Hard, Head, Intake, Know, Knowledge, Maths, Piano, Qualify, Stats., Stray, Stress, Study, Understand, Well

Learning
Education 17.1%
School 14.6%
Book(s) 7.3%
Curve 4.9%
Knowledge 4.9%
Teaching 4.9%
Words 4.9%
Difficulties 4.8%
2.4% Apparatus, Body, Development, Difficulty, Educate, Excel, For, Game, Giving, Health, Scholar, Stupid, Teach, Teacher, Wind, Young

Leather+
Belt 12.2%
Jacket 12.2%
Strap(s) 12.2%
Skin 7.3%
Armchair 4.9%
Coat 4.9%
Smell 4.9%
2.4% *, Bag, Black, Boy, Chair, Dress, Garment, Harness, Leather, Pants, Prostitute, Saddle, Shoes, Spanner, Tell, Wool, Yellow

Leave
Go 16.3%
Alone 14.0%
Depart 7.0%
Behind 4.7%
Come 4.7%
Desert 4.7%
Holiday 4.7%
Home 4.7%
Me 4.7%
2.3% All, Annual, Away, Book, Exit, French, Gone, Leave, Let, Quietly, Return, Sick, Stay, Take, Tree

Left
Right 57.8%
Hand 6.7%
Field 4.4%
Foot 4.4%
Out 4.4%
Wing 4.4%
2.2% Alone, Centre, Guard, Handed, Leg, Luggage, Sided, Station

Leg
Arm 33.3%
Foot 9.5%
Lamb 9.5%
Long 4.8%
2.4% Break, Bye, Calf, Cast, Fat, Flesh, Hand, Hop, Iron, Itch, Knee, Legless, Limb, Meat, Pull, Table, Warmer, Wooden

Lend
Borrow 27.7%
Money 27.7%
Hand 12.8%
Give 10.6%
Help 6.4%
2.1% Bank, Book, Me, Steal, Sum, Take, Usurer

Leniency
Easy 16.3%
Mercy 9.3%
* 7.0%
Soft 7.0%
Tolerance 4.7%
2.3% Allow, Allowance, Care, Clemency, Court, Generous, Hard, Hope, Kind, Law, Laziness, Lee-Way, Leniency, Liberal, Mellow, Moderately, Password, Pleasure, Poor, Rule, Senile, Strict, Teacher, Understanding

Leopard
Spot(s) 53.3%
Skin 13.3%
Cat 4.4%
Lion 4.4%
Run 4.4%
Tiger 4.4%
2.2% Concrete, Fast, Jaguar, Jungle, Safari, Snow, Spotty

Less
More 64.4%
* 4.4%
And 4.4%
Fewer 4.4%
Is 4.4%
Little 4.4%
None 4.4%
2.2% Likely, Of, Slim, Small, Than

Let
Allow 23.4%
House 14.9%
Flat 8.5%
Be 6.4%
Go 6.4%
Rent 6.4%
* 4.3%
In 4.3%
Lease 4.3%
2.1% Assign, By, Down, Have, Lone, Out, Property, Rented, Sake, Through

Lettuce+
Cabbage 21.4%
Leaf 21.4%
Salad 16.7%
Green 11.9%
Rabbit(s) 9.5%
Sandwich 4.8%
2.4% Celery, Cos, Plum, Radish, Tomato, Vegetable

Liberty
Freedom 56.1%
Free 24.4%
* 4.9%
France 4.9%
2.4% Bell, Chain, Equality, French, Statue

Library+
Book(s) 71.7%
Quiet 4.3%
2.2% Assistant, Calm, Card, College, Dust, Knowledge, Learning, Read, Reading, Study, Work

Lid+
Top 31.0%
Cover 14.3%
Jar 9.5%
Shut 9.5%
Tin 9.5%
Box 4.8%
Pot 4.8%
2.4% Bin, Container, Dustbin, Lover, Open, Pan, Toilet

Lie
Truth 21.4%
Cheat 14.3%
Down 9.5%
Fib 9.5%
Still 7.1%
Tell 4.8%
2.4% *, Criminal, Deceit, Deception, Detector, Little, Out, Pie, Pinocchio, Sex, Sleep, Tale, Teeth, To-Tell

Lieutenant+
Army 32.6%
Colonel 19.6%
Captain 8.7%
Soldier 6.5%
Woman 6.5%
2.2% *, British, Admiral, Awkward, Discipline, General, Lootenant, Major, Officer, Rank, Sergeant, War

Life
Death 26.2%
Force 7.1%
Line 4.8%
Live 4.8%
Long 4.8%
Time(s) 4.8%
2.4% *, Age, Buoy, Cycle, Daily, Day, Essence, Experience, Grey, Hard, Insurance, Living, Love, Maybe, Pleasure, Sentence, Skill, Story, Style, Whole

Light
Dark 20.0%
Bulb 17.8%
Heavy 13.3%
Day 4.4%
2.2% *, Airy, Bright, Cheese, Dappled, Feather, Foot, Headed, Heat, Lamp, Lighter, Lunch, Moon, Of, Sky, Sound, Stroke, Sun, Swan, Switch

Light bulb
Bright 20.0%
Light 20.0%
Switch 8.9%
Shade 6.7%
Idea 4.4%
Socket 4.4%
2.2% *, Bulb, Ceiling, Chair, Energy, Explode, Filament, Fitting, Flash, Glow, Ladder, Lamp, Room, Screw, Snap, Tungsten

Lightning+
Thunder 38.1%
Strike(s) 19.0%
Flash 11.9%
Bolt 4.8%
Sky 4.8%
2.4% Electricity, Fright, God, Light, Night, Speed, Storm, Tree

Like
Dislike 22.7%
* 18.2%
Love 13.6%
Hate 6.8%
As 4.4%
Enjoy 4.4%
Me 4.4%
Similar 4.4%
Unlike 4.4%
2.2% Amour, Good, Ike, Kind, Popular, Up, Yes

Lime
Lemon 26.5%
Green. 18.4%
Tree 10.2%
Juice 6.1%
Light 6.1%
Regis 6.1%
Cordial 4.1%
Stone 4.1%
2.0% American, Bitter, Bottle, Church, Citrus, Fruit, Scurvy, Sharp, Sweet

Limit
Speed 11.9%
End 7.1%
* 4.8%
Edge 4.8%
Limitless 4.8%
No 4.8%
Time 4.8%
2.4% Alcohol, Boundary, Ceiling, Damage, Distribution, Exercise, Finite, Half, Infinite, Less, Licence, Line, Maximum, None, Range, Restrict, Sky, Stop, Surpass, Take, Threshold, Top, Up, Upper

Line+
Draw 26.2%
Washing 9.5%
Circle 4.8%
Drawing 4.8%
Ruler 4.8%
Straight 4.8%
2.4% Clay, Clothes, Crease, Curve, Cycle, Drawn, Length, Match, Off, Opening, Pencil, Rule, Ship, Speed, Square, Stretch, Telephone, Time, Word

Link
Chain 34.0%
Connect 8.0%
Up 6.0%
Connection 4.0%
Join 4.0%
Together 4.0%
2.0% ?, Arms, Attach, Brick, Bridge, Cable, Data, Golf, Hug, It, Line, Missing, Mix, Road, Rope, Sausage, Sever, Tally, Tie, With

Lip
Mouth 21.3%
Service 8.5%
Kiss 6.4%
Cream 4.3%
Face 4.3%
Stick 4.3%
2.1% *, Bite, Bleed, Bottom, Cheek, Full, Gloss, Hair, Hook, Jug, Lipstick, Mick-Jagger, Mug, Mussels, Piercing, Read, Red, Salve, Seal, Sore, Stick, Teeth, Top, Tremble

Lips
Kiss 53.3%
Mouth 11.1%
Purse(d) 4.4%
2.2% Big, Eyes, Face, Hat, Hips, Kissing, Lipstick, Love, Mash, Red, Smile, Stick, Teeth, Wet

Liquid+
Water 24.2%
Solid 10.2%
Drink 9.4%
Fluid 6.3%
Nitrogen 6.3%
Wet 3.9%
Fairy 3.1%
Gas 2.3%
Washing-Up 2.3%
* 1.7%
Glass 1.7%
Gold 1.7%
Washing 1.7%
0.8% Assets, Bubble, Cleaner, Clear, Cold, Container, Cosh, Detergent, Earth, Flow, Fluidity, Food, Forum, Frozen, Glass, Gravity, Letters, Light, Love, Lunch, Mercury, Metal, Milk, Oxygen, Refreshment, River, Running, Sky, Smell, Soap, Tea, Viscous

List+
Shopping 21.7%
Paper 8.7%
Words 8.7%
* 6.5%
Item(s) 6.5%
Write 6.5%
Things 4.3%
2.2% Black, Brahms, Column, Computer, Dry, Itemise, Lips, Make, Memo, Names, Pad, Roster, Sheet, Shop, Tell, Work

Listen
Hear 54.2%
Birds 4.2%
Ear 4.2%
To 4.2%
2.1% *, Attend, Aural, Believe, Comprehend, Concentrate, Earphones, Here, Learn, Look, Say, See, Speak, Talk, TV, Understand

Little
Large 28.9%
Small 20.0%
Big 13.3%
Rain 4.4%
Tiny 4.4%
2.2% *, Amount, Bit, Boy, Dog, Hope, Known, Later, Much, Nell, Or-Large, Or-Not, Poor

Live
Die 21.3%
* 6.4%
Alive 6.4%
Band 6.4%
Aid 4.3%
Exist 4.3%
Long 4.3%
Wire 4.3%
2.1% Action, Be, Day, Dead, Embryo, Enjoy, Feel, Forever, Let-Live, Life, Love, Music, Sheep, Studio, Survive, TV, Under, Upon, Well, Yes

Lively
* 8.9%
Vivacious 8.9%

Active 6.7%
Alive 6.7%
Fun 6.7%
Energetic 4.4%
Happy 4.4%
Outgoing 4.4%
Person 4.4%
Quick 4.4%
2.2% Alert, Arts, Dance, Debate, Docile, Dull, Flippant, Friends, Good, Jolly, Joyful, Loud, Merry, Penelope, Pub, Soul, Young

Lobster
Pot 20.0%
Red 11.1%
Fish 8.9%
Crab 6.7%
Pink 6.7%
Prawn 4.4%
Sea 4.4%
Stew 4.4%
Thermidor 4.4%
2.2% Bait, Bisque, Chowder, Claws, Dinner, Eat, France, Luxury, Pincer, San-Sebastian, Shell, Swim, Wax

Lock
Key 55.6%
Hair 6.7%
Door 4.4%
Stock 4.4%
2.2% And-Key, Canal, Chain, Click, Fight, Hospital, Jed, Latch, Metal, Mortise, Pick, Secure, Up

Loft
Attic 56.2%
Roof 10.4%
High 8.3%
House 6.2%
Insulation 4.2%
2.1% Airy, Barn, Bread, Live, Rafters, Soft, Space, Top

Log
Cabin 18.8%
Fire 14.6%
Wood 12.5%
Tree 6.3%
Jam 4.2%
2.1% Anti-, Barn, Book, Branch, Captains, Chop, Data, File, Fine, Firewood, Free, In, Knobbly, Lie, On, Rhythm, Roll, Sleep, Table, Warm, Water

Logic
* 12.2%
Maths 7.3%
Philosophy 7.3%
Clear 4.9%
Illogical 4.9%
Mind 4.9%
Sense 4.9%
2.4% Book, Brain, Clarity, Computer, Cube, Feeling, Formal, King's, Laura, Mathematics, Method, Narrow, Orderly, Problem, Puzzles, Reason, Reasoning, Right, Science, Sensible, Story, Thought, Understand

Long+
Short 40.5%
Length 7.1%
Thin 7.1%
Desire 4.8%
2.4% Enormous, Far, Fellow, Her, Hope, Longer, Narrow, Ongoing, Pine, Road, String, Summer, T, Walk, Want, Winding, Yearn

Look
See 47.9%
Watch 6.3%
About 4.2%
Book 4.2%
Glasses 4.2%
2.1% *, At, Eye, Glance, Horrible, Learn, Left, Listen, Notice, Out, Regard, Sharp, Stare, Through, Up, Well

Loose
Tight 20.0%
Clothes 4.4%
End 4.4%
Fit 4.4%
Fitting 4.4%
Free 4.4%
Lost 4.4%
2.2% *, Cannon, Change, Clippings, Clothing, Dirt, Fast, Find, Flaking, Flowing, Foot, Forget, Goose, Joint, Leaf, Lips, Moose, Neck, Paint, Shirt, Slack, Solid, Talk, Tie

Lorry+
Truck 23.8%
* 9.5%
Load 7.1%
Van 7.1%
Big 4.8%
Car 4.8%
Driver 4.8%
Yellow 4.8%
2.4% Brake, Bus, Cart, Incline, Large, Lee, License, Mud, Noise, Road, Rubbish, Tracks, Wheels

Lose
Win 17.0%
Find 14.9%
* 6.4%
Lost 4.3%
Weight 4.3%
2.1% Call, Failure, Faith, Footing, Gain, Gene, Hard, Home, Hope, Job, Lead, Less, Life, Mislay, Misplace, Money, Out, Purse, Ring, Risk, Robe, Sight, Tight, Way, Woman

Loss
Death 14.3%
Found 14.3%
Grief 14.3%
Gain 7.1%
Adjuster 4.8%
Dread 4.8%
Find 4.8%
Sadness 4.8%
2.4% And-Found, At, Bereavement, Bereft, Comfort, Dead, Hair, Innocence, Life, Lose, Relative, Sold, Your

Lost
Found 57.1%
Cat 4.8%
Child 4.8%
Luggage 4.8%
Time 4.8%
2.4% *, Adrift, Boys, Dog, Dreams, Friend, Hope, Innocence, Love, Missed

Lot+
* 38.1%
Ink 14.3%
Car 4.8%
Many 4.8%
Parking 4.8%
Plot 4.8%
2.4% Auction, Drawing, Few, Landscape, More, Paper, Quantity, Small, Sortie, Sound, Spot, Tin

Loud
Noise 28.9%
Noisy 8.9%
Quiet 8.9%
Hailer 6.7%
Music 6.7%
Soft 6.7%
Clear 4.4%
Speaker 4.4%
Voice 4.4%
2.2% American, Bang, Boom, Cry, Cymbal, Party, Shout, Smart, Stereo

Love
Hate 36.2%
Heart 17.0%
* 4.3%
Happiness 4.3%
Romance 4.3%
Understanding 4.3%
2.1% Amour, Child, Comfort, Game, Life, Like, Marriage, Money, Nice, Red, Sad, Truth, Wife, Woman

Lovebird
* 10.0%
Song 10.0%
Cage 6.0%
Bird(s) 4.0%
Blue 4.0%
Colour(s) 4.0%
Dove 4.0%
Feathers 4.0%
Parrot 4.0%
Sing 4.0%
Sweet 4.0%
2.0% Chirp, Cockatiel, Dawn, Exotic, Gooey, Jay, Liverbirds, Love, Lovenest, Man, Nest, Noise, Parakeet, Peach-Faced, Person, Pigeon, Red, Romantic, Smooch, Sparrow, Sweetheart

Low+
High 40.5%
Down 21.4%
2.4% *, Bed, Behold, Depressed, Empty, Feeling, Floor, Ground, Income, Life, Little, Mood, Small, Under, Velocity, Work

Lower
Upper 24.4%
Class 8.9%
Down 6.7%
Higher 6.7%
Lip 6.7%
Abdomen 4.4%
Case 4.4%
Raise 4.4%
2.2% Back, Bottom, Deck, Demean, Fall, Floor, Flop, Jaw, Less, Level, Limb, Number, Orders, Path, Standards

Lubricate+
Oil 52.4%
Grease 9.5%
Ease 4.8%
Slip 4.8%
2.4% Durex, Engine, Gel, Jointy, Liquid, Moisten, Plastic, Rub, Rubber, Smooth, Soft, Vaseline

Luck
Fortune 17.1%
Chance 14.6%
Good 9.8%
* 7.3%
Charm 4.9%
Draw 4.9%
2.4% Chance, Dice, Fame, Flow, Fluke, Gold, Good-Fortune, Happy, Health, Horseshoe, Kind,

Looser, Lotto, Luck, Lucky,
Out, Try, Unlucky

Lust

Sex	33.3%
Love	31.0%
Desire	7.1%
Passion	4.8%

2.4% *, Animal, Emotion,
Envy, Flowers, Heart, Life,
Nature, Sin, Sweat

Lute+

Money	23.8%
Steal	11.9%
Rob	9.5%
Bounty	4.8%
Pillage	4.8%
Rape	4.8%

2.4% Bag, Banjo, Bank,
Dosh, Flute, Gold,
Instrument, Mag, Paper,
Plunder, Raid, Shop,
Stolen, Swag, Violin,
Wealth, Winning

Magazine+
Paper 14.3%
Article 11.9%
Book 7.1%
Journal 7.1%
Rack 7.1%
Newspaper 4.8%
Read 4.8%
Sunday 4.8%
2.4% *, Colour, Comic, Cover, Cutout, Elle, Flick, Glossy, Periodical, Pictures, Rag, Relax, Shop, Supplement, Table, Thin

Magic+
Box 9.5%
Magician 7.1%
Show 7.1%
Trick(s) 7.1%
* 4.8%
Hat 4.8%
Moment 4.8%
Paul 4.8%
2.4% Black, Cards, Circus, Clever, Dragon, Entertainment, Evil, Fine, Fun, Lantern, Mage, Mountain, Number, Reality, Rod, Roundabout, Spell, Wand, Witch, Wizard, Wonder

Magistrate+
Judge 45.2%
Court 26.2%
2.4% *, Beak, Bench, Castrate, Fine, Hood, Justice, King, Law, Police, Stipendary, Wig

Magnet+
Attract 21.4%
Iron 11.9%
Metal 11.9%
Pull 9.5%
Draw 4.8%
2.4% *, Attraction, Control, Draws, Electrify, Field, Filings, Flux, Force, Knife, Large, Maggot, Meta, Paper, Pole, Resonant, Solenoid

Magnitude
Size 29.3%
* 12.2%
Great 9.8%
Big 7.3%
Large 7.3%
Altitude 4.9%
Massive 4.9%
Strength 4.9%
2.4% Enormous, Height, Huge, Importance, King, Length, Magnify, Magnum, Ruler

Magnum+
Champagne 40.5%
Gun 11.9%
Bottle 7.1%
Television 7.1%
Force 4.8%
Great 4.8%
Large 4.8%
2.4% *, Big, Colt, Giant, Photo, Revolver, TV, Water

Maiden+
Aunt 19.0%
Name 19.0%
* 9.5%
Over 7.1%
Virgin 7.1%
Fair 4.8%
Girl 4.8%
Woman 4.8%
2.4% Bride, Cricket, Female, Hair, Iron, Lady, Marriage, Maw, Voyage

Mail
Post 18.8%
Order 16.7%
Letter(s) 10.4%
Chain 6.3%
Out 4.2%
Postman 4.2%
2.1% Bag, Bills, Bomb, Box, Catalogue, Direct, Electronic, Junk, Letterbox, On-Sunday, Open, Room, Send, Shot, Slot, Sort, Stamp, Train, Trap

Major+
Minor 33.3%
Sergeant 14.3%
Army 9.5%
General 7.1%
Big 4.8%
John 4.8%
2.4% *, Decision, Disaster, Discipline, Grade, Important, Key, Marriage, Officer, Operation, Prime

Make
Create 9.3%
Money 7.0%
Sure 7.0%
Break 4.7%
Cake 4.7%
Construct 4.7%
Produce 4.7%
Up 4.7%
2.3% Achieve, Amends, Believe, Bread, Break, Car, Complete, Dinner, Do, Dough, Force, Fortune, Garment, Ingredients, It, Love, More, Out, Pottery, Shift, Some, Tea, Try

Malice+
Aforethought 21.4%
Evil 16.7%
Bad 7.1%
Hate 7.1%
Nasty 4.8%
Spite 4.8%
2.4% Anger, Deceitful, Desert, Envy, Forethought, Grudge, Harm, Hurt, Ill-Content, Manipulate, Meanness, Ogre, Quaint, Revenge, Town, Wickedness

Mallet+
Hammer 54.8%
Hit 9.5%
Tent 7.1%
Croquet 4.8%
Peg 4.8%
2.4% Axe, Bash, Bonk, Death, Fish, Hatchet, Sales, Wood

Mammoth+
Elephant 35.7%
Tusk 16.7%
Woolly 9.6%
Big 7.1%
Huge 7.1%
Task 4.8%
2.4% Animal, Dead, Gargantuan, Gigantic, Hair, Large, Small, Tail

Man
Woman 51.1%
Boy 8.9%
Wife 6.7%
At-War 4.4%
2.2% *, Biped, Child, Distance, Down, Hat, Kind, Person, Silent, Tall, Uniform, Walk, Women

Manage
Cope 18.0%
* 6.0%
Able 4.0%
Control 4.0%
Handle 4.0%
Organize 4.0%
Run 4.0%
To 4.0%
2.0% Ably, Arrange, Bank, Better, Boss, Business, Capable, Chaos, Corrupt, Director, Do, Easy, Everything, Firm, Head, Job, Management, Manager, Ment, Money, Strange, Team, Them, Time, Try, Work

Manhandle
Rough 16.0%
Fight 6.0%
Touch 6.0%
* 4.0%
Abuse 4.0%
Assault 4.0%
Hold 4.0%
Push 4.0%
2.0% Arrest, Attack, Bad, Broom, Brutality, Bully, Carry, Dirty, Fuck, Grab, Handle, Hassle, Hurt, Injure, Maltreat, Man, Manoeuvre, Marmalade, Mistreat, Molest, No, Police, Shove, Spade, Tool, Woman-Handle

Manic+
Depressive 28.3%
Mad 13.0%
Man 8.7%
Depression 4.3%
Monday 4.3%
Wild 4.3%
2.2% *, Bad, Depress, Depressed, Elicited, Eyes, Glad, Hyper, Insane, Insanity, Jack, Manage, Mania, Miner, Rabid, Sad, Street

Manner
* 15.6%
Way 15.6%
Attitude 6.7%
Polite 6.7%
Bad 4.4%
Custom(s) 4.4%
2.2% -Ism, Abrupt, Act, Affection, Appearance, Behaviour, Bread, Character, Characteristic, Fashion, Good, House, Respectful, Rude, Stiff, Style, Table, Thought, Training, Type

Many
More 18.8%
Few 12.5%
* 8.3%
Much 6.3%
Plenty 6.3%
Things 6.3%
Hands 4.2%
Lots 4.2%
People 4.2%
Too 4.2%
2.1% About, Books, Day, Dozen, Grains, Loads, Months, Nanny, Numbers, Plentiful, Some, Times

Mar
Spoil 35.4%
* 22.9%
Ruin 8.3%
Bar 4.2%
2.1% Alter, Away, Bad, Destroy, Draw, Marathon, March, Mend, Prevent, Scar, Sea, Shame, Spot, Worse

Marble+
Arch 23.8%
Floor(s) 9.5%
Glass 9.5%

Cold 7.1%
Hall 7.1%
Statue 7.1%
Ball(s) 4.8%
Staircase 4.8%
Table 4.8%
2.4% Column, Hard, Look, Michaelangelo, Paper, Stone, Walls, White

Margaret
Thatcher 81.6%
* 6.4%
2.0% Atwood, Princess, Queen, Rutherford, Turner, Want

Margarine+
Butter 66.7%
Flora 4.8%
Jam 4.8%
Tub 4.8%
2.4% Bread, Oil, Polyunsaturated, Spread, Sunflower, Toast, Yellow, Yuck

Margin+
Paper 19.0%
Error 14.3%
Page 14.3%
Edge 9.5%
Ruler 7.1%
* 4.8%
Gap 4.8%
Right 4.8%
Write 4.8%
2.4% Border, Break, Campaign, Lined, Of-Error, Rule, Words

Marigold+
Flower 57.1%
Gloves 7.1%
Yellow 7.1%
2.4% *, Butter, Buttercup, Case, Cousin, Daisy, Glove, Greenfly, Orange, Sun, White, Wine

Marilyn
Monroe 93.9%
2.0% Chambers, Girl, Who

Marine
Sea 23.8%
Life 16.7%
Fish(es) 7.1%
Sailor 7.1%
Soldier 7.1%
Biology 4.8%
Boy 4.8%
Mammal 4.8%
2.4% Biologist, Boat, Commando, Land, Officer, Pollution, Ship, Sub, Submarine, Wildlife

Market+
Place 34.8%
Stall 10.9%
Fruit 8.7%
Food 4.3%
Garden 4.3%
Shop(s) 4.3%
2.2% *, Barter, Blind, Boxes, Busy, Buy, Cattle, Day, Market, Oranges, Price, Research, Sale, Saturday, Vegetable

Married
Single 31.1%
Man 8.9%
Wed 8.9%
Divorced 6.7%
Couple 4.4%
With-Children 4.4%
2.2% Again, Age, Confetti, Divorce, Gate, Getting, Hitched, House, Law, Not, Paper, Ring, Spouse, Trap, Widowed, Wife

Marry
Wedding 12.2%
Wed 11.1%
Divorce 10.0%
Wife 7.8%
Church 6.7%
Husband 6.7%
Me 6.7%
Girl 3.3%
Love 3.3%
Man 3.3%
* 2.2%
Engage 2.2%
Join 2.2%
Together 2.2%
1.1% Away, Bad, Dear, Die, Dowry, Forever, Happiness, Happy, Life, No, Off, Party, Regret, Ring, Sir, Spouse, Strange, Stranger

Marshall+
Law 21.4%
Court 16.7%
Aid 4.8%
Art 4.8%
General 4.8%
Sheriff 4.8%
2.4% *, Amp, Army, Collect, Cowboys, Field, Garage, Group, Major, Men, Racing, Rule, Saloon, Show, Steward, War, Warden, West

Martian+
Alien 23.8%
Mars 16.7%
Green 14.3%
Space 11.9%
Planet 4.8%
Venusian 4.8%
2.4% *, Antenna, Chronicle, Fiction, Moon, Odd, Planes, Spaceman, UFO, Venus

Masculine+
Feminine 40.5%
Male 16.7%
Man 7.1%
Butch 4.8%
Men 4.8%
2.4% Age, Female, Hair, Image, Macho, Manly, Muscle, Muscles, Priest, Strong, Woman

Mass
Church 14.6%
Murder 14.6%
Weight 12.5%
Media 6.3%
2.1% Appeal, Black, Burial, Carnival, Critical, Crowd, Deep, Grave, Heavy, Huge, Hysteria, Lots, Masses, Maths, More, Number, Priest, Spirit, Sunday, Surgery, Table, Type, Use, Velocity, Zero

Massacre
Kill 30.8%
Death 23.1%
Killing 7.7%
Blood 5.7%
* 3.8%
Murder 3.8%
1.9% ?, Bosnia, Crusade, Dead, Dead-Bodies, Devastation, Die, Holocaust, Hurt, Indians, Innocent, Iraq

Match
Light 22.9%
Stick 18.8%
Box 8.3%
Fire 8.3%
Equal 4.2%
Flame 4.2%
Football 4.2%
Game 4.2%
Tennis 4.2%
2.1% Cigarette, Different, Fag, Make, Maker, Play, Set, Strike, Team, Tie

Mate+
Friend 28.3%
Sex 19.6%
Partner 8.7%
* 6.5%
Animal 6.5%
Check 4.3%
Michael 4.3%
2.2% Bed, Copulate, Couple, Form, Fun, Good, Love, Male, Meet, Sleep, Zoo

Material
Cloth 19.5%
Fabric 19.5%
* 9.8%
Cotton 7.3%
Gain 4.9%
2.4% *, Canvas, Case, Clay, Clothes, Dress, Evidence, Girl, Money, Objects, Rag, Raw, Stuff, Superficial, Things, Wealth, Wool

Mature
Old 25.0%
Woman 12.5%
Cheese 8.3%
Man 6.3%
Sensible 6.3%
Adult 4.2%
Cheddar 4.2%
Student 4.2%
2.1% *, Aged, Boy, Dull, Grown, Horse, Immature, Lady, Manure, Mature, Person, Ripe, Tree, Wise

Maureen
Lipman 38.8%
* 19.0%
Crews 6.1%
O'Hara 4.1%
2.0% Actress, Bore, Fitzpatrick, Girl, Housewife, Jew, Johns, Johnson, Mcgovern, Mum, O'Neil, Redd, Smith, Stinks, Turner, Ugly

Mauve
Purple 40.0%
Colour 18.0%
Blue 10.0%
Red 4.0%
2.0% Away, Bland, Blue, Brown, Field, Glove, Green, Light, Like, Lila, Mourning, Pink, Sick, Ugly

Mayhem
Chaos 34.0%
* 6.0%
Bedlam 6.0%
Murder 6.0%
Noise 6.0%
Anarchy 4.0%
Madness 4.0%
Pandemonium 4.0%
2.0% Carnage, Caterpillar, Confusion, Crash, Crazy, Create, Day, Disturbance, Farce, Fiasco, Fuss, Maim, Minestrone, Muddle, Notting-Hill

Me
You 75.0%
* 8.3%
Mine 6.3%
2.1% And, And-You, I, Up, Yes

Meagre
Small 14.6%
* 13.5%
Bean(s) 6.3%
Little 6.3%
Rations 6.3%
Thin 6.3%
2.1% Amount, Diet, Earnings, Feast, Few, Generous, Less, Meal, Mean, Measly, Meek, Minor, Mix, Morsel, Old, Pay, Pittance, Poor, Position, Sum, Timid, Together, Weak

Mean
Stingy 10.6%
Nasty 8.5%
Evil 6.4%
Imply 6.4%
Miser 6.4%
* 4.3%
Average 4.3%
Man 4.3%
Money 4.3%
Say 4.3%
Tight 4.3%
2.1% Cruel, Doctor, Generous, Greed, Look, Miserly, Mode, Relevance, Rude, Scrooge, Streak, Streets, Stupid, Thought, Trick, Ugly, Understand

Meant+
* 23.9%
Mean(s) 10.9%
Intended 8.7%
Said 8.7%
2.2% Aimed, Cement, Ferment, For, Hope, Implied, Intend, Intent, Meaning, Need, Patient, Providence, Purpose, Really, Sent, Signify, Sincere, Supposed, Told, Tried, Will

Measles+
Mumps 23.8%
Illness 19.0%
Disease 14.3%
Spot(s) 14.3%
Ill 9.5%
Chickenpox 4.8%
2.4% Childhood, Contagious, Malaise, Pox, Sick

Meat
Red 14.3%
Animal(s) 9.5%
Steak 9.5%
Beef 7.1%
Vegetables 7.1%
Chicken 4.8%
Food 4.8%
Murder 4.8%
2.4% Cow, Dead, Dry, Eat, Eater, Flesh, Grey, Joint, Juicy, Less, Liver, Pig, Raw, Salt, Stock, Vegetarian

Median+
Middle 19.6%
Mean 10.9%
Average 8.7%
* 4.3%
Clairvoyant 4.3%
Mode 4.3%
Paper(s) 4.3%
2.2% Astrologer, Dead, Future, Gypsy, Half, Line, Mathematics, Media, Medium, Method, Mystic, News, Person, Psychic, Short, Small, Spiritual, Type, Water, Zodiac

Medic
Doctor(s) 65.9%
Ambulance 4.9%
Nurse 4.9%
2.4% *, Bag, Bottles, Emergency, Headache, Hospital, Patient, Siren, Smooth, White, Wizard

Meek
Mild 76.0%
Mouse 4.0%
2.0% Dog, Fragile, Heart, Inherit, Inherit, Lamb, Leek, Milk, Soul, Timid

Meet
Friend(s) 17.0%
People 17.0%
See 6.4%
Encounter 4.3%
Join 4.3%
Meeting 4.3%
Rendezvous 4.3%
Together 4.3%
Up 4.3%
2.1% *, Boy, Come, Correspond, Go, Handshake, Introduce, Learn, Life, Partner, Party, Person, Personal, Place, Soon, Stranger

Mel
Gibson 42.9%
Smith 14.3%
Brooks 10.2%
* 6.5%
Kim 4.1%
2.0% Appleby, Bell, Brown, Girl, Griffiths, Jones, Martin, Melvin, Singer, Stewart, Stuart

Member
Parliament 24.4%
Club 8.9%
Committee 4.4%
Function 4.4%
Group 4.4%
Organ 4.4%
Party 4.4%
Staff 4.4%
State 4.4%
2.2% *, Big, Chance, Cock, Dis-, Figure, File, Forces, House, Limb, Person, Remember, Sect, Society, Team, Willy

Memory
Loss 9.5%
* 7.1%
Bank 7.1%
Brain 7.1%
Computer 7.1%
Remember 7.1%
Mind 4.8%
Ram 4.8%
Thought 4.8%
2.4% Blank, Cognitive, Colin, Elephant, Fault, Forgetting, Happy, Head, Holiday(s), Jog, Language, Lapse, Photo, Picture, Short, Song, Sounds

Menace
Dennis 19.5%
Danger 12.2%
Fear 12.2%
Threat 9.8%
Kill 4.9%
2.4% *, Anger, Annoying, Cartoon, Cat, Creep, Danger, Fierce, Frighten, Growl, Hassle, Hooligan, Pain, Pain, Savage, Scared, Society, Vigilante

Mend
Fix 33.3%
Repair 15.6%
Sew 15.6%
Break 6.7%
2.2% Better, Borrow, Broken, Clothes, Cup, Dressmaking, Fast, Fuse, Patch, Plug, Throw, Zip

Mercy
Help 11.9%
Killing 7.1%
* 4.8%
Beg 4.8%
Love 4.8%
Seat 4.8%
2.4% At, Beseech, Christ, Church, Compassion, Distress, Emotion, Forgive, Forgiveness, God, Good, Heaven, Hope, Kind, Leniency, Me, Mission, No, Nuns, Pity, Plea, Sent, Strained, Sword, Thanks, Threat

Mere
Only 18.8%
* 14.6%
Lake 12.5%
Nothing 8.3%
Small 6.3%
Little 4.2%
Mare 4.2%
Slight 4.2%
2.1% Bagatelle, Child, Confident, Fantasy, Few, Kings, Not-Important, Pool, Sea, Simple, There, Trifle

Merry
Christmas 33.3%
Happy 20.0%
Drunk 4.4%
Father 4.4%
Go 4.4%
Loud 4.4%
Jolly 3.3%
2.2% Anti-Social, Drink, Glee, Holly, Make, Making, Men, Party, Quiet, Sherry, Weather, Wives

Mess
Untidy 15.4%
* 11.5%
Tidy 7.7%
Army 5.7%
Room 5.7%
Disorder 3.8%
Floor 3.8%
Messy 3.8%
Mud 3.8%
Rubbish 3.8%
1.9% Clean, Dirt, Food, Horrible, Hurt, Jam, Kitchen, Melee, Mess, Message, Neat, Noise, Sea, Soldier, Up, Water, Willy, Yard

Metal
* 11.9%
Gold 7.1%
Iron 7.1%
Cold 4.8%
Heavy 4.8%
Silver 4.8%
2.4% Alloy, Bandage, Body, Detector, Edge, Energy, Forecast, Frame, Game, Gun, Hammer, Helmet, Long, Mickey, Mineral, Plate, Sharp, Shiny, Solid, Steel, String, Tin, Wood, Work

Method
Madness 20.9%
Way 20.9%
Acting 14.0%
Reason 4.7%
2.3% *, Actor, Approach, Conclusion, Descartes, Mode, Organisation, Practise, Process, Qualitative, Rhythm, Scheme, Sequence, Thought, Type, Work

Michael
Jackson 65.3%
* 4.5%
Caine 4.1%
George 4.1%
2.0% Angel, Davies, Douglas, Heseltine, James, Lew, Longley, Maria, Name, Palin, Parkinson

Middle
Centre 34.9%
End 14.0%
* 4.7%
Road 4.7%
2.3% Age, Bat, Bit, Class, Compromise, Earth, Finger, Ground, Heart, Inner, March, Midway, Part, Pig, Pillar, Rift, Sandwich, Wicket

Might
Strength 16.0%
Maybe 12.0%
Not 12.0%
Strong 8.0%
Be 6.0%
* 4.0%
Do 4.0%
May 4.0%
Must 4.0%
Power 4.0%
2.0% Come, Doubt, Giant, Have, Is-Right, Live, Main, Might-Not, Muscle, Never, Possible, Possibility, Tight

Mild
Meek 30.0%
Mannered 12.0%
Gentle 6.0%
Manner(s) 6.0%
Milk 4.0%
Soft 4.0%
Weather 4.0%
2.0% Beer, Bitter, Brown, Bubbles, Calm, Cheese, Cigarettes, Cold, Dew, Drugs, Fairy-Liquid, Force, Genteel, Illness, Man, Tar, Weak

Mile+
Long 19.0%
Distance 14.3%
Yard 7.1%
Km 4.8%
Length 4.8%
Stone 4.8%
2.4% *, Cold, End, Far, Golden, Heaven, High, Journey, Jump, Measure, Mild, Minute, Miracle, Mum, Post, Road, Run, Storm, Tired

Milk
Cow 16.3%
Butter 8.2%
White 8.2%
Cheese 6.1%
Sugar 6.1%
Bread 4.1%
Cup 4.1%
Tea 4.1%
Top 4.1%
Water 4.1%
2.0% Applause, Baby, Bar, Bottle, Cake, Carton, Coffee, Disgusting, Dry, Eggs, Glass, Jug, Man, Of, Pan, Soap, Whiten

Milkshake
* 22.4%
Strawberry 14.3%
Macdonalds 12.2%
Chocolate 8.2%
Drink 8.2%
Thick 8.2%
Banana 4.1%
Sweet 4.1%
Vanilla 4.1%
2.0% Bubbles, Burger, Cola, Glass, Milk, Quick, Straw

Mill
Flour 26.0%
Saw 12.0%
Pepper 8.0%
Floss 6.0%
Wheel 6.0%
Grain 4.0%
Water 4.0%
Wind 4.0%
2.0% Bread, Cotton, Exe, Grind, Ground, Hand, Hill, Holland, Machine, Mill, Race, River, Stone, Stream, Windmill

Million+
Pounds 13.0%
Lots 10.9%
Money 8.7%
Thousand(s) 8.7%
Billion 6.5%
Dollar 6.5%
Many 6.5%
One 6.5%
Hundred 4.3%
Rich 4.3%
2.2% $, *, A, Cash, Loads, Millionaire, Mouths, People, To, Trillion, Unemployed

Millpond
* 18.8%
Water 10.4%
Duck(s) 6.3%
Calm 4.2%
Dew 4.2%
Fish 4.2%
Mill 4.2%
Still 4.2%
2.1% Chimney, Clear, Constable, Crane, Deep, Duckweed, Frog, Grindstone, Lane, Lily, Miller, Newt, Pool, Pottery, Sea, Stream, Suicide, Toad, Village, Waterwheel, Weeds

Mimic
Copy 39.6%
Mime 14.6%
Clown 6.3%
* 6.2%
Ape 4.2%
Laugh 4.2%
2.1% Comic, Funny, Gimmick, Imitate, Impersonate, Joke, Me, Parrot, Puppet, Show, Small, This

Mine
Yours 50.0%
Field 8.3%
Ours 6.3%
* 4.2%
2.1% Clown, Coal, Cole, Dein, Is, Jos, Me, Mind, Own, Own, Possess, Possession, Selfish, Shaft, Theirs

Mingy
* 16.7%
Mean 14.6%
Stingy 12.5%
Cat 10.4%
Tight 8.3%
Dingy 4.2%
Small 4.2%
2.1% Bugger, Damp, Dirty, Dull, Feet, Greed, Miserly, Mould, Musty, Poor, Scottish, Tatty, Wire, Wordy

Minion+
Servant 21.7%
* 10.9%
Slave 10.9%
Serf 8.7%
Small 4.3%
2.2% Area, Computer, Disdain, Domain, Dominion, King, Kingdom, Long, Lower, Mingle, Minute, Peasant, Person, Plebeian, Pull, Soldier, Subordinate, Under, Underlings, Worker

Misfortune+
Unlucky 21.7%
Luck 13.0%
Bad Luck 8.7%
* 6.5%
Sad 6.5%
Poor 4.3%
Sadness 4.3%
2.2% Accident, Bad, Bat, Chance, Disaster, Fate, Harsh, Ill Luck, Loss, Rich, Ring, Sorrow, Trouble, Undesirable, Unhappiness, Wonder

Mislay+
Lose 63.0%
Loose 19.6%
Keys 4.3%
2.2% Find, Forget, Lead, Leave, Lost, Misplace

Mislead+
Lie 10.9%
* 8.7%
Error 8.7%
Trick 6.5%
Deceive 4.3%
Follow 4.3%
Mistake 4.3%
Path 4.3%
Wrong 4.3%
2.2% Annoy, Away, Bad, Carry, Confusing, Deceive, Deny, Dismay, Encourage, Falsify, Fool, Hurt, Lose, Misinform, Mislay, Mistrust, No-Where, Others, Pronunciation, Them

Misplace+
Lose 57.1%
Loose 11.9%
Wrong 7.1%
Lost 4.8%
2.4% *, Bonnet, Dislodge, Forget, Loyalty, Position, Put, Steal

Miss
Hit 33.3%
* 4.8%
Me 4.8%
Target 4.8%
You 4.8%
2.4% Aim, Avoid, Cat, Escape, Found, Girl, Grieve, Hope, Information, Jean-Brodie, Kiss, Long, Lose, Loss, Murphy, Observe, Person, Shot, USA, -Ter

Mistake+
Error 48.9%
Wrong 14.9%
Fault 4.3%
Oh-Dear 4.3%
2.1% *, Bad, Callous, Cock-Up, Copy, Correction, Cross, Eraser, Fear, Folly, Government, Made, No

Misty
Fog 20.8%
Foggy 8.3%
Clint-Eastwood 6.2%
Morning 6.2%
Blurred 4.2%
Cold 4.2%

2.1% *, Air, Autumn, Breath, Cloudy, Crying, Damp, Dawn, Evening, Frost, Grey, Horse, Kitten, Lane, London, Murky, Night, November, Pail, Play, Rain, Romantic, Roots, Smog

Mitten
Glove 55.6%
Hand 15.6%
Kitten 6.7%
Cold 4.4%
2.2% *, Cat, Child, Loose, Smitten, Soft, Warm, Young

Mix
Match 16.7%
Blend 12.5%
* 10.4%
Up 10.4%
Stir 4.2%
Together 4.2%
Whisk 4.2%
2.1% All, Around, Bake, Bowl, Cake, Chop, Different, Food, Grind, Knife, Mash, Mix, Mixer, More, Porridge, Spoon, Stew, That

Modern
New 8.9%
Jazz 6.7%
Old 6.7%
Block 4.4%
Building 4.4%
City 4.4%
Day 4.4%
Post 4.4%
2.2% 1st, Ancient, Art, Athlete, Contemporary, Current, Dance, Ears, Flat, Highrise, Ideals, Life, Living, Music, New-York, Now, Poetry, Recent, Science, Sculpture, Talk, Times, Town, Traditional, World

Moist
Wet 44.0%
Damp 14.0%
Sex 4.0%
Tissue(s) 4.0%
2.0% *, Apples, Baby-Wipe, Cunt, Dry, Eyes, Grass, Hair, Inside, Lips, Pane, Pants, Snatch, Soft, Steam, Water, What

Monarch
King 57.1%
Queen 26.2%
2.4% Ball, Crest, Glamour, Pope, Royal, Royalty, Ruler

Money
Rich 19.0%
Bank 14.3%
Cash 14.3%
Notes 7.1%
Bag(s) 4.8%
Wallet 4.8%
2.4% Bad, Banknotes, Belt, Change, Cheque, Coins, Dollars, Funny, Gold, Life, Nice, Paper, Pocket, Pounds, Wins

Mongoose+
Animal 35.7%
Snake 16.7%
Bird 9.5%
* 4.8%
Civet 4.8%
2.4% Australia, Bite, Duck, Dump, Monsoon, Ostrich, Rattlesnake, Rikki, Rudyard, Santa, Shoot, Vermin

Monkey
Ape 14.9%
Nut(s) 10.3%
Tree(s) 10.3%
* 5.7%
Chimp 5.7%
Wrench 5.7%
Animal 3.4%
Fur 2.2%
Jungle 2.2%
Magic 2.2%
Puzzle 2.2%
Zoo 2.2%
1.1% Arms, Baby, Banana, Bite, Business, Cheek, Cheeky, Chimpanzee, Dance, Drum, Experiment, Eyes, Face, Gibbon, Grin, Human, Jump, Laugh, Man, Mischief, Pilot, Play, Primate, Shine, Show, Simian, Swing, Tail, Tricks

Monsoon+
Rain 45.2%
Season 11.9%
India 4.8%
Storm 4.8%
Wind 4.8%
2.4% China, Climate, Ditch, Dress, Indian, Music, Rains, Rainstorm, Shop, Weather, Wet, Whirlwind

Month+
Year 47.6%
Day 9.5%
Period 7.1%
Time 7.1%
* 4.8%
January 4.8%
Week 4.8%
2.4% April, March, May, Now, Season

Mood
Happy 13.3%
Bad 6.7%
Swings 6.7%
Temper 6.7%
* 4.4%
Blue 4.4%
Feeling 4.4%
Good 4.4%
2.2% Atmosphere, Attitude, Chain, Cheerful, Depression, Emotions, Faint, Glue, Grim, High, Humour, Indigo, Melancholic, Mind, Music, Sad, Smell, State, Stone, Sulk, Temperament, Thoughts

Moor
Land 14.9%
Bog 6.4%
Arab 4.3%
Boat 4.3%
Grouse 4.3%
Murder 4.3%
Othello 4.3%
Spanish 4.3%
Wind-Swept 4.3%
Yorkshire 4.3%
2.1% *, Alhambra, Black, Cock, Dale, Grass, Heather, Hen, Ilkley, Isolation, Murderer, Muslin, Open, Scotland, Sheep, Ship, Steppe, Tie, Wet, Wind, Windy

Moped
Bike 37.2%
Car 7.0%
Helmet 7.0%
Motorbike 7.0%
Cycle 4.7%
Mod 4.7%
2.3% *, Bicycle, Clean, Dream, Engine, France, Jim, Laughable, More, Ride, Speed, Sulked, Tricycle, Up

More
Less 40.0%
Extra 6.0%
Big 4.0%
Lot(s) 4.0%
Much 4.0%
Of 4.0%
Please 4.0%
2.0% *, Again, Arab, Greedy, Hunger, Many, Money, More, Or-Less, Plenty, Plus, Some, Stand, Tea, Than, Wants, Wood

Motive
Reason 23.8%
* 16.7%
Force 9.5%
Crime 4.8%
Goal 4.8%
Means 4.8%
2.4% Aim, Cause, Collect, Decision, Detective, Dodgy, Drive, Engine, Help, Lie, Mobile, Motivate, Murder, Ulterior, Why

Motocross
* 16.7%
Bike(s) 16.7%
Mud 12.5%
Motorbike(s) 8.3%
Car(s) 6.2%
Fast 4.2%
Race 4.2%
2.1% Accident, Brands-Hatch, Country, Cross-Country, Dirt, Drive, Fun, Ice, Moped, Motor, Motorway, Rally, Speed-Racing, Sport

Motor
Car 43.9%
Engine 19.5%
Boat(s) 4.9%
Vehicle 4.9%
2.4% Bike, Cog, Cycle, Drill, Engine, Fast, Guzzle, Oil, Outboard, Power, Show, Trade

Motorbike
Noise(y) 13.3%
Crash 8.9%
Speed 8.9%
Fast 6.7%
Rev 6.7%
* 4.4%
Engine 4.4%
Ride 4.4%
Sidecar 4.4%
2.2% Car, Cycle, Danger, Death, Go, Harley-Davidson, Hell, Helmet, Kick, Loud, Moped, Road, Rush, Wheels, Whir, Zoom

Mouse
Cat 20.9%
Rat 20.9%
Trap 14.0%
Tail 7.0%
Cheese 4.7%
House 4.7%
2.3% Brown, Cartoon, Clock, Computer, Eat, Elephant, Hole, Timid, Twitch, Vermin, Wee, Windmill

Mouth
Lip(s) 19.6%
Tooth/Teeth 17.4%
Big 8.7%

Face 8.7%
Kiss 4.3%
Nose 4.3%
Tongue 4.3%
Wash 4.3%
2.2% Eat, Foot, Full, Gob, Off, Organ, Red, Rinse, Shout, Speak, Tongue, Ulcer, Voice, Wash

Movie
Film 48.8%
Cinema 17.1%
-Drome 7.3%
2.4% Drive-In, End, Girl, Mogul, Moviedrome, Myth, Pictures, Premiere, Star, Theatre, TV, Watch

Much
More 32.0%
Many 16.0%
Ado 14.0%
Alot 6.0%
Little 6.0%
Lot(s) 6.0%
Too 4.0%
2.0% Big, Everything, Food, Money, Of, Often, Over, Very

Muff
Dive 10.0%
Ear(s) 10.0%
* 8.0%
Fur 8.0%
Fluff 6.0%
Glove(s) 6.0%
Warm 6.0%
Ball 4.0%
Cold 4.0%
Diver 4.0%
Diving 4.0%
2.0% Clean, Cotton, Feathers, Fingers, Furry, Hands, Large, Mistake, Mitt, Muffin, Mufflers, Pampered, Puff, Scone, Sound

Muffin
Mule 20.8%
Cake 12.5%
Crumpet 10.4%
Butter 8.3%
Bun 4.2%
Food 4.2%
Jam 4.2%
Scone 4.2%
2.1% Bacon, Blackberry, Blueberry, Breakfast, Chocolate, Dining, Dunkin'-Donuts, Eat, Intercourse, Martha, Round, Teacake, Teatime, Toast, Toasted

Mumps+
Measles 26.2%
Illness 19.0%
Ill 9.5%
Lumps 7.1%
* 4.8%
Childhood 4.8%
Disease 4.8%
Sick 4.8%
Spots 4.8%
2.4% Abbey, Bad, Bumps, Habits, Sterile, Swelling

Munch
Chew 26.0%
Eat 24.0%
Bunch 18.0%
Crunch 12.0%
Food 10.0%
Grass 4.0%
2.0% Munch, Swallow, Sweets

Museum+
Piece(s) 30.4%
British 10.9%
Old 8.7%
Curator 6.5%
* 4.3%
Art 4.3%
Artifacts 4.3%
Dinosaurs 4.3%
Pictures 4.3%
2.2% Ancient, Archive, Artwork, Dusty, Gallery, Large, Ornaments, Place, Show, Swords

Mush
Pea(s) 42.3%
Mess 7.7%
Potato 7.7%
* 5.7%
Potatoes 3.8%
Pulp 3.8%
Room 3.8%
Slush 3.8%
Wet 3.8%
1.9% Brain, Destroy, Lush, Mens, Peel, Romance, Rubbish, Squash, Vomit

Mushroom+
Omelette 16.7%
Fungus 14.3%
Magic 11.9%
Toadstool 11.9%
Fungi 7.1%
Cloud 4.8%
2.4% Bacon, Curry, Drugs, Edible, Food, Heap, Nice, Old, Plant, Poison, Taste, Tree, Vegetable, Wood

Music+
Sound 14.3%
Note(s) 11.9%
Pop 4.8%
Score 4.8%
Sheet 4.8%
Stave 4.8%
2.4% *, Bach, Book, Decibel, Guitar, Loud, Michael, Noise, Paper, Piano, Play, Pogues, Record, Shop, Sing, Singing, Song, Teacher, Time, Treble, Tune, Words

Nailbrush
Nail(s) 20.0%
Clean 8.0%
Dirt 6.0%
Dirty 6.0%
Hair 6.0%
Hand(s) 6.0%
Varnish 6.0%
File 4.0%
Finger(s) 4.0%
Sink 4.0%
2.0% Acetone, Basin, Bathroom, Brush, Comb, Groomed, Loofah, Manicure, Polish, Scrub, Sharp, Spruce, Teeth, Tooth, Water

Nailfile
Nail(s) 37.8%
* 6.7%
Emery board 4.4%
Finger 4.4%
Hand 4.4%
2.2% Bathroom, Bite, Care, Clip, Clipper, Comb, Emery, Escape, Hole, Lady, Manicure, Polish, Rough, Saw, Scrape, Sharp, Trees, Wear

Naked+
Nude 21.4%
Woman 9.5%
Body 7.1%
Sex 7.1%
* 4.8%
Bare 4.8%
Cold 4.8%
Lunch 4.8%
2.4% Aggression, Ape, Artist's, Bane, Beach, Blessed, Bore, Clothes, Dead, Dressed, Eye, Man, Me, Stark, Wet

Name
* 10.4%
Tag 8.3%
Call 6.3%
Sake 6.3%
Address 4.2%
Person 4.2%
Surname 4.2%
2.1% Age, Akua, Andrea, Bat, Card, Change, Christian, Draw, Elisabeth, Game, Handle, Illegible, Label, Martin, Mine, Monica, Namesake, Nom, Nomenon, Number, Place, Plate, Star, That, Title, Tune

Nap
Sleep 71.2%
Cat 5.7%
* 3.8%
Afternoon 3.8%
1.9% Kid, Knife, Napkin, Pan, Pillow, Smooth, Snooze, Tired

Narrate+
Story 39.1%
Tell 32.6%
Talk 8.7%
Read 6.5%
Speak 4.3%
2.2% Chatter, Narrow, Person, Voice

Narrow
Wide 26.7%
Thin 11.1%
Mind 8.9%
Minded 6.7%
Alley 4.4%
2.2% Bad, Barge, Bed, Bridge, Fit, Gate, Gauge, Gorge, Lane, Large, Path, Rigid, Road, Sighted, Slim, Slit, Stairs, Strand, Trim

Nasty
Nice 20.0%
Cold 15.6%
Cruel 6.7%
Horrid 6.7%
Mean 6.7%
Person 6.7%
2.2% Bad, Boy, Brown, Cautious, Drop, Foul, Girl, Good, Hateful, Hostile, Kind, Mother-Fucker, People, Smell, Sneer, Taste, Temper

Nation+
Country 31.0%
People 9.5%
State 9.5%
Wide 7.1%
Unto 4.8%
2.4% Again, City, Enemy, Flag, France, International, Join, Land, Language, League, Patriot, Pride, Split, UN, United, World

Native
Indian 8.9%
Speaker 8.9%
Foreign 6.7%
Person 6.7%
Island 4.4%
Land 4.4%
2.2% *, Aboriginals, American, Belong, Black, Country, Gavagai, Indigenous, Inhabitant, Inner, Interest, Local, Non, Origin, Original, Peasants, People, Primitive, Red-Indian, Return, Rural, Son, Speaking, Town, Tradition, Tribe, Vanuatu

Nature+
* 14.6%
Green 9.8%
Animal(s) 7.3%
Leaf(ves) 7.3%
Trail 7.3%
Nurture 4.9%
Reserve 4.9%
Watch 4.9%
Wildlife 4.9%
2.4% Alive, Biology, Birds, Ecology, Evolution, Generation, Land, Natural, Peace, River, Trees, Walk, Woods, World

Navy
Blue 49.0%
Sea 12.2%
Ship 12.2%
Lark 6.1%
Uniform 6.1%
2.0% *, Army, Boat, Jumper, Queer, Rum, Sailors

Near
Far 64.3%
Close 16.7%
Miss 4.8%
2.4% By, Death, Hit, Side, Sighted, There

Neat
Tidy 71.1%
Untidy 4.4%
2.2% American, Clean, Cooker, Fence, Fix, Hands, Room, Suit, Trick, White

Necklace
Neck 17.8%
Pearl(s) 17.8%
Bead(s) 8.9%
Diamond 8.9%
Earring(s) 6.7%
Jewellery 6.7%
Chain 4.4%
Glass 4.4%
Jewels 4.4%
2.2% *, Beautiful, Bracelet, Buy, Gold, Match, Ring, Sparkle, Tie

Need
Want 36.2%
* 14.9%
More 6.4%
Help 4.3%
Needle 4.3%
To 4.3%
2.1% Children, Come, Comfort, Community, Dough, Friend, Helpful, Must, Necessity, Nurse, Parenting, Response, Some, Yearn

Needy
Poor 39.6%
Want 8.3%
Need(s) 6.3%
Desperate 4.2%
Greedy 4.2%
Money 4.2%
2.1% *, Elderly, Give, Homeless, Homelessness, Knitting, Old, People, Rich, Sad, Sew, Tramp, Wanting, Wanton, Wealthy, Weedy

Negative+
Positive 40.5%
No 9.5%
Ion(s) 4.8%
Minus 4.8%
Vibes 4.8%
2.4% *, Anti, Attitude, Captain, Cathode, End, Film, Maths, Neutral, Number, Photograph, Photography, Positive, Result, Sums

Neglect
Leave 27.0%
Ignore 10.4%
Abandon 6.3%
Me 6.3%
Abuse 4.2%
Child 4.2%
Dog(s) 4.2%
2.1% *, Avoid, Boy, Disrespect, Duty, Forget, Forgot, Give-Up, Hair, House, It, Left, Let-Alone, Life, Neglectful, Pass, Poor, Throw

Neigh
Horse 66.0%
Neighbour 12.8%
2.1% Boor, Donkey, Moo, Near, Noise, Pony, Snore, Snort, When, Whinny

Neil
* 18.9%
Kinnock 14.3%
Diamond 12.2%
Brown 8.2%
Young 6.1%
? 4.1%
Armstrong 4.1%
Down 4.1%
2.0% Bent, Bradly, Brigg, Buchannan, Corridor, Dan, Death, Hippy, Name, Plumber, Simmons, Television, Tennant, Webb

Neither
Nor 64.0%
* 4.0%
Either 4.0%
No 4.0%
2.0% Both, Here, Neither, Never, Nobody, Non, None, Not, Nothing, Only, Or, Whether

Nephew+
Niece 47.6%
Uncle 14.3%
* 7.1%
Aunt 7.1%
Son 4.8%
2.4% Beat, Boy, Brother, Child, Cousin, Relation, Small, Tommy

Net+
Fish 31.0%
Curtain 14.3%
Catch 9.5%
Fishing 9.5%
Ball 7.1%
Butterfly 4.8%
2.4% Effect, Fisherman, Gross, Mesh, Nylon, Safety, Strawberry, Tennis, Wire, Work

Network
Computer 14.6%
South-East 14.6%
TV 6.3%
Friends 4.2%
Line 4.2%
Seven 4.2%
System 4.2%
2.1% Arts, Brief, Buses, Business, Call, Card, Channel, Connect, Connection, ITV, Micro, Model, News, Related, Ring, Tangle, Team, Telephone, Television, Train, Tube, Underground, Web

New
Old 40.9%
Shiny 11.4%
Clean 4.5%
Coat 4.5%
Fresh 4.5%
2.3% *, Apartment, Award, Car, Exciting, Expensive, Good, Kid, Mind, Now, Place, Rays, Second, Sparkling, Television

News
Paper 28.8%
Flash 7.7%
Information 3.8%
Old 3.8%
Television 3.8%
TV 3.8%
1.9% *, At-One, BBC-One, Black, Blues, Boy, Brief, Broadcast, Bulletin, Channel-Four, Event, Fast, First, Great, Headlines, Martin Lewis, Newspaper, Radio, Reporter, Reports, Room, Team, Views, Weather

Newscast
Television-TV 27.1%
News 16.7%
* 8.3%
Reader 6.2%
BBC 4.2%
Report 4.2%
2.1% Actor, Baker, CNN, Evening, Glass, Information, Man, Newscaster, News-At-Ten, Nine-O-Clock, Programme, Read, Set, Statement, Thunder, Trevor

Newspaper+
Print 21.9%
News 9.8%
Press 7.3%
Read 7.3%
Book 4.9%
Journal 4.9%
2.4% Boy, Clip, Clipping, Cutting, Editor, Journalist, Media, Murdoch, Page, Pen, Picture, Record, Store, Sun, Tabloid, Times, Work, Zeitung

New Zealand
Kiwi 19.1%
Australia 17.0%
Country 10.6%
Lamb 8.5%
Sheep 8.5%
Rugby 4.3%
2.1% Blacks, Bottom, Butter, Cliffs, Distance, Down-Under, Far, Ireland, Land, Losers, Shit, Under, Wellington, World

Next
Time 12.0%
One 10.0%
After 6.0%
Queue 6.0%
Shop 6.0%
Another 4.0%
Door 4.0%
First 4.0%
To 4.0%
Year 4.0%
2.0% *, Across, Adjacent, Again, Beside, But, But-One, Clothes-Shop, Interviewee, Last, More, Move, New, Now, Please, Too, Train, Two, Week, Who

Nice
Day 9.5%
Easy 7.1%
Good 7.1%
Nasty 7.1%
* 4.8%
Bad 4.8%
Food 4.8%
Lovely 4.8%
Naughty 4.8%
Pleasant 4.8%
Pretty 4.8%
2.4% Bland, Boring, Evil, Face, Foul, Fun, Hard, Horrible, Man, Person, Place, Prim, Sticky, Tea, View

Nigel
Lawson 20.4%
Kennedy 12.2%
Mansell 12.2%
Planer 10.2%
* 8.8%
Dempster 4.1%
Name 4.1%
2.0% ?, Davies, Fabric, Foster, Havers, Hawkins, Hawthorne, Morph, Newton, Owen, Peter, Plainer, Stephens, Taylor

Night
Day 37.8%
Time 17.8%
Dark 11.1%
Life 8.9%
Owl 8.9%
2.2% Black, Flight, Lamp, Light, Moon, Sabre, Sight/Vision

Nimble
Quick 40.0%
Agile 13.3%
Bread 4.4%
Fast 4.4%
Light 4.4%
Swift 4.4%
2.2% Ability, Athletic, Balloon, Cat, Clumsy, Feet, Fingers, Flexible, Fluent, Jack, Slight, Thimble

Nine+
Ten 59.5%
Number 14.3%
No 4.8%
2.4% Eight, Hundred, Lives, Lover, Morning, Not, Tailors, Tenths, Time

Noisy
Loud 43.8%
Quiet 14.6%
Row 4.2%
2.1% Bear, Brood, Bus, Busy, Car, City, Crowd, Din, Fast, Hear, Ignore, Messy, Noisome, Not, Radio, Shout, Sister, Traffic

Noodles
Chinese 16.7%
Food 7.1%
China 4.8%
Eat 4.8%
Rice 4.8%
Yellow 4.8%
2.4% *, Chop, Chopsticks, College, Cook, Curly, Eating, Egg, Fried, Honey, Long, More, Ostrich, Packet, Pasta, Pot-Noodles, Runny, Slurp, Soy-Sauce, Steam, Steaming, String, Water, Wiggly

Nor
Neither 62.0%
Not 8.0%
2.0% *, Black, But, Chew, I, Less, Nonsense, Northern, Norway, Or, Scandinavia, Snore, Soup, West, Yet

Norman
Wisdom 20.4%
Tebbit 16.3%
Conquest 10.2%
Fowler 8.2%
Bates 6.1%
Lamont 6.1%
Mailer 4.1%
* 2.6%
2.0% Blake, Davies, Hillins, Man, Manley, Name, Roman, Stevens, Stone, Stormin, Taylor, Whiteside, Willis

Nose
Face 23.8%
Dive 14.3%
Mouth 9.5%
Ear(s) 7.1%
Smell 7.1%
Eye(s) 4.8%
Job 4.8%
2.4% *, Big, Bleed, Blow, Drop, Gay, Hair, Head, Pierce, Small, Smile, Sneeze

Notebook
Pen 32.0%
Pad 10.0%
Write 10.0%
Diary 6.0%
Notes 6.0%
Pencil 6.0%
Journalist 4.0%
Paper 4.0%
2.0% Detective, Jotter, Lectures, Lined, Morse, Pocket, Police, Shorthand, Study, Trainspotter, Writing

Notice
Board 37.2%
See 23.3%
Sign 16.3%
Remark 7.0%
2.3% Anything, Espy, Eviction, Hoarding, Leave, Paper, Something

Notion
Idea 60.0%
Thought 17.8%

Motion 4.4%
Potion 4.4%
2.2% *, Commotion, Daft, Dream, Faint, Feeling

Novel
Book 60.0%
New 13.3%
Story 6.7%
2.2% Author, Idea, Large, Paperback, Plot, Read, Romance, Tale

Novice
Beginner 31.1%
New 24.4%
Nun 13.3%
Learner 4.4%
Newcomer 4.4%
Starter 4.4%
2.2% Apprentice, Beginning, Early, Maria, Neat, Training, Veteran

Now
Then 48.0%
Here 8.0%
Never 6.0%
Again 4.0%
Immediate 4.0%
Present 4.0%
2.0% *, And, Ever, Go, Happen, Here-And, Late, Next, Presently, That's, Today, Try, What

Nut
Cracker 20.0%
Case 11.1%
Bolt 8.9%
Shell 6.7%
Brazil 4.4%
Meg 4.4%
Roast 4.4%
Salt 4.4%
2.2% *, Bean, Brown, Christmas, Crack, Food, Fruit, Fruitful, Hard, House, Party, Pin, Squirrel, Sundae, Sweet, Tree

Oath
Swear 37.8%
Promise 8.9%
Vow 8.9%
Law 6.7%
Bible 4.4%
Court 4.4%
Truth 4.4%
2.2% *, Breaker, Commandment, Curse, Faith, Mind, Solemn, Solicitor, True, Under

Obedient
Servant 18.0%
Dog 16.0%
Good 8.0%
Obey 6.0%
Boy 4.0%
Slave 4.0%
2.0% *, ?, Away, Behaviour, Calm, Child, Complied, Cooperate, Discipline, Disloyal, Do, Donkey, Horse, Loyal, Merciful, Obey, Patient, Rules, Sheep, Strict, Subservient, Yes

Obese
Fat 75.0%
* 4.2%
2.1% Big, Bottom, Cheese, Fatness, Food, Gain, Gross, Huge, Large, Obsessive, Overweight

Obnoxious+
Horrid 9.5%
Nasty 9.5%
Horrible 7.1%
Bad 4.8%
Boy 4.8%
Git 4.8%
Rude 4.8%
Unpleasant 4.8%
2.4% Awful, Awkward, Conceited, Difficult, Disgusting, Fool, Hate, Idiot, Ignorant, Lecturer, Nose, Objectionable, People, Person, Pig, Prat, Smell, Smelly, Spite, Twit, Vile

Obscure
Strange 6.0%
Unknown 6.0%
Vague 6.0%
Black 4.0%
Dark 4.0%
Jude 4.0%
2.0% *, Abstract, Artist, Bizarre, Blacken, Blur, Camera, Complex, Desire, Dim, Dull, Esoteric, Fact, Glass, Hidden, Hide, It, Journal, Lie, Link, Mist, Nothing, Object, Obscene, Obsolete, Obstruct, Obvious, Opaque, Rare, Silly, That, Transparent, Unclear, Weird, Whale

Observe
See 37.5%
Watch 25.0%
Look 14.6%
* 4.2%
2.1% It, Look-At, Men, Observatory, Paper, Ponder, Sneaky, Spot, Stars

Obstacle+
Course 42.9%
Race 16.7%
Obstruction 7.1%
Barrier 4.8%
Hurdle 4.8%
2.4% Army, Block, Blocking, Climb, Jump, Obstacle, Path, Problem, Succeed, Way

Obvious
Clear 21.4%
* 11.9%
Easy 7.1%
Evident 4.8%
Obscure 4.8%
Open 4.8%
2.4% Answer, Apparent, Blatant, Blunt, Bright, Close, Clue, Connection, Course, Lucid, Mistake, Motive, Painful, Person, Really, Relationship, Response, See, Simple

Odd
Couple 20.0%
Even 17.8%
Strange 17.8%
Ball 6.7%
Number 4.4%
Out 4.4%
2.2% *, Ends, Fellow, Great, How, New, One, One-Out, Peculiar, Person, Queer, True, Weird

Of
* 14.6%
On 10.4%
Course 8.3%
Belong 6.3%
From 6.3%
And 4.2%
Mice 4.2%
To 4.2%
Yours 4.2%
2.1% Car, Generic, Here, In, Is, It, Land, Many, Multiply, No-One, Off, Own, Pertaining, Snow, Theirs, Them, Things

Off
On 68.0%
* 4.0%
Out 4.0%
2.0% Again, Dark, End, Floor, Fuck, Horse-Racing, Licence, Old, Side, Stump, Switch, Take

Offence
Crime 11.9%
Defence 11.9%
* 4.8%
Give 4.8%
Guilty 4.8%
Knife 4.8%
2.4% Anger, Assault, Attack, Courts, Fine, Grievous, Guilt, Insult, Intent, Leeway, Lust, Parking, Penalty, Police, Polite, Pride, Provoke, Rude, Speeding, Spit, The-Police, Traffic, Umbrage, Wrong

Offer
Give 26.0%
Help 6.0%
Refuse 6.0%
Bargain 4.0%
Me 4.0%
Money 4.0%
Sale 4.0%
Special 4.0%
2.0% *, Advert, Assistance, Deal, Everything, Extend, Hand, Honour, House, Lend, Make, Marriage, Nothing, Offer, Offertory, On, Once, Price, Take, Tender, Up

Official+
Uniform 8.7%
* 4.3%
Army 4.3%
Bureaucrat 4.3%
Document 4.3%
Government 4.3%
Order 4.3%
Unofficial 4.3%
-Dom 4.3%
2.2% Badge, Bastard, Body, Bossy, Bureaucracy, Capacity, Civil, College, Customs, Desk, Formal, Governmental, Guard, Important, In, Language, Law, Letter, Notice, Officer, Party, Right, Secret, Stamp, Whitehall

Old
Man 20.0%
Young 18.0%
New 16.0%
Age 4.0%
Codger 4.0%
Grey 4.0%
2.0% Aging, Antique, Archaic, Boy, Bugger, Building, Car, Crooked, Die, Flame, Frail, Git, New, Pension, Replace, Tired, Wrinkled

Oliver
Twist 42.9%
Reed 16.3%
Cromwell 10.2%
* 8.4%
North 4.1%
Stone 4.1%
2.0% Green, Me, Muslim, Popaje, Porridge, Show, Tobias

Omelette+
Egg(s) 85.7%
Cheese 4.8%
2.4% Food, Hamlet, Pan, Spice

Ominous+
Cloud 9.5%
Worrying 7.1%
Bad 4.8%
Dark 4.8%
Threat 4.8%
2.4% *, Awful, Black, Dangerous, Deadly, Dire, Disturbing, Dread, Forbidding, Forbode, Foreboding, Foreshadow, Foretelling, Gloom, Gross, Imposing, Large, Omelette, Portent, Scare, Scared, Scary, Sign, Strange, Tale, Terrible, Threatening, Thunder, Unknown

On
Off 68.0%
Top 8.0%
2.0% At, Bar, Fire, In, It, Onboard, Onward, Over, Standing, Switch, The-Table, Under

One
Two 58.7%
All 6.5%
Alone 4.3%
Only 4.3%
Single 4.3%
2.2% *, Above, Ace, Another, God, Night, O.K., Over, U2, Word

Open
Closed 28.6%
Door 19.0%
Close 11.9%
Shut 9.5%
Sesame 4.8%
Space 4.8%
2.4% *, Air, Book, Box, Case, Minded, Suit, Wide, Window

Optimism
Hope 21.4%

Pessimism 16.7%
Happy 14.3%
* 9.5%
Joy 4.8%
2.4% Cheerful, Cheerfulness, Cloud, Daft, Exam, Failure, Firm, Glasses, Glee, Happiness, Hopeful, Idea, Sunshine, Surprise

Orange
Apple 20.4%
Juice 20.4%
Peel 14.3%
Fruit 10.2%
Lemon 4.1%
Pip 4.1%
Squash 4.1%
2.0% *, Blood, Crush, Israel, Pear, Pie, Pith, Rand, Round, Tang, Water

Orchard+
Apple(s) 71.5%
Fruit 4.8%
Plant 4.8%
Tree(s) 4.8%
2.4% *, Cherry, Garden, Grove, Orange, Paddock

Ordeal+
Trial 14.3%
* 11.9%
Trauma 11.9%
Fire 9.5%
Torture 7.1%
Terrible 4.8%
Test 4.8%
2.4% Brave, Disaster, Dreadful, Effort, Hassle, Horrible, Hostage, Kidnap, Nightmare, Pain, Taxing, Terrify, Terror, Through, Tragedy

Order
New 8.4%
Menu 8.3%
Chaos 6.3%
Tell 6.3%
* 6.2%
About 4.2%
Get 4.2%
2.1% Army, Boss, Breakfast, Buy, Class, Day, Dinner, Disorder, From, Insane, In-The-Court, Last, Leave, Line, Meal, Meant, More, Novel, Of, Out, Over, Place, Receive, Structure, Told, Type, Waiter

Organise+
* 11.9%
Arrange 11.9%
Crime 7.1%
Boss 4.8%
Filofax 4.8%
Party 4.8%
Work 4.8%
2.4% Administrate, Against, Committee, Diary, Disorganised, General, Good, Neat, Order, Organiser, Organist, Plan, Rearrange, Regulate, Reliable, Rota, Run, Set-Up, Sort, Strict, Throw, Timetable

Organist+
Church 28.6%
Music 16.7%
Play 9.5%
Player 7.1%
Albert 4.8%
Choir 4.8%
Organ 4.8%
Piano 4.8%
2.4% Flautist, Grandma, Handel, Keys, Month, Musician, Pianist, Scholar

Oriental
Chinese 14.6%
China 10.4%
Food 8.4%
* 6.3%
Eyes 6.3%
Occidental 4.2%
People 4.2%
2.1% Bean, Boat, Carpet, Duck, East, Eastern, Foreign, Garden, Gold, Japan, Land, Looks, Meal, Person, Race, Red, Root, Rug, Style, Travel, Western, Yellow

Origin
Beginning 16.7%
Birth 9.5%
Species 9.5%
Ethnic 7.1%
Country 4.8%
Ragga-Man 4.8%
2.4% *, Aborigine, Background, Begin, Belief, Birth, Creation, Darwin, Destiny, End, Evolution, Fruit, Gender, Lace, Of, Old, Painting, Point, Source, Start

Ornament+
Mantelpiece 16.3%
Decoration 10.5%
Vase 10.5%
China 5.8%
Shelf 4.7%
Bird(s) 2.3%
Decorative 2.3%
Mantel 2.3%
Model 2.3%
Nicknack 2.3%
Shelves 2.3%
Trinket 2.3%
1.2% *, Bauble, Belonging, Birds, Break, Breakable, Chandelier, Decor, Decorate, Dog, Earring, Fireplace, Flowers, Fragile, Gaudy, Gift, Glove, Granny, Lounge, Necklace, Ormolu, Ornate, Picture, Piece, Sculpture, Superfluous, Table, Tacky, Thing, Unicorn, Useful, Whatnot

Ornate
Decorative 8.0%
Fancy 8.0%
Vase 8.0%
Grand 6.0%
Jewel(s) 6.0%
* 4.0%
Beautiful 4.0%
Chinese 4.0%
Intricate 4.0%
Jewellery 4.0%
2.0% Baroque, Byzantine, Carving, Ceiling, Church, Cup, Decor, Delicate, Design, Filigree, Fussy, Gaudy, Gilt, Gothic, Jug, Moulding, Ornament, Ostentatious, Simple, Small, Tidy, Ugly

Oscar
Wilde 49.0%
Award 14.3%
Winner 8.2%
Movies 6.1%
Nominations 4.1%
2.0% Cat, Comedy, Gold, Goldman, Nominee, Performance, Peterson, Prize, Tango

Out
In 43.8%
Side 10.4%
Let 6.3%
About 4.2%
House 4.2%
2.1% *, Air, Closet, Come, Desk, Go, In-The-Open, Not, Open, Out, Rain, Shake, Skin, Span, There

Outcome
Result 43.9%
End 24.4%
* 4.9%
Final 4.9%
2.4% Conclusion, Curtains, Death, Ending, End-Result, Events, God, Income, Spent, Win

Outer
Inner 37.8%
Space 22.2%
Layer 4.4%
Limit(s) 4.4%
Skin 4.4%
Wall 4.4%
2.2% Circle, Edge, Force, Imagination, Islands, Peripheral, Rim, Ring, Suburbs, Surrounding

Outrageous
* 12.5%
Mad 6.3%
Act 4.2%
Bold 4.2%
Funny 4.2%
Loud 4.2%
Show 4.2%
Wild 4.2%
2.1% Anger, Behaviour, Book, Calamatory, Cave, Clothes, Colour, Control, Crazy, Extravagant, Flamboyant, Gay, Glamorous, Guy, Incredible, Joke, Lie, Madonna, Me, People, Person, Queen, Rude, Ruth, Shocking, Shout, Slut

Oval
Cricket 20.4%
* 16.3%
Eggs 12.2%
Square 10.2%
Cubes 6.1%
Round 6.1%
Shape 6.1%
2.0% Camberwell, Circuit, Deformed, House, Moon, Olive, Ovum, Plate, Rugby, Stone, Tube

Oven+
Hot 26.2%
Cook 16.7%
Glove 11.9%
Bake 7.1%
Cooker 7.1%
Cooking 4.8%
Heat 4.8%
2.4% Baked, Bread, Buns, Door, Food, Many, Penmanship, Ready, Wok

Own
Mine 14.0%
Possess 8.0%
Car 6.0%
Have 6.0%
Home 6.0%
Yours 6.0%
* 4.0%
Belong 4.0%
House 4.0%
My 4.0%
Person 4.0%
Up 4.0%
2.0% Alone, Bicycle, Borrow, Boy, Buy, Claim, Happy, Hold, It, Land, Loan, Possession, Property, Thoughts, Your

Paint
Colour(s) 14.0%
Wall 14.0%
Brush 11.6%
Picture 7.0%
Draw 4.7%
Over 4.7%
2.3% *, Art, Canvas, Colour, Cover, Decorate, Dry, House, Job, Paper, Remover, Room, Shack, Smell, Stripes, Wet, White, Work, Yellow

Paintbrush
Paint 44.4%
Colour 8.9%
Art 6.7%
* 4.4%
Decorate 4.4%
Picture 4.4%
2.2% Bristle, Canvas, Dulux, House, Long, Man, Painting, Pigment, Sound, Splodge, Stroke, Wall

Painter
Artist 24.4%
Decorator 19.5%
Paint(s) 17.1%
Art 7.3%
Picture 4.9%
2.4% *, Dirty, Dungarees, Oil, Painting, Portrait, Provence, Rope, Sky, Vangogh, White

Painting
Artist 26.2%
Decorator 19.0%
Paint(s) 16.7%
Art 7.1%
Picture 4.8%
2.4% *, Dirty, Dungarees, Oil, Painting, Portrait, Provence, Rope, Sky, VanGogh, White

Pamela
Stephenson 30.6%
* 21.0%
Bordes 10.2%
Aunt 4.1%
Brown 4.1%
Ewing 4.1%
Stewart 4.1%
2.0% Dog, Girl, Harris, Jackson, Jones, Name, Ogilvy, Picasso, Shriver, Walls, Woman

Pamphlet
Booklet 17.1%
Leaflet 14.6%
Book 9.8%
Paper 7.3%
Brochure 4.9%
Leaflet 4.9%
Letter 4.9%
2.4% *, Agitate, Anarchy, Christianity, Evangelists, Fanzine, Information, Interest, Magazine, Missed, News, Politics, Sample, Slogan, Story, Tract

Pan
Fry 23.1%
Frying 9.6%
Handle 5.7%
Saucepan 5.7%
Cake 3.8%
Cooking 3.8%
Flash 3.8%
Pot(s) 3.8%
Sauce 3.8%
1.9% Bed, Bedpan, Bowl, Bread, Chips, Cook, Cooker, Cookery, Dish, Eggs, Flash-In-The, Flour, Fried, Gold, Nap, Omelette, Scrub, Short, Water

Par
Golf 30.0%
Course 16.0%
Excellence 8.0%
Level 8.0%
* 6.0%
By 4.0%
On-A 4.0%
2.0% Arion, Boil, Equal, Ever, Four, Green, On, On-Course, Parity, Six-, Through

Parachute
Jump 36.2%
Fall 10.6%
Fly 10.6%
Silk 8.5%
Drop 6.4%
Plane 6.4%
Man 4.3%
2.1% Adventure, Army, Cotton, Danger, Flight, Freedom, Land, Sky

Paradise
Heaven 24.4%
Island 14.6%
Eden 9.8%
* 4.9%
Beach 4.9%
Lost 4.9%
2.4% Beautiful, Beauty, Bottles, Bounty, Coconut, Dreams, God, Greek-Island, Hell, Ideal, Nirvana, Palm, Peace, Sand, Street, Trees

Parallel
Lines 40.5%
* 7.1%
Opposite 7.1%
Bars 4.8%
Side 4.8%
Straight 4.8%
Universe 4.8%
2.4% Connector, Curved, Distributed, Open, Parallelogram, Perpendicular, Processing, Serial, Square, Street, Wonky

Paratroop
Army 18.8%
Soldier 18.8%
* 8.3%
(N) Ireland 4.2%
Green 4.2%
Killer 4.2%
Parachute 4.2%
2.1% Beret, Boots, Camouflage, Civvies, Drop, Flak, Friend, Militia, Navy, Nazi, Para, Paratrooper, Plane, Silk, Territorial Army, Uniform, War, Yomp

Parcel+
Post 28.6%
Package 26.2%
Packet 9.5%
Present 9.5%
Bomb 4.8%
Box 4.8%
Letter 4.8%
2.4% Baggage, Magic, Pack, Pass, Surprise

Parental+
Care 13.0%
Father 13.0%
Guidance 10.9%
Mother 10.9%
Contribution 6.5%
Caring 4.3%
Dad 4.3%
2.2% *, Aid, Authoritative, Baby, Bond, Child, Egg, Guardian, Love, Mum, Parents, Paternal, Responsibility, Sibling, Strife, Support, Trust

Park+
Car 47.9%
Bench 12.5%
Trees 8.3%
2.1% Grass, Green, Holyrood, Hyde, Keeper, Municipal, Play, Road, Side, Space, Swings, Waiting, Walk, Warden, Way

Parrot
Bird 22.9%
Cage 8.3%
* 6.3%
Polly 4.2%
Repeat 4.2%
Yellow 4.2%
2.1% Colourful, Colours, Dog, Fashion, Macaw, Noise, Ornage, Parrot, Pollypolly, Psittacosis, Python, Railing, Red, Repeat, Sick, Sketch, Speak, Speech, Stick, Talk, Talking, Talks, Tree, Yapping

Parson+
Vicar 42.9%
Church 9.5%
Nose 9.5%
Priest 4.8%
2.4% *, Collar, Curate, Ecclesiastic, Flock, Green, Man, Parish, Parsnips, Pastor, Rector, Smile, Squire, Vicarage

Party+
Animal 17.4%
Fun 15.2%
Political 6.5%
Balloon(s) 4.3%
Good 4.3%
Hat 4.3%
Pooper 4.3%
Streamer 4.3%
Time 4.3%
2.2% *, Alcohol, Celebration, Dancing, Down, Drinks, Fiesta, Get, Goer, Late, Over, People, Piece, Present, Saturday, Third

Pass
Out 15.4%
Fail 9.6%
Port 7.7%
* 5.7%
By 5.7%
Go 5.7%
Exam 3.8%
Word 3.8%
1.9% Away, Bus, Bus-Pass, Dive, Gate, Jail, Leave, Lift, Mountain, Move, Overtake, Parcel, Play, Rate, Succeed, Time, Train, Tube, Valley, Walk, Win

Passage+
India 9.5%
Way 9.5%
* 7.1%
Corridor 7.1%
Route 7.1%
Ship 7.1%
Alley 4.8%
Book 4.8%
Sea 4.8%
2.4% Back, Boat, Chamber, Hall, House, Opening, Path, Pathway, Place, Rite, Sail, Sleep, Through, Translation, Travel, Tunnel

Passion
Love 29.3%
Fruit 12.2%
Lust 9.8%
* 4.9%
Desire 4.9%
Red 4.9%
Romance 4.9%
2.4% Amour, Anger, Cake, Feelings, Fire, Flower, Hot, Pit, Purity, Raging, Sex, Spent, Urge

Passive+
Active 35.7%
Kind 4.8%
Quiet 4.8%
2.4% *, Act, Cow, Docile, Female, Grammar, Inactive, Laid-Back, Lassitude, Lazy, Long, Lover, Resistance, Sad, Silent, Sitting, Sleep, Still, Submissive, Tense, Unbothered, Vacant, Verb

Past
History 20.0%
Present 17.8%
Future 13.3%
Life 6.7%
Tense 6.7%
Now 4.4%
Over 4.4%
Previous 4.4%
2.2% Ago, Go, Gone, Post, Reform, Term, Then, Threat, Time

Paste
Tooth 20.0%
Wallpaper 18.0%
Glue 12.0%
Fish 8.0%
Board 6.0%
Tomato 6.0%
Squeeze 4.0%
Toothpaste 4.0%
Tube 4.0%
2.0% Brush, Cement, Crab, Curry, Gloopy, Jar, Magnesium, Pesto, Wall

Pastry+
Cook 18.8%
Cake 16.7%
Pie 8.3%
Chef 6.2%
Food 6.2%
Bake 4.2%
Crust 4.2%
Roll 4.2%
2.1% Apple, Board, Brush, Cakes, Cutter, Danish, Dough, Fat, Flan, Flour, Make, Maker, Making, Puff, Rolling

Pasture
Green 38.1%
Field 19.0%
Grass 14.3%
Cow(s) 11.9%
2.4% Colts, Grain, Milk, New, New-Zealand, Peace, Play

Pat+
Dog 37.5%
Back 10.4%
Head 10.4%
Stroke 6.2%
Eastenders 4.2%
Praise 4.2%
2.1% Cake, Cat, Cousin, Encourage, Gentle, Gently, Girl, Hat, Horse, Kitten, Postman, Rub, Tap

Patch+
Jeans 16.7%
Sew 12.5%
Trousers 12.5%
Eye 8.3%
Mend 6.3%
Black 4.2%
Knee 4.2%
Spot 4.2%
2.1% Doll, Grass, Oxford, Pin, Pirate, Quilt, Rip, Seam, Skin, Sleeve, Soil, Tear, Up, Work

Path+
Way 27.1%
Road 16.7%
Garden 6.2%
Walk 6.2%
House 4.2%
Track 4.2%
2.1% Dragon, Foot, Footpath, Golf, Gravel, Kings, Lane, Magic, Mountain, Park, Pavement, Sand, Smoke, Steep, Stream, Trees, Wood

Patter+
Feet 35.4%
Pitter 10.4%
Talk 10.4%
* 8.3%
Rain 8.3%
2.1% Baby, Chat, Chatter, Chit-Chat, Mouse, Package, Pan, Pansy, Praise, Sales, Speech, Spiel, Toff

Paul
McCartney 18.4%
* 16.3%
Gawman 4.1%
Newman 4.1%
Peter 4.1%
Simon 4.1%
Young 4.1%
2.0% Andrew, Angus, Apostle, Cousin, David, Dickson, Friend, Gascoigne, John, Knob, Lennon, Line, Mark, Name, Newson, Nicholas, Owen, Price, Priest, Pry, Revelation, Zumama

Pause
Stop 33.3%
Think 7.1%
Wait 7.1%
Breath 4.8%
For-Thought 4.8%
Moment 4.8%
Silence 4.8%
Thought 4.8%
2.4% Break, Brief, Button, Comment, Gap, Hesitate, Meno, Mimic, Rest, Space, Tape, Video

Pavement
Stone(s) 31.0%
Slab(s) 23.8%
Crack(s) 9.5%
Road 7.1%
Street 7.1%
Ground 4.8%
2.4% Gold, Hard, Path, Rough, Sidewalk, Walkway, Wet

Payment
Money 26.7%
Cheque 13.3%
Wage(s) 11.1%
Cash 8.9%
Fee 4.4%
2.2% Bill, Book, Coinage, Date, Due, Fine, Full, Immediate, In-Advance, Loan, Now, On-Demand, Order, Packet, Pay, Rent

Pea
Pod 27.1%
Green 16.7%
Brain 14.6%
Shooter 6.3%
Soup 6.3%
Ham 4.2%
Small 4.2%
2.1% Allotment, Body, Fork, Knife, Mushy, Nose, Owl, Princess, Round, Wee

Peace
Love 16.7%
War 14.3%
Harmony 9.5%
Quiet 9.5%
Dove 7.1%
Tranquillity 7.1%
Tranquil 4.8%
2.4% Earth, Goodwill, Grass, Haven, Liar, Man, On, On-Earth, Relaxed, Separation, Talks, Treaty, World

Peach+
Fruit 20.8%
Plum 14.6%
Melba 12.5%
Apple 10.4%
Pear 8.3%
Stone 6.2%
Ripe 4.2%
Tree 4.2%
2.1% Blossom, Blush, Complexion, Cream, Grape, James, Round, Skin, Sweet

Peacock
Feathers 46.9%
Bird 18.4%
Beautiful 6.1%
Blue 6.1%
Eyes 4.1%
2.0% *, Boast, Cluedo, Colour, Colourful, Display, Pasta, Rajasthan, Tail

Peak+
Mountain 29.2%
Top 16.7%
District 8.3%
Summit 8.3%
Height(s) 6.3%
Hill 4.2%
2.1% Cap, Crest, Early, Fall, High, Hour, Lace, Lake, Look, Peach, Scafell, Spot, Trough

Peanut
Butter 46.7%
Nut(s) 11.1%
Cake 6.7%
Shell 6.7%
Brittle 4.4%
Chocolate 4.4%
Salt 4.4%
2.2% Ben, Dish, Hazelnut, Jam, Peanut, Sandwich, Walnut

Pebble+
Beach 37.5%
Stone 25.0%
Dash 14.6%
Mill 12.5%
2.1% Dashed, Newton, Rock, Shore, Smooth

Peek
Look 31.3%
Peer 12.5%
See 10.4%
A-Boo 6.3%
* 4.2%
Glimpse 4.2%
Hide 4.2%
Spy 4.2%
2.1% At, Cheat, Curtain, Gaze, In, Lift, Look-At, Peek, Poke, Seek, Voyeur

Peer
Lord(s) 27.1%

Look 22.9%
* 6.3%
Equal 6.3%
Glasses 4.2%
Peep 4.2%
2.1% Friend, Group, Gynt, House, In, Into, Knight, Over, Peek, Realm, Right, See, View

Peg+
Clothes 16.7%
Washing 16.7%
Line 10.4%
Coat 8.3%
Tent 8.3%
Leg 6.2%
Hold 4.2%
Wooden 4.2%
2.1% Anne, Hang, Hole, Hook, Nail, Out, Piton, Sue, Tooth, Unpeg, Woo, Word

Pelt+
Fur 33.3%
Skin 14.6%
Throw 12.5%
Hail 6.2%
Hit 6.2%
Rain 4.2%
2.1% Animal, Coat, Hard, Hurt, Oryx, Pour, Seal, Snowball, Stone, Stones, Tomatoes

Penance+
Sin 11.9%
Punishment 7.1%
* 4.8%
Church 4.8%
Confession 4.8%
Punish 4.8%
Sorry 4.8%
2.4% Bad, Contrition, Crime, Deliverance, Faith, Fine, Forfeit, Forgive, Guilty, Hell, Hurt, Monk, Nun, Pay, Paying, Pencil, Repay, Sacrifice, Scold, Sentence, Servitude, Suffer, Time, Wage

Pencil+
Pen 23.9%
Lead 13.6%
Case 11.4%
Paper 11.4%
Rubber 9.1%
Sharpener 8.0%
Sharpen 5.7%
Crayon 2.3%
Writing 2.3%
1.1% Blade, Blunt, Dent, Eraser, Grey, Holder, Neck, Ruler, Sharp, Wood, Write

Pennant
Flag 31.0%
* 14.3%

Necklace 7.1%
Sorry 7.1%
Sin 4.8%
2.4% Confession, Dangle, Football, Forgiving, Hanging, Jewellery, Pendant, Prize, Sad, Servile, Silk, Submissive, Triangle, Unhappy, Woman

Pension
Old 30.9%
Book 21.4%
Money 9.5%
Age 4.8%
Fund 4.8%
2.4% *, Allowance, Elderly, Mortgage, Off, Plan, Poor, Private, Retirement, Rights, Swiss, Wages

Pensive
Thoughtful 38.1%
Think 11.9%
Thinking 7.1%
Apprehensive 4.8%
Sorry 4.8%
Thought(s) 4.8%
Worried 4.8%
2.4% *, Anguish, Apprehensive, Mood, Old, Pencil, Quiet, Stoke, Tense, Worry

Penthouse
Suite 30.0%
Flat 28.0%
Magazine 8.0%
Apartment 4.0%
Rich 4.0%
2.0% Building, Door, Fleet, Hotel, House, Mag, Mayfair, Playboy, Suit, Tie, Top, View

Pepper
Salt 54.2%
Mill 18.8%
Corn 4.2%
2.1% Black, Cheese, Dash, Food, Ground, Peppercorn, Pot, Sargent, Sauce, Shaker

Peppermint
Sweet 36.5%
Tea 9.6%
Gum 5.7%
* 3.8%
Cream(s) 3.8%
Fresh 3.8%
Polo 3.8%
Smell 3.8%
Strong 3.8%
1.9% Candy, Flavour, Green, Leaf, Mint, Minty, Round, Stick, Strong-Mint, Tongue, Toothpaste, Train

Perceive
See 31.3%
Understand 20.8%
Look 8.3%
Think 8.3%
Notice 4.2%
Realise 4.2%
2.1% Difference, Distance, Expect, Keep, Observe, Sense, Spelling, Tell, View, Vision, Visualise

Perch+
Bird 33.3%
Parrot 16.7%
Sit 10.4%
Fish 6.2%
Tree 6.2%
Budgerigar 4.2%
2.1% Branch, Budgy, Cage, Loft, Nest, Pike, Rod, Stand, Tight, Top, Wait

Perfect
Good 13.6%
* 11.4%
Flawless 11.4%
Ideal 9.1%
Imperfect 9.1%
Day 4.5%
Right 4.5%
2.3% Beauty, Clean, Edge, Faultless, Lovely, Match, Nice, Partner, Pearl, Pitch, Place, Prefect, Sickening, Skin, Teeth, Tick

Perfume+
Smell 37.5%
Scent 27.1%
* 8.3%
Flower 4.2%
Sweet 4.2%
2.1% Apple, Bottle, Department, Grass, Murder, Narcotic, Odor, Saint, Scented

Peril
Danger 47.9%
* 6.2%
Beryl 4.2%
Fear 4.2%
Scared 4.2%
2.1% Cliff, Fate, Fright, Nasty, Now, Oyster, Peril, Persil, Powder, Shock, Snow, Trouble, Washing-Powder, Wits, Yellow

Person
People 20.0%
Man 11.1%
Friend 8.9%
Animal 6.7%
Child 4.4%
Human 4.4%
One 4.4%
To-Person 4.4%

2.2% *, Baby, Being, Belief, Believe, Fat, Global, Half, Happy, Head, Him, Holy, Lecturer, No, Ooh, Woman

Pet+
Dog 37.5%
Cat 12.5%
Animal 8.3%
Hate 6.2%
Stroke 6.2%
Touch 4.2%
2.1% Caress, Fish, Fondle, Head, Keep, Lamb, Love, Mate, Mouse, Pert, Plaything, Subject

Phantom+
Opera 66.7%
Ghost 21.4%
2.4% *, Dragon, Ghost-Of-The-Opera, Jet, Pregnancy

Pick
Nose 25.5%
Choose 21.3%
Up 12.8%
Axe 6.4%
Sweets 4.3%
2.1% *, Cherry, Clean, Crop, Day, Flower, Mix, Pick, Pluck, Scratch, Shovel, Tooth, Truck, Wheat

Pie+
Apple 33.3%
Sky 11.9%
Cake 4.8%
Circle 4.8%
Custard 4.8%
Shepherds 4.8%
2.4% American, Blackbirds, Chart, Cherry, Chicken, Crust, Dish, Filling, Fruit, Meat, Pastry, Pint, Pork, Pudding, -R^2

Pig+
Sty 10.4%
Hog 8.3%
Sow 8.3%
Cow 6.2%
Farm 6.2%
Pork 6.2%
Bacon 4.2%
Swine 4.2%
2.1% Animal, Bland, Chop, Dirt, Dog, Eat, Friendly, Goat, Greedy, Headed, Horse, Pen, Piglet, Pink, Poke, Shed, Sheep, Snort, Snout, Swill, Tail, Trough

Pigeon+
Pie 16.7%
Bird 14.6%
English 8.3%

Hole 8.3%
Fly 6.2%
Fancier 4.2%
Race 4.2%
Racing 4.2%
Stool 4.2%
2.1% Breast, Dove, Egg, Loft, London, Messenger, Rat, Seed, Sender, Shit, Step, Toe, Trafalgar, -Toed

Pigtail
Hair 34.0%
Girl 12.0%
Pig 8.0%
Plait(s) 6.0%
Pony 6.0%
Ponytail 6.0%
Ribbon 4.0%
2.0% Bacon, Bunny, Child, Curls, Farm, Fly, Little-Girl, Orange, Pink, School-Girl, Tress, Twee

Pike+
Fish 45.8%
Eel 25.0%
Staff 4.2%
Teeth 4.2%
Trout 4.2%
2.1% Bike, Kill, Lake, Length, Pine, Spear, Stick, Sword

Pill
Tablet 14.3%
Contraceptive 9.5%
Box 7.1%
Contraception 7.1%
Bitter 4.8%
Bottle 4.8%
Pregnancy 4.8%
Swallow 4.8%
The 4.8%
2.4% *, Anadin, Asprin, Birth-Control, Board, Combined, Drugs, LSD, Medicine, Pregnant, Support, Table, Take, Thrills, White, Yellow

Pillar+
Society 23.8%
Stone 11.9%
Strength 9.5%
Column 7.1%
Community 7.1%
Post 7.1%
Salt 7.1%
Temple 4.8%
2.4% *, Architecture, Bedding, Building, Establishment, Marble, Sleep, State, White

Pillion+
Passenger 31.2%
Rider 12.5%
Bike 6.2%
Horse 6.2%
Ride 6.2%
Motorbike 4.2%
Post 4.2%
2.1% Carriage, Carry, Cycle, Fall, Lambretta, Motorcycle, Piggy, Piles, Punishment, Romance, Saddle, Scooter, Siege, Spindle

Pillow+
Talk 19.7%
Sleep 18.5%
Case 9.8%
Fight 8.7%
Bed 7.4%
Soft 6.5%
Cushion 3.3%
Head 3.3%
Feather(s) 2.2%
Puff 2.2%
Sheet 2.2%
White 2.2%
1.1% *, Comfort, Comfortable, Cry, Fluff, Fluffy, Larva, Lay, Pad, Plump, Prayer, Rest, Willow

Pilot+
Plane 40.5%
Aeroplane 19.0%
Aircraft 4.8%
Airplane 4.8%
2.4% Airline, Auto, Cap, Driver, Drop, Father, Flight, Fly, Go, Light, Scheme, Ship, Test

Pimp+
Prostitute(s) 33.3%
Whore 18.8%
Tart 16.7%
Pink 4.2%
2.1% *, Male, Man, Pimple, Purse, Pusher, Scarlet, Scum, Sorrow, Spot, Street, Wally

Pin+
Head 18.8%
Needle 12.5%
Cushion 8.3%
Prick 8.3%
Drop 6.2%
Hole 6.2%
Sew 6.2%
Pick 4.2%
Point 4.2%
2.1% Angel, Bright, Down, Dress, Hold, Medal, Notice, On, Paper, Sharp, Shine, Tuck

Pine
Tree 42.2%
Needle 11.1%
Cone 6.7%
Wood 6.7%
Furniture 4.4%
2.2% Box, Coy, Dresser, Field, Forest, Kitchen, Lofty, Nut, Oak, Shelves, Smell, Table, Whine

Pineapple
Fruit 30.8%
Juice 5.7%
* 3.8%
Apple 3.8%
Chunk(s) 3.8%
Food 3.8%
Leaves 3.8%
Mango 3.8%
Melon 3.8%
Spikes 3.8%
Tropical 3.8%
1.9% ?, Cheesecake, Cubes, Delicious, Dug, Gammon, India, Island, Jelly, Juicy, Ripe, Shape, Sweet, Tree, Yellow

Pink+
Blue 14.3%
Red 14.3%
* 7.1%
Elephant 7.1%
Green 7.1%
Colour 4.8%
2.4% Candyfloss, Cheeks, Communist, Flower, Gin, Light, Panther, Pastel, Pig, Pretty, Purple, Rabbit, Rose, Rouge, Soft, Think, White, Yellow, Zone

Pious+
Religious 12.5%
Devout 6.2%
Good 6.2%
Holy 6.2%
Pope 6.2%
Priest 6.2%
Pompous 4.2%
Pray 4.2%
2.1% Aeneas, Cheap, Christian, Church, Coy, Crown, Evil, God, Godly, Greek, Honest, Hope, Irritating, Ninth, Prim, Rat, Religion, Rich, Righteous, Show, Sweet, Swimming, Wise

Pip+
Apple 29.2%
Orange 18.8%
Fruit 10.4%
Grape 6.2%
Seed 6.2%
Squeak 6.2%
Post 4.2%
2.1% Core, Dickens, Flatmate, Hoot, Lemon, Peel, Rabbit, Stone, Tone

Pipe
Smoke 46.7%
Cleaner 11.1%
Tobacco 6.7%
Tube 4.4%
2.2% Burst, Cherry, Cigar, Cigarette, Drain, Dream, Fire, Gauze, House, Peace, Plumber, Smoker, Water, Yard

Pirate+
Ship 26.2%
* 9.5%
Penzance 9.5%
Eyepatch 4.8%
Sea 4.8%
2.4% Berwick, Blackbeard, Criminal, Crossbones, Enemy, Eye, Film, Flag, Hat, Long, Musketeer, Navy, Patch, Sailor, Station, Thief, Treasure, Westward

Pistol+
Gun 50.0%
Shot 14.3%
Shoot 4.8%
Water 4.8%
2.4% Action, Bang, Bullet, Burroughs, Death, Fire, Plug, Pocket, Rifle, Sex, Weapon

Pitcher
Water 35.6%
Jug 31.1%
Baseball 4.4%
Fork 4.4%
Tequila 4.4%
2.2% *, Alcohol, Ball, Bowler, Bucket, Drum, Flask, Glass, Shake

Pity
Sorrow 17.1%
Shame 12.2%
Cry 9.8%
Sad 9.8%
Sympathy 9.8%
* 4.9%
Empathy 4.9%
2.4% Cat, Fear, Feeling, Grief, Horror, Loathsome, Nose, Patronise, Person, Poor, Power, Show, Sorry, Tragic

Place+
Fish 18.8%
Town 14.6%
Name 12.5%
Put 8.3%
Mat 6.3%
Cod 4.2%
Location 4.2%
Position 4.2%
2.1% Bet, Card, Chips, Free, Lay, Pattern, Play, Road, Setting, Situation, Spirit, Square

Plague+
Death 20.8%
Black 10.4%
Locust(s) 8.4%
Bubonic 6.2%
Rats 6.2%
Frogs 4.2%
2.1% Annoy, Crowd, Dark, Disease, Famine, Fleas, Horror, Horse, Houses, London, Maggots, Mice, Pestilence, Plague, Pox, Rare, Rat, Scourge, Sickness, Sore, Sorrow

Plaice
Fish 63.3%
Cod 10.2%
* 6.1%
Haddock 4.1%
White 4.1%
2.0% Chips, Local, Mat, My, Name, Water

Plain
Jane 7.4%
Ugly 7.4%
Flour 5.3%
Ordinary 5.3%
Boring 4.3%
Pretty 4.3%
* 3.2%
Sailing 3.2%
Bread 2.1%
Chocolate 2.1%
Clothes 2.1%
Dull 2.1%
Fancy 2.1%
Grey 2.1%
Language 2.1%
Paper 2.1%
Simple 2.1%
1.1% Beautiful, Biscuit, Blond, Bold, Brown, Colour, Cooking, Decorated, Desert, Digestives, Direction, Dress, Drifter, Dust, Girl, Hat, Ice-Cream, Illegible, Interesting, Long, Looks, Man, Normal, Patterned, Person, Same, Sand, Seat, Smooth, Straight, Talk, Tasty, Tiff, Tights, Uncomplicated, Virginia, White

Plan
Map 23.3%
Idea 7.0%
Action 4.7%
Method 4.7%
2.3% *, Ahead, Architect, Attack, Big, Blueprint, Build, Cash, Chest, Drawing, Far, Hatch, Instructions, Intend, Intention, Making, Nine, Organise, Plot, Project, Route, Sailing, Scheme, System, Tackle, Way

Plank+
Wood 60.4%
Walk 27.1%
2.1% Idiot, Plankton, Sawdust, Sea, Ship

Plate+
Cup 23.8%
Food 16.7%
Knife 9.5%
Dinner 4.8%
Fish 4.8%
Glass 4.8%
Saucer 4.8%
Table 4.8%
2.4% Cups, Dish, Eat, Fork, Lick, Mail, Meat, River, Solid, Spoon, Supper

Platform+
Station 29.2%
Train 16.7%
Shoes 12.5%
Stage 8.3%
Heel 4.2%
Railway 4.2%
Shoe 4.2%
2.1% Dais, Flat, Heels, Labour, Launch, Place, Public, Sole, Speaker, Speech

Playboy
Magazine 44.0%
Man 10.0%
* 4.0%
2.0% Bunny, Car, Casino, Club, Gentleman, Girl, Git, Greasy-Man, House, Jacket, James, Money, Nude, Penthouse, Philanderer, Porn, Rabbit-Logo, Rubber, Rude, Sticker, Toy

Playroom
Child 20.8%
Toy(s) 16.7%
Children 12.5%
* 10.4%
Baby 6.3%
Kid(s) 6.3%
Nursery 6.3%
Pen 4.2%
2.1% Cot, Door, Duster, Nurse, Playschool, Round, Sandpit, School

Playschool
Children 23.1%
Kids 11.5%
Child 7.7%
Nursery 7.7%
Window(s) 5.7%
Brian-Cant 3.8%
Programme 3.8%
TV 3.8%
1.9% ?, BBC, Break, Bricks, Brother, Chalkboard, Dayschool, Ground, Jackanory, Kindergarten, Leader, Noise, Play, Television, Toddler, Toys, Wendy

Plea
Bargain 22.2%
Beg 22.2%
Help 11.1%
* 4.4%
Flea 4.4%
Innocent 4.4%
Plead 4.4%
2.2% Advocate, Argument, Begging, Cry, For-Mercy, Guilty, Mercy, Paper, Pardon, Pledge, Request, Wish

Plead+
Beg 43.8%
Guilty 16.7%
Ask 10.4%
* 8.3%
Mercy 6.2%
Please 4.2%
2.1% Court, Game, Innocent, Plea, Want

Pleasant
Nice 20.9%
* 8.3%
Happy 6.3%
Person 6.3%
Pheasant 6.3%
Cheerful 4.2%
Surprise 4.2%
Time 4.2%
2.1% Agreeable, Comfy, Company, Drive, Ease, Experience, Fellow, Field, Fun, House, Manner, Nasty, Odor, Peasant, Quaint, Smell, Smile, Stream, You

Please+
Thank-You 25.0%
Thanks 12.5%
Help 8.3%
Beg 6.2%
Plead 6.2%
Ask 4.2%
Happy 4.2%
Pretty 4.2%
2.1% *, Gratify, Leave, Listen, Me, No, Plea, Pledge, Response, Sir, Sorry, Thank, Word, Yes

Pledge+
Promise 29.2%
Oath 10.4%
Vow 8.3%
Troth 6.2%
Allegiance 4.2%
Give 4.2%
Swear 4.2%
Truth 4.2%
2.1% Agree, Church, Clean, Cleaner, Donate, Honour, Lies, Money, Owe, Pay, Plead, Pleb, Sign, Struggle

Pliers
Wire 17.8%
Tool(s) 13.3%
Nail(s) 11.1%
Hammer 6.7%
Screw 6.7%
Teeth/Tooth 6.7%
Grip 4.4%
Pull 4.4%
2.2% *, Fires, Fork, Nuts, Pincers, Pinchers, Red, Snap, Squeeze, Toolbox, Turn, Twist, Wrench

Plod+
Policeman 22.9%
Slow 12.5%
Trudge 10.4%
PC 6.2%
Police 6.2%
Slowly 6.2%
Walk 6.2%
2.1% Along, Amble, Dull, Fields, Foot, Footstep, March, On, Shoe, Slog, Slowcoach, Step, Wearily, Wellies

Plug
Socket 35.4%
Hole 14.6%
Electricity 8.3%
Sink 6.3%
Bath 4.2%
Electric 4.2%
Wire 4.2%
2.1% Block, Fill, Fuse, Popularise, Spanner, Spark, Stop, Switch, Television, Wall, Water

Plunder+
Steal 27.1%
Rape 14.6%
Loot 8.3%
Pillage 6.3%
Pirate 6.3%
Rob 6.3%
Raid 4.2%
Treasure 4.2%
2.1% *, Colonise, Depths, Drop, Mistake, Money, Proletariat, Rapine, Rich, Strip, Wealth

Plush
Rich 16.7%
Carpet 8.3%
Sofa 8.3%
Luxury 6.3%
Velvet 6.3%
Armchair 4.2%
Cushion 4.2%
Fancy 4.2%
Nice 4.2%

2.1% Blush, Comfort, Comfortable, Comfy, Expensive, Fat, Furniture, Lush, Luxurious, Palace, Posh, Red, Seat, Settee, Smart, Soft, Suite, Swish

Poach
Egg(s) 54.2%
Steal 8.3%
Fish 6.3%
Pheasant 6.3%
Hunt 4.2%
Rabbit 4.2%
2.1% Catch, Cook, Game, Gamekeeper, Get, Gun, Hang, Hares

Pocket
Calculator 14.6%
Money 10.4%
Coat 8.3%
Watch 8.3%
Book 6.3%
Trousers 6.3%
Brass 4.2%
Pick 4.2%
Purse 4.2%
2.1% Camera, Change, Diary, Gofer, Hand, Handkerchief, Hanky, Keep, Knife, Locket, Pig, Snooker, Steal, Things, Type, Wallet

Point
Sharp 17.8%
Finger 13.3%
Pencil 8.9%
Ball 4.4%
Out 4.4%
2.2% *, Arrow, Blunt, Break, Dart, Indicate, Knife, Line, Mark, Marker, Nib, Order, Pin, Pointless, Pontificate, Pressure, Run, Stick, Still, Taken, Tip, To, To-Point

Poke+
Prod 31.3%
Stick 10.4%
Fun 10.4%
Hole 8.3%
Hit 6.3%
Pig 4.2%
* 4.2%
2.1% Dig, Eye, Finger, Hard, Jab, Nails, Peek, Push, Rod, Sharp, Turtle

Polar
Bear 58.3%
Ice 10.4%
Cold 6.3%
Expedition 4.2%
Ice-Cap 4.2%
2.1% *, Antarctic, Coordinates, Equatorial, Magnet, Pear, Regions, Star

Policy
Insurance 13.3%
Government 11.1%
* 4.4%
Document 4.4%
Law 4.4%
Maker 4.4%
Rule(s) 4.4%
2.2% Case, Confirm, Corrupt, Decision, Directive, Doubtful, Letter, Matter, Mechanism, Method, Minister, Number, Office, Pack, Paper, Plan, Police, Politics, Procedure, Report, School, Strict, Studies, Theft

Polite
Nice 16.0%
* 6.0%
Rude 6.0%
Boy 4.0%
Charming 4.0%
Girl 4.0%
Impolite 4.0%
Kind 4.0%
Shy 4.0%
2.0% Cautious, Charm, Child, Company, Conversation, Courteous, Formal, Gentle, Good, Hello, Helpful, Improper, Lie, Manners, Never, People, Pie, Polish, Politic, Proper, Quiet, Refusal, Smile, Suit

Pony
Horse 41.7%
Tail 16.7%
Trek 14.6%
Ride 4.2%
2.1% Cart, Club, Fat, Horace, Little, Money, Rider, Sloanes, Stable, Stool, Trekking

Pool
Water 29.2%
Swimming 12.5%
Blood 10.4%
Pond 8.3%
Swim 6.3%
Wet 4.2%
2.1% Byrons, Clear, Deep, Drown, Forest, Puddle, Push, Resources, Side, Snooker, Still, Sum, Sweat, Typing

Pop
Music 18.0%
Up 12.0%
Corn 8.0%
Tart 8.0%
Art 6.0%
Weasel 6.0%
Bang 4.0%
Star 4.0%
Top 4.0%
2.0% Burst, Cola, Concert, Explode, Eye, Gun, Open, Poppy, Record, Shop, Smack, Snack, Snap, Sock, Whistle

Pope+
Catholic(s) 12.5%
John 10.4%
Paul 10.4%
Rome 10.4%
Vatican 8.3%
Cardinal 6.3%
Church 4.2%
John Paul 4.2%
Pious 4.2%
Religion 4.2%
2.1% Cowl, Gregory, Hat, Holy, Joan, Mobile, Nick, Poke, Polish, Pomp, Priest, Rich

Port
Ship 12.0%
Wine 10.0%
Dock 8.0%
Boat 6.0%
Sea 6.0%
Sherry 6.0%
Harbour 4.0%
Starboard 4.0%
Storm 4.0%
Talbut 4.0%
2.0% Airplane, Bristol, Drink, Entry, Foreign, Hole, Ibiza, Left, Open, Piraeus, Quayside, Sail, Sailor, Sick, Steamer, Sunny, Tavern, Water

Post
Letter(s) 25.0%
Haste 10.4%
Man 8.3%
Party 6.3%
Guest(s) 4.2%
Mail 4.2%
Office 4.2%
Pillar 4.2%
Wood 4.2%
2.1% *, Box, Card, Christ, Communion, Dinner, Fences, Goal, Hole, Letterbox, Room, Wall, Wife, Winning

Postcard
Holiday 27.1%
Stamp 12.5%
Letter 8.3%
* 6.3%
Send 6.3%
Picture 4.2%
Write 4.2%
2.1% Abroad, America, Edge, Foreign, From-Edge, House, Italy, Message, Sea, Stand, Tune, Venice, View, Win

Pot
Plant 9.6%
Tea 9.6%
Pan 7.7%
Dish 5.7%
Kettle 5.7%
Noodle 5.7%
Container 3.8%
Jam 3.8%
Smoke 3.8%
1.9% *, Bowl, Break, Casserole, Dope, Flower, Full, Ganja, Hash, Holder, Jar, Jug, Luck, Of-Gold, Of-Tea, Pea, Pen, Pottery, Pourri, Shed, Shelf, Stew, Stone

Pottery
Clay 26.8%
Pot(s) 14.6%
Cup(s) 9.8%
Vase 7.3%
Ceramics 4.9%
Jar 4.9%
Jug 4.9%
Wheel 4.9%
2.4% Bowl, China, Craft, Kiln, Mad, Oven, Perugia, Pot, Sculptor, Soil

Pounce
Jump 35.4%
Cat(s) 16.7%
On 12.5%
* 4.2%
Ounce 4.2%
2.1% Animal, Dog, Grab, Grasp, Jeopardy, Leap, Lion, Over, Pence, Prowl, Seize, Tiger, Upon

Pour
Water 27.7%
Milk 19.1%
Jug 10.6%
Tea 6.4%
Drink 4.3%
Out 4.3%
2.1% *, Beer, Coffee, Cup, Flow, Hold, Jar, Rain, Scorn, Spill, Spout, Teem, Tilt

Poverty
Poor 40.4%
* 7.1%
Money 7.1%
Trap 7.1%
Wealth 7.1%
Stricken 4.8%
2.4% Dirt, Dole, Dust, Hardship, Homeless, House, Hunger, Poor-Woman, Rich, Squat, Strain

Power
Station 16.3%
Strength 9.3%

Electric 4.7%
Electricity 4.7%
Energy 4.7%
Engine 4.7%
Plug 4.7%
Strong 4.7%
2.3% *, Authority, Broker, Buzz, Cable, Chord, Fence, Full, Line, Lunch, Milk, Move, Muscle, Plus, Point, Room, Structures, Struggle, Submission, Switch

Powerful
Strong 34.9%
* 11.6%
Strength 4.7%
2.3% Almighty, Battery, Car, Eights, Electric, Fit, Great, Influence, Intoxicating, Lethal, Man, Mighty, Muscle, Person, Rich, Ruler, Smell, Stern, Thing, Urge, Weak

Powerlessness
Weak 30.2%
* 11.6%
Impotent 7.0%
Impotence 4.7%
2.3% Anger, Coward, Defeat, Empower, Empty, Feeble, Gender, Help, Helplessness, Hopeless, Immovable, Jeopardy, Little, Minority, Politics, Quiet, Serf, Sick, Wimp, Women

Pram+
Baby 67.4%
* 6.5%
Pushchair 6.5%
Wheel(s) 4.3%
2.2% Chair, Child, In, Nurse, Pud, Tray, Trolley

Prank
Joke 35.4%
Trick 33.3%
Play 8.3%
Game 4.2%
2.1% Children, Door, Jape, Jest, Joker, Spank, Turn, Wacky, Wrong

Pray
Church 25.5%
God 14.9%
* 6.4%
Kneel 6.4%
Priest 4.3%
Think 4.3%
2.1% Aloud, Beg, Bird, Book, Cross, Cry, Gently, Hands, Hard, Heaven, Jesus, Knees, None, Prayer, Quietly, Religion, Sing, Worship

Precious
Stone 27.1%
Metal(s) 14.6%
Rare 10.4%
Gem 6.3%
Jewel 6.3%
* 4.2%
Money 4.2%
2.1% Costly, Dear, Diamond, Expensive, Glass, Gold, Life, Little, Load, Mine, Person, Thing, Time

Prehistoric+
Dinosaur 32.6%
Ancient 17.4%
Old 17.4%
Animal 6.5%
History 4.3%
Monster 4.3%
2.2% Age, Antique, Cavemen, Early, Era, Ice Age, Stone, Study

Prejudice
Pride 25.6%
* 7.0%
Against 7.0%
Bias 7.0%
Racism 7.0%
Racist 7.0%
Black 4.7%
Hate 4.7%
2.3% Apartheid, Barrier, Blind, Book, Dishonour, Foolish, Gay, Jealousy, Judge, Police, Racial, Slanted, Sod

Press
Paper(s) 12.8%
Button 6.4%
Iron 6.4%
Squeeze 6.4%
Trousers 6.4%
Gang 4.3%
Hard 4.3%
Hold 4.3%
Orange 4.3%
2.1% Agent, Bell, Burger, Cameras, Card, Clothes, Dogs, Down, Flower, Free, Jackal, Love, Media, News, Newspaper, Popper, Print, Push, Release, Reporter, Squash

Pretend+
Play 17.4%
Fake 10.9%
False 10.9%
* 8.7%
Act 4.3%
Game 4.3%
Try 4.3%
2.2% Artifice, Disguise, Dissemble, Do, Falsity, Force, Imagine, Just, Kids, Lie, Make Believe, Play

Act, Pose, Put On, Seen, Show Off, Throne, Unreal

Previous
Before 28.6%
Past 7.1%
Conviction 4.8%
Day 4.8%
Experience 4.8%
Last 4.8%
2.4% Conditions, Earlier, Eastern, Encounter, Engagement, Events, First, Firstly, Former, Future, Job, Life, Marriage, Meeting, Next, Offence, Once, Record, Wife

Price
Cost 25.0%
Pay 25.0%
Right 16.7%
Tag 12.5%
Money 4.2%
2.1% Bought, Cut, Expense, Expensive, Label, Less, Rich, Shop

Pride
Fall(s) 35.4%
Joy 20.8%
Prejudice 10.4%
Lion 4.2%
Love 4.2%
2.1% *, Anger, Boast, Brag, Chest, Gay, Glory, High, Life, Lust, Mothers, Ponce

Priest
Church 16.7%
Bishop 4.2%
Black 4.2%
Father 4.2%
God 4.2%
High 4.2%
Religion 4.2%
Robe 4.2%
Vicar 4.2%
2.1% Altar, Cape, Cardinal, Catholic, Celibate, Cleric, Congregation, Cross, Dog-Collar, Fool, Hell, Holy, King, Lack, Magician, Mass, Pope, Prat, Prayer, Priestess, Sacrament, Scholar, Sermon, Worker

Prime+
Number 14.6%
Time 10.4%
Life 8.3%
Brodie 6.3%
First 6.3%
Youth 6.3%
Beef 4.2%
Cut 4.2%
Mover 4.2%
Peak 4.2%

2.1% Best, Candidate, Cause, Colour, Dance, Drive, Film, Forty, Glory, Mannerly, Meal, Ready, Scotland, Success, Superior, Suspect, Wart, Worm

Prince
Princess 20.8%
Charming 18.8%
King 14.6%
Charles 6.3%
Frog 6.3%
Pauper 4.2%
Queen 4.2%
Regent 4.2%
2.1% Album, Ball, Come, Country, Darkness, Duke, Peace, Phillip, Print, Romance

Princess+
Prince 35.4%
Anne 8.3%
Diana 8.3%
Pea 6.3%
Di 4.2%
Royal 4.2%
2.1% Andrew, Beautiful, Beauty, Castle, Crown, Joanna, Lady, Peach, Preen, Radiator, Sleep, Slipper, Thick, Tresses, Wales

Print
* 10.4%
Paper 10.4%
Book 8.3%
Write 8.3%
Shop 6.3%
Letter 4.2%
Newspaper 4.2%
Out 4.2%
Page 4.2%
Type 4.2%
Word 4.2%
2.1% At, Black, Clearly, Colour, Computers, Frock, Iconography, It, Material, News, Photo, Printer, Publish, Room, Test

Prison
Jail 22.0%
Bars 9.8%
Cage 7.3%
Cell 7.3%
* 4.9%
Prisoner 4.9%
Sentence 4.9%
Warder 4.9%
2.4% Bastille, Confinement, Dingy, Door, Escape, Force, Grey, Holloway, Lock, Metal, Sex, Space, Ugly, Walls, Water

Prisoner
Jail 19.5%
Cell 9.8%
Bars 7.3%
Cage 7.3%
* 4.9%
Captive 4.9%
Cell-Block-H 4.9%
Convict 4.9%
Inmate 4.9%
2.4% Caged, Captivity, Cell, Conscience, Depression, Free, Jailbird, Keeper, Number, Prison, Sentence, Six, Staid, War

Private
* 9.5%
Property 9.5%
House 7.1%
Public 7.1%
Secret 7.1%
Affair 4.8%
Closed 4.8%
Eye 4.8%
Garden 4.8%
Open 4.8%
Personal 4.8%
2.4% Function, Introvert, Joy, Keep-Out, Life(s), Mansion, Mine, Parts, Road, Room, Secretive, Trespass

Prize
Win 20.8%
Goal 8.3%
Winner 6.3%
Gain 4.2%
Giving 4.2%
Reward 4.2%
School 4.2%
Winnings 4.2%
2.1% *, Bull, Competition, Cup, Day, Esteem, Event, First, Game, Gift, Joy, Lost, Money, Open, Possession, Prick, Take, Target, Value, Weight, Won

Process
* 11.9%
Procedure 7.1%
Computer(s) 4.8%
Food 4.8%
Method 4.8%
Work(s) 4.8%
2.4% Biological, Car, Cheese, Content, Data, Due, Elimination, Experiment, Flour, Formula, Function, Job, Make, Metal, Mind, Mix, Power, Regress, Server, Stop, Success, Task, Theory, Thought, Use, Word

Prod
Poke 62.5%
Cattle 8.3%
Push 4.2%
Stick 4.2%
2.1% Awake, In, Jab, Prick, Probe, Score, Shove, Stab, Thump, Yes

Profit
Money 37.2%
Loss 16.3%
Cash 11.6%
Margin 9.3%
Gain 7.0%
2.3% Cost, Materialist, Motif, Motive, Share, Surplus, Take, Wealth

Promise
* 6.3%
Lie 6.3%
Truth 6.3%
Vow 6.3%
Child 4.2%
Give 4.2%
Kept 4.2%
Me 4.2%
Oath 4.2%
Swear 4.2%
To 4.2%
Trust 4.2%
2.1% Bond, Brownies, Faithfully, Forever, Forget, Fulfill, Gift, Keep, Love, Mend, Miracle, Pledge, Prospect, Remember, Seal, Someone, Something, Undertake, Wedding, Wish

Prompt
Quick 12.5%
Push 8.3%
Stage 8.3%
Play 6.3%
Actor 4.2%
Help 4.2%
Tell 4.2%
2.1% Act, Acting, Arrow, Box, Cast, Computer, Conductor, Correct, Encourage, Go, Line, Now, Pester, Precise, Prod, Propose, Question, Quickly, Reply, Response, Soon, Story, Swift, Urge, Word

Proof
Evidence 42.9%
* 4.8%
ID 4.8%
Positive 4.8%
Reader 4.8%
True 4.8%
2.4% Alcohol, Clue, Jury, Paper, Percent, Prove, Pudding, Reading, Shock, Show, Spoof, Text, Trial, Trust

Prop
Up 16.7%
Pit 12.5%
Stage 12.5%
Play 8.3%
Rugby 6.2%
Actor 4.2%
Hold 4.2%
Plane 4.2%
Stick 4.2%
Support 4.2%
2.1% Clothes, Crutch, Fall, Forward, Help, Line, Perch, Post, Stall, Table, Tip

Properly
Right 26.2%
* 11.9%
Correctly 11.9%
Correct 4.8%
Dress 4.8%
Well 4.8%
2.4% Addressed, Advise, Decent, Done, Exact, Fine, Good, Hope, Order, Orderly, Rightly, Straightforward, Thoroughly, Uniform

Property
House(s) 42.9%
Mine 7.1%
Own 7.1%
Owner 7.1%
Theft 7.1%
Land 4.8%
2.4% Belonging, Estate, Feature, Law, Possession, Rights, Shares, Someone's, Swindle, Tax

Propose
Marriage 32.6%
Suggest 25.6%
Marry 9.3%
Ask 7.0%
Ring 4.7%
Wedding 4.7%
2.3% Accept, Idea, Project, Proposal, Say, Smuggle, Speak

Prosperity
Rich 28.6%
Wealth 28.6%
Riches 7.1%
Happiness 4.8%
Money 4.8%
2.4% Abundance, Affluence, Cash, Gold, Hope, House, Inherited, Luck, Poverty, Prestige, Youth

Protect
Survive 11.6%
* 9.3%
Guard 7.0%
Gun 4.7%
Shield 4.7%
2.3% Against, Care, Commitment, Cover, Defect, Defend, Environment, Girl, Glove, Guardian, Harm, Helmet, Hide, Hurt, Incorporate, Intervene, Keep, Look-After, Purple, Safe, Safety, Save, Secure, Surround, Tame, Weak

Protection
Racket 14.6%
Security 12.2%
Money 9.8%
Guard 7.3%
Safe 7.3%
* 4.9%
Safety 4.9%
Shield 4.9%
2.4% Armour, Arms, Bars, Big-Man, Black, Canvas, Defence, Gate, Gun, Help, Insurance, Secure, Slide, Surround, Threaten

Pub
Drink(s) 32.2%
Beer 17.8%
Bar 7.8%
Lunch 4.4%
* 3.3%
Alcohol 3.3%
Crawl 3.3%
Inn 3.3%
Booze 2.2%
Cider 2.2%
House 2.2%
Lager 2.2%
Pint 2.2%
1.1% Act, Bomb, Brown, Club, Distaste, Drunk, Friends, Landlord, Monopoly, People, Smoke, Social

Public
Private 21.4%
Open 16.7%
House 9.5%
* 4.8%
Display 4.8%
Known 4.8%
2.4% Bus, Company, Convenience, Enemy, Everyone, Faces, Hall, Lavatory, Library, People, Perform, Property, Telephone, Toilet, Transport

Publish
Book 66.7%
Print 9.5%
Paper(s) 7.1%
2.4% Books, Dissertation, Distribute, Document, Novel, Printer, Write

Pull
Push 23.4%
Tug 12.8%
Ring 6.4%
String 6.4%
Up 6.4%

Cord 4.3%
Horse 4.3%
2.1% *, Away, Bell, Can, Chain, Chase, Draw, Drawer, Hard, Nose, Open, Out, Release, Rope, Success, Taught, Water

Pulley
Rope 31.2%
Wheel 10.4%
Lever 8.3%
System 8.3%
String 6.2%
* 4.2%
Winch 4.2%
2.1% Chain, Drag, Force, Haul, Heave, Hoist, Jumper, Laundry, Line, Push, Rack, Scullery, Weight

Pulp
Paper 18.8%
Apple 10.4%
Mash 10.4%
Fiction 6.2%
Fruit 6.2%
Mush 6.2%
Orange 6.2%
Wood 6.2%
2.1% Liquid, Marrow, Mashed, Mess, Paste, Pomp, Smoke, Soft, Sugar, Sun, Tooth, Tree, Turnip, Wet

Pulsar
Star 37.5%
* 12.5%
Watch 8.3%
Pulse 6.2%
Quasar 4.2%
Space 4.2%
2.1% Beacon, Beat, Car, CN, Flash, Heart, Lentil, Quartz, Radar, Solar-System, Telstar, Throb

Pump
Water 37.5%
Bike 10.4%
Bicycle 6.2%
Iron 6.2%
Tyre 6.2%
Burst 4.2%
Petrol 4.2%
2.1% Action, Broad, Extract, Gas, Pole, Pull, Punt, Push, Smoke, Up, Vacuum, Volume

Pumpkin
Pie 26.7%
Seed(s) 26.7%
Halloween 20.0%
Fruit 4.4%
Squash 4.4%
2.2% Balloon, Candle, Cinderella, Green, Mark, Orange, Soup, Vegetable

Pun
Joke 64.6%
Word(s) 8.3%
Punt 4.2%
2.1% Fun, Funny, Groan, Intended, Laugh, Poem, Silly, Slow, Three, Wit, Witty

Punch
Hit 33.3%
Judy 8.3%
Fight 6.2%
Suffolk 6.2%
Boxer 4.2%
Drunk 4.2%
Face 4.2%
Fist 4.2%
2.1% Box, Drink, Glove, Hurt, Injure, Kick, Nose, Out, Person, Poke, Rum, Stick, Throat, Thump

Puny
Weak 24.0%
Thin 12.0%
Skinny 8.0%
Small 6.0%
Boy 4.0%
Puny 4.0%
Weakling 4.0%
Wimp 4.0%
2.0% Action, Bastard, Body, Cissy, Girl, Man, Money, Nerd, Short, Slim, Soft, Sparrow, Spineless, Strong, Tiny, Tough, White

Pup
Dog 81.2%
Puppy 4.2%
2.1% Alsatian, Animal, Bitch, Do, Kitten, Small, Young

Pupil
Teacher 25.6%
School 20.9%
Eye(s) 16.3%
Student 9.3%
Boy 4.7%
Teach 4.7%
2.3% Black, Child, Girl, Kid, Lesson, Power, Uniform, Words

Puppet
String(s) 50.0%
Glove 14.6%
Show 6.2%
Dictator 4.2%
2.1% Children, Clown, Dance, Doll, Kids, King, Muppet, Punch, Puppy, Ruler, Sting, Wood

Purple
Colour 16.7%
Red 11.9%
Green 7.1%
Mauve 7.1%
Rain 7.1%
* 4.8%
Blue 4.8%
Pink 4.8%
Prince 4.8%
2.4% Cloak, Dress, Haze, Mountains, Orange, Puce, Rainbow, Ray, Robe, Rome, Royal, Suzy

Purpose
Aim 38.1%
Reason 7.1%
* 4.8%
Function 4.8%
Meaning 4.8%
2.4% All, Being, Built, Cause, Direction, Goal, Idea, Journey, Meaning, None, Object, Objective, Porpoise, Ready, Seal, Sorted, -Ful

Purr
Cat 97.7%
2.3% Joy

Put+
Place 35.4%
Down 22.9%
Get 6.2%
Lay 4.2%
On 4.2%
Take 4.2%
2.1% Back, Book, Give, Laid, Option, Out, Shot, Slot, Stack, There, Up

Pyjamas+
Bed 16.7%
Nightie 11.9%
Sleep 7.1%
Bottoms 4.8%
Nightdress 4.8%
Stripes 4.8%
2.4% Bananas, Bedtime, Bottle, Child, Dad, Dressing-Gown, Funny, Jump, Leg, Naked, Night, Nightshirt, Nighttime, Party, Shirt, Sleeping, Stripy, Time, Trousers, Useless, Why

Pylon+
Electricity 45.2%
Electric 11.9%
Wire 11.9%
Power 7.1%
Cable 4.8%
2.4% Landscape, Line, Male, Motorway, Post, Rod, Telephone, Ugly

Quack+
Duck 77.1%
Doctor 20.8%
2.1% Croak

Quantity
Amount 31.0%
Quality 14.3%
Lot(s) 9.5%
Number 7.1%
A-Lot 4.8%
2.4% Cost, Eggs, Full, Hundred, Large, Loads, Measure, Nothing, Pencils, Shopping, Surveyor, Volume, Water, Weight

Quarrel
Fight 31.2%
Argue 18.8%
Row 12.5%
Argument 6.2%
Shout 6.2%
2.1% *, Chickens, Couple, Family, Fire, Pain, Parents, Quagmire, Quart, Speak, Squirrel, Unhappy

Queen+
King 52.1%
Bee 10.4%
Hearts 4.2%
2.1% *, Anne, Cat, Chess, Country, England, Lord, Monarchy, Poof, Proud, Realm, Royal, Sheba, South, Spades, We

Quick+
Fast 33.3%
March 12.5%
Brisk 10.4%
Dead 8.3%
Slow 6.2%
Hurry 4.2%
2.1% Food, Fox, Nimble, On, Place, Run, Schnell, Speedy, Step, Sudden, Urgent, Walk

Quid+
Pound 61.9%
Money 19.0%
2.4% Cash, Cockney, Done, In, One, Pro, Sin

Quiet
Noisy 11.1%
Silent 11.1%
Loud 8.9%
* 6.7%
Silence 6.7%
Hush 4.4%
Noise 4.4%
Place 4.4%
Soft 4.4%
2.2% Alley, Alone, Call, Calm, Corner, Country, Countryside, Mouse, Now, Profound, Shy, Sly, Still, Talk, Tired, Tranquil

Quit
Leave 30.2%
Stop 14.0%
Smoking 9.3%
Finish 7.0%
End 4.7%
2.3% Cigarettes, Fire, Give-Up, Job, Now, Smoke, Stalling, Start, Stay, Still, Struggle, Terminate, Toad, Trying, Walk

Quiver
Arrow(s) 42.0%
Shake 26.0%
Cold 8.0%
Bow 6.0%
Shiver 4.0%
2.0% Boots, Fear, Feather, Indian, Quake, Still, Wobble

Rabbit+
Hare 12.6%
Bunny 8.0%
Hutch 5.7%
Warren 5.7%
Ear(s) 4.6%
Carrot(s) 3.4%
Hop 3.4%
Lettuce 3.4%
Run 3.4%
* 2.3%
Cage 2.3%
Dog 2.3%
Fox 2.3%
Furry 2.3%
Gun 2.3%
Hole 2.3%
Pie 2.3%
1.2% Animal, Breed, Burrow, Cat, Core, Den, Duck, Easter, Eat, Fast, Fluffy, Food, Fortune, Fur, Hut, Jump, Mammal, Mouse, Pea, Peter, Phone, Rodent, Roger, Snake, Stew, Talk, Tall

Raccoon
Stripe(d) 21.0%
* 8.9%
Tail 8.9%
Animal 6.7%
Hat 6.7%
Black 4.4%
2.2% America, Baboon, Bush, Canada, Cartoon, Claws, Coat, Desert, Dice, Double, Forest, Fridge, Furry, Garbage, Goat, Monkey, Skin, Steal, Tree, Wild

Racehorse
Win 16.0%
Jockey 8.0%
Red-Rum 6.0%
Winner 6.0%
Betting 4.0%
Colours 4.0%
Course 4.0%
Derby 4.0%
Fast 4.0%
Thoroughbred 4.0%
Track 4.0%
2.0% ?, Bet, Betting-Slip, Bookie, Bookmakers, Drugs, Epsom, Fix, Horse, Money, Pitch, Race, Racecourse, Run, Shergar, Speedy, Stallion, Whip

Radish+
Red 19.0%
Salad 14.3%
Lettuce 11.9%
Horse 9.5%
Bitter 4.8%
Hot 4.8%
Vegetable 4.8%
2.4% *, Cabbage, Carrot, Eat, Horrible, Rabbit, Radical, Root, Sandwich, Sauce, Source, Spicy, Tomato

Raft
River 16.3%
Boat 11.6%
Water 9.3%
Dingy 7.0%
Float 7.0%
Wood 7.0%
Logs 4.7%
Sink 4.7%
2.3% Bamboo, Barrels, Beam, Gorge, Huck, Kontiki, Major, Ocean, Oil-Drums, Race, Rapids, Ride, Roof, Sail

Rain+
Fall 14.5%
Wet 12.0%
Forest 8.4%
Snow 7.2%
Drop 4.8%
Shower 4.8%
Storm 4.8%
Water 3.6%
Cloud(s) 2.4%
Hail 2.4%
Shine 2.4%
Umbrella 2.4%
Wind 2.4%
1.2% *, Acid, Dance, Deer, Dirt, Down, Downpour, Drench, Forever, Glasses, Horse, Hour, Jewellery, London, Man, Manchester, Phone, Pour, Purple, Spring, Sun, Supreme, Weather

Raincoat
Wet 17.3%
Mac 9.6%
Umbrella 9.6%
Mack 5.7%
Mackintosh 5.7%
Plastic 5.7%
Ran 5.7%
Hat 3.8%
Jacket 3.8%
1.9% Beige, Belt, Black, Clothes, Dirty, Fall, Greatcoat, Heavy, Man, See-Through, Shelter, Sou'Wester, Trend, Unsure, Water, Weather, Web

Rake+
Garden 28.3%
Hoe 19.6%
Grass 8.7%
Leaves 8.7%
Drill 4.3%
Fork 4.3%
Soil 4.3%
Tool 4.3%
2.2% Earth, Grow, Hay, Lawn, Sapling, Saw, Spade, Turf

Rampage+
Bull 7.1%
Hooligan 7.1%
Drunk 4.8%
Pillage 4.8%
Run 4.8%
Stampede 4.8%
Wild 4.8%
2.4% *, About, Attack, Bedroom, Destroy, Fight, Flames, Force, Forward, Go, Mad, Mess, On, Rampant, Ravage, Riot, RSA, Shout, Siege, Steel, Storm, Streets, Teenage, Through, Tyranny, Warpath

Ran
Away 12.5%
* 8.3%
Run 8.3%
Down 6.3%
Far 6.3%
Fast 4.2%
Home 4.2%
2.1% Arrived, Bosun?, Bus, Dribble, Drown, Fled, Flowed, Hear, Hurry, Japan, Kurosawa, Man, Mile, Off, Out, Pelted, Race, Shoes, Sprint, Sprinted, Through, Tired, To, Walk, Walked

Rang+
Phone 31.0%
Telephone 28.6%
Bell 19.0%
Ring 4.8%
2.4% Called, Dale, Doorbell, Number, Phoned, Rung, Telephoned

Rapid
Fast 31.3%
Quick 18.8%
Fire 10.4%
River 4.2%
Shooting 4.2%
Slow 4.2%
2.1% *, Boat, Drying, Movement, Rapids, Relief, Response, Ride, Rise, Speak, Stream, Test, Wind

Rare
Bird 14.0%
Steak 10.0%
Breed 8.0%
Antique 4.0%
Extinct 4.0%
Uncommon 4.0%
Unknown 4.0%
2.0% Back, Beef, British-Museum, Common, Disease, Earth, Easy, Egg, Elephant, Expensive, Few, Foreign, Jewel, Meat, Money, Odd, Old, Plat, Precious, Radiant, Scarce, Species, Taste, Treat, Unusual, Valuable

Rate+
Tax 18.2%
Poll 9.2%
Speed 6.9%
* 5.7%
Exchange 4.6%
House 3.4%
Pay 3.4%
Payer 3.4%
Grade 2.3%
Inflation 2.3%
Interest 2.3%
Rape 2.3%
Rise 2.3%
1.1% Blue, Book, Bus, Change, Charges, Cry, Degree, Expensive, Fast, Growth, Heat, Highly, Mark, Measure, Monetary, Monument, Order, Payment, Percent, Pressing, Price, Rake, Rates, Rent, Slope, Time, Toll, View, Way

Raven
Black 47.9%
Bird 25.0%
Crow 8.3%
* 4.2%
Tower 4.2%
2.1% Blackbird, Hair, Haired, Shaven, Vixen

Raw
Meat 26.7%
Edge 13.3%
Cooked 11.1%
Egg(s) 8.9%
Fish 6.7%
Sewage 6.7%
Red 4.4%
Sore 4.4%
2.2% Bone, Cage, Carrots, Deal, Empty, Ripe, Steak, Uncooked

Razor+
Blade 37.0%
Sharp 26.1%
Shave 17.4%
Cut 8.7%
2.2% Brush, Edge, Hair, Soap, Stubble

Read
Book(s) 68.1%
Write 14.9%
Newspaper 4.3%
2.1% All, Enjoy, Hard, Learn, Quick, Words

Real
* 12.5%

Life 8.3%
True 8.3%
Thing 6.3%
World 6.3%
Estate 4.2%
False 4.2%
Fantasy 4.2%
Imaginary 4.2%
Unreal 4.2%
2.1% Actual, Apparent, Car, Fishing, Get, Gold, Imagined, Man, Me, Meal, People, Real, Reality, Reel, Surreal, Time, To, Virtual

Realm
Kingdom 21.4%
* 14.3%
King 9.5%
Fantasy 4.8%
Queen 4.8%
2.4% Area, Chaos, Company, Consciousness, Darkness, God, Hope, Land, Monarchy, Opportunity, Reason, Regal, Regime, Ruler, Senses, Space, Vision, Womans, World

Rearrange+
Tidy 14.3%
Change 11.9%
Order 7.1%
Furniture 4.8%
Move 4.8%
Organise 4.8%
2.4% Bring, Construct, Disorder, Fix, Flowers, Muddle, No, Objects, Pedantic, Permutate, Put-Up, Random, Realign, Reapply, Reorganize, Replace, Restructure, Sane, Shape, Shuffle, Sort, Suit

Reason
Why 14.0%
Excuse 11.6%
* 9.3%
Cause 4.7%
Doubt 4.7%
For 4.7%
Logic 4.7%
Mind 4.7%
Thought 4.7%
2.3% Age-Of, Because, Belief, Explanation, Head, Idea, Line, Motive, Rational, Reasonable, Rhyme, Science, Sense, Think, -Ing

Rebirth+
New 11.9%
Reincarnation 9.5%
Religion 9.5%
Born-Again 7.1%
Christian 7.1%
Renaissance 7.1%
Again 4.8%
Born 4.8%
Death 4.8%
2.4% Anew, Awaken, Begin, Con, Devil, Live, Reborn, Revival, Start, Therapy, To, Transfigure, Upsurge, What

Rebuild+
Construct 9.5%
House(s) 9.5%
Again 7.1%
* 4.8%
Bricks 4.8%
City 4.8%
Erect 4.8%
Fallen 4.8%
Reconstruct 4.8%
Renovate 4.8%
2.4% Bomb, Castle, Demolish, Destroy, Down, Jerusalem, M, Mend, Reconstruct, Remake, Repair, Ruin, Start, Structure, Tower, Up, Wall

Receipt
Bill 19.5%
Money 14.6%
Till 14.6%
Shop(s) 12.2%
Paper 7.3%
Ticket 7.3%
* 4.9%
2.4% Cheque, Gift, Invoice, Note, Paper, Rubbish, Tab, Voucher, Wares

Recent
New 18.0%
Past 14.0%
Event(s) 10.0%
* 6.0%
Death 6.0%
Now 6.0%
Soon 6.0%
Current 4.0%
Near 4.0%
Old 4.0%
Time(s) 4.0%
Today 4.0%
2.0% About, History, Issue, Just, Last, Late, Lately

Recoil+
Horror 11.9%
Back 7.1%
Remember 7.1%
Gun 4.8%
Snake 4.8%
2.4% Abhor, Avoid, Away, Backwards, Coil, Curl, Dismay, Draw, Fear, Go, Hide, Hose, Jump, Reject, Repel, Repugnant, Repulse, Retrieve, Return, Rope, Shrink, Shun, Shy-Away, Take, Terror, Uncurl, XXX

Recollect+
Remember 64.3%
Recall 21.4%
Memory 7.1%
2.4% Old, Stay, Time

Recollection
Memory 50.0%
Remember 19.0%
Dream 4.8%
Thought(s) 4.8%
2.4% *, Money, Natter, Of, Past, Plato, Recall, Remembrance, Tin

Record+
Tape 52.4%
Write 7.1%
Cassette 4.8%
Music 4.8%
Play 4.8%
2.4% Deliver, Disk, File, Noise, Playback, Pop, Register, Remember, Replay, Turntable, Voice

Record-player
Record 15.6%
Disk/c(s) 13.3%
Music 13.3%
Stereo 8.9%
Sound 6.7%
Compact-Disc 4.4%
Gramophone 4.4%
Tune 4.4%
2.2% *, Armature, Disc-Player, Electric, Loud, Old-Fashioned, Play, Player, Playing, Tape, Turn, Turntable, Up

Recycle+
Paper 33.3%
Green 11.9%
Waste 11.9%
Reuse 9.5%
Bottle 4.8%
Conserve 4.8%
Rubbish 4.8%
2.4% Change, Ecology, Fix, Food, Garbage, Misuse, Refresh, Remake, Save

Redress+
Balance 40.5%
* 11.9%
Amend 4.8%
Rebalance 4.8%
2.4% Address, Again, Angry, Back, Clothes, Come, Fix, Justice, Rectify, Refer, Rejoice, Repay, Stop, Take, Talk, Try

Reform+
Change 15.2%
School 15.2%
Law(s) 8.7%
Amend 4.3%
Mend 4.3%
Renew 4.3%
2.2% *, Army, Better, Bill, Borstal, Changed, Club, Courts, Government, House, Justice, Make, Movement, Oil, Party, Prison, Prisoner, Refer, Remake, Repeal, State, Straight

Refresh+
Drink 23.8%
Clean 7.1%
Memory 7.1%
Water 7.1%
* 4.8%
Wash 4.8%
2.4% Awaken, Battle, Break, Cleanse, Flowers, Fresh, Freshen, Lavender, New, Parts, Refreshing, Remind, Renew, Replenish, Revive, Screen, Sleep, Tea, You

Refuge+
Home 14.3%
Shelter 14.3%
Hide 9.5%
Hiding 9.5%
Asylum 4.8%
Escape 4.8%
Women 4.8%
2.4% Assurance, Camp, Dustbin, Gee, Haven, Hidden, Hideaway, Hole, Homeless, Hostage, Hut, Poor, Prisoners, Sinner, Tip, Women's

Refund+
Money 59.5%
Return 11.9%
Give 7.1%
2.4% *, Expend, Gift, Insurance, Pay, Rebate, Shop, Tax, Voucher

Reign
Queen 42.6%
King 25.5%
Rule 6.4%
* 4.3%
Over 4.3%
2.1% Acid, Crown, Deer, Emperor, Houses, Kingdom, Monarch, Monarchy

Rejoice+
Happy 23.8%
Celebrate 16.7%
Sing 9.5%
Glad 7.1%
Happiness 4.8%
Joy 4.8%

2.4% And, Denial, Exult, Good, Hymns, Laugh, Lord, Love, Merry, Parties, Praise, Tidings, Wow, Xmas

Rejoin+
* 14.3%
Mend 7.1%
Back 4.8%
Connect 4.8%
Gather 4.8%
Together 4.8%
2.4% Adjunct, Amend, Circle, Club, Conflate, Divide, Gain, Give, Glue, Join, Leave, Link, Link-Up, Marry, Meet, Partake, Rejoice, Replete, Return, Reunite, Stick, Stitch, Take, Union, Unite

Relax+
Sleep 11.9%
Bath 7.1%
* 4.8%
Easy 4.8%
Rest 4.8%
Sit 4.8%
2.4% Arms, Bed, Breathe, Calm, Chair, Coffee, Cram, Do, Ease, Enjoy, Hollywood, Lay, Massage, Muscle, Quiet, Rejoin, Release, Relieve, Remain, Repent, Soft, Stretch, Submit, Tea, Tense, Unwind

Release+
Free 25.0%
Freedom 7.1%
Let-Go 6.0%
Prisoner 4.8%
* 3.6%
Go 3.6%
Hostage(s) 3.6%
Leave 3.6%
Let 3.6%
Allow 2.4%
Drop 2.4%
Left 2.4%
Let-Out 2.4%
Prison 2.4%
1.2% Acoustic, Away, Capture, End, Escape, Escaped, Fly, Freed, Frustrate, Gentle, Give, Guildford, Him, Open, Out, Pinger, Relieved, Reprieve, Rescue, Slip, Throw, Urge, Welcome

Relic+
Old 38.1%
Ancient 11.9%
Antique 4.8%
Artifact 4.8%
Remain 4.8%
Ruin 4.8%
2.4% Cathedral, Death, Derelict, Engine, Fossil, Holy, Leftover, Religious, Remains, Saint, Site, Treasure, Wreck

Relief+
Sigh 11.9%
* 7.1%
Aid 4.8%
Headache 4.8%
Pain 4.8%
Relax 4.8%
2.4% Ache, Air, Blessed, Chiefs, Comic, Disaster, Ease, Felt, Field, Glad, Gratitude, Help, Hope, Hostage, Joy, Oh, OK, Phew, Piss, Pleasure, Release, Relieve, Rest, Siege, Thank, Toilet

Religion
Faith 15.6%
Church 13.3%
God 11.1%
Catholic 8.9%
Cross 6.7%
2.2% *, Christianity, Creed, Halo, Islam, Life, Mad, Museum, Mysticism, No, Nun, Oppression, Priest, Sheep, Spirit, Truth, Vicar, War, Weak

Relish+
Sauce 19.0%
Delight 14.3%
Burger 7.1%
Enjoy 7.1%
Like 7.1%
Love 7.1%
Corn 4.8%
Horseradish 4.8%
Tomato 4.8%
2.4% *, Chutney, Cucumber, Food, Lettuce, Nice, Pickle, Radish, Salad, Taste

Remain
Stay 54.2%
Still 6.3%
* 4.2%
Behind 4.2%
2.1% Alive, Coffin, Keen, Left, Put, Quiet, Remainder, Rest, Seated, Stay-Behind, There, Together, Vain, Wait, With

Remark+
Comment 35.6%
Say 11.1%
* 6.7%
Able 6.7%
Mention 4.4%
Notice 4.4%
2.2% Exclamation, Gossip, His, Insult, Make, Note, Observation, Pen, Rebuke, Remarkable, Speak, Stated, Think, Wrong

Remarry+
Divorce 54.8%
Again 7.1%
No 4.8%
Wife 4.8%
2.4% A, Couple, Fear, Happiness, Love, Make, Marry, Reclaim, Ring, Second, Why, Widow

Remember+
Forget 24.4%
Memory 13.3%
Recall 7.8%
* 4.4%
Think 4.4%
Past 3.3%
To 3.3%
Everything 2.2%
Me 2.2%
Mind 2.2%
November 2.2%
Well 2.2%
Word(s) 2.2%
1.1% Brain, Date, Desire, Dream, Elephant, Fifth, It, Knot, Learn, Memoirs, Mnemonics, Never, Nothing, Now, Recollect, Reflect, Remind, Scheme, Sunday, Thoughts, Time, Unforgettable, What, Who

Remind+
Remember 33.3%
Tell 11.9%
Forget 7.1%
Memory 7.1%
Library 4.8%
Me 4.8%
2.4% *, Acknowledge, Again, Letter, Memo, Nag, Note, Pluck, Prompt, Register, Remit, Stress, You

Remodel+
Remake 14.3%
Change 9.5%
Make 9.5%
Reshape 9.5%
Build 4.8%
Car 4.8%
New 4.8%
Revamp 4.8%
2.4% *, Again, Boat, Building, Computer, Decorate, Fit, Plasticine, Rebuild, Reform, Renovate, Restructure, Sculpt, Shape, Wax, Window

Remote
Control 44.0%
Far 10.0%
Island 10.0%
Distant 6.0%
Near 6.0%
2.0% *, ?, Alone, Cold, Faraway, Hill-Top, Lonely, Own, Peninsular, Place, Sensor, Skye

Remove
Take 37.5%
Take-Away 18.8%
Van 8.3%
2.1% *, Belongings, Chair, Clothes, Clothing, Delete, Furniture, Out, Reconciliate, Removal, Rid-Of, Steal, Trousers, Undress, Wart, Wipe

Rent
Money 16.0%
Boy 14.0%
House 14.0%
Pay 10.0%
Book 6.0%
Flat 4.0%
Rates 4.0%
Tear 4.0%
2.0% Appeal, Arrears, Attic, Borrow, Cheque, Cost, Hole, Home, Key, Let, Living, Mortgage, Pain, Tenant

Rental+
TV 32.6%
Television 13.0%
Car(s) 10.9%
Hire 8.7%
Radio 6.5%
Flat 4.3%
Lend 4.3%
Pay 4.3%
Van 4.3%
2.2% *, Agreement, Change, Rate, Video

Repair+
Mend 47.6%
Fix 19.0%
Car 9.5%
Man 7.1%
2.4% Bike, Cars, Correct, Damage, Puncture, Remake, Washing

Repeal+
* 11.9%
Appeal 9.5%
Law(s) 9.5%
Stop 7.1%
Change 4.8%
Plea 4.8%
Withdraw 4.8%
2.4% Abolish, Ask, Attack, Cancel, Corn, Court, Forgive, Give, Go, Help, Kill, Live, Plead, Release, Remove, Renege, Repeat, Take, Top, Try

Repeat+
Again 69.0%

Twice 4.8%
2.4% Beat, Boring, Enunciate, It, Iterate, Often, Phrase, Reiterate, Repeat, Repetitive, Word

Report+
Tell 14.3%
Paper 11.9%
School 11.9%
News 7.1%
* 4.8%
Bad 4.8%
Newspaper 4.8%
Reporter 4.8%
2.4% Bore, Crime, Document, Essay, Journalist, Note, Official, Police, Sneak, Sports, Story, Talk, Term, Write, Written

Reprint+
Book 14.3%
Again 11.9%
Paper 7.1%
Copy 4.8%
Edit 4.8%
Publish 4.8%
2.4% *, Article, Computer, Edition, New, Newspaper, Of, Pages, Photo, Press, Redo, Reissue, Release, Republish, Request, Restart, Rewrite, Science, Type, Write, Wrong

Request+
Ask 66.7%
Demand 4.8%
Please 4.8%
2.4% Beg, Dance, Denied, Deny, Plead, Recall, Record, Require, Requisition, Suggestion

Reside+
Live 73.8%
Dwell 4.8%
Home 4.8%
Stay 4.8%
2.4% Abide, House, Over, Queen, Sit

Resign+
Leave 26.2%
* 7.1%
Give-Up 7.1%
Out 7.1%
Quit 7.1%
End 4.8%
Work 4.8%
2.4% Allow, Cabinet, Disown, Give, Give-In, Immediately, Lawson, Minister, Move, Off, Post, Sacked, Stop, Towel, Wait

Respect
* 10.4%
Yourself 8.3%
Me 6.3%
Admire 4.2%
Love 4.2%
2.1% Adult, Authority, Behaviour, Cove, Dignity, Disrespect, Due, Enough, Fist, For, Friend, Give, Grateful, Honour, It, Judge, Like, Mother, Normski, No-One, Obey, People, Regard, Revere, Reverence, Rings, Senior, Spectacle, Suspect, Tall, Us, You

Rest
Sleep 27.1%
Relax 6.3%
Bed 4.2%
Run 4.2%
Still 4.2%
Tired 4.2%
2.1% *, Assured, Breather, Chair, Couch, Exercise, Holiday, Less, Lie, Lie-Down, Music, Others, Play, Remain, Repose, Room, Slumber, Snooze, Sofa, Stay, Stop, Up, Well, With

Restore+
Fix 9.5%
Old 7.1%
Clean 4.8%
House 4.8%
Order 4.8%
Rebuild 4.8%
2.4% Antique, Back, Bring, Building, Chair, Change, Church, Computer, Conservation, Conserve, Faith, Furniture, Give, Glory, Hair, Health, New, Number, Paint, Painting, Regain, Renew, Renovate, Repair, Revamp, Save, Work

Restrain+
Hold 33.3%
Stop 11.9%
Control 4.8%
Hold-Back 4.8%
Leash 4.8%
Withhold 4.8%
2.4% Back, Bra, Dog, Fight, Force, Horse, Lead, Order, Prevent, Pull, Restrict, Stake, Tie, Tie-Up, Trouble

Result
End 18.0%
Score 14.0%
Exam 10.0%
Outcome 8.0%
Test 6.0%
Football 4.0%
2.0% Conclusion, Consequence, Experiment, Fail, Final, Finding, Finish, Full-Time, Goal, Great, In, Maths, Numbers, Of, Product, School, Section, Try, Wait, Win

Retail+
Shop 26.2%
Price 19.0%
Sell 19.0%
Sale 7.1%
Wholesale 4.8%
2.4% Makers, Management, Manufacture, Outlet, Profit, Salesman, Selling, Store, Tailor, Value

Retreat+
Back 9.5%
Hide 7.1%
Army 6.0%
* 4.8%
Go 4.8%
Leave 4.8%
Return 4.8%
Run 4.8%
Advance 2.4%
Away 2.4%
Backwards 2.4%
Back-Off 2.4%
Battle 2.4%
Flee 2.4%
Forward 2.4%
Home 2.4%
Lose 2.4%
Withdraw 2.4%
1.2% Attack, Bomb, Conquer, Drawback, End, Fall, Go-Away, Go-Back, Hideout, Holiday, Holy, Hovel, Loss, Monastery, Nun, Out, Refuge, Retire, Retract, Reverse, Safety, Scared, Surrender, Tactical, Turnback, Walk, War

Retrieve+
Find 23.8%
Fetch 19.0%
Get 19.0%
Dog 7.1%
Take 7.1%
Return 4.8%
2.4% Get-Back, Log, Look, Lost, Pheasant, Regain, Remove, Where

Return+
Back 11.9%
Give 7.1%
Native 7.1%
Again 4.8%
Go 4.8%
Home 4.8%
Key 4.8%
Retrieve 4.8%
Ticket 4.8%
2.4% *, A, Button, Carriage, Come, Escape, Fare, Give-Back, Journey, King, Letter, Post, Prodigal, Reply, Retreat, Revisit, Stage, Supply, Train

Reunion+
Meeting 19.0%
Friend(s) 9.5%
Meet 9.5%
Party 9.5%
School 9.5%
Together 7.1%
Join 4.8%
2.4% *, Age, Back, Class, Erasure, Family, Gather, Get, Happy, Marriage, Old, Pals, Uni

Revision+
Work 21.7%
Exam(s) 17.4%
Study 8.7%
Homework 6.5%
Learn 4.3%
2.2% *, A, Agh, Boring, Correct, Depression, Desk, Heck, Horrible, Night, Redo, Renew, Review, Revise, Rewrite, Swotting, Tedious, Try, Write

Revolve
Turn 27.1%
Spin 14.6%
Door(s) 10.4%
Around 8.3%
Gun 6.2%
* 4.2%
Fan 4.2%
Round 4.2%
2.1% Chair, Circus, Go-Round, Green, LP, Move, Rotate, Take, Turn-Around, Wheel

Rewrite+
Book 10.9%
Draft 6.5%
Work(s) 4.4%
Again 4.3%
Change 4.3%
Correct 4.3%
Edit 4.3%
Essay 4.3%
Revise 4.3%
Script 4.3%
Start 4.3%
2.2% *, Amend, Better, Boring, Chance, Corrections, Lines, Play, Redo, Redraft, Redraw, Rehash, Rephrase, Review, Rewind, Rework, Story, Summary, Write

Rhino
Horn 37.8%
Animal 6.7%

* 6.7%
Big 4.4%
Charge 4.4%
Elephant 4.4%
Mud 4.4%
Safari 4.4%
2.2% Africa, Bush, Grey, Hide, Horny, Jungle, Lion, Rhino, Veldt, Wild, Wrinkly, Zoo

Ribs
Bone(s) 14.9%
Cage 14.9%
Spare 12.8%
Chest 8.5%
Barbecue 6.4%
Break 6.4%
Meat 6.4%
Body 4.3%
Food 4.3%
Tickle 4.3%
2.1% Adam, Beef, Eat, Empty, Food, Knuckle, Skin, Skinny

Rich
Poor 38.7%
Money 12.9%
Wealthy 8.6%
Man 6.5%
Bastard(s) 4.3%
* 2.2%
1.1% Aunt, Bitch, Chocolate, Colours, Er, Fat, Filthy, Food, Fruity, Full, Gold, Grandeur, Happy, Kids, Maxwell, Millions, Overpowering, People, Perspective, Queen, Rob, Small, Success, Tart, Tea

Richard
* 16.3%
Harris 12.2%
The-Third 12.2%
Branson 6.1%
Harrison 6.1%
Cliff 4.1%
Ford 4.1%
2.0% Adam, Bornat, Boy, Briers, Coote, Dad, Dreyfus, Harvey, Innuendo, Irvine, John, Jones, Keith, King, Lennon, Nothing, O'Brien, Wagner

Rick
Mayall 28.6%
* 22.9%
Astley 16.3%
Wakeman 8.2%
2.0% Bar, Boy, Brick, Hay, James, Name, Nelson, Newton, Parfitt, Rent, Shaw, Young-Man

Rid+
* 16.7%
Away 9.5%
Get 9.5%
Gone 7.1%
Lose 4.8%
Of 4.8%
2.4% Bin, Cure, Disease, Dispose, Drive, Dump, Eradicate, Excise, Good, Jar, Off, Relieve, Remove, Ride, Rim, Rubbish, Throw, Throwaway, Top, Waste

Ride+
Horse 42.9%
* 7.1%
Bike 4.8%
Up 4.8%
2.4% Angry, Bus, Elevate, Fall, Horses, Lift, Moan, Narrow, Rage, Rant, Sex, Snake, Struggle, Swim, Turn, Twist, Wriggle

Rider
Horse 51.2%
Bike 12.2%
Horseman 7.3%
Jockey 4.9%
2.4% *, Cavalier, Competition, Cowboy, Easy, Jilly-Cooper, Motorbike, Romance, Series, Shaun, Storm

Right
Wrong 52.4%
Left 19.0%
Hand 7.1%
On 7.1%
2.4% Answer, Correct, Fine, Lane, Opportunity, Up

Rigid
Stiff 44.4%
Hard 6.7%
Solid 6.7%
Flexible 4.4%
Straight 4.4%
2.2% *, Balloon, Cold, Conservative, Control, Erect, Firm, Fixed, Frigid, Girder, Inflexible, Rough, Sharp, Start

Ring
Finger 17.8%
Wedding 11.1%
Bell 8.9%
Round 8.9%
Call 6.7%
Diamond 4.4%
Gold 4.4%
Telephone 4.4%
2.2% Bile, Boxer, Bracelet, Bride, Circle, Doorbell, Hand, Jewellery, Married, Marry, Noise, Phone, Water, Widow, Worm

Rinse
Hair 29.8%
Clean 8.5%
Wash 8.5%
Out 6.4%
Clothes 4.3%
Mouth 4.3%
Off 4.3%
2.1% *, Aid, Away, Basin, Bath, Blue, Cleanse, Shampoo, Soap, Spin, Suds, Taps, Through, Washing, Water

Rise
Sun 18.6%
Up 16.3%
Fall 7.0%
Above 4.7%
Bread 4.7%
Get-Up 4.7%
Hill 4.7%
2.3% *, Arisen, Day, Dough, Elevate, Float, Follow, High, Hole, Kneel, Lift, Morning, Power, Raise, Ride, Shine, Tide

Risk
Danger 22.2%
Chance 6.7%
Gamble 6.7%
Take 6.7%
Taker 6.7%
Dare 4.4%
Taking 4.4%
2.2% Adventure, Bad, Business, Caught, Change, Company, Dangerous, Dice, Factor, Give, High, Live, Math, Probability, Security, Small, That, Tricky, Your

Roach
Cock- 19.2%
Cockroach 9.6%
Fish 9.6%
* 5.7%
Beetle 5.7%
Insect 5.7%
? 3.8%
Paper 3.8%
Spliff 3.8%
1.9% Broach, Bug, Card, Cigarette, Coach, Drugs, End, Hash, Joint, Kitchen, Material, Morocco, Perch, Spider, Stamp, Ugh

Roar
Lion 68.0%
Loud 10.0%
Sea 4.0%
2.0% *, Crowd, Growl, Lad, Mouth, Noise, Shout, Thunder, Tiger

Rob
Steal 42.6%
Bank 10.6%
Blind 4.3%
2.1% *, Burglar, Burglary, Gun, House, Jewelery, Jim, Mugger, Neighbours, Nick, Rachael, Roy, Run, Slob, Someone, Strip, Take, Theft, Thieve

Rock
Stone 38.1%
And-Roll 4.8%
Granite 4.8%
Hard 4.8%
Roll 4.8%
Sea 4.8%
2.4% *, Ages, Baby, Boat, Box, Brighton, Climbing, Concert, Cradle, Face, Grey, Hardplace, Island, Mountain, Music, Sway

Rocket
Ship 18.6%
Moon 11.6%
Man 9.3%
Sky 9.3%
Fire 7.0%
Launch 7.0%
Fireworks 4.7%
Missile 4.7%
Space 4.7%
2.3% Danger, Explosion, Fuel, Pocket, Power, Propelled, Ruse, Scientist, Spaceship, Strip

Rocking chair
Granny 13.3%
Old 8.9%
Cushion 6.7%
Grandma 6.7%
Rock 6.7%
Wood 6.7%
* 4.4%
Porch 4.4%
Seat 4.4%
2.2% Bamboo, Blanket, Calm, Creak, Gran, Grandfather, Grandmother, Lounge, Sit, Sitting Room, Sleep, Sight, Slug, Soothing, Stable, Swing

Rodent+
Rat(s) 71.4%
Mouse 7.1%
2.4% Animal, Cat, Crocodile, Dirt, Hamster, Rabbit, Roland, Smell, Verminous

Roller-skate
Wheel(s) 20.0%
Ice 8.9%
Rink 8.9%
Fall 6.7%
Skateboard 6.7%
* 4.4%
Child 4.4%
Fast 4.4%
2.2% Ball, Cities, Drift, Feet, Floor, Game, Man,

Movement, Park, Path, Road, Rolling board, Skid, Skinny, Slide, Snake

Rolling pin
Pastry 33.3%
Dough 8.9%
Flour 6.7%
Kitchen 6.7%
Bread 4.4%
Cake 4.4%
Flatten 4.4%
Hit 4.4%
2.2% Apron, Bake, Beat, Coat, Cook, Cooking, Flat, Mice, Mother, Roll, Round, Wood

Romance
Love 31.7%
Novel 14.6%
Book(s) 4.9%
Flowers 4.9%
Marriage 4.9%
Mills-&-Boon 4.9%
2.4% Beauty, Coleridge, Fantasy, Happy, Heart, Holiday, Kiss, Lover, Mush, Passion, Place, Rose, Stone, Thriller, Wedding

Ronald
Reagan 73.5%
Mcdonald 16.3%
X 4.1%
2.0% Dan, Prick, Rat

Rooster
Hen 20.6%
Crow(s) 14.9%
Cock 13.8%
Cockerel 12.6%
Chicken 10.3%
Red 9.1%
Morning 5.7%
Bird 2.3%
Dawn 2.3%
Farm 2.3%
1.1% *, Feathers, Left, Noise, Sleep, Song

Rope+
Hang 26.1%
String 10.9%
Twine 8.7%
Knot 6.5%
Tie 6.5%
Hanging 4.3%
2.2% *, Boat, Climber, Cut, Hemp, Ladder, Lasso, Macrame, Money, Old, Outward, Pull, Pulley, Sails, Swing, Thick

Rose
Thorn(s) 20.0%
Petal 10.0%
Flower 8.0%
Red 8.0%
Smell 8.0%
Bud 6.0%
Bush 6.0%
Garden 6.0%
Hip 6.0%
Pink 4.0%
2.0% ?, Beauty, Ceiling, Dragonfly, Lily, Mother, Name, Sweet, Water

Rosebud
Flower 16.7%
Petal 10.4%
Citizen-Kane 6.3%
Pink 6.3%
Film 4.2%
Kane 4.2%
Scent 4.2%
Smell 4.2%
2.1% ?, Beautiful, Bloom, Blooming, Blossom, Cinderella, Cottage, Delivery, Flame, Flowering, Jelly, May, Movie, Orson-Welles, Red, Romance, Small, Sweet, Thorn, Tight, Welles

Rot
Wood 14.9%
Decay 10.6%
Apple 4.3%
Green 4.3%
Mouldy 4.3%
2.1% Cabbage, Damp, Death, Decompose, Die, Dry, Earth, Egg, Fester, Flesh, Food, Fruit, Fungi, Garden, Hell, High, Jot, Leaves, Mushroom, Old, Politics, Putrid, Rubbish, Smell, Smelly, Snot, Stink, Stump, Weed

Rotate
Spin 32.6%
Turn 32.6%
Around 4.7%
Circle 4.7%
Round 4.7%
2.3% Arm, Blade, Fan, Finger, Helicopter, Planet, Screw, Space, Washing-Line

Rough
Smooth 40.5%
Ready 9.5%
Ground 4.8%
2.4% Cut, Dog, Hands, House, Justice, Patchy, Sandpaper, Sea, Sex, Sleep, Sore, Stuff, Surface, Terrain, Trade, Violent, Weather, Windy, Work

Round
Ball 31.0%
Circle 21.4%
Table 9.5%
Corner 7.1%
Shape 4.8%
2.4% About, Bowl, Face, Hole, Mulberry-Bush, Small, Smooth, Soft, Square, Wheel, Yellow

Row
Boat 40.0%
Argue 15.6%
Argument 15.6%
Fight 6.7%
Seat(s) 4.4%
2.2% *, Angry, Beach, Fast, Oars, Over, Race, Shout

Row+
Boat 28.6%
Column 14.3%
Seats 9.5%
Houses 4.8%
2.4% Classroom, Cod, Cold, Deer, Fish, Group, Hard, Mornings, Oar, Paddle, River, Run, Sea, Snail, Stream, Terrace, Theatre, Trees

Rub
Down 8.0%
Ointment 8.0%
Out 8.0%
Hard 6.0%
* 4.0%
A-Dub-Dub 4.0%
Oil 4.0%
Polish 4.0%
2.0% Brass, Cream, Dub, Eyes, Finger, Genie, Good, Hamlet, Here, Horse, Hub, Itch, Mark, Massage, Neck, On, Rubber, Salt, Scrub, Shake, Shoulder, Smooth, Tub, Tummy, Vicks, Warmth, Wrong

Rubbish bin
Rubbish 15.6%
Smell 11.1%
Trash 8.9%
Bag 4.4%
Garbage 4.4%
Sack 4.4%
Smelly 4.4%
* 4.4%
2.2% Bin, Bin Men, Black, Black Bag, Can, Christmas, Chuck, Dustbin, Eggs, Full, Kitchen, Mess, My Bedroom, Out, Park, Pedal Bin, Stink, Street, Waste

Ruby+
Red 21.4%
Diamond 14.3%
Wax 14.3%
Gem 9.5%
Jewel 7.1%
Stone 7.1%
* 4.8%
Ring 4.8%
Tuesday 4.8%
2.4% Anniversary, Precious, Sapphire, Wealth

Rug
Carpet 31.0%
Mat 19.0%
Floor 7.1%
Big 4.8%
2.4% *, Afghanistan, Bear, Blanket, Cloth, Cushion, Fire, Green, Leopard, Persian, Rag, Raggy, Turkish, Wool, Woolly, Woven

Rugby
* 22.4%
Ball 16.3%
Field 6.1%
Player 6.1%
Football 4.1%
Scrum 4.1%
Sport 4.1%
Union 4.1%
2.0% England, Game, Hall, Hate, League, New-Zealand, No, Pitch, Red, School, Shirt, Sweat, Team, Test, Violent, World-Cup

Ruin
Castle 15.6%
Destroy 15.6%
Building 8.9%
Break 4.4%
Pompeii 4.4%
Remains 4.4%
Stone 4.4%
2.2% *, Ancient, Brag, Build, Corrupt, Damage, Debris, End, Finished, Life, Mend, Mother, Repair, Road, Rome, Rubble, Trash, Wreck

Rule
Law 11.1%
Of-Thumb 11.1%
* 8.9%
Ruler 8.9%
Line 6.7%
Break 4.4%
Out 4.4%
Reign 4.4%
2.2% Authority, Badly, Book, Command, Country, Desk, Govern, Governed, Guard, King, Over, Paper, Protractor, Regulation, School, Tape, World

Ruler
Straight 22.2%
Pencil 13.3%
King 11.1%
Line(s) 11.1%
Measure 8.9%

Pen 4.4%
School 4.4%
Wood 4.4%
2.2% Above, Leader, Maths, Plastic, Rubber, Rule, Sovereign, Walk

Rumour
Gossip 26.2%
Whisper 14.3%
* 4.8%
Lie 4.8%
Story 4.8%
2.4% Factory, False, Heard, Hint, Hoax, Message, Monger, Rigourous, Riot, Rumour, Scandal, Spread, Started, Tale, Tell, True, Truth, Try, Vicious

Run
Walk 26.1%
Fast 14.1%
Away 10.9%
Legs 5.4%
Jog 4.3%
Hide 3.3%
Jump 3.3%
Out 3.3%
Race 3.3%
Sprint 3.3%
* 2.2%
Far 2.2%
Mile 2.2%
1.1% Breathless, Dash, Free, Hard, Hurry, Javelin, Leap, Madly, Rabbit, Road, Speed, Sport, Track, Up, Well

Rural
Country 23.8%
Urban 11.9%
Cottage 4.8%
Countryside 4.8%
Home 4.8%
Idyll 4.8%
Landscape 4.8%
2.4% Area, Boredom, England, Environment, Farm, Fields, Health, Land, Life, Past, Pastures, Peaceful, Pretty, Scene, Setting, Town, Tracks

Rush
Run 20.0%
Hurry 15.6%
Hour 8.9%
Reeds 6.7%
Out 4.4%
2.2% About, Air, Around, Fast, Greed, Helter-Skelter, Job, London, Needle, Past, Quick, Rash, Record, Slow, Speed, Through, Traffic, Train, Wind

Sadism
Masochism 12.8%
Pain 10.6%
Masochist 8.5%
* 6.4%
Cruel 6.4%
Whip 6.4%
Bad 4.3%
Hurt 4.3%
Marquis 4.3%
Men 4.3%
Torture 4.3%
2.1% Bondage, Fun, Mad, Marat, Mean, Party, Pervert, Rope, S&M, Saddam, Sadist, Satin, Sick

Sadness
Tears 12.8%
Cry 10.6%
Misery 6.4%
Depression 4.3%
Frown 4.3%
Glum 4.3%
Joy 4.3%
Low 4.3%
Unhappy 4.3%
2.1% *, Awe, Care, Crying, Day, Death, Dismay, Down, Entrenched, Happiness, Happy, Help, Lost, Madness, Melancholy, Miserable, Pain, Pride, Sadness, Sorrow, Unhappiness

Safety
* 11.9%
First 11.9%
Belt 9.5%
Net 9.5%
Danger 4.8%
Health 4.8%
Helmet(s) 4.8%
Pin 4.8%
Seat-Belt 4.8%
2.4% Blanket, Catch, Chair, Conscious, Harness, House, Margin, Numbers, Safe, Security, Valve, Vest, Womb, Workman

Sagacity
* 53.5%
Wisdom 23.3%
Wise 7.0%
Cheek 4.7%
2.3% Calm, Honesty, Insight, Knowledge, Omit

Sailboat
Sea 33.3%
Water 11.1%
Sail(s) 8.9%
Ship 8.9%
Yacht 8.9%
Wind 6.7%
Ocean 4.4%
2.2% Float, Freedom, Lake, Moving, Race, Sailing, Steam, Waves

Sake
God(s) 22.0%
Goodness 14.0%
For 8.0%
* 6.0%
Drink 6.0%
Japan 6.0%
Wine 6.0%
Heaven's 4.0%
Keep 4.0%
Pete's 4.0%
2.0% Case, Christ, Forgive, Hake, His, House, My-Thine, Opinion, Snake, Your

Saloon+
Bar(s) 69.1%
Car 26.2%
2.4% Room, Western

Salt shaker
Pepper 40.0%
* 11.1%
Salt 8.9%
White 4.4%
2.2% Cellar, Container, Cruet, Devil, Food, Glass, Grind, Hole, Kitchen, Mill, Rum, Sjaleshake, Snake, Stuck, Table

Salute+
Army 19.0%
Soldier 11.9%
Greet 6.0%
Wave 4.8%
Flag 3.6%
Hand 3.6%
Hello 3.6%
Military 3.6%
Signal 3.6%
Applaud 2.4%
Captain 2.4%
Colonel 2.4%
General 2.4%
Queen 2.4%
Sailor 2.4%
1.2% Acknowledge, Admire, Attention, Cap, Complement, Encounter, Formal, Guard, Gun, Gunshot, Him, Honour, Italian, Obey, Officer, Police, Rank, Respect, See, Sign, Why, Worship

Sandwich
Bread 17.8%
Eat 13.3%
Lunch 13.3%
Cheese 8.9%
Board 4.4%
Ham 4.4%
2.2% *, Bar, Beef, Bite, Coat, Cucumber, Filling, Food, Lettuce, Marmite, Meat, Nice, Salad, Shop, Spread, Squash, Starch

Sarah
* 17.2%
Brightman 8.2%
Green 8.2%
Jane 6.1%
Smith 6.1%
Ferguson 4.1%
Woman 4.1%
2.0% Abraham, Bennet, Bernhard, Doris, Fergie, Hannah, Harrison, Hunt, Jacobs, Jones, Lee, Love, Miles, Newton, Sahara, Sara, Shepherd, Singer, Sister, Smile, Sweet, Tracie, White

Sarcasm
Wit 27.7%
Irony 10.6%
Humour 8.5%
Funny 6.4%
Joke 6.4%
* 4.3%
Envy 4.3%
Nasty 4.3%
2.1% Annoyance, Block, Canny, Cruel, Cutting, Dislike, Hate, Mean, Rude, Snide, State, Wrong, Yup

Saucepan+
Pot 21.4%
Lid 9.5%
Cook 7.1%
Cooker 7.1%
Pan 7.1%
Food 4.8%
Kettle 4.8%
Oven 4.8%
2.4% *, Bach, Boil, Boiled, Clatter, Cup, Custard, Dinner, Frying, Handle, Kitchen, Spoon, Stove

Saucer+
Cup 66.7%
Tea 9.5%
2.4% *, China, Flying, Food, Milk, Pan, Plate, Saucepan, Utensil

Sausage+
Meat 16.7%
Egg 14.3%
Bacon 7.1%
Chips 7.1%
Mash 7.1%
Pork 7.1%
Roll 4.8%
2.4% Beans, Breakfast, Dog, Eat, Factory, Fry, Frying-Pan, Long, Machine, Meaty, Pig, Potato, Skin, Spider, Yuck

Save
Money 20.9%
Bank 4.7%
Income 4.7%
Invest 4.7%
Life 4.7%
Rescue 4.7%
Seal(s) 4.7%
2.3% *, Coins, Death, Economy, Energy, Face, Goal, Keep, Me, Net, Paper, Prosper, Purpose, Respect, Ring, Spend, Squander, Thrift, Time, UCH, Up, Whales

Savour
Taste 50.0%
Flavour 14.6%
Food 8.3%
* 6.3%
Enjoy 6.3%
2.1% Bud, Meal, Mull, Saint, Salt, Savoury-Rice, Sight

Savoury+
Crisp(s) 13.0%
Tasty 10.9%
Cheese 8.7%
Sweet 8.7%
Taste 8.7%
Biscuit(s) 4.3%
Nice 4.3%
Pie 4.3%
Snack 4.3%
Sour 4.3%
2.2% Cracker, Customer, Delicious, Delight, Eat, Edible, Pig, Rice, Salt, Sausage, Tartlet, Toast, Unsavoury

Saw
See 20.8%
Wood 16.7%
Doctor 12.5%
Mill 12.5%
Chain 4.2%
Cut 4.2%
Tooth 4.2%
2.1% *, Axe, Band, Chisel, Core, Dust, Hack, Log, Metal, Nail, Saw, Screw

Sawmill
Wood 36.5%
* 9.6%
Log(s) 9.6%
Sawdust 9.6%
Dust 3.8%
Saw 3.8%
Tree 3.8%
1.9% Axe, Candyfloss, Country, Countryside, Dusk, Out, Shavings, Teeth, Timber, Tooth, Windmill, Wood-Shavings

Saxophone
Jazz 25.5%
Player 16.3%
Music 14.3%
Brass 6.1%
Trumpet 6.1%
Band 4.1%
Instrument 4.1%
2.0% *, Blues, Day, Groovy, Joke, Melody, Moody, Note, Play, Reed, Silver, Tenor

Say
Speak 25.5%
So 10.6%
Tell 8.5%
Do 6.4%
Said 6.4%
It 4.3%
No 4.3%
Something 4.3%
Talk 4.3%
Word 4.3%
2.1% Again, Hear, More, Nothing, Now, Opinion, Prayer, Sell, State, Utter, Voice

Scaffold+
Building 35.4%
Build 11.0%
Hang 6.1%
Iron 3.7%
Builder 2.4%
Repair 2.4%
Steel 2.4%
Tower 2.4%
1.2% Band, Bars, Board, Brace, Brick, Builders, Buildings, Climb, Construct, Death, Execution, Gibbet, Grad-Pad, Hangman, Head, High, Lift, M, Metal, Plank, Pole, Poles, Rectangle, Redecorate, Scaffolding, Structure, Wooden, Workmen

Scarf
Neck 18.0%
Warm 12.0%
Cold 6.0%
Glove(s) 6.0%
Hat 6.0%
Head 6.0%
Silk 4.0%
Wool 4.0%
Wrap 4.0%
2.0% Checked, Clothes, Dress, Dr-Who, Football, Green, Hot, Knot, Laugh, Long, Muffler, Red, Ronald, Spurs, Tie, Wear, Woolly

Scarlet
Red 44.0%
Pimpernel 16.0%
Fever 8.0%
O'Hara 6.0%
Letter 4.0%
Woman 4.0%
2.0% Black, Bloody, Cloak, Colour, Dress, Errol, Pen, Purple, Whore

Scenery
Tree(s) 21.0%
Landscape 19.0%
Green 9.5%
View 7.2%
* 7.1%
Countryside 7.1%
Picturesque 4.8%
Woods 4.8%
2.4% Beautiful, Change, Fields, Hill, Mountain, Panoramic, Play, Set, Shift,

Scent
Smell 45.8%
Perfume 31.3%
Rose(s) 6.3%
2.1% *, Aroma, Fifth, Flavour, Fragrance, Hideous, Jasmine, Sniffed

Scheme
Plan 26.2%
* 16.7%
Idea 7.1%
Play 7.1%
Plot 4.8%
2.4% Bad, Bonus, Bureaucrat, Business, Con-Man, Cunning, Endless, Insurance, Order, Pension, Roads, Salesman, Schedule, Schemer, Solve, Thought

School
Day 14.6%
College 8.3%
Uniform 8.3%
Teacher 6.3%
Time 6.3%
Book(s) 4.2%
Bus 4.2%
Yard 4.2%
2.1% *, Awful, Bag, Cap, Children, College, Comprehensive, Games, Holiday, Inspector, Learn, Leaver, Lesson, Out, Playground, Project, Shop, Shout, Streatham, Torment, Work

Schoolgirl
Uniform 17.3%
Skirt 11.5%
School 9.6%
Child 7.7%
Teacher 5.7%
* 3.8%
Boy 3.8%
Little 3.8%
Satchel 3.8%
Schoolboy 3.8%
Socks 3.8%
1.9% ?, Flowers, Girlie, Hat, Kid, Kiss, Ma'am, Noisy, Pigtails, Run, Sexy, Tunic, Young

Scooter+
Bike 26.2%
Mod 14.3%
Moped 9.5%
Motorcycle 4.8%
Ride 4.8%
Wheels 4.8%
2.4% Bicycle, Boys, Funfair, Lambretta, Mike, Mobile, Mode, Motor, Motorbike, Pedal, Sleigh, Speed, Toy, Transport, Use

Scoundrel+
Rascal 14.3%
Dog 9.5%
Rogue 9.5%
Cad 7.1%
Rotten 7.1%
Bad 4.8%
Bastard 4.8%
Naughty 4.8%
Rogue 4.8%
Scallywag 4.8%
2.4% *, Bugger, Criminal, Crook, Dirty, Fiend, Pest, Pig, Scally, Thief, Vagabond, Wag

Scratch
Itch 25.6%
Nail(s) 7.0%
Sniff 7.0%
* 4.7%
Arms 4.7%
Card 4.7%
Head 4.7%
Rash 4.7%
2.3% Back, Blood, Car, Enjoyment, Etch, Hands, Harm, Maim, Mark, Neck, Out, Pad, Paint, Post, Puzzle, Scrape

Scream
Shout 17.4%
Yell 13.0%
Loud 8.7%
Cry 6.5%
Fright 4.3%
Murder 4.3%
2.2% *, Dark, Fear, Help, Horror, Howl, Jet, Loudly, Mouth, Noise, Out, Pain, Pierce, Primal, Ream, Shrill, Siren, Up, Whisper, Woman

Screw
Driver 22.2%
Nail(s) 8.9%
Screwdriver 6.7%
Turn 6.7%
* 4.4%
Ball 4.4%
Loose 4.4%
Tight 4.4%
You 4.4%
2.2% Around, Close, Decorating, Enjoy, Fuck, In, Mechanical, Pyramid, Round, Secure, Slot, Spanner, Thumb, Top, Twist

Screwdriver
Screw 20.0%
Turn 17.8%
Nail 15.6%
Drink 6.7%
Tool 6.7%
Wood 6.7%
* 4.4%
Fix 4.4%
2.2% Arm, Bash, Electric, Fascists, Fasten, Mending, Tighten, Useful

Scrub
Clean 29.2%
Brush 10.4%
Floor 6.3%
Wash 6.3%
* 4.2%
Bush 4.2%
Down 4.2%
Soap 4.2%
Up 4.2%
2.1% Away, Bruise, Dry, Ears, Hands, Hard, Land, Off, Rub, Scrubber, Slag, Step, Surgical

Sea
Shore 15.6%
Ocean 11.1%
Side 11.1%
Water 8.9%
Wave(s) 6.7%
Blue 4.4%
Choppy 4.4%
Saw 4.4%
2.2% Calm, Deep, Moving, Print, Sailing, Scape, Shell, Slug, Stormy, Sun, Surround, Swim, Urchin, Weymouth, White

Seabird
Gull 48.0%
Seagull 10.0%
Sea 8.0%
Albatross 6.0%
Cliff 4.0%
Tern 4.0%
2.0% Atlantic, Blue-Skies, Carrier, Egret, Fish, Fulmer, Glide, Nest, Sky, Waves

Seafood
Prawn 18.8%
Crab 6.3%
Fish 6.3%

Shrimp 6.3%
* 4.2%
Oyster(s) 4.2%
Pasta 4.2%
Restaurant 4.2%
Seaweed 4.2%
Shell(s) 4.2%
2.1% Calimares, Casserole, Chowder, Corsica, Dinner, Harbours, Holiday, Horrible, Kelp, Pink, Platter, Shellfish, Shop, Starter, Surprise, Tuna, Water, Yuck

Seahorse
Sea 11.1%
* 8.9%
Fish 6.7%
Water 6.7%
Ride 4.4%
Swim 4.4%
Wave 4.4%
2.2% Beautiful, Beauty, Charming, Coral, Deep, Delicate, Dragon, Dune, Elegant, Fairy Tale, Glide, Green, Salt, Scripture, Seagull, Seawater, Sex, Smart, Tail, Tiny, Toy, Turquoise, Twitch, Underwater

Seal
Sea 13.3%
Skin 13.3%
Pup 8.9%
Grey 6.7%
Animal 4.4%
Wax 4.4%
2.2% *, Album, Ball, Bark, Close, Cold, Elephant, Fish, Flippers, Fur, Ice, Lion, Many, Might, Oil, Sea-Lion, Sing, Swim, Tight, Water, Wrap, Yelp

Seaport
Boat(s) 19.2%
Ship 15.4%
Harbour 13.5%
* 9.6%
Ferry 5.7%
Town 5.7%
Brighton 3.8%
Dock 3.8%
Dover 3.8%
Water 3.8%
1.9% Airport, Biera, Coast, Fish, Hartlepool, Salt, Sea, Slip

Search
Find 21.4%
Look 19.0%
* 11.9%
Seek 9.5%
Light 4.8%
2.4% Captive, Computer, Destroy, Fear, Help, Hunt, Locate, Look-For, Network, Party, Retrieve, Seeker, Serial, Word

Season
Spring 21.4%
Autumn 14.3%
Summer 14.3%
Greeting(s) 9.5%
Winter 9.5%
Ticket 4.8%
Weather 4.8%
Year 4.8%
2.4% *, Cake, Disorder, Last, Man, Pepper, Salt

Seat
Chair 28.9%
Pant(s) 8.9%
Down 6.7%
Bench 4.4%
Bottom 4.4%
Bus 4.4%
Sat 4.4%
Sit 4.4%
2.2% -Ed, Back, Belt, Car, Comfy, Cover, Empty, Hard, Learning, Leather, My, Power, Reserved, Settee, Stand

Second+
First 38.1%
Minute(s) 13.3%
Last 7.1%
Best 4.8%
Out 4.8%
Third 4.8%
Time 4.8%
2.4% *, Confirm, Fight, Hand, Lose, Nature, None, Place, Rate

Secret
Garden 19.0%
Hidden 9.5%
* 4.8%
History 4.8%
Private 4.8%
Quiet 4.8%
Service 4.8%
2.4% Affair, Ballot, Cave, Chocolate, Date, Door, False, Hideaway, Hush, Letter, Lives, Locket, Mystery, Open, Public, Self, Story, Top, Whisper, Wish

Section
Part 39.5%
Piece 9.3%
Off 7.0%
Segment 7.0%
2.3% *, Asylum, Baker, Book, Corner, Cut, Editor, Head, Mad, Of, One, Partition, Quarter, Slice, Society, Table

Security
Safe 19.5%
Lock(s) 12.2%
* 9.8%
Guard(s) 9.8%
Man 9.8%
Bars 4.9%
2.4% Alarm, Baby, Fence, Forces, Number, Peace, Person, Poverty, Prison, Safety, Save, Van, Warmth, Wrapped

Sedate+
Sleep 17.4%
Drug(s) 15.2%
Calm 13.0%
Quiet 10.9%
Asleep 4.3%
Chair 4.3%
Injection 4.3%
Pill(s) 4.3%
2.2% City, Drowsy, Genteel, Hospital, Knock-Out, Ladylike, Medical, Penal, Relaxed, Sad, Serene, Slow

See
Look 22.9%
Eye(s) 14.6%
Hear 10.4%
Saw 8.3%
Clearly 6.3%
* 4.2%
It 4.2%
Notice 4.2%
Sight 4.2%
2.1% Beach, Binoculars, Glance, How, Me, Perceive, Pretty, View, Vision, Well

Seedless+
* 16.7%
Grape(s) 14.3%
Pip(s) 11.9%
Fruit 7.1%
Orange 7.1%
2.4% Empty, Forever, Fruitful, Fruitless, Grass, Impotent, Infertile, Jaffa, Jam, Kings, Plant, Pod, Pulp, Ripe, Seeds, Sterile, Vacuum

Seedy+
* 11.9%
Dirty 7.1%
Bar 4.8%
Dive 4.8%
Sleazy 4.8%
Tacky 4.8%
2.4% Bad, Birds, Dark, Dingy, Down, Film, Grim, Horrible, Hotel, Joint, Lurking, Nasty, Orange, Pub, Run, Scala, Scruffy, Shallow, Shameful, Sick, Sleaze, Slow, Soho, Tomato, Yuk

Seek
Find 27.9%
Hide 20.9%
Look 18.6%
Destroy 7.0%
2.3% Fortune, Friendship, Help, Knowledge, Longingly, Quest, Religion, Search, Seek, Someone, There

Seem
Appear 28.0%
* 6.0%
To 6.0%
Appears 4.0%
Dress 4.0%
Like 4.0%
Look 4.0%
2.0% Almost, Apparent, Be, Believe, Fake, Grasp, Is, Looks, Mean, Reality, Seemly, Smile, So, Stitch, Stress, Such, Team, Together, Trouser, Unsure, Weird, Why

Seesaw
Swing(s) 16.0%
Margery-Daw 14.0%
Playground 14.0%
Park 8.0%
Children 6.0%
Play 6.0%
Child 4.0%
Game 4.0%
Kids 4.0%
Slide 4.0%
Tip 4.0%
2.0% Jigsaw, Play-Park, Ride, Rock, Seaweed, Sit, Topsy-Turvy, Up-Down

Segment+
Orange 33.3%
Piece 26.2%
Part 9.5%
Circle 4.8%
Sector 4.8%
2.4% *, Block, Divide, Portion, Section, Stack, Tangerine, Winter, Worm

Selina
Scott 83.7%
* 6.3%
2.0% Cook, Girl, Moon, Name, Semolina

Sell
Buy 44.7%
House 10.6%
Shop 8.5%
Goods 6.4%
Money 6.4%
Make 4.3%
2.1% Agent, Business, Fast, Own, Seek, Stall, Street, Vend, Vendor

Send
Letter 32.6%
Post 14.0%
Money 9.3%
Mail 7.0%
Go 4.7%
Home 4.7%
2.3% Back, Dismiss, Dispatch, Envelope, Envoy, Luck, Prophet, Push, Remit, Telegram, To, Up

Senior
Citizen 26.2%
Junior 11.9%
Elder 9.5%
Service 9.5%
Old 7.1%
Older 7.1%
Prefect 4.8%
2.4% *, Dad, Granny, Nurse, Officer, Partner, Pensioner, Person, Prom, Respect

Sense
Smell 22.9%
* 12.5%
Feel 10.4%
Touch 8.3%
Nonsense 6.3%
Commonsense 4.2%
2.1% Common, Empathise, Fifth, Five, Forget, Guess, Hear, Less, Meaning, Of-Joy, Perception, See, Sensibility, Sound, Taste, Understanding

Separate
Apart 20.8%
Divorce 16.7%
Divide 6.3%
Part 6.3%
* 4.2%
Different 4.2%
Twins 4.2%
2.1% Away, Bill, Change, Circulate, Cut, Detach, From, Join, Liquid, Milk, People, Remove, Rooms, Spelling, Strands, Tables, Together, Unjoin

Sergeant+
Major 61.9%
Army 11.9%
Corporal 4.8%
Man 4.8%
2.4% General, Order, Pepper, Police, Private, Rank, War

Serial
Killer 46.7%
Television(TV) 13.3%
Parallel 11.1%
Number 6.7%
Line 4.4%
2.2% Dilution, Event, Many, Process, Repeat, Series, Show, Time

Serious+
Solemn 16.7%
* 9.5%
Grave 7.1%
Straight 7.1%
Thoughtful 4.8%
2.4% Bandit, Clear, Conversation, Crime, Difficult, Discussion, Expression, Fatal, Firm, Frivolous, Grey, Intense, Intent, Problem, Real, Sensible, Severe, Sombre, Talk, Trouble, Unfunny, Wet, Wise

Service
Waiter 13.3%
Bus 6.7%
Station 6.7%
Car 4.4%
Charge 4.4%
Church 4.4%
Hotel 4.4%
Industry 4.4%
Room 4.4%
2.2% *, Bank, Business, Clean, Delivery, Desk, Engine, Fix, Lift, Maid, Man, National, Petrol, Provided, Public, Ritual, Shaker, Shop, Silent, Till, Token

Set
Jelly 11.6%
Down 9.4%
Piece 9.4%
Back 7.0%
Badger(s) 7.0%
Game 4.7%
Television 4.7%
2.3% Cast, Class, Complete, Concrete, Cup, Geometry, Hair, Hard, Match, Plaster, Right, Same, Stage, Stand, Table, Tennis, To, Up, Upon, Video, Watch

Seven
Eight 9.3%
Up 9.3%
Dwarves 7.0%
Eleven 7.0%
Teen 7.0%
Time 7.0%
* 4.7%
Nine 4.7%
Number 4.7%
River 4.7%
2.3% Dive, Drink, Fingers, Gate, Kings, Lucky, Men, O'Clock, People, September, Sisters, Six, Week, Yellow

Sew
Needle 19.6%
Thread 19.6%
Dress 6.5%
Knit 6.5%
Stitch 6.5%
Material 4.3%
2.2% *, Bird, Box, Button, Cloth, Clothes, Cut, Drew, Find, Machine, Make, Mend, Reap, Repaid, Rib, Shirt, Trousers

Sexploitation
Woman/en 12.5%
Exploitation 10.4%
Sex 10.4%
* 6.3%
Porn 6.3%
Film 4.2%
Magazine(s) 4.2%
Money 4.2%
Pornography 4.2%
2.1% Germaine Greer, Madonna, Abuse, Advertisement, College, Disgusted, Exploit, Girl, Harass, Lib, Male, Pornographic, Sexism, Sexual Harassment, Using, Word, Work, Yes Please

Shake
Milk 18.8%
Hand 12.6%
Rattle 10.4%
Shiver 8.3%
* 6.2%
Leg 4.2%
2.1% About, Bate, Cocktail, Down, Head, Loose, Me, Mix, Rattle-And-Hum, Shatter, Stir, Take, Thing, Tremble, Up, Vat, Vibrate, Wild, Wring

Shall
Will 18.8%
We 16.7%
Have 14.6%
Not 8.3%
Shan't 6.3%
* 4.2%
Be 4.2%
Do 4.2%
2.1% Coat, Find, I, Intend, Intention, Shell, Should, Stall, Want, Wedding, Work

Shallot+
Onion 28.3%
Lady 17.4%
* 10.9%
Vegetable 10.9%
2.2% Aubergine, Castle, Chocolate, Clothe, Food, Garden, Garlic, Harlot, Mushroom, Pants, Pea, Plant, Skirt, Tart, Veggie

Shallow
Water(s) 37.8%
Deep 24.4%
Stream(s) 4.4%
2.2% Breathing, Dog, Edge, Empty, Flat, Ground, Hole, Lake, Paddling-Pool, Pebbles, Person, Pond, Sea, Tree, Trench

Shame
Guilt 14.6%
* 9.8%
Embarrassment 9.8%
Blush 9.0%
Honour 7.3%
Red 7.3%
Embarrassed 4.9%
Faced 4.9%
Sad 4.9%
2.4% Dishonour, Embarrass, Fame, Far, Feeling, Hang, Hide, Humiliation, Old, Pity, Proof, Shroud

Shampoo+
Hair 52.2%
Wash 10.9%
Set 6.5%
Conditioner 4.3%
Shower 4.3%
Soap 4.3%
2.2% Animals, Bath, Bubbles, Drop, Hairspray, Johnson's, Rabbit, Water

Share
Give 10.0%
Equal 6.0%
Stock(s) 6.0%
Together 6.0%
Certificate 4.0%
It 4.0%
Out 4.0%
2.0% *, All, Bear, Bonds, Bread, Cake, Children, Common, Crop, Cropper, Cropping, Deal, Flat, Holder, House, Keep, Lend, Lot, Me, No, Overall, Part, Partner, Pound, Split, Sweets, That, Twin, Us, Wear

Sharp
Knife 17.8%
Edge 15.6%
Blunt 13.3%
Point 11.1%
Tongue 6.7%
2.2% Blade, Cold, Cut, End, Flint, Intake, Jagged, Needle, Pain, Pin, Prick, Smooth, Stick, Stone, Tooth, Weapon

Sheep
Wool 17.8%
Cow(s) 13.3%
Farm 6.7%
Field 6.7%
Flock 6.7%
Dip 4.4%
Shepherd 4.4%
2.2% Baa, Conformity, Cowards, Dog, Dr-Weitundbreit, Ewe, Farmer, Hill, Horn, Lamb, Park, Pig, Rural, Shear, Skin, Stare, White, Woolly

Shelf
Book(s) 26.9%
Life 13.5%
Bracket 7.7%
Ledge 7.7%
* 5.7%
Wall 3.8%
Wood 3.8%
1.9% Dust, Hammer, Hide, High, Hook, Latch, Mark, Pin, Pine, Pot, Stacking, Storage, Timber, Tin, Top, Wooden

Shimmer
Shine 26.0%
Light 8.0%
Shake 8.0%
Glimmer 6.0%
Glow 6.0%
* 4.0%
Bright 4.0%
Glisten 4.0%
2.0% Beautiful, Dark, Glass, Glint, Gold, Golden, Lake, Leaf, Moonlight, Ripple, Scintillate, Silver, Sun, Tree, Warm, Water, Water

Shine
Sun 37.0%
Shoe(s) 15.2%
Bright 10.9%
Light 4.3%
Moon 4.3%
2.2% Brilliant, Brilliantly, Buff, Clean, Cut, Glitter, On, Polish, Reflect, Sheen, Star, Through, Work

Shiny
New 10.4%
Bright 8.3%
Plastic 8.3%
* 4.2%
Clean 4.2%
Gloss 4.2%
Happy 4.2%
Metal 4.2%
Silver 4.2%
2.1% Black, Blue, Boots, Clothes, Coin, Gleam, Gleaming, Glowing, Illuminate, Knob, Light, Metallic, Paper, Penny, Pool, Reflective, Shoes, Slimy, Smooth, Sparkle, Spoon, Tinny, Tinsel

Ship+
Boat 21.4%
Wreck 21.4%
Sea 16.7%
Sail 11.9%
Ocean 4.8%
Sink 4.8%
2.4% Captain, Journey, Liner, Port, Sailing, Sailor, Shape, Wrecked

Shiver
Shake 42.0%
Cold 40.0%
* 4.0%
Timbers 4.0%
Tremble 4.0%
2.0% Coat, Goosepimples, Sick

Shock
Horror 23.8%
Electric 11.9%
* 9.5%
Scare 4.8%
Terror 4.8%
2.4% Bomb, Crisis, Faint, Fear, Fright, Hurt, Jump, Kettle, Pink, Prod, Rock, Surprise, System, Therapy, Treatment, Tremble, Troop, Waves, You

Shoot
Kill 31.9%
Gun(s) 21.3%
Bang 6.4%
Down 6.4%
Duck 6.4%
Dead 4.3%
Target 4.3%
2.1% Birds, Die, Fire, Hit, Man, Pheasants, Rabbit, Rifle, Up

Shop
Front 8.6%
Buy 7.5%
Assistant 6.5%
Window 6.5%
Store 5.4%
Street 5.4%
Corner 4.3%
Sweet(s) 4.3%
* 3.2%
Around 3.2%
Keeper 3.2%
Light(s) 3.2%
Money 3.2%
Clothes 2.2%
Door 2.2%
Fitter 2.2%
Food 2.2%
Goods 2.2%
Supermarket 2.2%
1.1% Basket, Boots, Buying, Closed, Consume, Counter, Delicatessen, Floor, Lifter, Look, Lunch, Run, Sell, Shoe, Shut, Sign, Soiled, Steward, Talk, Wait, Yellow

Shore
Beach 31.7%
Sea 31.7%
Line 9.8%
Pebbles 7.3%
Sand 4.9%
2.4% Coast, Leave, Michael, Seaside, Shell, Side, Stones

Short
Long 26.7%
Tall 8.9%
Brief 6.7%
Leg(s) 6.7%
Story 6.7%
* 4.4%
Course 4.4%
Small 4.4%
Straw 4.4%
Time 4.4%
2.2% Brothers, Curlies, Fall, Film, Hair, Hand, Pants, Quick, Staff, Tiny

Shortbread
Biscuit 37.5%
Cake 12.5%
* 8.3%
Scotland 8.3%
Butter 6.3%
Sugar 4.2%
Tin 4.2%
2.1% Bake, Cookies, Crusty, Ginger, Nice, Oat, Scottish, Tea, Toast

Shortcake
Biscuit(s) 34.6%
Bread 5.7%
Eat 5.7%
Food 5.7%
Pastry 5.7%
Tea 5.7%
* 3.8%
Scotland 3.8%
Sweet 3.8%
1.9% ?, Cookies, Crumbly, Dry, Fingers, Packet, Raisin, Recipe, Scottish, Strawberry, Sugar, Tartan

Shot
Gun 37.8%
Dead 15.6%
Hit 6.7%
Dark 4.4%
Putt 4.4%
2.2% Arrow, At, Bourbon, Bullet, Death, Down, Ground, Hot, Lead, Line, Long, Put, Shield, Wounded

Shoulder
Cry 23.4%
Arm 10.6%
Lamb 10.6%
Pad 6.4%
Bone(s) 4.3%
2.1% *, Anatomy, Blade, Body, Edge, Ham, Hand, Hard, Heart, Holster, Joint, Length, Load, Pain, Pork, Ride, Scapula, Shoulder, Strap, Time, Yoke

Shout
Loud 31.9%
Yell 12.8%
Aloud 6.4%
At 4.3%
Out 4.3%
2.1% About, Anguish, Bellow, Cry, Football, Hard, Holler, Hoorah, Horn, Joy, Lulu, Lungs, Mouth, Name, Now, Roar, Scream, Twist, Voice

Shriek
Scream 22.9%
Cry 16.7%
Shout 14.6%
Back 8.3%
Yell 8.3%
* 4.2%
Aagh 4.2%
Ghost 4.2%
Loud 4.2%
Shrill 4.2%
2.1% Girl, Ouch, Out, Small

Shut
Door 48.9%
Close 12.8%
Up 12.8%
Out 10.6%
Closed 6.4%
2.1% Damn, Down, Gate, Mouth

Shy
Timid 20.5%
Quiet 13.6%
Bashful 9.1%
Coy 6.8%
Retiring 6.8%
* 4.5%
Blush 4.5%
Person 4.5%
2.3% Away, Child, Conceit, Confident, Deer, Diffident, Fear, Introvert, Lonely, Retire, Shy, Subdued, Woman

Sick
Bad 35.6%
Bastard 11.1%
Bed 4.4%
Day 4.4%
Dog 4.4%

Health 4.4%
Healthy 4.4%
Heart 4.4%
2.2% Humour, Ill, Note, Nurse, Parrot, Person, Pig, Sea, Sight, Vomit, Well, White

Side
Board 8.9%
Front 8.9%
Way(s) 8.9%
* 6.7%
Door 6.7%
Long 4.4%
View 4.4%
2.2% Ache, Building, By, Edge, Garden, Head, Kick, Ledge, Left, Log, Lying, Off, Out, Overthere, Saddle, Shape, Shot, Show, Step, Stretch, Wind, Winder, With

Sigh
* 12.5%
Relief 10.4%
Breath 8.3%
Cry 8.3%
Groan 6.3%
Moan 6.3%
Sad 6.3%
Breathe 4.2%
2.1% Annoyed, Blow, Deeply, Feelings, Gasp, Heave, Huff, Lament, Laugh, Love, Mouth, Remark, Sleep, Snort, Throat, Whisper, Wish, Yawn

Sight
Eye(s) 29.2%
See 20.8%
Sound 12.5%
Hearing 8.3%
Vision 8.3%
Glasses 4.2%
2.1% Binoculars, Lens, Look, Of, Rifle, Seeing, Sore

Sighted
Short 26.7%
Blind 15.6%
Seen 11.1%
Far 8.9%
Near 8.9%
Saw 4.4%
2.2% Deaf, Eyes, Gift, Hearing, Intelligent, Long, Lost, Misery, Spectacles, Target, Vision

Significance
Importance 23.4%
* 12.8%
Statistics 12.8%
Important 6.4%
Meaning 4.3%
Point 4.3%
2.1% Big, Change, Error, Experiment, Focus, Greed, Knowing, Knowledge, Level, Mean, Reading, Relevance, Sign, Signify, Size, Trophy, What

Silent
Night 34.9%
Quiet 27.9%
Still 7.0%
Film 4.7%
2.3% Calm, Dark, Introspective, Loud, Noise, Peace, Room, Scheuppen, Tale, Touch, Water

Silver+
Gold 41.5%
Metal 7.3%
Smith 4.9%
Spoon 4.9%
2.4% Arrow, Bonging, Brass, Bronze, Bullet, Candlestick, Cutlery, Heirlooms, Jewellery, Lace, Lining, Plate, Plated, Ring, Shiny, Teapot, Waiter

Simple
Easy 26.2%
Simon 14.3%
Complex 9.5%
* 4.8%
Basic 4.8%
2.4% Clear, Complicated, Dim, Egg, Hard, Phrases, Pleasures, Problem, Quick, Silly, Small, Song, Straight, Thick, Thought, Truth, World

Sin
Bad 17.8%
Evil 8.9%
* 6.7%
Church 4.4%
Devil 4.4%
God 4.4%
Sex 4.4%
2.2% Bin, Catholic, Crime, Fire, Fun, Gin, Good, Guilt, Happy, Lie, Living, Mortal, Original, Peace, Religion, Reward, Rules, Satan, Vice, Wages, Wicked

Sing
Song 42.6%
Choir 6.4%
Along 4.3%
Bird 4.3%
Loud 4.3%
Play 4.3%
Praise 4.3%
Pray 4.3%
2.1% Dance, Fat, Julie-Andrews, Laugh, Loudly, Lullabye, Prayer, Talk, Tune, Voice, Wail, Yowl

Single
Person 15.6%
Double 8.9%
Married 6.7%
Mother 6.7%
One 6.7%
Cream 4.4%
Man 4.4%
2.2% Bad, Bed, Brow, Celled, Cheap, Club, Cone, Couple, File, Life, Minded, Pair, Plural, Room, Run, Shingle, Shot, Solitary, Stroke, Twins, Woman

Sink
Water 10.6%
Drown 8.5%
Ship 8.5%
Kitchen 6.4%
Swim 6.4%
Boat 4.3%
Drain 4.3%
Hole 4.3%
Plug 4.3%
Tap(s) 4.3%
Weight 4.3%
2.1% *, All, Basin, Belgrano, Block, Choke, Clean, Clothes, Down, Feeling, Float, Plunger, Stone, Washbasin, Washing-Up

Sip+
Drink 26.7%
Tea 15.6%
Cup 14.4%
Water 5.6%
Gulp 4.4%
Slurp 4.4%
Taste 4.4%
Wine 3.3%
1.1% Beer, Champagne, Coffee, Cool, Daintily, Dainty, Down, Glass, Gulp, Hip, Ill, Lick, Mouthful, Quaff, Sap, Sip, Slip, Straw, Suck, Up

Sister
Brother 59.5%
* 9.5%
Girl 4.8%
2.4% Family, Half, Hood, Mother, Nun, Pretty, Relative, Sibling, Tara, Two

Sit
Down 25.0%
Chair 22.9%
Stand 18.8%
Still 8.3%
Tight 4.2%
2.1% Bottom, Cushion, Dog, Here, Low, Pose, Rest, Seat, Table, Walk

Sitcom
Television-TV 39.6%
Comedy 12.5%
Soap 10.4%
* 6.2%
Movie 4.2%
Sofa 4.2%
2.1% Boredom, Chair, Comedian, Dull, Funny, Poor, Rubbish, Sad, Situation, Terry-And-June, Vietnam

Six
Seven 53.5%
Pence 11.6%
* 7.0%
Number 7.0%
Dozen 4.7%
2.3% Eggs, Fingers, Letters, News, Sense, Sextuplets, Three

Size+
Large 16.7%
Big 11.9%
Shape 11.9%
Small 9.5%
Clothes 7.1%
Elephant 4.8%
2.4% *, Aspect, Cut, Difference, Dimension, Enormous, Exclusion, Huge, Important, Magnitude, Of, Paper, Space, Tall, Up, Well

Skeleton+
Bone(s) 31.0%
Cupboard 23.8%
Closet 7.1%
Skull 7.1%
Death 4.8%
2.4% Anatomy, Biology, Body, Dead, Dig, Grave, Person, Structure, Undead, White, Zombie

Skill
Ability 14.3%
* 11.9%
Talent 9.5%
Art 7.1%
Carpenter 4.8%
Expertise 4.8%
2.4% Acumen, Appliance, Connect, Control, Craft, Factor, Football, Game, Gladiator, Knitting, Labourer, Lack, Music, Opt, Quality, Tact, Tennis, Trade, Typing, Worker

Skin
Deep 14.9%
Disease 8.5%
* 4.3%
Bone 4.3%
Brown 4.3%
Crawl 4.3%
Freckles 4.3%
Peel 4.3%

Soft 4.3%
2.1% Alive, Body, Bumpy, Care, Caucasian, Cold, Complexion, Fair, Feel, Fresh, Hair, Movie, Nose, Organ, Permatone, Pores, Rash, Rub, Sun, Sweat, Test, Tremble

Skinhead
Boot(s) 7.7%
Fascist 7.7%
Hair 7.7%
Punk 7.7%
Bald 5.7%
Nazi 5.7%
Short 5.7%
* 3.8%
Head 3.8%
Hippie 3.8%
Rough 3.8%
Shave 3.8%
Ugly 3.8%
Violence 3.8%
1.9% ?, Bald-Head, Danger, Fool, Jeans, Knuckles, Lout, Nut, Pest, Racist, Rocker, Shaved, Yob

Skinny
Thin 56.2%
Dip 6.2%
* 4.2%
Fat 4.2%
Stick 4.2%
Twiggy 4.2%
2.1% Lean, Legs, Me, Not, Rake, Skeleton, Small, Smoke, Tall

Skip
Rope 30.0%
Jump 24.0%
Hop 10.0%
Kangaroo 6.0%
Rubbish 4.0%
2.0% *, Child, Dance, Girl, Hopscotch, Light, Loo, Lorry, Over, Tango, Through, Tip, Wood

Skirt+
Dress 26.2%
Blouse 14.3%
Hem 11.9%
Clothes 7.1%
Women 7.1%
Mini 4.8%
Top 4.8%
Woman 4.8%
2.4% Jupe, Knee, Legs, Lift, Material, Short, Shoulder

Skunk
Smell 55.6%
Stink 6.7%
Animal 4.4%
Stripe(s) 4.4%
2.2% Black, Dirt, Drunk, Forest, Funk, Fur, Laser, Norman-Lamont, Pepe-Le-Pew, Punk, Rodent, Sea, Smelly

Slack
Loose 32.0%
Tight 8.0%
Trouser(s) 8.0%
Rope 6.0%
Lazy 4.0%
Slacks 4.0%
2.0% *, Alice, As-Fuck, Bad, Chimney, Coal, Cords, Fail, Floppy, Free, Generation, Limp, Muscle, Raven, Slacker, Tights, Untidy, Useless, Weak

Slap
Hit 28.0%
Hand 12.0%
Face 10.0%
* 8.0%
Hard 6.0%
Tickle 6.0%
Happy 4.0%
Hurt 4.0%
2.0% Back, Bitch, Boys, Branch, Cheek, Dash, Her, Him, It, Leak, Sting

Sledge
Snow 44.2%
Hammer 34.9%
Sleigh 4.7%
2.3% Dog, Ice, Santa, Shit, Sister, Skis, Slay

Sleep
Dream(s) 34.8%
Bed 8.7%
Night 6.5%
Pillow 6.5%
Awake 4.3%
Peace 4.3%
Rest 4.3%
Slumber 4.3%
2.2% Deep, Deeply, Easy, Fast, Fence, Night, Nightmare, Now, Out, Star, Wake, Walk

Sleepy
Tired 40.0%
Bed 6.7%
Drowsy 6.7%
Head 4.4%
Sleep 4.4%
2.2% Alert, Awake, Cat, Dreams, Dumb, Dwarf, Eyes, Grumpy, Lull, Overwork, Pillow, Pyjamas, Quiet, Town, Village, Weepy

Slice
Bread 35.4%
Cake 25.0%
Cut 8.3%
Knife 4.2%
Meat 4.2%
Piece 4.2%
2.1% Brie, Cheese, Luck, Nice, Orange, Pie, Take, Toast, Tomato

Slide
Slip 18.8%
Swing(s) 18.8%
Down 12.5%
Door 6.3%
Rule 6.3%
Water 6.3%
Projector 4.2%
Show 4.2%
2.1% *, Banana, Child, Children, Photo, Picture, Playground, Push, Shut, Skid, Snow

Slim
Fat 26.7%
Thin 20.0%
Figure 6.7%
Slight 6.7%
Girl 4.4%
Line 4.4%
Skinny 4.4%
2.2% *, Chance, Cigar, Elegant, Fellow, Hips, Jim, Shirt, Stout, Tonic, Tree, Waist

Sling
Shot 23.3%
Arm 16.3%
Arrows 9.3%
Bandage 7.0%
Hook 7.0%
Broken 4.7%
Rock(s) 4.7%
2.3% Backs, Bow, Catapult, David, Hammock, Match, Mud, Over, Satchel, Stone, Throw, White

Slip
Fall 31.3%
Slide 14.6%
Up 14.6%
Away 4.2%
Down 4.2%
Off 4.2%
2.1% Disc, Dress, Drop, Girl, Ice, In, Mistake, Out, Over, Sliding, Small, Stumble, Underwear

Slope
Ski 33.3%
Hill 19.0%
Down 7.1%
Skiing 7.1%
Downwards 4.8%
Mountain 4.8%
2.4% *, Descend, Forward, Gradient, Level, Piste, Smooth, Sudden, Valley, Wall

Sloth
Lazy 23.3%
Animal 14.0%
Slow 9.3%
Laziness 7.0%
* 4.7%
Monkey 4.7%
Trees 4.7%
2.3% Anger, Beast, Creep, Dull, Full, Furry, Lie, Mess, Shaggy, Slowness, Soft, Two-Toed, Untidy, Warm

Slow
Fast 33.3%
Down 20.0%
Quick 8.9%
Snail 4.4%
Stop 4.4%
2.2% Boat, Bus, Dance, Fish, Foolish, Hand, Journey, Movement, Sluggish, Speech, Speed, Traffic, Wait

Slug
Snail 20.4%
Slime 14.3%
Worm 6.1%
Lettuce 4.1%
Pellets 4.1%
Slow 4.1%
Yuk 4.1%
2.0% Apple, Beetle, Black, Cabbage, Caterpillar, Crawl, Creepy, Greasy, Grommet, Gun, Hit, Horrible, Insect, Moist, Pest, Salt, Sea, Shell, Shyama, Slimy, Stamina

Smack
Hit 30.0%
Hard 10.0%
Slap 10.0%
Lip(s) 8.0%
Hand 4.0%
Heroin 4.0%
Kiss 4.0%
2.0% *, Anger, Bottom, Child, Cry, Drug, Fishing, Horse, Hurt, Mouth, Red, Sound, Spank, Stroke, Teeth

Small
* 26.5%
Large 10.2%
Little 10.2%
Tiny 10.2%
Big 8.2%
2.0% Back, Best, Box, Cat, Cute, Frame, House, Hurt, Insignificant, Is-Beautiful, Minded, Mouse, Nose, Petite, Print, Shape, Size

Smart
Dress 18.8%

Clever 16.7%
Alec 6.3%
Suit 6.3%
* 4.3%
2.1% Ass, Card, Clothes, Elegant, Fellow, Formal, Idea, Kid, Man, Move, Old, Outfit, Pain, Pretty, Quick, Shiny, Smarties, Soldier, Straight, Stupid, Tidy, Tie, Tramp

Smash
Break 20.8%
Grab 14.6%
Hit(s) 8.3%
Up 8.3%
Window 6.3%
* 4.2%
Plate 4.2%
2.1% Brace, Car, Crush, Destroy, Down, Eggs, Fall, For-Mash-Get, Glass, It, Kill, Loud, Mash, Squash

Smell
Nose 19.1%
Odour(s) 8.5%
Taste 8.5%
Bad 6.4%
Food 6.4%
Horrible 6.4%
Sniff 6.4%
Aroma 4.3%
Fart 4.3%
Pong 4.3%
2.1% Acrid, Fragrance, Horrid, Nostril, Pooh, Reeves, Rose, Rot, Scent, Snort, Stench, Strong

Smog
Fog 35.4%
Smoke 16.7%
L.A. 8.3%
London 8.3%
City 4.2%
Pollution 4.2%
2.1% Asthma, Atmosphere, Death, Dog, Log, Mist, Pea, Sea, Victorian, Weather

Smooth
Rough 37.8%
Surface 13.3%
Skin 6.7%
Silk 4.4%
Soft 4.4%
2.2% Cream, Empty, Habutai(?), Hairy, Mmmm, Out, Paste, Pearl, Rumpled, Service, Shin, Silky, Stone, Water, Wood

Snail
Shell 20.0%
Slow 17.8%
Garden 13.3%
Slug 13.3%
Slime 11.1%
Crawl 8.9%
Trail 4.4%
2.2% Bent, Bite, Earth, Pace, Squidgy

Snake
Grass 23.2%
Bite 16.2%
Skin 9.3%
Long 4.6%
Queue 4.6%
2.3% Adder, Asp, Coil, Hat, In-The-Grass, Ladder, Oil, Poison, Rasping, Rattle, Reptile, Saw, Slime, Slimy, Sling, Slipper, Smooth, Snake

Snap
Shot 16.0%
Crackle 14.0%
Dragon 10.0%
Break 8.0%
Cards 6.0%
Happy 4.0%
Photo 4.0%
2.0% *, Anger, Angry, Argue, Brandy, Camera, Card-Game, Cold, Crack, Crocodile, Disc, Finger, Fish, Game, Group, Gun, Shut, Sugar, Thistle

Snapshot
Photo 31.3%
Picture 18.8%
Camera 14.6%
Album 6.3%
Moment 4.2%
2.1% *, Click, Flash, Kodak, Life, London, Memories, Mugshot, Peek, Silly, SLR, Smiles

Snarl
Dog(s) 31.9%
Growl 25.5%
Sneer 8.5%
Teeth 4.3%
Cat 4.3%
2.1% *, Anger, Curl, Gribe, Grimace, Grrr, Lips, Mouth, Rottweiler, Savage, Threaten, Wolf

Snatch
Grab 28.0%
Take 26.0%
Bag 8.0%
Thief 4.0%
2.0% *, Cunt, From, Get, It, Open, Pinch, Pocket, Pull, Purse, Sleep, Snipe, Steal, Stop, Swatch, Swift, Vagina

Sneeze
Cold 18.6%
Hankie 18.6%
Nose 14.0%
Cough 11.6%
Tissue 9.3%
Hard 4.7%
2.3% Aloud, Blow, Dust, Fast, Light, Loudly, Sniff, Snooker, Snort, Snuffle

Sniff
Smell 39.6%
Glue 16.7%
Nose 10.4%
Cold 6.3%
Snuff 4.2%
2.1% *, Air, Aroma, Dog, Onomatopoeia, Pong, Scent, Scratch, Snuffle, Tissue, Whiff

Snooker
Ball 30.6%
Table 18.4%
Cue 10.2%
Player 8.2%
Pool 8.2%
2.0% *, Billiard, Black, Board, Championship, Cricket, Game, Geometry, Hurt, Pole, Steve, We

Snort
Coke 16.0%
Cocaine 14.0%
Nose 14.0%
Pig 10.0%
Sniff 10.0%
Sneeze 6.0%
Bull 4.0%
Oink 4.0%
2.0% Abort, Blow, Drugs, Grunt, Laugh, Nasal, Quiet, Snore, Snot, Snuff, Speed

Snow
White 48.1%
Cold 9.6%
Flake 9.6%
Fall 7.7%
Ice 7.7%
Ball 3.8%
1.9% Christmas, Frost, Hail, Logic, Man, Winter

Snowman
Melt 11.1%
White 11.1%
Ball 8.9%
Snow 8.9%
Winter 8.9%
Cold 6.7%
Ice 6.7%
Carrot 4.4%
Hat 4.4%
Scarf 4.4%
2.2% *, Booty, Briggs, Childhood, Coal, Film, Fly, Frosty, Mittens, Playing, Sand

Snug
Bug 32.0%
Warm 14.0%
Cosy 10.0%
Fit 8.0%
* 4.0%
Comfortable 4.0%
Slug 4.0%
2.0% Bar, Bed, Booth, Close, Comfort, Comfy, Cuddle, Dug, Heat, Home, Hug, Quiet

Soak
Wet 35.4%
Up 14.6%
Bath 6.3%
Drench 6.3%
Skin 4.2%
Water 4.2%
2.1% -Ing, Beans, Cloak, Clothes, Coat, Douse, Dry, Flannel, It, Jacket, Oat, Peas, Socks, Steep, Wash

Sob
Cry 66.0%
Tear(s) 4.0%
Weep 4.0%
2.0% Alone, Ball, Eyes, Heart, Lad, Pity, Sad, Sniff, Sorrow, Sorry, Uncontrollably, Wail, Wet

Sober
Drunk 55.6%
Up 11.1%
Judge 8.9%
Drink 4.4%
Straight 4.4%
2.2% Clear, Cold, Dry, Dull, Mind, Pissed, Thought

Soda+
Water 45.2%
Pop(s) 11.9%
Stream 7.1%
Siphon 4.8%
Whiskey 4.8%
2.4% Bottle, Clean, Coke, Cream, Drink, Fizzy, Gin, Lime, Thirst, Washing

Sofa+
Bed 23.8%
Chair 19.0%
Couch 9.5%
Settee 9.5%
Seat 7.1%
Comfy 4.8%
Sit 4.8%
2.4% Home, Lost, Nest, Recline, Sitting, Sleep, Squidgy, Wood

Soft
Hard 18.4%
* 8.8%
Warm 4.4%
Comfort 3.7%

Cushion 3.7%
Feather(s) 3.7%
Pillow 3.7%
Strong 3.7%
Toy 3.7%
Bed(s) 2.2%
Cuddly 2.2%
Gentle 2.2%
Head 2.2%
Touch 2.2%
Wool 2.2%
Cheese 1.5%
Egg 1.5%
Fluffy 1.5%
Furry 1.5%
Hearted 1.5%
Round 1.5%
Small 1.5%
Smooth 1.5%
Soap 1.5%
0.7% Baby, Bedding, Body, Bouncy, Breast, Brick, Cloth, Cold, Cotton, Cuddle, Fur, Little, Long, Mallow, Melt, Mushy, Pencil, Porn, Prod, Puff, Smell, Sponge, Spot, Squeezy, Tactile, Tissue, Velvet, Wear

Solemn+
Sad 26.2%
Serious 16.7%
Grave 9.5%
Funeral 4.8%
Glum 4.8%
Morose 4.8%
Promise 4.8%
2.4% *, Boring, Dire, Gloomy, Gommorah, Holy, Lofty, Occasion, Poor, Procession, Severe, Vows

Solid+
Rock 19.0%
Hard 10.7%
Liquid 9.5%
Object 4.8%
Wood 4.8%
Block 3.6%
Brick 3.6%
Gold 3.6%
Strong 3.6%
Sturdy 3.6%
Brass 2.4%
Firm 2.4%
Support 2.4%
1.2% Bone, Complete, Door, Earth, Hefty, Hollow, Horse, Large, Lead, Lump, Mass, Metal, Neck, Opaque, Phase, Solid, Space, Sphere, Square, Steep, Stone, Whole

Solo
Alone 42.2%
Flight 6.7%
Own 6.7%
Single 4.4%
Together 4.4%
Violin 4.4%
2.2% *, Art, Attached, Bicycle, Career, Effort, Group, Lone, One, Only, Saxophone, Singer, Yacht

Some
More 12.0%
Many 8.0%
Time(s) 8.0%
* 6.0%
All 6.0%
Any 6.0%
Money 6.0%
Others 6.0%
A-Few 4.0%
Few 4.0%
None 4.0%
Thing 4.0%
2.0% Amount, A-Lot, Day, Eggs, Food, Gather, Have, Less, Like-It-Hot, Little, Quantity, Reason, Several

Son
Daughter 56.3%
Father 8.3%
Heir 4.2%
Male 4.2%
2.1% -Day, Baby, Boy, Family, In, In-Law, Light, Lover, Man, Mine, Mother, Never, Sound

Song
Sing 23.1%
Bird 15.4%
Music 13.5%
Tune 13.5%
* 3.8%
Singer 3.8%
Swan 3.8%
1.9% Aria, Happy, Hymn, Pop, Sang, Singing, Smith, Title, Verse, What, Word, Write

Soon
Now 29.4%
Later 12.5%
Come 6.3%
* 4.2%
Enough 4.2%
Never 4.2%
Possible 4.2%
2.1% After, Clock, Directly, Early, Immediate, It, Late, Maybe, Near, Nearby, Please, Time, Watch, When, Yesterday

Sorrow
Grief 24.4%
Sad 19.5%
Tear(s) 17.1%
Sadness 9.8%
Pain 4.9%
2.4% Cry, Death, Distress, Hang, Heart, Misery, Pity, Remorse, Shame, Unhappy, Weep

Soul
Mate 20.0%
Music 11.1%
* 6.7%
Heart 6.7%
Mind 6.7%
Body 4.4%
Brother 4.4%
Inner 4.4%
White 4.4%
2.2% Blues, David, Essence, Finger, God, Good, Immortal, Nuns, Rebel, Searching, Silence, Sister, Survivor, Third-Eye

Spade+
Shovel 19.1%
Bucket 14.8%
Dig 10.6%
Fork 8.5%
Ace 6.4%
Club 6.4%
Heart 6.4%
Garden 4.3%
2.1% Black, Card, Cold, Earth, Graves, Negro, Plough, Space, Tool, Trump, Work

Spanish+
Inquisition 11.9%
Language 9.5%
Foreign 7.1%
* 4.8%
Armada 4.8%
French 4.8%
Harlem 4.8%
Portuguese 4.8%
2.4% Army, Council, Country, Eye, Flamenco, Gardenia, German, Hispanic, Hola, Italian, Legion, Liquorice, Madrid, Mum, Omelette, Onion, Rose, Senorita, Sherry, Sunny

Spanner
Works 31.1%
Car 11.1%
Tool(s) 11.1%
Nut 6.7%
Wrench 6.7%
Bolt(s) 4.4%
2.2% Bang, Dyke, Garage, Head, Help, Idiot, Jack, Key, Operation, Screw, Silver, Turn, Undo

Spare
Tyre 27.1%
Rib(s) 8.4%
Time 8.3%
Extra 6.3%
Room 6.3%
Wheel 6.3%
* 4.2%
Part 4.2%
2.1% Another, Change, Coin, Dime, Excess, Free, Left-Over, Life, Need, None, Other, Some, Tool, Us

Speak
Say 12.8%
Talk 10.6%
Voice 10.6%
Mouth 6.4%
Word 6.4%
Bellow 4.3%
Loud 4.3%
Out 4.3%
Tell 4.3%
Utter 4.3%
Well 4.3%
2.1% Announce, Corner, Double, Easy, Fast, Language, Lies, Listen, Me, Message, Phone, Public, Said, Speech

Spear+
Head 9.5%
Arrow 7.1%
Round 7.1%
Circle 4.8%
Fear 4.8%
Globe 4.8%
Throw 4.8%
Weapon 4.8%
2.4% Aborigine, Area, Ball, Cut, Dagger, Death, Gun, Hurl, Hurt, Javelin, Knife, Lance, Octopus, Off, Orb, Pointed, Primate, Shoot, Soldier, Sword, War

Speech
Talk 16.7%
Therapy 14.3%
Impediment 11.9%
Language 11.9%
Say 4.8%
Therapist 4.8%
Voice 4.8%
2.4% *, Announce, Defect, Dinner, Drama, End, Handy, Listen, Mark, Music, Pattern, Silence, Silent

Speed
Fast 26.1%
Car 17.4%
Drug 8.7%
Kills 4.3%
King 4.3%
2.2% Ahead, Chase, Crash, Drive, Fiend, Fine, Great, Limit, Quick, Race, Rapid, Run, Space, Tractor, Up, Velocity, Wing, With

Spell
Word(s) 32.6%
Witch 23.3%

Bind 4.7%
Bound 4.7%
Speak 4.7%
Write 4.7%
2.3% Abound, Black-Board, Bound, Crazy, Curse, Dream, It, Reading, Wand, Wizard, Written

Spend
Money 63.8%
Buy 4.3%
Thrift 4.3%
2.1% *, Clothes, Earn, It, Lots, Overdraft, Sentence, Shop, Spree, Time, Up, Want, Whirl

Spicy
Hot 24.5%
Curry 20.4%
Food 20.4%
Indian 6.1%
Nice 4.1%
2.0% *, Brash, Cinnamon, Fruity, Huh, Nice-And, Peppers, Prawns, Rice, Sauce, Soup, Taste

Spill
Milk 12.8%
Over 12.8%
Water 10.6%
* 6.4%
Beans 6.4%
Drop 4.3%
Liquid 4.3%
Stain 4.3%
2.1% Chemical, Cloth, Coffee, Drink, Floor, Food, Jug, Lager, Life, Light, Mess, Oil, Out, Pour, Puddle, Slick, Spilt

Spirit
Ghost 33.3%
Sky 6.7%
Whiskey 6.7%
Drink 4.4%
Free 4.4%
Level 4.4%
Turps 4.4%
2.2% Alcohol, Church, Cleanse, Demon, Elfin, Gas, Ghoul, Hang, Happy, Horse, Ignite, Liquor, Mind, Religion, World

Spit
Gob 10.6%
Saliva 10.6%
* 6.4%
Out 6.4%
Foul 4.3%
Ground 4.3%
Mouth 4.3%
2.1% America, Apple, Chips, Cough, Dog, Dummy, Flog, Floor, French, Grave, Greenie, Grosse, Juice, Man, Meat, Over, Phlegm, Pot, Punk, Repulse, Roast, Split, Tuberculosis, Up, Wet

Spite
Hate 17.0%
* 9.8%
Spit 7.3%
Venom 7.3%
Evil 4.9%
Malice 4.9%
Nasty 4.8%
2.4% Anger, Contempt, Cruel, Cynicism, Disdain, Grind, Hatred, Haze, Hurt, Irritate, Malice, Mean, Of, Pain, People, Sharp, Snake, Spiteful, Vicious

Spitfire
Plane(s) 46.0%
Aeroplane 10.0%
Car 8.0%
Engine 6.0%
2.0% Battle, Fire, Fly, Gargle, Guns, Horse, Jet, My-Car, Phone, Plain, Propeller, Red-Arrows, Roast, Soft-Top, Yes

Splash
Water 54.3%
Down 8.7%
Dive 4.3%
Out 4.3%
Pool 4.3%
Swim 4.3%
Wet 4.3%
2.2% Around, Blue, Dolphin, Film, Mermaid, Paint, Splash, Waves

Spoil
Ruin 17.0%
Child(ren) 10.6%
Food 6.4%
* 4.3%
Fruit 4.3%
Heap(s) 4.3%
Rotten 4.3%
Soil 4.3%
2.1% Bad, Black, Brat, Broth, Damage, Destroy, Dirt, Eggs, For-Choice, Hurt, I, Indulgent, Kitchen, Meat, Mess, Milk, Neglect, Run, Spend, War, Work

Spoon+
Fork 39.1%
Knife 13.0%
Egg 6.5%
Fed 4.3%
Silver 4.3%
Soup 4.3%
2.2% Baby, Cutlery, Dessert, Feed, Food, Jelly, Metal, Metallic, Oval, Play, Smooth, Stir

Sportsman
Athlete 24.4%
Cricket 9.8%
Cricketer 9.8%
Botham 4.9%
Footballer 4.9%
Jockey 4.9%
Runner 4.9%
2.4% *, Batter, Boxer, Clothes, Fit, Fitness, Game, Gun, Horses, Joker, Money, Player, Racquet, Runner, Win, Woman

Sprig
Holly 25.0%
Twig 22.9%
Leaf 6.2%
Parsley 6.2%
Tree 6.2%
Mistletoe 4.2%
Spring 4.2%
2.1% *, Branch, Bream, Down, Flowers, Girl, Kiss, New, Onion, Piece, Vine, Water

Spring
Summer 23.4%
Water 10.6%
Jump 8.5%
Onion 8.5%
Flowers 6.4%
Time 6.4%
Action 4.3%
Up 4.3%
2.1% Autumn, Blossom, Bounce, Clean, Coil, Green, Happy, Loaded, Rabbit, Roll, Season, Weather, Winter

Sprint
Run 66.7%
Fast 4.2%
Olympics 4.2%
2.1% *, Ben-Johnson, Champion, Dash, Mile, Race, Relay, Slow, Start, Trainers, Walk, White

Squeeze
Orange 12.0%
Hug 10.0%
Lemon(s) 8.0%
Squash 8.0%
Tight 8.0%
Hold 6.0%
Crush 4.0%
Hard 4.0%
Please 4.0%
Push 4.0%
2.0% Acne, Cats, Clasp, Crunch, Grab, Grape, Hand, Held, Hold, Juice, Me, Out, Sponge, Toothpaste, Up, Waist

Squirrel
Nut(s) 35.6%
Tree 11.1%
Tail 8.9%
* 6.7%
Nutkin 6.7%
Red 6.7%
2.2% Acorn, Away, Furry, Grey, Park, Pine, Rat, Run, Shit, Syric, Woods

Stage
Struck 16.3%
Theatre 14.0%
Fright 11.6%
Play 7.0%
Act 4.7%
Actor 4.7%
Dias 4.7%
2.3% *, Back, Block, Coach, Curtain, Drama, Manage, Manager, Performance, Phase, Scene, Screen, Script, Set, Show, Speaker

Stall
Market 30.8%
Horse 5.7%
Stop 5.7%
* 3.8%
Book 3.8%
Car 3.8%
Sell 3.8%
Stable 3.8%
1.9% ?, Camden, Cow, Crash, Delay, Fall, Goods, Head, Holder, Lot, Noise, Own, Ox, Pause, Plane, Seller, Shop, Slow, Sweet, Theatre

Stampede+
Horses 16.7%
Elephants 11.9%
Rush 11.9%
Run 9.5%
Buffalo 7.1%
Elephant 7.1%
Bull 4.8%
Cattle 4.8%
Herd 4.8%
2.4% *, Buffaloes, Cows, Death, Hoard, Hooves, Horde, Rousted, Wildebeest

Stand
Up 27.7%
Sit 14.9%
Still 14.9%
By 6.4%
Deliver 6.4%
2.1% Apart, Down, Erect, Fall, Foot, Hat, Legs, Light, Queue, Stood, Straight, Table, Tall, Wash

Stare
Eyes 21.7%
Look 21.7%
At 8.7%
Out 8.7%

Gaze 4.3%
Glare 4.3%
Hard 4.3%
2.2% Ahead, Down, Face, Glasses, Humiliate, Into, Nothing, Rude, Scan, Space, Stare, Sun

Start
Begin 46.7%
Stop 8.9%
Finish 6.7%
Jump 6.7%
Now 4.4%
Race 4.4%
2.2% *, Afresh, Again, End, Forward, Gun, New, No, Over, Run

Starve
Eat 15.6%
Food 15.6%
Hunger 13.3%
Die 11.1%
Hungry 11.1%
Death 4.4%
Famish 4.4%
2.2% *, Africa, Cambodia, Children, Dead, Dying, Education, Ethiopian, Hurt, Sudan, The

State+
Country 15.2%
Say 10.9%
USA 6.5%
* 4.3%
Government 4.3%
King 4.3%
Of 4.3%
Union 4.3%
2.2% Alabama, America, Army, California, Defence, Department, Depressed, Enemy, Estate, Mind, Monaco, Nation, Palace, Pension, People, President, Sovereign, Stem, Tell, United, Visit

Station+
Train(s) 45.7%
Master 15.2%
Wagon 10.9%
Railway 6.5%
Euston 4.3%
Stop 4.3%
2.2% *, Airport, Bomb, Post, Stationary, Waiting

Status
Symbol 23.8%
Quo 11.9%
Position 9.5%
Equal 4.8%
Hierarchy 4.8%
Level 4.8%
2.4% Car, Class, Community, Dr, Exempt, High, Imply, Importance, King, Man, Money, Rank, Rock, Single, Society, Student, Wealth

Stay
Remain 20.9%
Behind 11.6%
Away 7.0%
Go 7.0%
Here 7.0%
Home 4.7%
Leave 4.7%
2.3% *, Around, Arrive, Belong, Bone, Corset, Good, Long, Longer, Main, Put, Steer, Support, There, Weekend

Steady
Firm 11.6%
Ready 9.3%
Rock 7.0%
Stable 7.0%
Still 7.0%
* 4.7%
Calm 4.7%
Go 4.7%
Hand 4.7%
Regular 4.7%
Straight 4.7%
2.3% Balance, Constant, Easy, Even, Fall, Feet, On, Person, Safe, Smooth, Stop, Sure, Wobble

Steal
Money 21.3%
Rob 12.8%
Thief 12.8%
Take 8.5%
Wrong 6.4%
Beg 4.3%
Burglar 4.3%
2.1% *, Borrow, Car, Coffee, Crook, Find, Glass, Law, Mugger, Nothing, Pinch, Steal, Theft, Worth

Steffi
Graff 65.3%
* 24.6%
Grant 6.1%
2.0% Patts, Tennis

Stepladder
Climb 16.0%
Loft 6.0%
Wall 6.0%
* 4.0%
Stairs 4.0%
2.0% Aluminium, B&Q, Bed, Danger, Decorate, Decorating, Dig, Falling, Gold, Height, Help, High, Jacob, Ladder, Library, Man, Metal, Paint, Rise, Roof, Rope, Ropeladder, Rungs, Splendour, Steel, Steep, Stool, Under, Up, Weak-Bladder, Window, Wooden

Stereo
Mc(s) 16.7%
Sound 14.6%
Hi-Fi 8.3%
Radio 6.3%
Record(s) 6.3%
Speaker 6.3%
Music 4.2%
System 4.2%
2.1% Black, Blast, Car, Cassette, Echo, Equipment, Loud, Man, Noise, Player, Quality, Recorder, Tape, Two, Unit, Walkman

Stereotype
* 13.5%
Same 7.7%
Typical 7.7%
Cliche 5.7%
Archetype 3.8%
Black 3.8%
Image 3.8%
1.9% ?, Biased, Bimbo, Blond, Boring, Caricature, Character, Easy, False, Genetics, Girly, Glasses, Madonna, Man, Person, Photo, Pop, Prejudice, Race, Record, Recording, Secretary, Special, Unique, Usual, View, Woman, Wrong

Stern
Strict 12.9%
Angry 8.6%
Hard 7.5%
Boat 5.4%
Ship 5.4%
Cross 4.3%
Look 3.2%
Rear 3.2%
Serious 3.2%
Back 2.2%
Face 2.2%
Firm 2.2%
Frown 2.2%
Harsh 2.2%
Severe 2.2%
Stiff 2.2%
1.1% Authority, Bank-Manager, Bough, Bow, Contorted, Eyebrows, Faced, Fierce, Gallery, Growl, Headmistress, Head-Teacher, Hold, Lax, Lip, Loud, Master, Mortar, Old, Parent, Person, Schoolmaster, Start, Stubborn, Teacher, Tough

Stick
Glue 21.3%
Blu-Tack 4.3%
Branch 4.3%
Man 4.3%
Wood 4.3%
2.1% Back, Ball, Big, Down, Finger, Hit, Inject, Insect, In-The-Mud, Lolly, Mud, On, Parachute, Peach, Pin, Posters, Rod, Sellotape, Snare, Stamp, Stone, Straw, Thin, Throw, Tree, Twig, Unstick, Up

Stiff
Hard 13.6%
Rigid 11.4%
Neck 9.1%
Drink 6.8%
Collar 4.5%
Finger(s) 4.5%
Leg 4.5%
Upper 4.5%
2.3% *, Ache, Arthritis, Board, Bones, Corpse, Erect, Lip, Loose, Push, Records, Snob, Soft, Sore, Start, Stiffle, Stuck, Upper-Lip

Sting
Bee 61.7%
Wasp 12.8%
Hurt 4.3%
Police 4.3%
Scorpion 4.3%
2.1% Arch, Man, Pain, Peak, Prick, Song

Stink
Smell 44.4%
Bomb 15.9%
Nose 4.5%
Rot 4.5%
2.2% *, Bathroom, Bug, Cot, Dog, Drain, Dump, Fart, Foul, Kitchen, Odour, Pipe, Sink, Stench

Stockroom
Store 14.0%
Box 10.0%
Books 4.0%
Shelf 4.0%
Stock 4.0%
Take 4.0%
Warehouse 4.0%
Work 4.0%
2.0% *, Attic, Basement, Big, Black, Cans, Classroom, Closed, Cows, Dirty, Files, Film, Goods, Jacket, Keys, Ladder, Lock, Paper, Pencil, Room, School, Sticky, Stock-Take, Things, Tie, Toy

Stomach+
Pain(s) 15.5%
Pump 13.1%
Food 7.1%
Ulcer 5.9%
Ache 4.8%
Belly 4.8%
* 3.6%

Muscle(s) 3.6%
Bowel(s) 2.4%
Chest 2.4%
Eat 2.4%
Empty 2.4%
Intestine 2.4%
Pit 2.4%
Tummy 2.4%
1.2% Acid, Appetite, Body, Boil, Bug, Churn, Contents, Cow, Digest, Entrails, Fight, Gut, Insides, Intestine, Lining, Meal, Poison, Pumped, Puncture, Tongue, Upset

Stop
Go 23.3%
Start 16.3%
Halt 11.6%
Now 7.0%
Arrest 4.7%
2.3% *, Barrier, Cease, Dead, Desist, End, Full, Police, Press, Quit, Red, Road, Shop, Sign, Terminate

Stopcock
* 19.2%
Water 19.2%
Tap 15.4%
Ballcock 5.7%
Valve 5.7%
Plumber 3.8%
Plumbing 3.8%
1.9% ?, Bung, Cockstop, Cork, Drain, Faucet, Flood, Robin, Shelf, Sink, Stop, Switch, Temporary, Watch

Store
Keep 16.7%
Shop 16.7%
Cupboard 10.4%
Hide 6.3%
House 6.3%
Hoard 4.2%
Room 4.2%
Squirrel 4.2%
2.1% *, Computer, Co-Op, Fat, File, Market, Memory, Pantry, Safe, Save, Shopping, Supermarket, Sweets, Take, Tin

Stork
Bird 32.0%
Baby 30.0%
Margarine 10.0%
Butter 4.0%
Heron 4.0%
2.0% *, Birth, Calm, Cloud, Crane, Lie, Long, Marg, Nest, S.B.

Storm
Wind 14.6%
Cloud(s) 12.5%
Rain 8.3%
Teacup 8.3%
Weather 8.3%
* 6.2%
Tempest 4.2%
2.1% Abate, Bird, Brew, Cyclone, Drain, Force, Gale, Hold, Hurricane, Lightning, Over, Sea, Stilled, Tea, Together, Trooper, Warning, Windy

Stormy
Weather 45.2%
Monday 9.5%
Sea(s) 9.5%
Clouds 4.8%
Lightning 4.8%
Wind 4.8%
Windy 4.8%
2.4% Balmy, Calm, Cloudy, Night, Row, Thunder, Wednesday

Story
Tale 41.9%
Book 23.3%
Fable 7.0%
Board 4.7%
Fairy 4.7%
2.3% Fairy-Tale, Legend, Name, Novel, Short, Tell, Teller, Yarn

Stove
Oven 26.7%
Cooker 17.8%
Heat 11.1%
Cook 8.9%
Fire 8.9%
Pipe 4.4%
2.2% *, Aga, Coal, Home, Hood, Kitchen, Pudding, Sink, Wood

Straight
Narrow 24.5%
Line 20.4%
* 6.1%
Gay 6.1%
Bent 4.1%
Crooked 4.1%
Curve 4.1%
Forward 4.1%
Lace 4.1%
Road 4.1%
2.0% Ahead, Curved, Hair, Jacket, Jail, Long, Normal, Out, Up

Strange
Weird 16.7%
Odd 10.4%
Man 8.3%
Brew 6.3%
* 6.2%
People 4.2%
Person 4.2%
Unknown 4.2%
Unusual 4.2%
2.1% Alternative, Bizarre, Boy, Creature, Days, Doctor, Fellow, Fruit, Funny, Love, Music, News, Normal, Obscure, Outlook, Time, Uncanny

Streamline
Car 12.0%
Boat 8.0%
Smooth 8.0%
* 4.0%
Aeroplane 4.0%
Air 4.0%
Fish 4.0%
Jet 4.0%
Plane 4.0%
River 4.0%
Thin 4.0%
2.0% Aerodynamic, Bike, Buses, Dolphin, Fast, Guard, Privatisation, Service, Ship, Sleek, Slim, Slim-Down, Speed-Stripes, Swimmer, Traffic, Train, Vehicle, Version, Water, Woman

Street
Road 28.6%
Wise 12.2%
Car 6.1%
Coronation 6.1%
Pavement 6.1%
City 4.1%
Lamp 4.1%
2.0% *, Corner, Crime, Funny, Holbeingate, Kid, Lamp-Post, Life, Name, Oxford, Place, Rue, Star, Sweeper, Urchin, Way

Strength
Muscle 14.3%
* 11.9%
Power 11.9%
Weakness 11.9%
Force 7.1%
Strong 7.1%
Man 4.8%
Weak 4.8%
2.4% Aim, Arms, Bar, Hard, Iron, Jaw, Pillar, Rambo, Strength, Valour, Vigour

Stress
Strain 17.0%
Work 17.0%
Worry 6.4%
* 4.3%
Anxious 4.3%
Emphasise 4.3%
Pain 4.3%
Pressure 4.3%
2.1% Agitation, Anxiety, Back, Disorder, Elastic, Freak, Hard, Incontinence, Relief, Straw, Stressor, Sweat, Syndrome, Tension, Tired, Tiring, Trials, Urgent

Stretch
Pull 18.6%
Elastic 9.3%
Bend 7.0%
Rubber 7.0%
* 4.7%
Fabric 4.7%
Lycra 4.7%
Marks 4.7%
2.3% Arms, Break, Curl, Eke, Flex, Leg, Long, Movement, Out, Putty, Slowly, Spin, Tight, Tone, Tug, Turn, Yawn

Strict
Severe 10.0%
Discipline 8.0%
Hard 8.0%
Order 6.0%
Teacher 6.0%
Cane 4.0%
Harsh 4.0%
Man 4.0%
Mother 4.0%
Stern 4.0%
2.0% Authoritarian, Authority, Behaviour, Dad, Disciplined, Education, Exact, Father, Firm, Heart, Hitler, Kind, Mild, Ouch, Parents, Police, Regime, School, Schoolmistress, Teacher, Upbringing

Stride
Walk 26.1%
Step 23.9%
Legs 8.7%
Big 4.3%
Boot(s) 4.3%
Carefully 4.3%
Confident 4.3%
2.2% After, Around, Astride, Feet, Long, On, Onwards, Open, Out, Over, Quickly

Strike
Hit 23.4%
Match 12.8%
Baseball 4.3%
Miners 4.3%
Out 4.3%
Violence 4.3%
2.1% *, Back, Ballot, Bowling, Coal, Hard, Hunger, Iron, Low, Luck, Lucky, Me, Money, Picket, Scorpion, Someone, Stand, Unions, Weapons, Work, Workers

String+
Ball 23.9%
Knot 6.5%
Piece 6.5%
Twine 6.5%
Along 4.3%
Vest 4.3%

2.2% *, Bean, Book, Conker, Cord, End, Highly, Length, Line, Long, Man, Models, Paper, Parcel, Pearls, Pull, Quartet, Rope, Sellotape, Taut, Tie

Stroke
Cat 12.5%
Hand 12.5%
Heart 10.4%
* 8.3%
Breast 4.2%
Caress 4.2%
Pet 4.2%
Skin 4.2%
2.1% Back, Brush, Calm, Death, Dog, Hair, Hit, Ill, Leg, Match, Pat, Person, Rub, Sheet, Sick, Speech, Stroke, Thigh, Victim

Stroll
Walk 64.6%
Park 6.2%
Run 6.2%
Wander 4.2%
2.1% Along, Away, Meander, Pall-Mall, Pleasant, Promenade, Spring, Stride, Strolling

Strong
Weak 30.6%
Man 12.2%
* 4.1%
Giant 4.1%
Muscle 4.1%
Week 4.1%
2.0% Ape, Arm, Arnold, Big, Black, Bow, Chain, Fight, Fort, Gale, Good, Hand, Heavy, Liaison, Lion, Medicine, Minded, Muscular, Tea, Wind

Stronghold
Castle 30.8%
Fort 21.2%
Fortress 11.5%
* 9.6%
House 3.8%
Tight 3.8%
1.9% Barrack, Gaddafi, Grip, Gun, Hand, Hold, Prison, Rope, Safe, Wood

Stubborn+
* 16.7%
Mule 16.7%
Donkey 7.1%
Obstinate 7.1%
Awkward 4.8%
Silly 4.8%
2.4% Angry, Arrogant, Aw, Awful, Bull, Child, Coerce, Dad, Firm, Honest, Mulish, No, Obdurate, Obtuse, Proud, Reluctant, Stomach, Strong

Stuffing
Chicken 31.7%
Turkey 31.7%
Christmas 4.9%
Food 4.9%
2.4% Chestnut, Cushion, Eating, Filling, Goose, Grain, Herb, Meat, Pigeon, Pillow, Pips, Plum

Stumble
Fall 56.3%
* 8.3%
Across 6.3%
Over 6.3%
Block 4.2%
Trip 4.2%
Upon 4.2%
2.1% About, Across, Bumble, Humble, Word

Stupid
Thick 17.8%
Clever 13.3%
Fool 8.9%
Silly 8.9%
Person 6.7%
* 4.4%
Cow 4.4%
Cupid 4.4%
Idiot 4.4%
2.2% Ass, Bright, Creature, Cunt, Daft, Dull, Foolish, Ignorant, Inane, Pillock, Senseless, Slow

Stupor
Drunken 21.4%
* 14.3%
Drunk 11.9%
Drink 7.1%
Coma 4.8%
Fall 4.8%
2.4% Beer, Blind, Block, Boring, Daze, Disgusting, Drugged, Friendly, Gone, Haze, Mind, Silly, Sleep, Stupid, Wooze

Style
Fashion 28.6%
* 4.8%
Art 4.8%
Chic 4.8%
Clothes 4.8%
Council 4.8%
2.4% Appearance, Cool, Cosmopolitan, Got-It, Graceful, Guru, Individual, Layout, Like, Merchant, New, Pattern, Pen, Shade, Sheet, Skill, Theme, Type, Victim, Wars

Subject
Object 27.7%
Topic 8.5%
Book 4.3%
Experiment 4.3%
Lesson 4.3%
Maths 4.3%
Matter 4.3%
Person 4.3%
2.1% Boredom, Cube, Domain, Experimentation, History, Number, One, Pain, Participant, Predicate, Royal, School, Teach, Test, To, Torture, Touch, Type

Submarine
Yellow 13.0%
Boat 10.9%
Underwater 10.9%
Sea 8.7%
Under 8.7%
Water 8.7%
Ship 6.5%
Deep 4.3%
War 4.3%
2.2% Beatles, Cable, Captain, Claustrophobia, Das-Boot, Down, Grey, Metal, Russian, Torpedo, Troy, Vessel

Submerge
Sink 19.0%
Submarine 19.0%
Water 14.3%
Drown 9.5%
Bury 4.8%
Hide 4.8%
Immerse 4.8%
Soak 4.8%
2.4% Cover, Deep, Dive, Diver, Doctrine, Sea, Under, Underwater

Subtle
Flavour 4.4%
Hint 4.4%
Obvious 4.4%
Quiet 4.4%
Sledgehammer 4.4%
Soft 4.4%
2.2% As-Hell, Bad, Blunt, Brick, Brutal, Clear, Clever, Clouched, Coarse, Crude, Cue, Defeat, Difficult, Doubt, Envy, Flexible, Gentle, Harmony, Hue, Indirect, Loud, Rough, Sensitive, Shield, Simple, Slight, Song, Style, Suggest, Suggestion, Unseen, Unsubtle, Vibes

Success
Failure 12.8%
Money 12.8%
Happiness 6.4%
Win 6.4%
Breeds 4.3%
Business 4.3%
Job 4.3%
Light(s) 4.3%
Work 4.3%
2.1% *, Ability, Achievement, Approval, End, Envy, Fame, Ful, Gain, Glory, Greed, Growth, Happy, Hard, Height, Hope, Suit, Top, Yes

Successfully
* 31.0%
Well 14.3%
Right 9.5%
2.4% Brilliant, Completed, Correctly, Credit, Did, Did Well, Done, Exam, Fun, Great, Hunger, Pass, Rich, Swindle, Unsuccessfully, Wealth, Winner, Yes

Succession
King(s) 13.6%
Next 9.1%
Throne 9.1%
Follow(ed) 7.1%
Chain 6.6%
After 4.6%
Generation(s) 4.6%
Line 4.6%
Series 4.6%
2.3% *, Climate, Family, Following, Monarchy, Order, Process, Repeated, Row, Stairs, Success, Take, Train, Years

Suck
Sweet(s) 25.6%
Lolly 16.3%
Dry 4.7%
Dummy 4.7%
Nipple 4.7%
Orange 4.7%
See 4.7%
2.3% *, Dick, Drink, Eggs, Honey, It, Kiss, Lemon, Lick, Lollipop, Pencil, Stinks, Straw, Teat, Thumb

Sudden
Shock 19.0%
Quick 11.9%
Immediate 9.5%
Death 7.1%
Flash 7.1%
Fast 4.8%
2.4% *, Abrupt, At-Once, Bang, Change, Close, Crash, Instant, Jolt, Noise, Now, Pull, Sharp, Slow, Stance, Start, Stop

Sue
Lawley 22.4%
* 14.1%
Barker 6.1%
Girl 4.1%
Peggy 4.1%
Pollard 4.1%
Townsend 4.1%
2.0% Anderson, Arnold,

Bing, Blonde, Booth, Clark, Dee, Dew, Expand, Hickey, Jameson, Leigh, Maull, Morris, Muller, Name, Reynolds, Rogers, Ryder, Sister, Stone

Suggest+
Idea(s) 15.6%
* 12.2%
Propose 7.8%
Imply 5.5%
Hint 4.4%
Offer 4.4%
Ask 3.3%
Say 3.3%
Persuade 2.2%
Question 2.2%
Tell 2.2%
1.1% Claim, Comment, Convey, Equal, Expect, Gift, Help, Her, Intimate, Know, Might, Nudge, Opinion, Place, Ponder, Preferential, Prod, Prompt, Proposal, Put-Forward, Remark, Request, Response, Seduce, Sex, Sexuality, Suggestion, Surreptitious, That, Think, Try, Why, Wonder, Word

Suicide+
Death 42.9%
Kill 11.9%
Dead 7.1%
Depression 4.8%
Murder 4.8%
2.4% Bid, Bridge, Cancer, Case, Drown, End, Fatal, Hamlet, Jump, Pact, Sadness, Self

Suitcase
Holiday 22.2%
Travel 17.8%
Clothes 11.1%
Pack 11.1%
* 4.4%
Bag 4.4%
Box 4.4%
2.2% Away, Carry, Case, Handbag, Hatbox, Heat, Luggage, Plane, Run, Shit, Valise

Sun
Shine 17.8%
Hot 13.3%
Moon 11.1%
Burn 8.9%
Ray(s) 6.7%
Stroke 6.7%
Sea 4.4%
Sky 4.4%
Tan 4.4%
2.2% Glasses, God, Heat, Newspaper, Planets, Rise, Sew, Ultra-Violet, Up

Sunburn
Red 27.1%
Pain 8.3%
Tan 6.3%
* 6.3%
Heat 4.2%
Hot 4.2%
Lotion 4.2%
Skin 4.2%
Sore 4.2%
2.1% Arm, Back, Beach, Bum, Burn, Cream, Death, Factor, Headache, Itch, Lobster, Malignant-Melanoma, Sun, Sunbathing, UV

Sunflower
Seed(s) 32.7%
Yellow 25.0%
Oil 9.6%
* 3.8%
Flower 3.8%
1.9% Big, Brain, Field, Garden, Glory, Grow, High, Love, Petal, Plant, Summer, Sun, Van-Gogh

Sunshine
Hot 12.0%
Bright 10.0%
Warm 8.0%
Light 6.0%
Good-Day 4.0%
Heat 4.0%
Rain 4.0%
Sky 4.0%
Warmth 4.0%
Yellow 4.0%
2.0% *, ?, Beaches, Beam, Cloud, Cold, Glow, Green, Happy, Lazy, Love, Morning, Rays, Shimmer, Stars, Summer, Sun, Tan, Wind, Wonder

Super
Great 18.8%
Man 12.5%
-Duper 10.4%
Ego 6.3%
* 6.2%
2.1% -Annuation, Brilliant, Dog, Eat, Fast, Fly, Food, Huge, Human, Incredible, Intend, Intendant, On, Plus, Sonic, Super, Superb, Supper, Time, Ultimate, Wonderful, -Ted

Surf
Sea 22.9%
Board 10.4%
Wave(s) 10.4%
Beach 4.2%
Foam 4.2%
2.1% Australia, Beach-Boys, Burn, California, Clean, Cold, Froth, Land, Line, Music, Nose, Powder, Sand, Spray, Stupidity, Sun, Turf, Twig, USA, Washing-Powder, Water, White, Wind

Surface+
Top 23.8%
Flat 7.1%
Plane 4.8%
Smooth 4.8%
Tension 4.8%
Under 4.8%
Water 4.8%
2.4% Area, Blemish, Bottom, Charge, Circle, Cover, Edge, Feel, Floor, Layer, Level, Orange, Reaction, Skimmer, Submarine, Surfactant, Surgeon, Table, Value

Surfboard
Sea 30.8%
Neighbours 7.7%
Water 7.7%
Australia 5.7%
Wave(s) 5.7%
Surf 3.8%
1.9% ?, Bali, Beach, Brad, California, Cold, Crest, Fun, Hard, Ninja, Salt, Skateboard, Ski, Slip, Smooth, Sport, Sun, Surfers, Tube, USA

Surfeit+
Excess 33.3%
* 19.0%
Enough 4.8%
More 4.8%
2.4% Above, Beachboy, Extra, Full, Loose, Lots, Much, Overmuch, Palfreys, Quantity, Racing, Stop, Surf, Surface, Surplus, Too

Surplus
Extra 30.0%
Army 8.0%
Excess 6.0%
More 6.0%
Requirement(s) 6.0%
Spare 6.0%
Stock 4.0%
2.0% Baggage, Clothes, Clothing, Dearth, Enjoyment, Feelings, Food, Many, Much, Old, Over, Paper, Produce, Profit, Remainder, Value, Waste

Surprise
Shock 33.3%
Present 11.9%
* 9.5%
Party 9.5%
Surprise 7.1%
2.4% Amazement, Birthday, Bright, Cilla-Black, Elation, Jump, Leap, List, Not, Package, Pleasant, Wow

Suspicion
Suspect 13.3%
* 11.1%
Doubt 8.9%
Guilt 6.7%
Envy 4.4%
Evil 4.4%
Spy 4.4%
Trust 4.4%
2.2% Anger, Crime, Detective, Edgy, Eyes, Genuine, Girl, Guile, Hitchcock, Idea, Inspector, Lie, Mind, Mistrust, Of, Police, Think, Trustlessness

Swamp
Bog 14.0%
Marsh 11.6%
Fever 7.0%
Thing 7.0%
Alligator 4.7%
Land 4.7%
Monster 4.7%
Mud 4.7%
2.3% *, Dank, Dell, Drainage, Fungi, Hot, Hug, Mangrove, Me, Mess, Mosquitos, Muddy, Murky, Overwhelm, River, Rushes, Water, Wet

Swan
Lake 35.6%
White 8.9%
Swim 6.7%
Bird 4.4%
Cygnet 4.4%
Lager 4.4%
2.2% Beak, Black, Cigarettes, Dinner, Down, Elegant, Feathers, Geese, Good, Graceful, Matches, Neck, Next, Pond, Song, Water

Swear
Oath 11.6%
Word 9.3%
Blind 7.0%
Curse 7.0%
Fuck 7.0%
Loud 7.0%
Bad 4.7%
Cuss 4.7%
Shit 4.7%
2.3% *, About, Anger, Angry, Blab, Bloody, Bollocks, Box, Loudly, Out, Rude, Shout, Surprise, Time, Truth, Wrong

Sweaty+
Hot 21.4%
Palm(s) 14.3%
Wet 11.9%

Armpit(s) 7.1%
Smelly 7.1%
* 4.8%
Perspire 4.8%
2.4% Cold, Dirt, Dress, Dry, Exercise, Exertion, Perspiring, Sweater, Tacky, Tired, Uncomfortable, Water

Sweep
Chimney 21.3%
Broom 19.1%
Clean 14.9%
Brush 12.8%
Sooty 6.4%
Floor 4.3%
Road 4.3%
2.1% Away, Carpet, Error, Mine, Stake, Stair, Swept, Up

Sweet
Sour 19.0%
Sugar 16.7%
Tooth 16.7%
Bonbon 4.8%
Bread(s) 4.8%
Chocolate 4.8%
Paper 4.8%
Tea 4.8%
Wrapper 4.8%
2.4% Bitter, Cake, Chewy, Life, Meat, Sickly, Suck, Toffee

Sweetheart
Love 30.0%
Lover 12.0%
Heart(s) 6.0%
Sweet(s) 6.0%
Boy 4.0%
Letter 4.0%
Valentine 4.0%
2.0% ?, Black, Boyfriend, Broken, Candy, Child, Darling, Doll, Flowers, Free, Girlfriend, Old, Sugar, Teenager, True, Wedding, Woman

Swift
Bird 22.0%
Fast 20.0%
Quick 16.0%
Slow 12.0%
Swallow 10.0%
2.0% *, Air, Car, Cut, Fleet, Fly, Limp, Sail, Ship, Wings

Swim
Water 15.2%
Pool 13.0%
Sink 8.7%
Sea 6.5%
Dive 4.3%
Drown 4.3%
Lake 4.3%
Splash 4.3%
2.2% Around, Band, Bath, Blue, Cool, Crawl, Fast, Float, Goggles, Height, Over, Relax, River, Run, Sing, Slowly, Stroke, Wear

Swing
* 6.7%
High 6.7%
Park 6.7%
Rope 6.7%
Children 4.4%
Playground 4.4%
Roundabouts 4.4%
Slide 4.4%
2.2% About, Beat, Breeze, Chains, Child, Dance, Ding, Four, Gate, Grass, Gulf, Jump, Low, Motion, Music, Out, Ping, Rhythm, Round, Saw, Shift, Sixties, Swung, Up, Wind

Sword
Fight 10.4%
Knife 10.4%
Knight 8.3%
Scabbard 8.3%
Stone 8.3%
Cut 6.3%
Sharp 6.3%
* 4.2%
Fish 4.2%
Sheath 4.2%
Stick 4.2%
2.1% Buckle, Dagger, Death, Handle, Holly, Kill, Man, Pen, Play, Samurai, Shield, Wilkinson

Swordfish
Fish 13.5%
Steak 11.5%
* 7.7%
Sea 7.7%
Dangerous 3.8%
Food 3.8%
Sharp 3.8%
Trombone 3.8%
1.9% Bill, Danger, Diving, Dubai, Fishing, Fond, Jelly, Line, Marlin, Nets, Note, Ocean, Saw, Shark, Sleek, Spine, Starfish, Sword, Tropical, Tuna, Water, White

Symptom+
Disease 35.7%
Illness 23.8%
Cure 7.1%
Ill 7.1%
Cause 4.8%
Doctor 4.8%
2.4% Diagnosis, Flu, Illness, Phenotype, Sickness, Sign, Underlying

System+
Computer 14.3%
Analysis 11.9%
* 7.1%
Defect 4.8%
Method 4.8%
Water 4.8%
Way 4.8%
2.4% Analyst, Control, Esta, Failure, File, Go, Library, Operating, Operations, Oppression, Process, Rota, Rules, School, Set, Systematic, Tank, Theory, Toilet, Words

Tablecloth
Check(s) 10.0%
Table 8.0%
White 8.0%
Napkin 6.0%
Checked 4.0%
Gingham 4.0%
Plate(s) 4.0%
Red 4.0%
2.0% *, Checkered, Cheese, Chequers, Clean, Cloth, Cover, Cutlery, Dinner, Egg-Cup, Flowers, Food, Forks, Home-Parental, Kitchen, Lay, Pattern, Picnic, Plaid, Sabbath, Set, Square, Stains, Supper, Tea, Things

Tablet
Pill 38.1%
Stone 14.3%
Drug(s) 4.8%
Medicine 4.8%
2.4% *, Altar, Aspirin, Book, Capsule, Dispirin, Doctor, Ecstasy, Ill, Illness, Lozenge, Pop, Sick, Slate, Water, White

Taboo+
* 8.7%
Drink 8.7%
Wrong 8.7%
Forbidden 6.5%
Subject 6.5%
Bad 4.3%
No 4.3%
Sex 4.3%
2.2% Africa, African, Anthropology, Borneo, Box, Cannibal, Don't, Evil, Forbade, Hate, High, Malibu, Mask, Naughty, Not, Put, Secretive, Sexual, Totem, Undiscussed, Unwanted, Voodoo

Tack+
Pin 25.0%
Nail 16.7%
Sew 8.3%
Sail 6.2%
Attack 4.2%
Carpet 4.2%
Horse 4.2%
Stick 4.2%
Tin 4.2%
2.1% Advance, Change, Course, Hammer, Onto, Stable, Tog, Turn, Weave, Wind, Yacht

Tadpole+
Frog(s) 69.0%
Fish 7.1%
Jar 4.8%
Pond 4.8%
2.4% *, Guppy, Life, Sperm, Tiny

Tail
End 15.4%
Feather 7.7%
Animal 5.7%
Long 5.7%
Back 3.8%
Cat 3.8%
Fin 3.8%
Fish 3.8%
Rabbit 3.8%
1.9% *, Bird, Bone, Brush, Coat, Dog, Geek, Head, Hit, Legs, Monkey, Mouse, Nose, Plane, Rear, Snake, Spin, Swish, Thin, Wag, Way, Wind, Wing

Tailor+
Made 35.7%
Suit 23.8%
Clothes 11.9%
2.4% Coat, Cut, Dress, Knit, Make, Needle, Pin, Sew, Soldier, Taylor, Tinker

Take+
Give 19.4%
Steal 10.1%
Away 8.6%
Off 7.2%
Grab 3.6%
Over 3.6%
Snatch 2.9%
Five 2.2%
Remove 2.2%
* 1.4%
Borrow 1.4%
Mine 1.4%
Note(s) 1.4%
Out 1.4%
Part 1.4%
Receive 1.4%
0.7% Apart, Ask, Back, Bite, Blow, Break, Bring, Chance, Charge, Clapperboard, Demand, Down, Drugs, From, Get, Grasp, Greed, Handle, Help, Hold, It, Lift, Live, Make, Many, Money, Move, Now, Pick, Play, Prise, Shop, Stage, Steel, Stock, Swipe, Too, Turn, Two, Up

Talent+
Skill 14.3%
Good 11.9%
Contest 9.5%
Gift 9.5%
Competition 4.8%
Girl 4.8%
Show 4.8%
2.4% Ability, Actress, Attractive, Clever, Five, Gifted, Here, Jew, Match, Musician, Silver, Sing, Singer, Song, Spot, Spotting, Talon

Talk
Speak 17.1%
About 9.8%
Chat 7.3%
To 4.9%
2.4% *, Always, A-Lot, Back, Chatter, Converse, Gabble, Listen, Loud, Loudly, Mouth, Openly, Phone, Point, Prattle, Quickly, Shit, Show, Sound, Speech, T.V., Tell, Time, Voice, Well

Tall
Short 29.2%
Long 8.3%
Man 8.3%
High 6.3%
Man 6.3%
* 4.2%
Boy 4.2%
Building 4.2%
Small 4.2%
Story 4.2%
2.1% Big, Elegant, Girl, Glass, Guy, Lanky, Me, Strength, Thin, Trees

Talon
Claw(s) 40.5%
Eagle 16.7%
* 9.5%
Nail 7.1%
Bird 4.8%
Hook 4.8%
2.4% Clam, Coin, Heel, Spike, Talc, Tooth, What

Tame+
Lion 45.8%
Wild 18.8%
Animal 8.3%
Pet 4.2%
2.1% Beast, Befriend, Calm, Dog, Domesticate, Fierce, Heal, Learn, Shrew, Teach, Train

Tangerine+
Orange 54.8%
Dream 19.0%
Apple 7.1%
Fruit 7.1%
Mandarin 4.8%
2.4% Citrus, Lemon, Satsuma

Tangle+
Mess 18.8%
Web 16.7%
String 10.4%
Knot 8.3%
Twist 6.2%
Wire(s) 6.2%
Weed 4.2%
2.1% Blue, Dance, Difficult, Entwined, Hair, Knotted, Rope, Stoke, Twisted, Untangle, Up, With, Wood, Wool

Tanker
Oil 38.8%
Fuel 6.1%
Petrol 6.1%
* 4.1%
Army 4.1%
Engine 4.1%
Ship 4.1%
Top 4.1%
Water 4.1%
2.0% Big, Bill, Boat, Destruction, Drink, Full, Iraq, Lorry, Tank, Thomas, Tinker, War

Tantrum+
Temper 23.8%
Fit 19.0%
Child 14.3%
Anger 7.1%
Rage 4.8%
2.4% Baby, Hysterics, Immature, Mad, Mood, Murder, Noisy, Scream, Spoilt, Test, Through, Throw, Wobbler

Tape+
Measure 26.2%
Music 16.7%
* 11.9%
Record 9.5%
Play 4.8%
Sellotape 4.8%
2.4% Adhesive, Cassette, Deck, Race, Recorder, Sew, Songs, Sticky, String, Thin, Worm

Tar+
Road(s) 30.8%
Brush 9.5%
Coal 9.5%
Feather 9.5%
Baby 7.1%
Black 4.8%
Pit 4.8%
Thanks 4.8%
2.4% *, Bucket, High, London, Mac, Oil, Punt, Sailor

Target+
Practice 35.8%
Arrow 14.3%
Aim 11.9%
Bullseye 9.5%
Shoot 9.5%
Hit 4.8%
School 4.8%
2.4% Bow, Darts, Gun, Prey

Tarnish+
Spoil 14.3%
Silver 11.9%
Blemish 7.1%

Varnish 7.1%
* 4.8%
Rust 4.8%
2.4% Besmirch, Brass, Brush, Burn, Burnish, Destroy, Dull, Fail, Glint, Gold, Hero, Leather, Man, Polish, Reputation, Scratch, Shiny, Stain, Tan, Tattered, Unsightly

Tarpaulin+
Tent 31.0%
Cover 9.5%
* 7.1%
Boat 4.8%
Canvas 4.8%
Plastic 4.8%
Rubber 4.8%
Sheet 4.8%
2.4% Black, Camping, Campsite, Cloth, Covering, Fence, Groundsheet, Mar, Net, Rain, String, Waterproof

Tart+
Jam 29.2%
Cake 16.7%
Apple 12.5%
Prostitute 8.3%
Whore 6.2%
Pie 4.2%
2.1% Cream, Female, Fruit, Let, Pimp, Red, Sex, Sharp, Skim, Sour, Women

Tartan+
Kilt 26.2%
Scottish 19.0%
Plaid 14.3%
Scotland 9.5%
Cloth 4.8%
Scot 4.8%
2.4% Check, Dress, Fabric, Package, Scotsman, Shirt, Skin, Skirt, Stripes

Task+
Job 35.4%
Work 29.2%
Force 12.5%
Try 4.2%
2.1% Act, Aim, Attempt, Difficulty, Hard, Help, Outset, Trial, Trivial

Taste
Smell 12.5%
Tongue 10.4%
Bud(s) 8.3%
Food 6.3%
Sweet 6.3%
Wine 6.3%
* 4.2%
Eat 4.2%
Lick 4.2%
Mouth 4.2%
Nice 4.2%
Sour 4.2%
2.1% Bad, Cake, Culture, Flavour, Good, Horrible, It, Less, Milk, Pear, Sense, Vinegar

Taunt+
Tease 29.2%
Jeer 8.3%
Tempt 8.3%
Sneer 6.2%
Jibe 4.2%
2.1% *, Castle, Child, Destroy, Devil, Dread, Flaunt, Jibes, Joke, Laugh, Liz, Misery, Poke, Provoke, Rag, Rib, Ridicule, Thin, Torment, Try, Yell

Tavern+
Pub 42.9%
Inn 28.6%
Beer 9.5%
Cave 7.1%
Drink 4.8%
2.4% Drunk, Greece, Pints

Tax+
Money 22.9%
Poll 6.2%
Collector 4.2%
Cut(s) 4.2%
Dodge 4.2%
Evasion 4.2%
Form 4.2%
Government 4.2%
Man 4.2%
Pay 4.2%
Vat 4.2%
2.1% Bracket, Caesar, Collect, Exile, Feudal, Free, Heavy, Income, Insist, Inspector, Rates, Rebate, Redistribution, Remit, Return, Take

Taxi
Cab 44.2%
Car 16.3%
Ride 11.6%
Expensive 4.7%
Fare 4.7%
Rank 4.7%
2.3% Black, Driver, Home, London, Road, Stuff, Urgent

Tea
Coffee 40.4%
Cup 17.3%
Pot 11.5%
Cake 3.8%
1.9% *, Bag, Break, Brew, Brown, Cushion, Leaf, Milk, Mug, Sugar, Teasmaid, Time, Toast, Warm

Teach+
Learn 33.3%
School 10.4%
Children 6.2%
Pupil(s) 6.2%
Teacher 6.2%
Lecture 4.2%
Lesson 4.2%
Student 4.2%
2.1% -Er, Blackboard, Follow, Learn, Learning, Listen, Me, People, Taught, Teeth, Train, Word

Tear+
Rip 60.4%
Hole 4.2%
Paper 4.2%
2.1% Away, Cloth, Damage, Dress, Half, Hurt, Material, Mend, Muscle, Ruin, Sheet, Shreds, Split, Twist, Up

Tear
Rip 23.4%
Cry 14.9%
Eye 8.5%
Paper 8.5%
Cloth 4.3%
Drop 4.3%
Off 4.3%
Up 4.3%
2.1% Break, Clothes, Coat, Dress, Hole, Material, Mend, Slip, Split, Wear, Weep, Wet

Tease
Joke 6.5%
* 4.3%
Child 4.3%
Fun 4.3%
Kid 4.3%
Me 4.3%
Out 4.3%
2.2% About, Amuse, Annoy, Bate, Bicker, Cat, Cruelty, Cry, Cut, Flirt, Goad, Hassle, Her, Irritate, Like, Mirth, Moment, Play, Poke, Prick, Rubbish, Seduce, Sexy, Strip, Taunt, Test, Tickle, Torment, Trick, Unkind

Teasle+
* 16.7%
Thistle 8.3%
Brush 6.3%
Flower 6.3%
Plant 6.3%
Grass 4.2%
Hedgehog 4.2%
Tassle 4.2%
Weasel 4.2%
2.1% Art, Bushy, Chief, Cloth, Coat, Dry, Easel, Embankment, Flower Arrangement, Out, Prickly, Rush, Spike, Squirrel, Stand, Take, Tease, Weed, Wild

Teaspoon
Sugar 38.0%
Tea 12.0%
Coffee 8.0%
Silver 6.0%
Stir 6.0%
Table 4.0%
2.0% Brown, Cup, Dirty, Egg, Fork, Knife, Loon, Medicine, Mix, Saucer, Small, Sugar-Cube, Teacup

Technofear
* 18.8%
Computer(s) 14.6%
Phobia 8.3%
Machines 4.2%
Scared 4.2%
2.1% VDU, Acid, Afraid, Boring, Computer Phobic, Cybernetic, Ear, Fright, Geek, Gizmo, Granny, Horror, Ignorant, Me, New, Nothing, Poor, Rave Music, Technical, Technician, Technological, Technology, Videos

Technophobic
Computer(s) 22.9%
* 14.6%
Fear 6.3%
Technical 4.2%
2.1% Agoraphobic, Allergic, Anti-phobia, Arsehole, Artist, Back, Dad, Dim, Film, Fools, Idiot, Ignorance, Intelligent, Luddite, Modern, Music, Musical, Myself, Out of Date, Ow, Science, Spiders, Technology, What, Women

Teeth+
Mouth 14.6%
Dentist 12.5%
Bite 10.4%
Clean 10.4%
Gums 7.3%
Dentures 4.2%
Gnaw 4.2%
Jaw 4.2%
Lip(s) 4.2%
Mark(s) 4.2%
White 4.2%
2.1% Brush, Claws, Comb, Decay, Gleam, Gnash, Molars, Pain, Yellow

Teetotal+
Drink 23.9%
Alcohol 15.2%
* 8.7%
Beer 4.3%
Drunk 4.3%
2.2% Abstainer, Alcoholic, Bit, Booze, Boring, Bull, Coke, Drinker, Drunkard, Dull, Methodist, Non-Alcohol, Non-Drinker,

Orange, Pubs, Sister, Stoned, Strength, Water, Whisky

Telecast
* 16.7%
Television-TV 14.6%
News 12.5%
Broadcast 6.2%
Transmit 4.2%
2.1% 1984, Actor, Aerial, Announce, Guitar, Ian-McCaskill, Message, New, Newsreader, Newsreel, People, Pod, Programme, Reader, Report, Scene, Show, Telecom, Telephone, Visual, Weather

Telegram
Letter 20.0%
Sam 8.8%
Important 6.6%
Message 6.6%
Queen 6.6%
Mail 4.4%
News 4.4%
Wire 4.4%
2.2% *, Abroad, Birthday, Communicate, Country, Envelope, Joy, Overseas, Pen, Postman, Russia, Send, Sri-Lanka, Stripper, Telephone, Urgent, Yellow

Telephone
Ring 44.4%
Call 11.1%
Box 6.7%
Line 4.4%
2.2% Aunt, Bell, Book, Cable, Conversation, Directory, Disturbance, Fax, Illegible, Message, Number, Plastic, Rabbit, Talk, Voice

Telethon
Charity 18.8%
* 16.7%
Television-TV 14.6%
Tele-Phone 10.4%
Money 6.2%
Marathon 4.2%
2.1% Aerial, Boring, Dull, Exercise, ITV, Noel-Edmonds, Presenter, Run, Sport, Terry-Wogan, TV-Broadcast, Wank, Yellow

Television
Programme 17.8%
Set 8.9%
Box 6.7%
Radio 6.7%
Screen 6.7%
Watch 6.7%
Film 4.4%
News 4.4%
Show 4.4%
2.2% Boring, Colour, Crap, Distraction, Drag, Gameshow, Hewn, Inspector Morse, Moving, On, Picture, Presenter, Rubbish, Station, Video

Tell
Tale(s) 21.3%
Me 8.5%
Kiss 6.4%
William 6.4%
Ask 4.3%
Give 4.3%
Lie 4.3%
Story 4.3%
Talk 4.3%
2.1% *, Bank, Blind, Convey, Describe, Disclose, Gossip, Grass, Instruct, Know, People, Phone, Relate, Say, Speak, Teach, Told

Template+
Pattern 14.3%
Model 7.1%
Print 7.1%
Copy 4.8%
DNA 4.8%
Metal 4.8%
Mould 4.8%
Plan 4.8%
Stencil 4.8%
2.4% *, Blueprint, Cardboard, Cutout, Dish, Draw, Drawing, Engineer, Follow, Future, Matching, Molecule, Patchwork, Publish, Script, Shape, Starter, Think

Tempt+
* 10.4%
Sin 10.4%
Apple 6.2%
Devil 6.2%
Try 6.2%
Eve 4.2%
Satan 4.2%
Seduce 4.2%
Succumb 4.2%
Temple 4.2%
Tempter 4.2%
2.1% Beckon, Christ, Desire, Fate, Fruit, Girl, Greed, Have, Look, Steal, Taunt, Test, Vine-Leaf, Want, Wilde, Will, Yes

Ten
Eleven 17.0%
Number(s) 12.8%
Nine 10.6%
Twenty 6.4%
Five 4.3%
Pounds 4.3%
2.1% *, Bells, Bottles, Days, Feathers, Green, Hands, Men, Music, News, Noughts, Pence, People, Phone, Pins, Swedish, Thirty, Thousand, Toes, Tonne, Two

Tenant+
Landlord 30.4%
Rent 17.4%
Flat 6.5%
House 6.5%
Lager 6.5%
* 4.3%
Lodger 4.3%
2.2% Farmer, Householder, Law, Let, Lodge, Me, Money, Pills, Property, Room, Steven

Tend+
Care 26.1%
Nurse 13.0%
Sheep 10.9%
* 8.7%
2.2% Aid, Bed, Calf, Cherish, Cultivate, Garden, Give, Hurt, Leave, Look, Mend, Mind, Minister, Money, Sick, Take, Tender, Try

Tennis+
Ball(s) 21.7%
Court 17.4%
Racquet 13.0%
Match 10.9%
Game 8.7%
Player 6.5%
Table 6.5%
Wimbledon 4.3%
2.2% Champion, Green, Net, Ph, Red-Clay

Tennis racquet
Ball(s) 33.3%
String(s) 8.9%
Court 6.7%
Game 6.7%
Sport 6.7%
Tennis 6.7%
Play 4.4%
* 4.4%
2.2% Boredom, Club, Deuce, Friend, Hard, Serve, Squash, Summer, Tennis ball, Volley

Tense+
Nervous 37.5%
Stress 6.2%
Camp 4.2%
Tight 4.2%
Uptight 4.2%
Worried 4.2%
2.1% Alert, Anxious, Crack, Fearful, Headache, Moment, Mood, Muscle, Neck, Present, Quiet, Scout, Shiatsu, Taut, Terse, Thin, Uneasy, Verb, Wait

Tent+
Camp 33.3%
Peg 20.8%
Camping 4.2%
Canvas 4.2%
Pole 4.2%
2.1% Arabia, Bedouin, Flap, Green, Hike, Hole, Outside, Place, Ridge, Scout, Sleep, Small, Stay, Wet, Wigwam, Wound

Tepid+
Warm 47.8%
Water 28.9%
Lukewarm 12.2%
Cold 2.2%
Cool 2.2%
Hot 2.2%
Luke 2.2%
1.1% Blood, Waters

Term+
School 27.1%
End 10.4%
Endearment 6.2%
Cambridge 4.2%
Condition 4.2%
Holiday 4.2%
Time 4.2%
2.1% Bitter, Card, College, Ended, Ending, Ends, Exams, Exchange, Full, Gull, Name, Over, Semester, Start, Tower, Trimester, Twist, Weeks, Year

Terrain+
Land 26.2%
Ground 23.8%
Country 9.5%
Rough 9.5%
Landscape 7.1%
* 4.8%
Hills 4.8%
2.4% Desert, Earth, False, Flat, Surroundings, Wilderness

Terry
Waite 26.5%
Wogan 24.5%
* 10.7%
June 10.2%
Chocolate 6.1%
2.0% Anderson, Eagleton, Hall, Higgins, Jackson, Long, Scott, Teresa, Thomas, Venables, White

Teutonic+
* 30.4%
German 30.4%
Germanic 15.2%
Tutor 4.3%
2.2% Ancient, Authority, Baltic, Cheeks, Knight, Plate, Powerful, Race, Volcano

Text+
Book 50.0%
Words 10.9%
Read 8.7%
Writing 6.5%
Reading 4.3%
Write 4.3%
2.2% Bible, Knowledge, Play, Print, Printing, Share, Story

That
This 28.0%
Take 12.0%
* 8.0%
One 8.0%
There 8.0%
Hat 4.0%
Is 4.0%
Was 4.0%
2.0% Connective, Day, Definite, Object, Over, Person, Specific, The, Then, Those, Wall, Which

The
End 12.0%
The 12.0%
* 10.0%
It 10.0%
One 6.0%
A 4.0%
Best 4.0%
First 4.0%
Man 4.0%
2.0% Begin, Boy, Definite-Article, Frost, Hat, Is, Moon, News, Next, Of, Small, Story, They, This, Time, Town, What

Theatre+
Play 30.4%
Actor(s) 6.5%
Goer 6.5%
Ticket 6.5%
Curtain 4.3%
Show 4.3%
2.2% *, Audience, Bar, Cinema, Comedy, Critic, Fun, Gallery, Go, National, Operate, Operations, People, Red, Round, Seat, Shakespeare, Studies, Thespian

Them
Us 66.7%
* 6.2%
There-Eyes 4.2%
2.1% All, Ants, Coaxe, Out, Sad, Their, Theirs, There, These, Those, We

Theme
Park 17.0%
Music 12.8%
Tune 12.8%
Story 8.5%
Film 4.3%
Idea 4.3%
Play 4.3%
2.1% *, Concerto, Design, Drama, Evening, Frieze, Gene, Good, Motif, Over, Paris, Plan, Plot, Refrain, Show, Song, Television

Then
Now 60.4%
* 12.5%
There 6.3%
When 4.2%
2.1% And, And-There, I, Past, Them, Then, Till, Was

There
Here 29.2%
There 12.5%
* 10.4%
Now 8.3%
Over 8.3%
Then 8.3%
Is 4.2%
Place 4.2%
Where 4.2%
2.1% Are, Away, Home, Was, You

Thick
Thin 48.9%
Bread 8.9%
Cream 6.7%
And-Thin 4.4%
2.2% Brick, Cut, Dense, Forest, Head, Lip, Mane, Shake, Skin, Skull, Slow, Wire, Wood, Yoghurt

Thimble
Sew 24.4%
Needle 20.0%
Thumb 20.0%
Sewing 8.9%
Finger 6.7%
Thread 6.7%
2.2% Cotton, Full, Nimble, Pipe, Shaker, Small

Thin
Fat 31.2%
Skinny 8.6%
Thick 8.6%
* 3.2%
Man 3.2%
Slim 3.2%
Small 3.2%
Fine 2.2%
Ice 2.2%
Stick 2.2%
Wedge 2.2%
1.1% Andrex, Arm, Bones, Bread, Ethernet, Figure, Girl, Hair, Knife, Laurel, Layer, Legs, Line, Lips, Lizzy, Matchstick, Pencil, Person, Sexy, Sinew, Skinned, Spindly, Steak, Tall, Wafer, Watery, Woman, Yes

Think
* 16.7%
About 8.3%
Brain 8.3%
Tank 8.3%
Hard 4.2%
Mind 4.2%
Thought 4.2%
2.1% Ahead, Ask, Believe, Carefully, Cogitate, Concentrate, Consider, Fast, Feel, Good, Headache, Hear, Idea, Logic, Paper, Pause, Pink, Reflect, Slow, Tink, Up, Wonder

This
That 70.8%
* 4.3%
Is 4.2%
2.1% And, And-That, Garden, Instance, Object, Then, There, This, Time, World

Thought
Idea 21.1%
Think 15.6%
Mind 11.1%
Brain 8.9%
After 4.4%
Dream 4.4%
Process 4.4%
2.2% *, About, Action, Forget, Give, Less, Memory, Nice, Non, Now, Speed, Thoughtful, Time

Threat
Danger 16.7%
* 9.5%
Evil 4.8%
Fear 4.8%
Men 4.8%
2.4% Annihilation, Blackmail, Dagger, Death, End, Fight, Fist, Frightened, Gun, Hit, Kill, Knife, Menace, Panic, Point, Power, Pressure, Retreat, Scared, Scary, Threaten, Threatening, Thug, War, Warning

Three
Four 20.4%
Number 12.2%
Two 10.2%
* 6.1%
Bears 6.1%
Blind 4.1%
Mice 4.1%
2.0% Action, Bags, Goat, Luck, Mason, Men, One, Pigs, Small, Some, Times, Tree, Triad, Trinity, Triplets, Up, Wiser, Wise-Men

Thrill
Excitement 26.2%
Rollercoaster 16.7%
Seeker 7.1%
Cheap 4.8%
Excite 4.8%
Scare 4.8%
2.4% *, Buy, Enthrall, Fairground, Feeling, Fun, Happiness, Nice, Nothing, Scream, Sex, Shriek, Smile, Speed, Whee

Throw
Ball 25.0%
Away 12.5%
Catch 10.4%
Chuck 10.4%
Up 10.4%
Cast 4.2%
Cricket 4.2%
Hurl 4.2%
2.1% *, Back, Dart, Discus, Far, Javelin, Muscle, Put, Rubbish

Thumb
Finger 20.0%
Nail 20.0%
Hand 15.6%
Print 6.7%
Up 6.7%
* 4.4%
Press 4.4%
Screw 4.4%
Tom 4.4%
2.2% Grip, Hitchhike, John-Thumb, Moribund, Nose, Tack

Thummbnail
Sketch 16.0%
Finger 8.0%
* 4.0%
Bite 4.0%
Print 4.0%
Varnish 4.0%
2.0% ?, Big, Broken, Bruised, Cuticle, Cuttings, Daddy, Dirty, Fat, Fingernail, Grail, Grease, Hand, Hit, Hob, Hurt, Mark, Nail, Nail-Brush, Needle, Scissors, Scratch, Screw, Sharp, Split, Tack, Tear, Thumb, Two, Volley

Thump
Hit 30.0%
Punch 8.0%
Bang 6.0%
Hard 6.0%
Rabbit 6.0%
Bash 4.0%
2.0% *, Bambi, Bully, Crash, Drop, Fall, Finger, Fist, Her, Nose, Pillow, Punish, Stairs, Success, Swing, Them, Thud, Whack, Worm, You

Thunder
Lightning 60.4%
Rain 6.3%
Black 4.2%
Bolt 4.2%
Cloud 4.2%
Storm 4.2%
2.1% Barn, Clap, Crash, Dark, God, River, Road, -Drome

Thunderbird
Puppet(s) 17.3%
Go 15.4%
Cartoon 9.6%
Wine 7.7%
* 5.7%
Are-Go 5.7%
Car 5.7%
Televsion 3.8%
Tv 3.8%
1.9% Bottle, Captain-Scarlett, Drink, Fab, Ford, Four, Gerry, Plane, Space, Tv-Programme, Two, Virgil, Vodka

Tidy
Neat 22.9%
Room 22.9%
Clean 16.7%
Up 12.5%
* 6.2%
Untidy 4.2%
2.1% Carpet, Flat, Near, Organised, Scruffy, Smart, Sum

Tie
Knot 22.9%
Shirt 22.9%
Clip 4.2%
Dye 4.2%
Neck 4.2%
Rack 4.2%
Up 4.2%
2.1% Bind, Bow, Cast, Collar, Down, Jacket, Lace, Loose, Me, Rope, Scarf, Shoelace, String, Suit, Untie, Wear

Tight
Fit 24.5%
Squeeze 16.3%
* 10.2%
Loose 6.1%
Jeans 4.1%
Lycra 4.1%
Rope 4.1%
Skirt 4.1%
2.0% ?, Baggy, Close-Together, Drum, Fisted, Neat, Pants, Pinching, Small, Stingy, Suffocate, Taut

Tighten
Belt 25.5%
Up 12.8%
Grip 10.6%
Rope 6.4%
* 4.3%
Squeeze 4.3%
2.1% Clash, God, Hard, Knot, Noose, Nut, Pull, Rope, Screw, Secure, Slack, Stiff, Strangle, String, Throat, Trousers

Tile+
Roof 38.9%
Bathroom 21.1%
Wall 7.8%
Floor 5.6%
Kitchen 4.4%
Ceramic 3.3%
1.1% Bath, Brick, Garden, Grout, Hill, Lay, Light, Mat, Paint, Plate, Pottery, Red, Roofing, Room, Slate, Tiling

Timid
Shy 57.8%
Mouse 6.7%
Confident 4.4%
2.2% Afraid, Bold, Child, Fear, Fox, Love, Nature, Nervous, Outgoing, Person, Quiet, Scared, Strum

Tin+
Can 35.6%
Mine 6.7%
Man 5.6%
Box 4.4%
Opener 4.4%
Pot 4.4%
Foil 3.3%
Pan 3.3%
Plate 3.3%
Baked-Beans 2.2%
Biscuits 2.2%
Hat 2.2%
Lead 2.2%
Mug 2.2%
1.1% Aluminium, Beans, Container, Copper, Drum, Lid, Metal, Michael, Open, Paint, Steel, Tagel, Tin, Tuna

Tina
Turner 79.6%
* 6.4%
2.0% Charlie, Friend, Harris, Regnard, Stern, Tiny, Welham

Tiny
Small 39.6%
Baby 4.3%
Tim 4.3%
Tot 4.3%
Big 3.3%
Hand(s) 3.3%
Little 3.3%
Mind 3.3%
Minuscule 2.2%
Petite 2.2%
1.1% Blink, Boy, Brain, Children, Delicate, Feet, Fish, Giant, Hard, Huge, Mature, Midget, Minute, Mouse, Person, Roland, Room, Shell, Tall, Tears, Thin, Tina, Titchy, Toes, Wee

Tip+
Rubbish 14.6%
Waiter 12.5%
Money 10.4%
Top 10.4%
Dump 8.3%
Taxi 4.2%
Tilt 4.2%
2.1% Driver, End, Fibre, Hint, Ice, Iceberg, Lorry, Out, Over, Peak, Pour, Races, Throw, Tippex, Tongue, Wing, Wop

To
From 22.9%
* 12.5%
Go 8.3%
Fro 6.3%
There 6.3%
Me 4.2%
Where 4.2%
You 4.2%
2.1% Annul, Be, Give, It, Last, M, One, Place, Ten, The, Toward, Town, Twit, Two, Yours

Toad+
Hole 39.6%
Frog 35.4%
Stool 6.2%
2.1% Amphibian, Girl, Hall, Kiss, Olga, Prince, Rat, Slimy, Witches

Toaster
Toast 28.9%
Bread 15.6%
Breakfast 6.7%
Burnt 6.7%
Kitchen 4.4%
Pop 4.4%
2.2% Bounce, Burn, Butter, Crumpets, Eat, Grill, Jam, Machine, Marmalade, Mexico, Oven, Plug, Small, Warm

Toe
Foot 55.3%
Nail 19.1%
Line 4.3%
Suck 4.3%
2.1% Gout, Heel, Hold, Job, Painful, Rope, Tip, Touch

Toffee+
Apple 45.8%
Sweet(s) 12.5%
Chew 10.4%
Fudge 6.2%
Nose 4.2%
Nosed 4.2%
Sticky 4.2%
Teeth 4.2%
2.1% Crisp, Fairground, Sugar, Trucker

Tolerate
* 14.6%
Allow 12.5%
Accept 4.2%
Give 4.2%
Patience 4.2%
2.1% Accommodate, Calm, Child, Difficult, Dislike, Endure, Give-In, Him, It, Just, Let, Like, Majority, Misery, Moan, Mother, Nothing, Open, Person, Problem, Put, Put-Up, Put-Up-With, Stand, Take, Understand, Us, Withstand, You

Toll+
Bridge 16.7%
* 12.5%
Gate 12.5%
Booth 10.4%
Pay 10.4%
Money 6.2%
Bell 4.2%
2.1% Battle, Fine, Foot, Hand, House, Number, Payment, Price, Puddle, Said, Small, Twenty-Five, Way

Tongue+
Cheek 18.8%
Lick 12.5%
Mouth 12.5%
Ham 6.3%
Taste 6.3%
Kiss 4.2%
Lip(s) 4.2%
Red 4.2%
Teeth 4.2%
2.1% Check, Cross, Eat, Lambs, Long, Mount, Out, Poke, Sheep, Speak, Touch, Train, Wet

Tonic+
Gin 38.3%
Water 38.3%
Medicine 4.3%
2.1% Bottle, Freshen, Glass, Good, Lotion, Save, Sort, Wine, Write

Tool
Hammer 42.0%
Kit 4.0%
Shed 4.0%

Spanner 4.0%
Weapon 4.0%
2.0% Body, Box, Car, Case, Gun, Idiot, Implement, Jig, Lathe, Machine, Mill, Pliers, Plumber, Spade, Stone, Store, Toolbox, Trade, Up, Wooden

Toolbox
Hammer 20.8%
Kit 16.7%
Spanner 16.7%
Tool(s) 10.4%
Father 4.2%
2.1% Blue, Conkers, Container, Fringe, Garage, Gift, Knife, Metal, Nail, Saw, Screwdriver, Toolkit, Woodwork, Work

Tooth
Brush 11.5%
Ache 9.6%
Decay 7.7%
Gum 7.7%
Mouth 7.7%
Fairy 5.7%
White 5.7%
Dentist 3.8%
Nail 3.8%
Pick 3.8%
Teeth 3.8%
1.9% And-Claw, Bite, Canine, False, Fang, Filling, Hole, Molar, Month, Pain, Paste, Sabre, Saw, Tongue, Toothbrush

Toothbrush
Clean 15.6%
Paste 15.6%
Brush 11.1%
Toothpaste 11.1%
Bathroom 6.7%
Bristle(s) 6.7%
Teeth 6.7%
Tooth 6.7%
2.2% Dentist, Holder, Mouth, Mug, Overnight, Peg, Scrub, Tube, Water

Toothpaste
Brush 22.0%
Teeth 14.0%
Clean 8.0%
Tube 8.0%
Toothbrush 6.0%
Mint 4.0%
Sink 4.0%
White 4.0%
2.0% *, Bite, Fresh, Kingfisher, Maclean, Minty, Mornings, Pot, Squirt, Stripes, Stripy, Strontium, Taste, Tooth, Yuk

Top+
Bottom 56.2%
Spin 8.3%
Spinning 8.3%
Hat 4.2%
2.1% *, End, First, Gun, Less, Lid, Sh?, T-Shirt, Tool, Turning, Turvy

Topic
Subject 48.8%
Chocolate 12.2%
Conversation 7.3%
Idea 4.9%
Story 4.9%
2.4% *, Bar, Book, Controversial, Essay, Mars, News, Scrap-Book, Seminar, Spots

Torment
* 8.9%
Pain 6.7%
Tease 6.7%
Abuse 4.4%
Anguish 4.4%
Black 4.4%
Hurt 4.4%
Storm 4.4%
2.2% Anger, Angry, Annoy, Beat, Blood, Children, Despair, Divorce, Fight, Fortune, Hassle, Hate, Inquisition, Jibe, Me, Mock, Nag, Pester, Plead, Torture, Trouble, Unhappiness, Upset, Wound

Torso
Body 61.9%
Chest 11.9%
Muscle 7.1%
2.4% Belt, Belvedere, Leornado, Spine, Sternum, Stomach, Strong, Wealth

Toss+
Coin 27.1%
Throw 20.8%
Turn 16.7%
Ball 6.2%
Caber 6.2%
Catch 4.2%
2.1% Fire, Heads, Masturbate, Off, Pancake, Penny, Spin, Twist, Up

Total+
All 30.4%
Recall 21.7%
Complete 10.9%
Sum(s) 8.7%
Petrol 6.5%
Control 4.3%
2.2% *, Collapse, Destroy, Power, Result, Teetotal, Whole, Wreck

Touch
Feel 29.2%
Finger(s) 16.7%
* 6.3%
Hand(s) 6.3%
Me 4.2%
2.1% Body, Go, Handle, Hold, It, Love, Pad, Paper, Rough, Sense, Skin, Soft, Stroke, Sweat, Tactile, Thrill, Type, Up

Tough
Hard 24.0%
Strong 18.0%
Guy 12.0%
Nut 4.0%
Rough 4.0%
Weak 4.0%
2.0% *, Chewy, Cookie, Enough, First, Gristly, Hide, Leather, Luck, Meat, Muscle, Rope, Rugby, Steak, Steel, Tender, Titty

Tour+
Holiday 12.5%
Bus 10.4%
Guide 10.4%
Travel 8.3%
Tourist 6.2%
Trip 6.2%
Coach 4.2%
Operator 4.2%
Round 4.2%
World 4.2%
2.1% City, Cooks, Country, Cry, Cycling, Drive, Europe, France, Look, Move, Paris, Stage, Town, Trek

Town
Folk 24.4%
City 20.0%
Council 17.8%
Village 8.9%
Hall 4.4%
London 4.4%
Planning 4.4%
Ship 4.4%
2.2% House, Life, People, Street, Townsfolk

Toy
Children 16.7%
Boy 11.9%
Doll 11.9%
Soft 11.9%
Car 7.1%
Baby 4.8%
Shop 4.8%
2.4% Bear, Boat, Box, Bus, Cards, Cuddly, Fun, Jack-In-A-Box, Pen, Plastic, Play, Sweet, Train

Track+
Path 22.9%
Race 8.3%
Run 8.3%
Train 8.3%
Follow 6.2%
Running 6.2%
Field 4.2%
Trail 4.2%
2.1% Animal, Athlete, Athletics, Circuit, Dirt, Dogs, Dust, Hunt, Mind, Railroad, Rails, Scan, Search, Trek, Turn

Trade+
Swap 10.4%
Barter 8.3%
Market 8.3%
Sell 6.2%
Shop(s) 6.2%
Business 4.2%
Buy 4.2%
Merchant 4.2%
Ware(s) 4.2%
2.1% Affair, Balance, Bargain, Bond, Capitalism, Economy, Give, Goods, Man, Mark, Money, Profession, Profit, Spend, Tear, Train, War, Wealth, Wind, Wooded, Work

Tradition
Old 22.0%
* 12.2%
Custom 9.8%
Past 9.8%
Music 4.9%
2.4% Age, Bound, Ceremony, Church, Conservation, Culture, England, Family, History, Jewish, Line, Monarchy, Respect, Ritual, Royal, Story, Tight, Tory

Traffic+
Car(s) 35.7%
Jam 33.3%
Light(s) 4.8%
Noise 4.8%
Warden 4.8%
2.4% Busy, Chaos, Circulation, Cone, Direct, Jams, Policeman

Tragedy
Comedy 11.9%
Sad 11.9%
Loss 7.1%
Accident 4.8%
Death 4.8%
Tragic 4.8%
War 4.8%
2.4% *, Awful, Bee-Gees, Car, Drama, Emotion, Fatal, Flood, Fragile, Gone, Greek, Grief, Hamlet, Heroine, Life, Queen, Romeo, Shame, Sorrow, Suffering, Upset

Tragic
Sad 14.3%
Comedy 9.5%
Accident 7.1%

Death 7.1%
Consequences 4.8%
Fall 4.8%
Macbeth 4.8%
2.4% *, Affair, Case, Circumstances, Comic, Dancer, Depressing, Drama, End, Event, Loss, Performance, Queen, Serious, Story, Terrible, Town, Trauma, War, Worsen

Train+
Station 8.3%
Bus 6.2%
Line 6.2%
Rail 6.2%
Teach 6.2%
Tram 6.2%
Carriage 4.2%
Learn 4.2%
Spot 4.2%
Track 4.2%
2.1% Away, Boat, Car, Dog, Go, Guard, Halt, Journey, Platform, Rails, Railway, Ride, Set, Shoe, Spotter, Steam, Stop, Tech, Time, Tube, Whistle

Tram+
Line(s) 27.1%
Bus 22.9%
Train 12.5%
Car 6.2%
Rail 4.2%
Track 4.2%
Vienna 4.2%
2.1% Abroad, Basel, Electric, London, Old, Trolley-Car, Way, Wires

Tranquil
Quiet 38.0%
Peaceful 13.0%
Calm 9.8%
Peace 8.7%
Silent 3.3%
* 2.2%
Lake 2.2%
1.1% Atmosphere, Bedlam, Birdsong, Butterfly, Clear, Country, Drink, Feather, Green, Mood, Mountains, Noisy, River, Scene, Sea, Serene, Sleep, Still, Tired, Water

Tranquillity
Peace 40.4%
Quiet 19.1%
Calm 8.5%
Serenity 6.4%
Countryside 4.3%
2.1% Blue, Ecstasy, Green, Harmony, Passive, Peacefulness, Rest, Serene, Warmth

Trap+
Mouse 22.9%
Animal 12.5%
Catch 12.5%
Door 10.4%
Caught 4.2%
Fur 4.2%
Snare 4.2%
2.1% *, Cage, Dog, Ensnare, Fall, Kill, Otter, Pheasant, Rabbit, Set, Tight, Train, Trend, Water

Trash+
Rubbish 41.7%
Can 33.3%
Bin 4.2%
Garbage 4.2%
2.1% American, Bad, Bang, Cheap, Dustbin, Junkyard, Waste, White

Travel
Plane 7.1%
Train 7.1%
Agent 4.8%
Companion 4.8%
Holiday(s) 4.8%
Light 4.8%
Log 4.8%
Trip 4.8%
2.4% Arrive, Away, Boat, Brochure, Experience, Fly, Go, Map, Overseas, Plus, Roam, Sailing, Ship, Shop, Show, Sick, Stay, Suitcase, Ticket, Time, Tips, Voyage, Wander, World

Trawl+
Fish 39.6%
* 14.6%
Catch 6.2%
Drag 6.2%
Ship 6.2%
Boat 4.2%
2.1% Bog, Evil, False, Fisherman, Herring, Sea, Short, Sing, Song, Sweet, Thorough

Tread+
Carefully 18.8%
Foot 10.4%
Tyre 10.4%
Softly 8.3%
Step 8.3%
Feet 4.2%
Gently 4.2%
Mill 4.2%
Plod 4.2%
Shoe 4.2%
Walk 4.2%
2.1% Fear, Footfall, Footprint, Over, Pattern, Slowly, Sole, Warily, Wheel

Treat+
Trick 25.6%
Sweet 13.3%
Present 8.9%
Special 5.6%
Surprise 4.4%
* 3.3%
Child 2.2%
Cure 2.2%
Doctor 2.2%
Fun 2.2%
Patient 2.2%
Peanut 2.2%
Spoil 2.2%
Toffee 2.2%
1.1% Apple, Birthday, Cake, Care, Chocolate, Enter, Heal, Help, Ice, Joy, Myself, Nice, Pleasure, Reward, Swim, Test, Treaty, Well, You

Tree
Leaf 20.4%
Branch 14.3%
Leaves 10.2%
Trunk 8.2%
* 6.1%
Oak 6.1%
Root 4.1%
Wood 4.1%
2.0% Acorn, Bark, Big, Bud, Forest, Garden, Green, Grow, Life, Oasis, Plant, Stick, Tall

Trek+
Hike 12.5%
Journey 12.5%
Star 12.5%
Walk 8.3%
Mountain(s) 6.2%
Climb 4.2%
Path 4.2%
2.1% Across, Desert, Far, Footprint, Forest, Hiker, Kathmandu, March, Moors, North, Pony, Ride, Search, Tour, Upwards, Valley, Voyage, Way, Wild

Tremble
Shake 40.0%
Fear 14.0%
Quiver 8.0%
Shiver 8.0%
2.0% *, Afraid, Boots, Calm, Cold, Earthquake, Hand, Leaf, Lip, Music, Parkinsons, Quake, Shudder, Weak, Window

Trench+
War(s) 29.2%
Coat 14.6%
Dig 14.6%
Warfare 8.3%
Ditch 6.2%
Soldier(s) 6.2%
Deep 4.2%
Fight 4.2%
Hole 4.2%
2.1% Army, Dyke, Man, Water

Trend
Fashion 31.0%
Setter 16.7%
Follow 4.8%
2.4% *, Association, Clothes, Down, Idea, Old, Past, Pattern, Relationship, Ritual, Router, Sequence, Set, Significance, Significant, Temporary, Tendency, This, Thought, Up

Tress+
Hair 47.9%
* 12.5%
Table 10.4%
Dress 4.2%
Locks 4.2%
Trestle 4.2%
2.1% Chicken, Clothes, Head, Pass, Skirt, Stress, Trail, What

Tribune+
Herald 28.6%
Roman 9.5%
* 7.1%
Newspaper 7.1%
Paper 7.1%
Rome 4.8%
2.4% Communism, Communist, Daily, Decide, Empire, Heard, House, Labour, Law, Legion, Marxism, Paper, Romans, Soldier, USA

Tribute+
* 14.3%
Offering 7.1%
Acclaim 4.8%
Gift 4.8%
Honour 4.8%
Praise 4.8%
Song 4.8%
Wreath 4.8%
2.4% Accolade, Award, Commendation, Compliment, Dedication, Event, Fame, Farewell, Homage, King, Pasadena, Pay, Prevail, Respect, Roman, Spanner, Statement, Talisman, To, Trumpet, Well-Done

Trick+
Treat 20.8%
Fool 14.6%
Joke 12.5%
Magic 10.4%
Trade 6.2%
Magician 4.2%
2.1% Clown, Con, Deceit, Deceive, Fox, Fun, Guile,

Light, Out, Party, Play, Ploy, Question, Slip, Tail

Trigger+
Gun 54.2%
Happy 16.7%
Pull 8.3%
Horse 6.2%
Finger 4.2%
2.1% Fire, Guard, Mechanism, Shoot, Start

Trill+
Sing 18.8%
Bird 10.4%
Budgie 6.2%
High 6.2%
Seed(s) 6.2%
Shrill 6.2%
Song 6.2%
Flute 4.2%
Music 4.2%
Sound 4.2%
2.1% *, Double, Fun, Natter, Noise, Note, Phone, Piano, Sweet, Thrill, Trilby, Whine, Whistle

Trip+
Fall 52.1%
Wire 10.4%
Drug 6.2%
Holiday 6.2%
Day 4.2%
Up 4.2%
2.1% *, Acid, Excursion, Foot, Journey, Mile, Move, Seaside

Triumph
Win 19.0%
Victory 16.7%
Car 7.1%
Motorbike 7.1%
Success 4.8%
2.4% *, Adversity, Arch, Bike, Cup, Defeat, Evil, Failure, Great, Hope, Motor, Personal, Roman, Spitfire, Succeed, Truth, Victor, Will, Wreak

Trombone+
Trumpet 16.7%
Instrument 14.3%
Player 9.5%
Band 7.1%
Music 7.1%
Brass 4.8%
Horn 4.8%
Jazz 4.8%
Play 4.8%
2.4% Artist, Clarinet, Drum, Noise, Orchestra, Paperclip, Pete, Pomp, Second, Seventy, Wind

Trot+
Horse(s) 45.9%
Run 16.7%
Canter 6.2%
Gallop 6.2%
Along 4.2%
Pig 4.2%
Pony 4.2%
2.1% Frock, Jog, Jump, March, Paddock, Slowly

Trouble
Maker 15.6%
Double 6.7%
In 6.7%
* 4.4%
Northern 4.4%
Strife 4.4%
With 4.4%
Problem 3.3%
2.2% Bad, Bother, Bubble, Business, Causer, Children, Cry, Danger, Deadline, Deep, Fool, Harm, Peace, Police, Riff-Raff, School, Shooter, Storm, Terrible, War, Work, You

Trousers
Leg(s) 11.1%
Man 8.9%
Press 8.9%
Shorts 6.7%
Baggy 4.4%
Belt 4.4%
Jeans 4.4%
Pocket 4.4%
2.2% *, Down, Flares, Flies, Grey, Hem, Jacket, Jumper, Make, Material, Mouth, Pants, Pink, Problem, Shirt, Shoes, Skirt, Smart, Stripy, Wear, Zip

Trout+
Fish 54.2%
Farm 18.8%
2.1% Almond, Eat, Fishing, Fly, Mask, Pellets, Pond, Rise, River, Schubert, Shark, Swim, Woman

Truck+
Lorry 45.8%
Car 6.2%
Load 4.2%
Road 4.2%
Van 4.2%
2.1% Bus, Cart, Door, Driver, Dump, Flap, Hedgehog, Highway, Mack, Nine, Speed, Stop, Train, Trucking, Wheel, With, Yorkie

True
False 53.3%
Story 8.9%
Belief 4.4%
Lie 4.4%
Love 4.4%
2.2% Believe, Dementia, Fact, Faith, Faithful, Light, Luck, Right, Song, To-Life, Veracity

Trumpet+
Horn 21.4%
Blow 16.7%
Blast 4.8%
Bugle 4.8%
Music 4.8%
Play 4.8%
Sound 4.8%
Trombone 4.8%
2.4% Band, Bassoon, Blower, Brass, Call, Concerto, Instrument, Musician, Noise, Orchestra, Player, Playing, Tribune, Voluntary

Trunk+
Elephant 47.9%
Case 14.6%
Holiday 4.2%
Room 4.2%
Tree 4.2%
2.1% Cabin, Car, Chest, College, Lorry, Luggage, Metal, Nose, Suitcase, Sway, Torso, Train

Trust+
Faith 12.7%
Friend 8.5%
Believe 7.4%
Love 5.3%
Fund 4.3%
Me 4.3%
* 3.2%
Bond 2.1%
Equity 2.1%
Friendship 2.1%
House 2.1%
1.1% Belief, Believe-In, Care, Confidence, Entrust, Fidelity, Fix, Fool, Glad, Glue, God, Good, Grace, Heart, Help, Honest, Honour, Income, Keep, Lie, Life, Lord, Loyal, Luck, Mistrust, National, Obey, Pledge, Savings, Sing, Sweet, Sympathy, T?, Trick, Tryst, Turn, Unit, Vulnerable, Water, Well, Will, Worthy

Truth
Lie(s) 45.2%
Honest 7.1%
False 4.8%
Game(s) 4.8%
Tell 4.8%
2.4% Bible, Dare, Drug, Fact, Fortune, Honesty, Hypothesis, Love, Many, Not-A-Lie, Tale, Truth, Value, Virtue

Truthfulness
Honesty 25.5%
Lie(s) 21.3%
Honest 12.8%
Good 4.3%
Right 4.3%
Truth 4.3%
2.1% *, Clergy, Court, Deceit, Faith, Falsehood, Friend, Help, Life, Loyalty, Sin, Sincere, Sincerity

Try
Again 12.0%
Attempt 12.0%
Hard 10.0%
Able 6.0%
Effort 6.0%
Harder 6.0%
* 4.0%
Again 4.0%
Rugby 4.0%
Strain 4.0%
2.0% Another, Endeavour, Essay, Fail, Fry, More, Not, Now, On, Out, Refuse, Score, Tempt, To, Why, Work

Tub
Bath 38.0%
Lard 20.0%
Ice-Cream 6.0%
Wash 6.0%
Washing 6.0%
Margarine 4.0%
Water 4.0%
2.0% Bathroom, Beer, Hot, Marge, Of-Margarine, Rinse, Round, Swift

Tube
Train 25.5%
Underground 17.0%
Paste 4.3%
Toothpaste 4.3%
2.1% *, -Igrip, Bicycle, Bike, Cylinder, Dust, Fix, Grip, Inner, London, Neck, Puncture, Roll, Siphon, Strike, Stuffy, Subway, Test, Testtube, Transport, Travel, Trouble, Tub

Tuck+
Bed 14.6%
Box 6.2%
In 6.2%
Pin 6.2%
Under 6.2%
Food 4.2%
Jump 4.2%
Neat 4.2%
Nip 4.2%
Pleat 4.2%
Shirt 4.2%
Shop 4.2%
2.1% Away, Bend, Bib, Donald, Friar, Hamper, Hide, Sew, Skirt, Snip,

Surgery, Sway, Tail, Touch, Turn

Tulip+
Flower 38.6%
Amsterdam 15.9%
Bulb 6.8%
Holland 6.8%
Daffodil 4.5%
Field(s) 3.4%
Red 3.4%
Spring 3.4%
1.1% *, Bell, Black, Blossom, Bud, Cup, Dutch, Floridae, Hash, Mint, Nasty, Petal, Petunia, Plant, Rose, Tiptoe

Tumble
Fall 50.0%
Down 16.0%
Dryer 8.0%
Over 4.0%
Roll 4.0%
2.0% Acrobat, Dry, Rough, Rough, Round, Somersault, Stumble, Toss, Weed

Tummy+
Button 31.2%
Stomach 20.8%
Rumble 12.5%
Ache 10.4%
Bug 6.2%
Upset 4.2%
2.1% *, Belly, Muscles, Pain, Smooth, Trouble, Warm

Turbulent+
Rough 23.8%
Water 14.3%
Stormy 7.1%
Waters 7.1%
Aircraft 4.8%
Wave(s) 4.8%
Wavy 4.8%
2.4% Air, Bumpy, Calm, Flow, Flowing, Passionate, Relationship, Storm, Swirling, Upset, Violent, Wild, Windy, Wing

Turf+
Grass 50.0%
Lawn 6.2%
Out 4.2%
Racing 4.2%
Sod 4.2%
Soil 4.2%
2.1% Clod, Cricket, Field, Garden, Golf, Horseracing, Peat, Pitch, Territory, Throw, Throwaway, Tower, Turn

Turn+
Around 20.7%
Twist 10.8%
Over 5.4%
Round 5.4%
Up 5.4%
About 4.3%
Away 4.3%
Corner 3.3%
Move 3.3%
Screw 3.3%
Bird(s) 2.2%
Change 2.2%
On 2.2%
Page 2.2%
Rotate 2.2%
Spin 2.2%
Stile 2.2%
1.1% Act, Divert, Fell, Fit, Funny, Off, Revolve, Seagull, Sixpence, Spell, Swatch, Swivel, Tide, Turntable, Wheel

Turquoise+
Blue 45.2%
Colour 11.9%
Green 11.9%
Sea 7.1%
2.4% Azure, Beauty, Egypt, Like, Lilac, Mauve, Purple, Shell, Tiles

Turtle
Shell 22.2%
Dove 11.1%
Neck 11.1%
Sea 6.7%
Soup 6.7%
Tortoise 4.4%
Water 4.4%
2.2% *, Beach, Bin, Caribbean, Flippers, Frog, Money, Mutant, Ninja, Queen, Slow, Swim, Terrapin, Turn, Wax

Turtleneck
Jumper 50.0%
Sweater 36.5%
1.9% *, Blazer, Cardboard, Collar, Poloneck, Shirt, Soup

Tusk+
Elephant 64.6%
Ivory 4.2%
Teeth 4.2%
Tooth 4.2%
2.1% *, Boar, Dead, Horn, Mammoth, Pig, Snow, Tarzan, Tree, Trunk, Walrus

Twine+
String 30.4%
Rope 13.0%
* 8.7%
Cord 4.3%
Needle 4.3%
Wool 4.3%
2.2% Bailer, Bale, Cotton, Farmer, Grin, Interlink, Meet, Mix, Separate, Twain, Twist, Vine, Weave, Wind, Wrap

Twist+
Turn 58.3%
Shout 14.6%
Dance 6.2%
Bend 4.2%
2.1% Candy, Cards, Catch, Slide, Spin, Stick, Tear, Twig

Twitch+
Itch 16.7%
Muscle 6.2%
Nervous 6.2%
Fidget 4.2%
Finger 4.2%
Jump 4.2%
Nerve(s) 4.2%
Tic 4.2%
2.1% *, Cheek, Epilepsy, Eye, Face, Fall, Jerk, Lip, Move, Nose, Shake, Shrug, Skin, Snap, Snatch, Sniff, Spasm, Stick, Sun, Tail, Turn, Twist, Wiggle, Wink

Two
Three 22.4%
Four 16.3%
* 10.2%
Pair 6.1%
Tea 6.1%
Couple 4.1%
Tango 4.1%
2.0% By-Two, Duo, Feet, Gloves, Long, Man-Crew, Of-A-Kind, People, Small, Times, Twice, Twins, Two, Up, You

Tyre
Car 33.3%
Wheel 19.0%
Rubber 16.7%
Tread 7.1%
Round 4.8%
2.4% Air, Black, Burst, Flat, Iron, Marks, Necklace, Road

Umbrella+
Rain 63.0%
Stand 8.7%
Black 4.3%
2.2% *, Dance, Hat, Holder, Open, Parasol, Shower, Snow, Spokes, Term, Wet

Uncertain+
Unsure 38.1%
Sure 16.7%
Dither 4.8%
Doubt 4.8%
Scared 4.8%
What 4.8%
2.4% Contract, Doubtful, Fluid, Help, Knowledge, Not, Pensive, Question, Tenuous, Tired, World

Uncle
Aunt 52.4%
* 4.8%
Relative 4.8%
2.4% Cousin, Again, Auntie, Bob, Brother, Family, Friend, Jack, Joe, John, Kill, Men, Nephew, Rob, Terrible

Uncommon+
Rare 33.3%
Unusual 23.8%
Strange 14.3%
Odd 4.8%
2.4% *, Common, Good, Illness, Life, Occurrence, Posh, Seldom, Valour, Weird

Under
Over 18.8%
Fire 12.5%
Wood 8.3%
Bed 6.3%
* 6.2%
-Neath 4.2%
Above 4.2%
Below 4.2%
Weather 4.2%
What 4.2%
2.1% Beneath, Bridge, Down, Grave, Pillow, Shelter, Stair, Stand, Stress, Top, Tree, World, You

Understand
Know 19.6%
Comprehend 15.2%
Care 8.7%
Help 4.3%
2.2% *, Comfort, Consider, Deep, Desire, Explore, Feeling, Female, Forgive, Height, Kind, Knowledge, Language, Nice, One, Peace, Problem, Read, See, Song, Sympathy, Think, Will, Women

Uneasy+
* 26.1%
Uncomfortable 10.9%
Afraid 4.3%
Bad 4.3%
Ill 4.3%
Nervous 4.3%
Sad 4.3%
2.2% Anxious, Calm, Difficult, Easy, Fear, Feel, Fright, Help, Matter, Silence, Sure, Unnerve, Unrest, Unsettled, Unsure, Upset, Uptight, Worried

Unhook+
Fish 15.2%
Coat 13.0%
Undo 8.7%
* 4.3%
Loosen 4.3%
Take-Off 4.3%
2.2% Bra, Clothes, Dislodge, Dress, Hook, Key, Liberate, Line, Lower, Meat, Peg, Pull, Release, Scab, Take, Take-Down, Tie, Tree, Unattach, Underwear, Undress, Unhinge, Unleash

Unique+
Only 28.6%
Alone 16.7%
One 9.5%
Me 7.1%
Single 7.1%
Special 7.1%
Original 4.8%
2.4% *, Individual, Oneness, Own, Salesman, Singular, Unusual, Whole

University
College 36.6%
School 12.2%
Books 4.9%
Degree 4.9%
Life 4.9%
London 4.9%
Student(s) 4.9%
Study 4.9%
2.4% Academic, Brick, Building, Cambridge, Language, Learn, Paper, Scarf, Spire, UCL

Unkind+
Cruel 31.0%
Nasty 9.5%
* 4.8%
Evil 4.8%
Mean 4.8%
Word(s) 4.8%
2.4% Bad, Bastard, Dislike, Horrible, Hurt, Hurtful, Nice, Remorse, Rotten, Sad, Sane, Savage, Strong, To, Unfriendly, Unpleasant, Unsympathetic

Unofficial+
* 23.9%
Official 13.0%
Informal 6.5%
Casual 4.3%
Dodgy 4.3%
2.2% A, Alternative, Bad, Declaration, Desultory, Disallowed, Frank, Guardian, Illegal, Lax, No, Norm, Off The Record, Okay, Old, On The Side, Ordinary, Rebel, Reminder, Suspect, Title, Unrecognised

Unpopular+
* 23.9%
Bad 8.7%
Person 6.5%
Hated 4.3%
Illegible 4.3%
Unliked 4.3%
2.2% Boy, Decision, Depressing, Dictator, Disliked, Feelings, Friends, Hate, Horrible, Infamous, Maggie, Nasty, Not, Out, Outcast, Popular, Sad, Solitude, Thatcher, Unfavourable, Unlikeable, Unlucky

Unreal+
False 11.9%
Fantasy 9.5%
Fiction 7.1%
Imaginary 7.1%
* 4.8%
Imagine 4.8%
Real 4.8%
Surreal 4.8%
Truth 4.8%
Untrue 4.8%
2.4% Crazy, Fairy, Fake, Flawed, Imagined, Like, Magical, Mystical, Philosophy, Pretend, Story, True, Way-Out, Weird, Wire

Unsavoury+
Nasty 13.0%
Sweet 13.0%
Taste 10.9%
Character 6.5%
Crisps 6.5%
* 4.3%
Sour 4.3%
2.2% Awful, Bad, Cheese, Dirty, Dislike, Flat, Food, Fruit, Hacky, Inedible, Lock, Odorous, Seedy, Smelly, Spread, Stink, Unappetising, Unpleasant, Unwanted

Unusual+
Strange 40.5%
Different 14.3%
Odd 11.9%
Weird 7.1%
Original 4.8%
Unique 4.8%
2.4% Dress, Extraordinary, Novel, Rare, Thing, Tom, True

Unwise+
Silly 31.0%
Stupid 19.0%
Foolish 9.5%
Fool 4.8%
Ill-Advised 4.8%
Move 4.8%
Owl 4.8%
2.4% *, Bad, Clever, Ignorant, Imprudent, Not, Prodigal, Unintelligent, Unwind

Up
Down 60.0%
Stairs 4.4%
Umbrella 4.4%
2.2% Arm, Balloon, Beat, Feather, Go, High, Hill, Look-Up, Scale, Shot, Side, Start, To, Toward

Upper
Lower 28.6%
Hand 23.8%
Cut 9.5%
Arm 7.1%
* 4.8%
Class 4.8%
Storey 4.8%
2.4% Body, High, Level, Shoulder, Stair, Street, Teeth

Upset
Sad 17.8%
Cry 11.1%
Stomach 11.1%
Happy 4.4%
Hurt 4.4%
2.2% *, Anger, Box, Bucket, Cart, Crime, Crying, Distraught, Distress, Distrust, Disturbed, Down, Funeral, Knock, Nappy, Not, Quiet, Sick, Spill, Spilled, Tearful, Tip

Upward
Mobile 20.0%
Downward(s) 17.8%
Down 13.3%
High 4.4%
Motion 4.4%
Movement 4.4%
Onward(s) 4.4%
Slope 4.4%
Thrust 4.4%
2.2% Escalator, Falling, Go, Going, Height, Hill, More, Sky, Slant, Swing

Urban

City	11.1%
Rural	11.1%
Town	11.1%
House(s)	6.7%
Jungle	6.7%
Myth	6.7%
Species	6.7%
Street	4.4%
Warrior	4.4%

2.2% *, Centre, Country, Environment, Grey, Landscape, Population, Setting, Sprawl, Suburb, Trial, Urban, Waste, Wasteland

Urbane+

*	23.9%
Order	8.7%
Boring	6.5%
City	4.3%

2.2% Acknowledge, Answer, Authority, Boss, Civil, Civilised, Cowardice, Disobey, Dull, House, Judgement, Listen, Obedience, Obese, Obey, Rule, Rural, Smart, Subservient, Timid, Urban, Wedding, Wife, Wise, Witty, Wordy

Urchin+

Sea	21.4%
Street	16.7%
Child	11.9%
Boy	9.5%
Kid	7.1%
Orchard	4.8%
Orphan	4.8%

2.4% Flower, Lad, Little, Me, Poor, Ragged, Scoundrel, Scruffy, Terror, Waif

Urge

Push	14.6%
*	8.3%
Overkill	6.3%
Persuade	6.3%
You	6.3%
Encourage	4.2%
On	4.2%
To	4.2%
Want	4.2%

2.1% Body, Clap, Discourage, Feeling, Force, Him, Idea, Incite, Insist, Loss, Lust, Me, Merge, Procreate, Prod, Strong, Tell, Think, Try, Yearn

Vacant+
Empty 38.1%
Look 7.1%
Pretty 7.1%
Open 4.8%
Stupid 4.8%
2.4% Application, Area, Expression, Lost, Lot, Mind, Orbital, Pistols, Place, Position, Possession, Room, Shop, Space, Spot, Stare

Vagabond+
Tramp 31.0%
Thief 14.3%
Vagrant 7.1%
Ragamuffin 4.8%
Rogue 4.8%
Ruffian 4.8%
2.4% Beggar, Dodgy, Drunk, Gab, Leader, Minstrel, Mission, Muffin, Person, Robber, Rouge, Scoundrel, Stray, Urchin

Vagrant+
Tramp 52.4%
Wanderer 9.5%
Vagabond 4.8%
2.4% Beggar, Corrupt, Dirt, Gypsy, Hobo, Immigrant, Loiterer, Migrant, Nomad, Nomadic, Runaway, Smell, Spy, Stray

Valiant
Brave 29.2%
Knight 14.6%
* 8.3%
Soldier 6.3%
Attempt 4.2%
Effort 4.2%
2.1% Bang, Be, Behaviour, Bold, Bright, Defender, Drugs, Gallant, Good, Hero, Horse, Kind, Prince, Strong, Time, Victor

Value
Worth 24.4%
Money 15.6%
* 6.7%
Added 6.7%
Cost 6.7%
Less 6.7%
Oscar 4.4%
Price 4.4%
2.2% Amount, Cash, Free, Good, Love, Moral, Pay, Real, Treasure, Worthwhile

Vanessa
Redgrave 61.2%
* 30.8%
2.0% Girl, Jones, Nearly, Paradis

Vase
Flower(s) 73.3%
Break 4.4%
China 4.4%
2.2% *, Amphora, Broken, Glass, Pot, Symposium, Urn, Weddings

Vat+
Tax 26.2%
Wine 19.0%
Man 7.1%
Money 7.1%
Tank 4.8%
Tub 4.8%
Urn 4.8%
2.4% *, Acid, Cider, Drum, Flask, Jug, Pot, There, This, Which, Whisky

Venom+
Snake 64.3%
Poison 19.0%
2.4% Acid, Cobra, Evil, Fatalistic, Hate, Neon, Sting

Veranda
Balcony 27.1%
Porch 10.4%
* 4.2%
Patio 4.2%
Spain 4.2%
2.1% Australia, Beach, Chair, Cheese, France, Garden, Hot-Weather, House, India, Italy, Kiss, Miranda, New-Orleans, Plantation, Plants, Rocking-Chair, Settee, Snooker, Terrace, Wealth, White, Window, Wood

Vicious
Dog 11.9%
Circle 7.1%
Kick 7.1%
Violent 7.1%
* 4.8%
Attack 4.8%
Evil 4.8%
Mean 4.8%
Nasty 4.8%
Sid 4.8%
Teeth 4.8%
Violence 4.8%
2.4% Angry, Cruel, Cycle, Dangerous, Fierce, Gentle, Horrid, Kind, Malicious, Savage, Thoughts, Thug

Victim+
* 21.4%
Rape 11.9%
Attack 9.5%
Death 4.8%
Liar 4.8%
2.4% Assault, Attacker, Blood, Conqueror, Crime, Criminal, Cruel, Dead, Help, Hurt, Injured, Murder, Murdered, Prey, Prisoner, Scared, Sex, Terrorist, Victor, Violence

Victory
Win 28.0%
Defeat 9.8%
War 9.8%
Success 4.9%
2.4% -Vs, Alleluia, Battle, Boat, Celebrate, Celebration, Churchill, Conquer, Cry, Cup, Fear, Flag, Great, Happiness, Napoleon, Rocket, Ship, Sword, Triumph, Won

Violin
Music 20.5%
Play 11.4%
Cello 9.1%
String 9.1%
Bow 6.8%
Instrument 6.8%
Concert 4.4%
Concerto 4.4%
Fiddle 4.4%
Screech 4.4%
2.3% Bass, Case, Lessons, Maker, Player, Please, Sweet, Voice, Wood

Virginia
* 28.9%
Woolf 28.6%
Bottomley 12.2%
Water 8.2%
Wade 6.1%
2.0% Astley, Cox, Plain, Queen, Scott, Slim's, USA, West

Virtual+
* 21.4%
Nearly 14.3%
Almost 11.9%
All 4.8%
Complete 4.8%
Reality 4.8%
True 4.8%
2.4% Good, Hidden, Image, Many, Oblivion, Only, Practical, Practically, Real, Stop, Total, Virtuous, Write-Off

Virtuality
Real 14.6%
* 12.5%
Reality 12.5%
Almost 10.4%
Computer(s) 6.3%
Game 4.2%
Nearly 4.2%
Virtual 4.2%
Virtual Reality 4.2%
2.1% Black, Equality, Good, Image, Insistence, Life, Screen, Sensor, Space, Three dimensions, Unreal, Video, Virtue

Virtuous+
Good 20.0%
* 6.7%
Kind 4.4%
Pious 4.4%
Pure 4.4%
Woman 4.4%
2.2% Attributes, Bad, Characteristics, Chaste, Church, Circle, Faith, Girl, Goody, Holy, Honest, Immoral, Lady, Me, Moral, People, Piety, Prissy, Righteous, Saint, Sneering, Virgin, Voluptuous, Well-Behaved, Wife

Vision+
Sight 28.3%
See 17.4%
Eye 10.9%
On 10.9%
Seer 4.3%
View 4.3%
2.2% 20/20, Drugs, Gift, Glasses, Goal, Look, Mary, Of, Picture, Screen, Senses

Visit+
See 14.3%
Prison 9.5%
Hospital 7.1%
Aunt 4.8%
Family 4.8%
Friend 4.8%
Go 4.8%
Meet 4.8%
Stay 4.8%
Trip 4.8%
2.4% *, Castle, City, Country, Doctor, Guest, Home, Old, Parents, Relations, Relative, Return, Stranger, Welcome, Wink

Vivacious
Lively 33.3%
Bubbly 8.9%
* 4.4%
Girl 4.4%
Outgoing 4.4%
2.2% Active, Charming, Crazy, Curls, Cute, Eager, Energetic, Gorgeous, Happy, Jolly, Loud, Noisy, Pretty, Quiet, Shy, Sly, Sociable, Vivid, What

Voice
High 9.5%
Over 9.5%
Speech 9.5%
Loud 7.1%
Box 4.8%
Sing 4.8%
Song 4.8%
Sound 4.8%
2.4% *, Alto, Break, Clean, Deep, Friend, Hard, Head, Hear, Noise, Opera,

Opinion, Pitch, Singing, Speak, Speaker, Talk, Therapy, Thought

Volcano

Erupt	28.9%
Eruption	17.8%
Lava	15.6%
Island	4.4%
Mountain	4.4%

2.2% *, Ash, Explode, Explosion, High, Hot, Italy, Joe, Molten, Pompeii, Rock, Stromboli, Vesuvius

Vow

Promise	23.8%
Marriage	21.4%
Wedding	11.9%
Oath	7.1%
Silence	7.1%
Pledge	4.8%
Swear	4.8%

2.4% *, Aver, Break, Many, Never, Reason, Solemn, To-My-Country

Wagon+
Wheel 26.2%
Train 23.8%
Cart 14.3%
Car 9.5%
Horses 4.8%
2.4% *, Cowboy, Horse, Indian, Load, Moving, Tarpaulin, Tie, Western

Waistcoat
Jacket 13.3%
Shirt 11.1%
Suit 11.1%
Smart 8.9%
* 6.7%
Buttons 6.7%
2.2% Clothing, Dandy, Decorative, Dress, Fashion, Front, Grey, Knit, Leather, Man, Nice, Snooker, Stripy, Tapestry, Tight, Top, Trousers, Watch, Wear

Wait
* 10.4%
Stay 10.4%
Stop 6.3%
Around 4.2%
Long 4.2%
Remain 4.2%
Room 4.2%
See 4.2%
Sit 4.2%
Terry 4.2%
There 4.2%
2.1% And-See, At, Attend, Awhile, Bus, Bus-Stop, Buy, Cafe, Doctor, Expect, Go, Hang-Around, Here, Outside, Platform, Queue, Read, Shop, Up

Wake
Up 27.9%
Sleep 9.3%
Arise 4.7%
Death 4.7%
Early 4.7%
Morning 4.7%
Open 4.7%
Sea 4.7%
2.3% Alarm, Alive, Bed, Behind, Charm, Day, Dream, Funeral, Rise, Ship, Snore, Start, Up-Time, Wake, Wide

Walk
Run 30.4%
Stroll 6.5%
Tall 6.5%
Fast 4.3%
Away 3.3%
Dog 3.3%
Go 3.3%
Talk 3.3%
* 2.2%
Country 2.2%
Countryside 2.2%
Far 2.2%
On 2.2%
Out 2.2%
1.1% Across, Along, Around, Brisk, Down, Dry, Jump, Meander, Move, Over, Pleasure, Ramble, Ride, River, Road, Saunter, Shoe, Sleep, Through, Tree, Trip, Way, With-Whom, Woods

Wallet+
Money 54.8%
Purse 33.3%
2.4% Cash, Hanky, Line, Pocket, Steal

Wallpaper
Paste 16.0%
Paint 14.0%
Flowers 10.0%
Pattern 10.0%
Hanging 8.0%
Print 4.0%
Room 4.0%
2.0% *, Blues, Brush, Cherub, Chintz, Clouds, Covering, Decorating, Design, Flowery, Green, Horrible, House, Peeling, Wall, Yellow

Walnut+
Nut 19.0%
Cracker(s) 9.5%
Shell 9.5%
Tree 9.5%
Cake 7.1%
Xmas 4.8%
2.4% *, Allergy, Cancer, Chocolate, Crack, Fruit, Hazelnut, Head, Kernel, Nuts, Oil, Pie, Squish, Tongue, Whip, Whirl, Wrinkly

Walrus+
Seal 19.0%
Tusk(s) 19.0%
Carpenter 16.7%
* 7.1%
2.4% Animal, Boat, Bone, Catcher, Cow, Dog, Egg, Fat, Kings, Mammal, Nightingale, Sea, Sealion, Teeth, Whale, Wonder

Want
Need 25.0%
Have 8.4%
Desire 8.3%
More 8.3%
Wish 8.3%
To 6.3%
It 4.2%
2.1% Ache, Everything, Food, Get, Give, Greed, Know, Like, Money, Require, That, This, War, Yearn, You

War
Peace 29.2%
Fight 10.4%
Death 8.3%
Cry 6.3%
* 4.2%
Crime 4.2%
Guns 4.2%
2.1% America, Army, Battle, Bosnia, Cult, Hate, Horrible, Lord, On-Want, Rage, Sadness, Strife, Time, Torn, Troops, Want

Ward
Hospital 42.3%
Nurse 15.4%
Sister 7.7%
Court 5.7%
Fend 3.8%
Guard 3.8%
1.9% *, Area, Baby, Bed, Girl, Minor, Number, Off, Sick, Stone, Wardrobe

Warm
Cold 15.5%
Hot 9.5%
Bed 6.0%
Weather 6.0%
Cosy 4.8%
Soft 4.8%
Blanket 2.4%
Body 2.4%
Bread 2.4%
Cat 2.4%
Comfortable 2.4%
Cool 2.4%
Gloves 2.4%
Sun 2.4%
Toast 2.4%
1.2% Beer, Blood, Bounce, Coat, Coffee, Cuddle, Fire, Foot, Hair, Hands, Heady, Heart, Hearted, Heat, Hug, Mild, Moist, Plates, Room, Socks, Summer, Tepid, Tingle, Up, Water, Wet

Warmth
Heat 31.3%
Fire 16.7%
Cold 6.3%
Hot 6.3%
Wool 6.3%
* 4.2%
2.1% Bed, Blanket, Comfort, Cool, Glow, Heater, Kind, Lager, Moist, Moisture, Moth, Sex, Tired

Wash
Clean 24.4%
Hands 13.3%
Dry 11.1%
Face 6.7%
Soap 6.7%
Up 6.7%
Basin 4.4%
2.2% *, -Ing, Brush, Clothes, Dirty, Moslem, N'Go, Scrub, Sink, Splash, Steam, Wet

Washing
Machine 22.0%
Up 19.5%
Dirty 7.3%
Laundry 7.3%
Line 7.3%
Clean 4.9%
Dishes 4.9%
Liquid 4.9%
Powder 4.9%
2.4% Clothes, Cold, Drying, Laundry, Room, Washing-Line, Washing-Up, Wind

Watch
Time 46.7%
Tower 11.1%
Look 8.9%
Hand 4.4%
2.2% *, Arm, Clock, Digital, Observe, Out, Plain, See, Swiss, Switzerland, This, Tick, Wrist

Water
Wet 14.3%
* 6.1%
Bucket 6.1%
Drink 6.1%
Fall 6.1%
Glass 4.1%
Rain 4.1%
Tap 4.1%
2.0% Baby, Bath, Bottle, Butt, Cup, Dry, Duck, Fitter, Hot, Ice, Live, Log, Melon, Resistant, River, Running, Sea, Sports, Stream, Swim, Wave, White, Wings, Works

Waterfall
Water 31.9%
Splash 6.8%
* 4.5%
Cascade 4.5%
Ground 4.5%
Rock(s) 4.5%
Wet 4.5%
2.3% Bird, Blue, Cliff, Force, Forest, Heavy, Holiday, Jump, Niagara, Noise, Pond, Pool, Rapids, River, Serene, Stream, Swimming

Watering can
Water 26.7%
Garden 22.2%
Flower(s) 15.6%
Plant(s) 11.1%

Spray 4.4%
2.2% Fountain, Gardener, Grass, Lawn, Man, Rust, Speed, Sprinkle, Sprinkler

Watermelon
Juice(y) 26.7%
Seeds 11.1%
Water 8.9%
Fruit 6.7%
Man 6.7%
Red 6.7%
2.2% *, Beach, Bowl, Food, Fresh, Greece, Green, Honeydew, Lemon, Ooze, Pineapple, Ripe, Run, Tourmaline, Wet

Wavy
Hair 31.2%
Curly 16.7%
Sea 16.7%
Line(s) 10.4%
Gravy 4.2%
Straight 4.2%
Wave(s) 4.2%
2.1% Curved, Davey, Fluid, Foam, Moving, Wonky

Weak
Strong 40.8%
* 10.2%
Tea 10.2%
Feeble 8.2%
Will 4.1%
2.0% Anaemia, Arms, Face, Grim, Lethargic, Meagre, Mighty, Minded, Muscle, Never, Poor, Pulse, Water

Weakness
Strength 28.9%
* 4.4%
Feeble 4.4%
Ill 4.4%
Soft 4.4%
Weak 4.4%
2.2% Deflate, Drink, Failing, Fall, Fault, Flaw, Fold, Fragile, Hate, Kindness, Knees, Laziness, Limbs, Limp, Link, Me, Old, Small, Thin, Vice, Vulnerable

Wealth
Money 51.2%
Rich 9.3%
Health 7.0%
Power 7.0%
Riches 4.7%
2.3% *, Empire, Ferrari, Greed, Information, Poor, Poverty, Waste

Wealthy
Rich 70.8%
Money 12.5%
Poor 6.2%
Cash 4.2%
2.1% *, Man, Wealth

Weapon
Gun 33.3%
Sword 8.9%
War 8.9%
Arms 6.7%
Arrow 4.4%
2.2% *, Attack, Axe, Chisel, Dagger, Hot, Kill, Knife, Lethal, No, Rifle, Shield, Shoot, Spear, Stick, Strong, Tank

Weather
Forecast 11.1%
Rain 8.9%
Cold 6.7%
Fine 6.7%
Report 6.7%
Cloudy 4.4%
Girl 4.4%
Stormy 4.4%
Sun 4.4%
2.2% Atmosphere, Bright, Centre, Cloud, Cock, Control, Dark, Endure, Fair, Gate, Grey, Hot, Light, Man, Nature, Season, Sky, Storm, Windy

Weave
Cloth 11.6%
Wool 11.6%
Carpet 7.0%
Knit 7.0%
Basket 4.7%
Clothe 4.7%
Mat 4.7%
Rugs 4.7%
2.3% *, Blanket, Cotton, Dream, Dry, Hair, Loom, Make, Nest, Net, Sew, Spell, Spider, Stitch, Sweater, Threads, Warp, Weft, Yarn

Wedding+
Bell(s) 30.4%
White 13.0%
Present 8.7%
Ring 8.7%
Cake 6.5%
Bride 4.3%
Dress 4.3%
Gown 4.3%
2.2% Day, Groom, March, Marriage, Married, Night, Reception, Scales, Sister

Weep
Cry 61.7%
Tear(s) 12.8%
Willow 6.4%
* 4.3%
Sad 4.3%
2.1% Bitter, Hanky, Sob, Wail, Worn

Weird
Strange 30.0%
Odd 8.0%
Wonderful 8.0%
Science 6.0%
Funny 4.0%
Tales 4.0%
2.0% *, ?, Bizarre, Corny, Crazy, Eerie, Freak, Grey, Hippy, Insane, Mad, Normal, Not, Outrageous, People, Shit, Stuff, Test, Witch, Wizard

Welcome+
Hello 26.2%
Home 19.0%
Greet 11.9%
Mat 7.1%
Greeting 4.8%
Hail 4.8%
2.4% Arms, Come, Committee, Doormat, Enter, Foreigner, Foundation, Friendly, Greetings, Party, Trust

Well
Water 37.8%
Deep 8.9%
Wishing 6.7%
Being 4.4%
Done 4.4%
Ill 4.4%
2.2% *, Better, Fine, Garden, Health, Hole, Ink, Of-Dreams, Sick, Spring, Then, Treacle, Wisher, Wishes, Woman

Western
Cowboy(s) 22.2%
Eastern 11.1%
Film 8.9%
Movie 8.9%
World 8.9%
Clint 4.4%
Isles 4.4%
Music 4.4%
2.2% Accident, Approaches, Block, Breeze, Front, Gun, Ideas, Ocean Shore, Open, Oriental, Theatre, Wild

Wet
Dry 21.5%
Water 18.3%
Rain 14.0%
Damp 7.5%
Cold 6.5%
Fish 4.3%
Blanket 2.2%
Paint 2.2%
1.1% Bath, Beach, Bed, Cloth, Cool, Dream, Drops, Flannel, Floor, Miserable, Rag, Slippery, Soaked, Soaking, Soft, Soggy, Tap, Warm, Wash, Weather, Weekend

Whale
Bone 12.2%
Sea 12.2%
Animal 6.1%
Big 6.1%
Blubber 6.1%
Fish 6.1%
Mammal 6.1%
Meat 6.1%
Blue 4.1%
Oil 4.1%
2.0% *, Again, Big-Fish, Dog, Dolphin, Endanger, Extinct, Fat, Huge, James, Jonah, Nave, Pool, Spurt, Time

What
Where 18.0%
When 12.0%
Why 10.0%
Who 8.0%
Ever 4.0%
If 4.0%
Is 4.0%
Which 4.0%
2.0% *, Comes, Deaf, For, Hip, How, Next, No, Pardon, Question, See, Son, That, The-Hell, This, Tyler, Wrong, You

Wheel
Car 40.0%
Turn 13.3%
Fortune 11.1%
Round 4.4%
Spin 4.4%
2.2% Barrow, Brace, Cart, Clamp, Life, Rim, Spokes, Sprocket, Steel, Turning, Tyre, Wright

When
Now 26.4%
Where 14.6%
How 8.3%
Then 8.3%
Time 8.3%
* 6.3%
Why 6.3%
Ever 4.2%
2.1% ?, Comes, Day, History, Soon, Temporal, They, We, What

Where
When 16.7%
There 12.5%
Here 10.4%
* 6.2%
-Abouts 4.2%
Are 4.2%
How 4.2%
Now 4.2%
To 4.2%
2.1% About, And-When,

At, Ever, For, Is, Look, New, On, Over-There, Place, Question, We, Were, What, Why

Which
One 24.0%
Way 18.0%
When 10.0%
Where 8.0%
Magazine 6.0%
Who 6.0%
Ever 4.0%
Why 4.0%
2.0% Choose, Fold, Nose, One, Question, Was, Way-Now, What, Whose, Wood

Whispers
Chinese 14.9%
Quiet 8.5%
Secret 6.4%
Soft 6.4%
Quietly 4.3%
Silent 4.3%
Speech 4.3%
Sshh 4.3%
Voice 4.3%
2.1% Annoying, Breath, Careless, China, Clothes, Gallery, Gossip, Lies, Low, Mass, Mouth, Murmurs, Mutters, Noise, Shy, Slowly, Sound, St-Pauls, Talks, Wind

Whistle
Blow 20.0%
Stop 8.9%
Noise 6.7%
Tune 6.7%
* 4.4%
Call 4.4%
Loud 4.4%
2.2% Blower, Demonstration, Dog, Down, Gristle, Heat, Jacket, Lips, Metal, Round, School, Shrill, Silver, Sing, Song, Sport, Train, Tuneless, Up, Wet

White
Black 62.2%
Snow 4.4%
Teeth 4.4%
2.2% Blouse, Face, Glow, Heart, Leg, Lies, Light, Noise, Sheet, Shining, Wall, Wash, Wedding

Whole
Entire 16.3%
Earth 9.3%
Part 9.3%
Round 9.3%
Complete 7.0%
Story 4.7%
Total 4.7%
2.3% *, All, Apple, Big, Body, Bread, Entity, Fat, Grain, Half, Nut, Pear, Some, Wheat, Wholesome, World

Why
Not 30.0%
When 12.0%
Question 8.0%
What 8.0%
Because 6.0%
Me 4.0%
Where 4.0%
2.0% Bird, Do, Hide, How, Oh, Question-Mark(?), Reason, Sea, Tell, That, What-For, Wherefore, Who, Would

Wicked+
Evil 52.4%
Witch 14.3%
Bad 7.1%
Nasty 4.8%
2.4% Despicable, Easy, Good, Great, Lady, Mad, Man, Naughty, Spartan

Wicket+
Cricket 40.5%
Bad 9.5%
Stump 7.1%
Bail(s) 4.8%
Evil 4.8%
2.4% Ball, Bowl, Devious, Good, Hate, Help, Hit, Justice, Keeper, Nasty, Queen, Vicious, Witch, Woman

Wide
Open 18.8%
Narrow 10.4%
Mouth 6.3%
* 4.2%
Angle 4.2%
Berth 4.2%
Broad 4.2%
Far 4.2%
Load 4.2%
Range 4.2%
Road 4.2%
2.1% Ball, Big, Chasm, Choice, Cover, Distant, Eyed, Fat, Large, Long, Ocean, River, Wider, World, Yawning

Wife
Husband 46.7%
Mother 6.7%
Marriage 4.4%
2.2% *, Astray, Batter, Batterer, Beater, Daughter, Dowry, Farce, Femme, Hair, Home, Life, Man, Needed, Oh-No, She, Spouse, Widow, Woman

Wild
* 24.5%
Animals 8.2%
Flowers 6.1%
At-Heart 4.1%
Strawberry 4.1%
Thing 4.1%
2.0% Cat, Child, Country, Danger, Duck, Easy, Extravagant, Ferocious, Field, Fierce, Fiery, Free, Fruit, Hair, Happy, Horses, Kill, Oats, One, Person, Ragged, Swans, West, Windy

Win
Lose 39.5%
Game 11.6%
Money 7.0%
Prize 7.0%
Race 4.7%
Victory 4.7%
2.3% Competition, Face, Fast, Finish, Gamble, Horse, Jackpot, Lottery, Over, Success, War, Yes

Wind+
Blow 20.2%
Rain 7.1%
Storm 4.8%
Break 3.6%
Cold 3.6%
Tree(s) 3.6%
Tunnel 3.6%
* 2.4%
Fall 2.4%
Fart 2.4%
Gale 2.4%
Swept 2.4%
Weather 2.4%
Willows 2.4%
1.2% Air, Bag, Blast, Blowing, Blustery, Chime, City, Cloud, Cool, Damage, Desert, Fan, Fire, Force, Hurricane, Instrument, Kite, Machine, Mill, Pipe, Raw, Sailor, Scale, Sing, Speed, Strong, Sun, Very, Wind-In-The-Willows, Womb

Windmill
Holland 20.0%
Sail(s) 13.3%
Wind 13.3%
Flour 8.9%
Round 4.4%
2.2% *, Air, Bread, Breeze, Can, Circle, Country, Countryside, Dutch, Flowers, Grain, Grind, Move, Sky, Turn, Vane, Water

Wine glass
Drink 28.9%
Wine 20.0%
* 11.1%
Crystal 4.4%
2.2% Asti Spumante, Bottle, Brandy, Broken, Clink, Dinner Party, Fence, Full, Glass, Red, Sherry, Smash, Stains, Stem, Tall, Whine

Winston
Churchill 91.8%
* 4.2%
2.0% Silcott, Wells

Wisdom+
Wise 17.0%
Knowledge 14.9%
Teeth/Tooth 14.9%
Age 6.4%
Clever 4.3%
Learning 4.3%
Norman 4.3%
Sage 4.3%
Wit 4.3%
2.1% *, Beard, King, Learn, Man, Old, Practical, Sagacity, Scholar, Socrates, Stupidity, Truth

Wise
Old 21.4%
Owl 16.7%
Man 11.9%
Clever 9.5%
* 4.8%
Knowledge 4.8%
Person 4.8%
Woman 4.8%
2.4% Experienced, Foolish, Knowledgeable, Monkey, Morecambe, True, Up, Wisdom, Wrinkly

Witch
Broomstick 14.3%
Broom 9.5%
Craft 9.5%
Hat 9.5%
Black 7.1%
Hazel 7.1%
Hunt 7.1%
Wizard 4.8%
2.4% Bitch, Cow, Dark, Evil, Magic, Night, Switch, Wardrobe, Warlock, Way, White, Wicked, Woman

With
Out 24.0%
Without 14.0%
And 6.0%
What 6.0%
Who 6.0%
You 6.0%
Me 4.0%
That 4.0%
Us 4.0%
Whom 4.0%
2.0% *, Association, Avec, Belong, Child, In, Nail,

Not, Salad, Stand, Whenever

Withdraw
Away 8.7%
Go 8.7%
Remove 8.7%
Money 6.5%
Deposit 4.3%
Pull-Back 4.3%
Retreat 4.3%
2.2% Backup, Back-Off, Balance, Cane, Clear, Disappear, From, Leave, Life, Lose, Pistol, Quiet, Recede, Regularly, Retract, Sex, Shell, Shield, Shy, Stop, Stroke, Support, Tactical, Take, Take-Out

Withstand
* 12.8%
Hold 8.5%
Pressure 6.4%
Strong 6.4%
Endure 4.3%
Fall 4.3%
Put-Up 4.3%
Stand 4.3%
Survive 4.3%
2.1% Against, Armour, Beat, Cope, Defend, Gale, Hat, Impact, Just, Manage, Pain, Resist, Shock, Strain, Stress, Stubborn, Tolerate, Trouble, Uphold, Wall, Withhold

Witness+
Court 12.2%
Crime 12.2%
Accident 7.3%
See 7.3%
Film 4.9%
Jury 4.9%
Prosecution 4.9%
Stand 4.9%
2.4% *, Box, Case, Dock, Eye, Ford, Important, Justice, Law, Notice, Person, Prosecutor, Seeing, Spectator, Suspect, Trial

Witty+
Funny 57.1%
Clever 7.1%
* 4.8%
Amusing 4.8%
Laugh 4.8%
2.4% Droll, Dull, Fun, Howard, Pleasant, Repartee, Repertoire, Riposte, Wild

Wonder
Think 10.4%
Why 10.4%
Amaze 6.3%
Amazement 6.3%
Marvel 6.3%
Stuff 6.3%
* 4.2%
At 4.2%
Awe 4.2%
Gaze 4.2%
How 4.2%
2.1% Aloud, Ask, Child, Debate, Dream, Full, If, Imagination, Nature, Ponder, Sight, Strange, Surprise, Wise, Wonderful, World

Wood
Tree(s) 41.7%
Balsa 6.2%
Forest 6.2%
2.1% Brunt, Dark, Dead, Effect, Furniture, Grain, Knot, Leaf, Lice, Loft, Metal, Mouldy, Oak, Paper, Pile, Pine, Plank, Steel, Table, Warm, Work, Worm

Woodworm
Hole(s) 17.3%
Wood 15.4%
Rot 11.5%
* 5.7%
Antique(s) 5.7%
Bug 3.8%
Lice 3.8%
Wardrobe 3.8%
1.9% Bitter, Dark, Decay, Dry-Rot, Eating-Away, Furniture, Grubs, House, Maggot, Pest, Rotten, Sawdust, Sick, Slimy, Timber, Tree, Worm

Work
Hard 26.6%
Labour 11.1%
Job 8.9%
Place 6.7%
Play 6.7%
Study 4.4%
2.2% *, Boredom, Change, Difficult, Hate, Horse, Leisure, Load, Long, Love, Money, Strain, Today, Toil, Unlikely, While

World
Wide 20.0%
View 8.9%
Earth 4.4%
Order 4.4%
Round 4.4%
Universe 4.4%
2.2% Bad, Big, Circus, Class, Country, Crazy, Famous, Games, Global, Globe, Hand, Hope, Map, Old, Peace, Planet, Problems, Service, Sphere, Spinning, Travel, Turning, War, Weary

Worm
* 24.5%
Earth 10.2%
Soil 8.2%
Turn 8.2%
Wiggle 6.1%
Wriggly 6.1%
Long 4.1%
2.0% Food, Garden, Grub, Horrible, Hot, Hydra, Mud, Pink, Slime, Slow, Slug, Snail, Snake, Straight, String, Wood

Worst
Best 42.2%
* 6.7%
Last 6.7%
Nightmare 6.7%
Bad 4.4%
Case 4.4%
Day 4.4%
Enemy 4.4%
2.2% Disaster, Dreadful, Fall, Of-All, Terrible, The, Thing, Time, Wear

Worth
Value 29.5%
Money 13.6%
Less 9.1%
* 6.8%
While 6.8%
Rich 4.5%
2.3% All, Allegiance, Bracelet, Cheque, Down, Gold, Good, More, Self, Wool, Worry, Worthless, Worthy

Wrath
Anger 51.2%
* 12.2%
God(s) 12.2%
2.4% Bone, Chaos, Cross, Enemy, Fear, Grapes, Grapes, Hatred, Ire, Peace, Tornado

Wrist
Watch 44.0%
Arm 20.0%
Hand 12.0%
Ankle(s) 4.0%
Band 4.0%
2.0% *, Bone, Elbow, Limp, Neck, Rash, Smack, Thicken

Wristwatch
Time 41.7%
Clock 8.3%
* 4.2%
Strap 4.2%
Swatch 4.2%
Watch 4.2%
Wrist 4.2%
2.1% Analogue, Arm, Band, Black, Brown, Chocolate, Click, Deadline, Leather, Love, Orange, Scan, Tick-Tock, Timer

Write+
Wrong 37.0%
Letter 10.9%
Book 6.5%
Pen 6.5%
Read 6.5%
A 4.3%
Correct 4.3%
Left 4.3%
2.2% Away, Down, Essays, Play, Saw, Say, Scribble, Script, Words, Write

Write
Book 17.0%
Letter 17.0%
Read 14.9%
Pen 12.8%
* 4.3%
Learn 4.3%
Now 4.3%
Scrawl 4.3%
2.1% Down, Essay, Legible, Scribe, Speak, Spell, Story, Type, Words, Wrong

Writer
Author 31.7%
Journalist 12.2%
Pen 7.3%
Book 4.9%
Story 4.9%
2.4% *, Block, Creator, Drama, Female, Green, Journal, Money, Pages, Paper, Producer, Quill, Reader, Scribble, Scribe, Thought, Words

Wrong
Right 76.2%
2.4% Answer, Cross, Decision, Doing, Incorrect, Mistake, Night, Price, Way, Word

Yard+
Mile 23.8%
Stick 21.4%
Foot 9.5%
Metre 7.1%
Inch 4.8%
Long 4.8%
2.4% *, Ale, Arm, Distance, Feet, Grass, Length, Measure, Music, Stone, Width

Year+
Month 19.0%
Age 11.9%
Day 11.9%
Date 9.5%
Book 4.8%
Long 4.8%
Time 4.8%
2.4% *, 1991, Anno, Birthday, By, Calendar, Century, Far, Leap, Lobe, Not, Now, School

Yearn
Long 18.0%
Desire 12.0%
For 12.0%
Want 10.0%
Love 6.0%
Earn 4.0%
2.0% Bored, Dream, Eat, Hope, Learn, Life, Longs-For, Lost, Lust, Miss, Need, Sigh, Sleep, Strive, Thirst, To, Wish, Wishful, Yield

Yellow
Sun 19.0%
Banana 14.3%
Green 7.1%
Red 7.1%
Blue 4.8%
Butter 4.8%
Custard 4.8%
2.4% Band, Bird, Brick, Brick-Road, Cab, Canary, Car, Colour, Daffodil, Flower, Gold, Line, Paint, Rose, Sheet, Sick

You
Me 66.7%
Are 6.3%
* 4.3%
Them 4.2%
2.1% About, And-Me, Bastard, Die, I, Not-Me, Too, Us, Yours

Young
Old 42.9%
Man 6.1%
Baby 4.1%
Child 4.1%
Guns 4.1%
2.0% Attractive, At-Heart, Chinese, Couple, Cub, Deer, Fresh, Girl, Hair, Hundred, Jimmy, Kid, Ones, Person, Sapling, Screwed, Soft, Thing, Twenty-Something

Yours
Mine 58.3%
Theirs 8.3%
* 6.2%
Ours 4.2%
2.1% Beast, From, Give, His, Its, Others, Sincerely, This, Tours, Up, Yours

Zebra

Stripes	51.1%
Crossing	28.9%
Horse	6.7%

2.2% *, Asp, Cross, Skin, Strip, Stripy

Zip+

Fastener	16.7%
Trousers	16.7%
Up	16.7%
Button	4.8%
Coat	4.8%
Code	4.8%
Fasten	4.8%
Fly	4.8%
Shut	4.8%

2.4% *, Clothes, Flight, Metal, Neatness, Strike, Strip, Stuck, Zipper

Zoo+

Animal(s)	50.0%
Zebra	8.7%
Bear	4.3%
Cage	4.3%
Lion	4.3%

2.2% *, Baby, Balloon, Bars, Capture, Gardens, Look, Monkey, Park, Place, Walking, Watch, Zulu

Stimulus words

A

A
Abandon
Abate
Abdomen
Abduct
Ability
Able
Abrupt
Absolute
Accept
Accordingly
Accuse
Ache
Acre
Acrobat
Active
Actor
Actual
Acute
Address
Admire
Admit
Adolph
Advantage
Aerobicise
Aeroplane
Africa
Age
Agile
Agree
Airport
Alcohol
Alike
Alive
All
Alley
Alligator
Allow
Alone
Also
Amaze
Amazement
Ambassador
Amble
Ambulance
America
Amount
Amputate
Anchor
Ancient
And
Anger
Animal
Animate
Ankle
Anne
Annihilation
Announce
Annoyance
Another
Antidote
Anxiety
Apathy
Ape
Appeal
Appear
Appease
Apple
Applicant
Apricot
Apron
Aptitude
Argue
Arid
Arise
Arm
Armistice
Aroma
Array
Arthritis
Arthur
Artichoke
Artist
Asbestos
Ascertain
Ashtray
Ask
Asparagus
Aspirin
Asset
Assist
Assistance
Astonish
At
Athlete
Atlas
Atrocious
Attach
Attack
Attempt
Attic
Auction
Audition
Auditor
Aunt
Authentic
Author
Authority
Automobile
Avalanche
Avid
Await
Awake
Award
Awkward
Axe

B

Baby
Back
Backbite
Backbone
Background
Bacteria
Bad
Badminton
Bag
Bake
Balance
Balcony
Ball
Ballad
Ballet
Balloon
Ballot
Ban
Band
Bandage
Bandit
Bane
Banish
Banquet
Baptise
Barbara
Bare
Bargain
Barge
Bark
Barn
Baron
Barrack
Barrel
Bars
Basement
Basic
Basin
Basket
Bastard
Bat
Batch
Bath
Bathroom
Bathtub
Batter
Battle
Bayonet
Beach
Beak
Bear
Beat
Become
Bee
Beehive
Beer
Beg
Begin
Beginner
Beginning
Belief
Believe
Bell
Belt
Benefit
Bent
Beseech
Besiege
Best
Bet
Beverage
Bias
Bib
Bicycle
Big
Bigamy
Bike
Billiard
Billion
Billow
Billy
Bin
Bind
Bingo
Biology
Birch
Birdcage
Birth
Birthday
Biscuit
Bishop
Bit
Bite
Bitter
Black
Blackboard
Blame
Bland
Blank
Blatant
Bleat
Bleed
Blend
Bless
Blind
Blitz
Blizzard
Blond
Blood
Blossom
Blot
Blow
Blue
Blueprint
Blunder
Blunt
Blush
Board
Boast
Boat
Body
Bog
Boil
Bomb
Bond
Bone
Bonnet
Bony
Boo
Book
Boomerang
Boot
Bootleg
Boredom
Boris
Born
Boss
Both
Bother
Bottom
Bough
Boulder
Bounce
Bowl
Bowler
Box
Boy
Boyfriend
Branch
Brave
Brawl
Bread
Break
Breathalyser
Breathe
Breed
Breeze
Brew
Bride
Bridge
Brief
Briefcase
Bright
Brigitte
Brisk
Brittle
Broad
Broadcast
Bronze
Broom
Broth
Brother
Brown
Brunch
Brush

Bubble
Bud
Bug
Build
Building
Bull
Bullet
Bulletin
Bully
Bump
Bun
Bunch
Buoyant
Burn
Burst
Bus
Bush
Business
But
Butcher
Butterfly
Buttermilk
Button
Buy
By

C

Cabbage
Cabin
Cable
Cafe
Cage
Cake
Calculate
Calf
Call
Calm
Calmness
Calorie
Camel
Camera
Canal
Cancel
Cancer
Candid
Candle
Cane
Canine
Canvas
Canyon
Cap
Capability
Cape
Capsize
Captain
Caption
Captive
Car
Card
Cardboard
Caretaker
Cargo
Carl
Carnation
Carol
Carpenter
Carpet
Carrot
Carry
Cart
Carton
Carve
Cary
Case
Cash
Castle
Casual
Casually
Casualty
Cat
Catch
Catchword
Cathedral
Cauldron
Cause
Cave
Celery
Cellar
Cello
Cement
Century
Ceramic
Cereal
Chagrin
Chain
Chalk
Challenge
Chance
Change
Chaos
Chaotic
Chase
Chat
Cheerfulness
Chef
Cherry
Chest
Chew
Chief
Child
Childbirth
China
Chisel
Chocolate
Chocaholic
Choice
Choir
Choose
Chop
Christmas
Chuckle
Chunnel
Church
Cigar
Cinema
Circus
Cistern
Citizen
City
Claim
Clamour
Clap
Clarinet
Clasp
Class
Classical
Classroom
Claw
Clean
Cleanse
Clever
Cliff
Climate
Climb
Cling
Clog
Clone
Closed
Clothes-peg
Clothing
Cloud
Clown
Cluck
Clue
Clumsy
Coach
Coal
Coarse
Coast
Coat
Cob
Cobweb
Cock
Cockerel
Cocktail
Coconut
Cod
Coin
Cola
Cold
Collar
College
Collide
Comb
Come
Comedian
Comet
Comic
Commence
Commend
Commerce
Common
Commonwealth
Commute
Competence
Complex
Computer
Conceal
Concede
Conceit
Conceive
Concept
Concern
Conclusion
Concrete
Confess
Confetti
Confide
Confidential
Confine
Connect
Consent
Consequence
Consume
Contend
Content
Converse
Convert
Cook
Cooked
Cooker
Cookie
Cool
Cope
Copy
Core
Correct
Cosmetic
Cost
Costume
Cosy
Cot
Cotton
Cotton reel
Couch
Could
Country
Couple
Courage
Courtship
Cousin
Cove
Cover
Crack
Craft
Cram
Crane
Cranny
Crash
Crater
Cravat
Crave
Crawl
Craze
Cream
Crease
Create
Creation
Creature
Creed
Creek
Creep
Cremate
Cricket
Crime
Crimson
Crisis
Croak
Crooked
Cross
Crow
Crowd
Crown
Cruel
Crumble
Crush
Crust
Cry
Cryptic
Cuddle
Cup
Cupboard
Cur
Curfew
Curly
Currant
Current
Curse
Cushion
Custard
Custom
Cut
Cute
Cutlass
Cutlet
Cycle
Cyclone

D

Daffodil
Dairy

Dam
Damage
Damp
Dance
Dangle
Dare
Dark
Dart
Dash
Dashboard
Date
Day
Daylight
Dazzle
Dead
Deal
Death
Decade
Decker
Declare
Decoration
Defence
Deft
Delicate
Delicatessen
Delirium
Demand
Den
Dennis
Dense
Dent
Depose
Depression
Depth
Desert
Desk
Destitute
Destruction
Detective
Devil
Devise
Dew
Dial
Diamond
Did
Die
Diesel
Diet
Difficult
Dig
Din
Dingy
Dip
Diplomat
Dirty
Disagree
Disappear
Disarray
Disclose

Discord
Discount
Discourse
Discover
Disease
Disgrace
Dish
Disk
Dismount
Disobey
Disorder
Dispatch
Distant
Distemper
Distress
Distrust
Divide
Divine
Do
Document
Dodge
Dog
Dogcart
Dogwood
Doll
Dolphin
Domain
Dominion
Don
Donate
Donkey
Door
Doorbell
Doorknob
Doss
Double
Doubt
Dove
Down
Downtown
Downward
Drab
Draft
Drag
Dragon
Dragonfly
Drain
Dram
Draw
Dread
Dream
Dredge
Drench
Dress
Dresser
Drift
Drill
Drone
Drool

Drop
Drought
Drown
Drug
Drunk
Drunken
Dry
Dual
Duck
Duke
Dull
Dullness
Dummy
Dung
Dusk
Dust
Duster
Dwarf
Dwell

E

Each
Eager
Ear
Early
Earn
Eastern
Easy
Eat
Ecstasy
Educate
Education
Edwina
Effluent
Egg
Eggplant
Eight
Elastic
Elbow
Electrocute
Elegant
Elephant
Elizabeth
Elvis
Emerald
Emergency
Emotion
Empty
Encrust
End
Endanger
Enfold
Engine
English
Engrave
Enlist
Enormous
Enterprise
Enthusiastic
Entwine
Envelope
Envious
Envy
Enzyme
Equal
Error
Estate
Estimate
Estuary
Europe
Eurosceptic
Evade
Even
Eventually
Every
Evidence
Evil
Examine
Excel
Excess
Exchange
Excise
Excitement
Exclaim
Excuse
Exile
Expansion
Expensive
Explain
Explore
Explosive
Exposure
Express
Exquisite
Extend
Extra
Extreme
Eye

F

Fabric
Fabulous
Facetious
Fade
Failure
Faint
Faith
Falcon
Fall
Fallible
Fallout
False
Falsehood
Famish
Famous
Fancy
Fantasy
Far
Farm
Farmhouse
Farmland
Fashion
Fast
Fat
Father
Fathom
Fault
Feast
Feed
Feedback
Feel
Feeling
Feline
Fence
Ferment
Fertile
Fervent
Fetch
Few
Fiddle
Fidget
Field
Fierce
Fight
Fill
Filling
Film
Fine
Finger
Fire
Firebomb
Fireman
First
Fish
Fishcake
Fishpond
Fit
Five
Fix
Flag
Flagrant
Flannel
Flash
Flashback
Flat
Flawless
Fling
Float
Flood
Flower
Fluid
Fluoride
Fly

Foggy
Fold
Folk
Follow
Fondant
Food
Foot
Football
For
Forbid
Force
Foreign
Forest
Forget
Forgive
Fork
Form
Formal
Formation
Former
Fortune
Found
Four
Fragile
Fragrance
Fragrant
Frail
Frailty
Franchise
Franglais
Frank
Free
Freedom
Freeze
French horn
Fridge
Friend
Frighten
Frivolous
Fro
Frock
Frog
Frolic
From
Front
Frontal
Frontier
Frustrate
Fry
Frying-pan
Fugitive
Full
Fur
Furlong
Furnace
Furnish
Further
Fuse
Future

G

Gable
Gag
Gain
Galaxy
Gale
Gallant
Gallery
Gallon
Gallop
Gamble
Gap
Gape
Garment
Garret
Gary
Gas
Gasp
Gate
Gauge
Gauze
Gaze
Generator
Gentle
Gentleman
Genuine
George
Germ
Germanic
Gestation
Get
Ghost
Gift
Giggle
Gin
Ginormous
Giraffe
Give
Glad
Glamour
Glance
Glass
Glasses
Gleam
Glenda
Glimpse
Globe
Glory
Gloss
Glove
Glow
Glue
Go
Goal
Goat
God
Gold
Good
Goon
Gore
Gorilla
Gossip
Grab
Grace
Grade
Gradual
Graduate
Graft
Grain
Gram
Grand
Granny
Grant
Grape
Grapefruit
Grasp
Grass
Grasshopper
Grater
Grave
Gravel
Gravy
Graze
Grease
Great
Greed
Greek
Green
Greenhouse
Grief
Grill
Grim
Grime
Grin
Grind
Grip
Groan
Groin
Grotesque
Group
Growl
Growth
Grub
Gruel
Grumble
Grunt
Guard
Guess
Guesstimate
Guide
Guilty
Guitar
Gull
Gunshot
Gut
Guy
Gymnast

H

Habit
Hair
Hairbrush
Half
Halt
Ham
Hamlet
Hammock
Hamper
Hamster
Hand
Handbag
Handful
Handicap
Handle
Handsome
Hanger
Happiness
Happy
Hard
Hardship
Hare
Harm
Harrison
Hasten
Hat
Hatchet
Hatred
Have
Havoc
Hawk
Hazard
Head
Headlong
Headscarf
Heal
Healthy
Hear
Heart
Heat
Heathen
Heaven
Heavy
Hedgehog
Helen
Helicopter
Heliport
Helmet
Help
Hem
Hen
Her
Here
Herring
Hesitate
Hesitation
Hide
High
Hijack
Him
Hire
Hiss
Historic
History
Hit
Hockey
Hog
Hold
Holland
Hollow
Home
Honesty
Honey
Honeybee
Honeydew
Honour
Hook
Hooligan
Hoot
Hop
Hope
Horizon
Horn
Horrid
Horseplay
Hospital
Hot
Hotbed
Hotel
Hound
House
Household
How
Howl
Hug
Huge
Hum
Humble
Humbug
Humiliation
Hunt
Hurdle
Hurricane
Hurry
Hurt
Husband
Hygiene
Hymn
Hypnotic

I

Ice
Idea
Idle

Ignition
Ignore
Imagine
Immediate
Immoral
Implement
Importance
Impose
Impotence
In
Inanimate
Inch
Incite
Incorrect
Increase
Indifference
Indigo
Infallible
Infant
Infantile
Infantry
Infirm
Informal
Infringe
Inhabit
Inhibit
Initial
Initiative
Injustice
Inn
Innate
Inner
Innocent
Insane
Inside
Insincere
Insist
Install
Instigate
Intend
Intense
Interpol
Interview
Invite
Invoice
Irate
Iron
Ironing board
Irony
Irritation
Isaac

J

Jack
Jackpot
Jail
James
Janitor
Jargon
Jealous
Jealousy
Jeffrey
Jockey
Jog
Join
Joker
Journal
Journey
Jovial
Joy
Judge
Jump
Jumper
Jumpy
Junior
Justice
Juvenile

K

Kale
Kangaroo
Keep
Kennel
Key
Keyboard
Kick
Kidnap
Kill
Kin
King
Kingdom
Kipper
Kippers
Kiss
Kit
Kitchen
Kite
Kitten
Kneel
Knit
Knock
Know
Knowledge

L

Labour
Lack
Lacrosse
Lad
Ladder
Lady
Ladybird
Lagoon
Lake
Lament
Land
Landscape
Lane
Language
Lantern
Large
Late
Latin
Laugh
Laundry
Law
Lawrence
Lay
Laziness
Lazy
Lead
Lead (auditory)
Leaflet
Lean
Leap
Learn
Learning
Leather
Leave
Left
Leg
Lend
Leniency
Leopard
Less
Let
Lettuce
Liberty
Library
Lid
Lie
Lieutenant
Life
Light
Light bulb
Lightning
Like
Lime
Limit
Line
Link
Lip
Lips
Liquid
List
Listen
Little
Live
Lively
Lobster
Lock
Loft
Log
Logic
Long
Look
Loose
Lorry
Lose
Loss
Lost
Lot
Loud
Love
Lovebird
Low
Lower
Lubricate
Luck
Lust
Lute

M

Magazine
Magic
Magistrate
Magnet
Magnitude
Magnum
Maiden
Mail
Major
Make
Malice
Mallet
Mammoth
Man
Manage
Manhandle
Manic
Manner
Many
Mar
Marble
Margaret
Margarine
Margin
Marigold
Marilyn
Marine
Market
Married
Marry
Marshall
Martian
Masculine
Mass
Massacre
Match
Mate
Material
Mature
Maureen
Mauve
Mayhem
Me
Meagre
Mean
Meant
Measles
Meat
Median
Medic
Meek
Meet
Mel
Member
Memory
Menace
Mend
Mercy
Mere
Merry
Mess
Metal
Method
Michael
Middle
Might
Mild
Mile
Milk
Milkshake
Mill
Million
Millpond
Mimic
Mine
Mingy
Minion
Misfortune
Mislay
Mislead
Misplace
Miss
Mistake
Misty
Mitten
Mix
Modern
Moist
Monarch
Money
Mongoose
Monkey
Monsoon
Month

Mood
Moor
Moped
More
Motive
Motocross
Motor
Motorbike
Mouse
Mouth
Movie
Much
Muff
Muffin
Mumps
Munch
Museum
Mush
Mushroom
Music

N

Nailbrush
Nailfile
Naked
Name
Nap
Narrate
Narrow
Nasty
Nation
Native
Nature
Navy
Near
Neat
Necklace
Need
Needy
Negative
Neglect
Neigh
Neil
Neither
Nephew
Net
Network
New
News
Newscast
Newspaper
New Zealand
Next
Nice
Nigel
Night
Nimble
Nine
Noisy
Noodles
Nor
Norman
Nose
Notebook
Notice
Notion
Novel
Novice
Now
Nut

O

Oath
Obedient
Obese
Obnoxious
Obscure
Observe
Obstacle
Obvious
Odd
Of
Off
Offence
Offer
Official
Old
Oliver
Omelette
Ominous
On
One
Open
Optimism
Orange
Orchard
Ordeal
Order
Organise
Organist
Oriental
Origin
Ornament
Ornate
Oscar
Out
Outcome
Outer
Outrageous
Oval
Oven
Own

P

Paint
Paintbrush
Painter
Painting
Pamela
Pamphlet
Pan
Par
Parachute
Paradise
Parallel
Parcel
Parental
Park
Paratroop
Parrot
Parson
Party
Pass
Passage
Passion
Passive
Past
Paste
Pastry
Pasture
Pat
Patch
Path
Patter
Paul
Pause
Pavement
Payment
Pea
Peace
Peach
Peacock
Peak
Peanut
Pebble
Peek
Peer
Peg
Pelt
Penance
Pencil
Pennant
Pension
Pensive
Penthouse
Pepper
Peppermint
Perceive
Perch
Perfect
Perfume
Peril
Person
Pet
Phantom
Pick
Pie
Pig
Pigeon
Pigtail
Pike
Pill
Pillar
Pillion
Pillow
Pilot
Pimp
Pin
Pine
Pineapple
Pink
Pious
Pip
Pipe
Pirate
Pistol
Pitcher
Pity
Place
Plague
Plaice
Plain
Plan
Plank
Plate
Platform
Playboy
Playroom
Playschool
Plea
Plead
Pleasant
Please
Pledge
Pliers
Plod
Plug
Plunder
Plush
Poach
Pocket
Point
Poke
Polar
Policy
Polite
Pony
Pool
Pop
Pope
Port
Post
Postcard
Pot
Pottery
Pounce
Pour
Poverty
Power
Powerful
Powerlessness
Pram
Prank
Pray
Precious
Prehistoric
Prejudice
Press
Pretend
Previous
Price
Pride
Priest
Prime
Prince
Princess
Print
Prison
Prisoner
Private
Prize
Process
Prod
Profit
Promise
Prompt
Proof
Prop
Properly
Property
Propose
Prosperity
Protect
Protection
Pub
Public
Publish
Pull
Pulley
Pulp
Pulsar
Pump
Pumpkin
Pun
Punch
Puny

Pup
Pupil
Puppet
Purple
Purpose
Purr
Put
Pyjamas
Pylon

Q

Quack
Quantity
Quarrel
Queen
Quick
Quid
Quiet
Quit
Quiver

R

Rabbit
Raccoon
Racehorse
Radish
Raft
Rain
Raincoat
Rake
Rampage
Ran
Rang
Rapid
Rare
Rate
Raven
Raw
Razor
Read
Real
Realm
Rearrange
Reason
Rebirth
Rebuild
Receipt
Recent
Recoil
Recollect
Recollection
Record
Record-player
Recycle
Redress
Reform
Refresh
Refuge
Refund
Reign
Rejoice
Rejoin
Relax
Release
Relic
Relief
Religion
Relish
Remain
Remark
Remarry
Remember
Remind
Remodel
Remote
Remove
Rent
Rental
Repair
Repeal
Repeat
Report
Reprint
Request
Reside
Resign
Respect
Rest
Restore
Restrain
Result
Retail
Retreat
Retrieve
Return
Reunion
Revision
Revolve
Rewrite
Rhino
Ribs
Rich
Richard
Rick
Rid
Ride
Rider
Right
Rigid
Ring
Rinse
Rise
Risk
Roach
Roar
Rob
Rock
Rocking chair
Rocket
Rodent
Roller-skate
Rolling pin
Romance
Ronald
Rooster
Rope
Rose
Rosebud
Rot
Rotate
Rough
Round
Row
Row (auditory)
Rub
Rubbish bin
Ruby
Rug
Rugby
Ruin
Rule
Ruler
Rumour
Run
Rural
Rush

S

Sadism
Sadness
Safety
Sagacity
Sailboat
Sake
Saloon
Salt shaker
Salute
Sandwich
Sarah
Sarcasm
Saucepan
Saucer
Sausage
Save
Savour
Savoury
Saw
Sawmill
Saxophone
Say
Scaffold
Scarf
Scarlet
Scenery
Scent
Scheme
School
Schoolgirl
Scooter
Scoundrel
Scratch
Scream
Screw
Screwdriver
Scrub
Sea
Seabird
Seafood
Seahorse
Seal
Seaport
Search
Season
Seat
Second
Secret
Section
Security
Sedate
See
Seedless
Seedy
Seek
Seem
Seesaw
Segment
Selina
Sell
Send
Senior
Sense
Separate
Sergeant
Serial
Serious
Service
Set
Seven
Sew
Sexploitation
Shake
Shall
Shallot
Shallow
Shame
Shampoo
Share
Sharp
Sheep
Shelf
Shimmer
Shine
Shiny
Ship
Shiver
Shock
Shoot
Shop
Shore
Short
Shortbread
Shortcake
Shot
Shoulder
Shout
Shriek
Shut
Shy
Sick
Side
Sigh
Sight
Sighted
Significance
Silent
Silver
Simple
Sin
Sing
Single
Sink
Sip
Sister
Sit
Sitcom
Six
Size
Skeleton
Skill
Skin
Skinhead
Skinny
Skip
Skirt
Skunk
Slack
Slap
Sledge
Sleep
Sleepy
Slice
Slide
Slim
Sling

Slip
Slope
Sloth
Slow
Slug
Smack
Small
Smart
Smash
Smell
Smog
Smooth
Snail
Snake
Snap
Snapshot
Snarl
Snatch
Sneeze
Sniff
Snooker
Snort
Snow
Snowman
Snug
Soak
Sob
Sober
Soda
Sofa
Soft
Solemn
Solid
Solo
Some
Son
Song
Soon
Sorrow
Soul
Spade
Spanish
Spanner
Spare
Speak
Spear
Speech
Speed
Spell
Spend
Spicy
Spill
Spirit
Spit
Spite
Spitfire
Splash
Spoil
Spoon
Sportsman
Sprig
Spring
Sprint
Squeeze
Squirrel
Stage
Stall
Stampede
Stand
Stare
Start
Starve
State
Station
Status
Stay
Steady
Steal
Steffi
Stepladder
Stereo
Stereotype
Stern
Stick
Stiff
Sting
Stink
Stockroom
Stomach
Stop
Stopcock
Store
Stork
Storm
Stormy
Story
Stove
Straight
Strange
Streamline
Street
Strength
Stress
Stretch
Strict
Stride
Strike
String
Stroke
Stroll
Strong
Stronghold
Stubborn
Stuffing
Stumble
Stupid
Stupor
Style
Subject
Submarine
Submerge
Subtle
Success
Successfully
Succession
Suck
Sudden
Sue
Suggest
Suicide
Suitcase
Sun
Sunburn
Sunflower
Sunshine
Super
Surf
Surface
Surfboard
Surfeit
Surplus
Surprise
Suspicion
Swamp
Swan
Swear
Sweaty
Sweep
Sweet
Sweetheart
Swift
Swim
Swing
Sword
Swordfish
Symptom
System

T

Tablecloth
Tablet
Taboo
Tack
Tadpole
Tail
Tailor
Take
Talent
Talk
Tall
Talon
Tame
Tangerine
Tangle
Tanker
Tantrum
Tape
Tar
Target
Tarnish
Tarpaulin
Tart
Tartan
Task
Taste
Taunt
Tavern
Tax
Taxi
Tea
Teach
Tear
Tear (auditory)
Tease
Teasle
Teaspoon
Technofear
Technophobic
Teeth
Teetotal
Telecast
Telegram
Telephone
Telethon
Television
Tell
Template
Tempt
Ten
Tenant
Tend
Tennis
Tennis racquet
Tense
Tent
Tepid
Term
Terrain
Terry
Teutonic
Text
That
The
Theatre
Them
Theme
Then
There
Thick
Thimble
Thin
Think
This
Thought
Threat
Three
Thrill
Throw
Thumb
Thumbnail
Thump
Thunder
Thunderbird
Tidy
Tie
Tight
Tighten
Tile
Timid
Tin
Tina
Tiny
Tip
To
Toad
Toaster
Toe
Toffee
Tolerate
Toll
Tongue
Tonic
Tool
Toolbox
Tooth
Toothbrush
Toothpaste
Top
Topic
Torment
Torso
Toss
Total
Touch
Tough
Tour
Town
Toy
Track
Trade
Tradition
Traffic
Tragedy
Tragic
Train
Tram
Tranquil
Tranquillity
Trap
Trash
Travel
Trawl
Tread

Treat
Tree
Trek
Tremble
Trench
Trend
Tress
Tribune
Tribute
Trick
Trigger
Trill
Trip
Triumph
Trombone
Trot
Trouble
Trousers
Trout
Truck
True
Trumpet
Trunk
Trust
Truth
Truthfulness
Try
Tub
Tube
Tuck
Tulip
Tumble
Tummy
Turbulent
Turf
Turn
Turquoise
Turtle
Turtleneck
Tusk
Twine
Twist
Twitch
Two
Tyre

U

Umbrella
Uncertain
Uncle
Uncommon
Under
Understand
Uneasy
Unhook
Unique
University
Unkind
Unofficial
Unpopular
Unreal
Unsavoury
Unusual
Unwise
Up
Upper
Upset
Upward
Urban
Urbane
Urchin
Urge

V

Vacant
Vagabond
Vagrant
Valiant
Value
Vanessa
Vase
Vat
Venom
Veranda
Vicious
Victim
Victory
Violin
Virginia
Virtual
Virtuality
Virtuous
Vision
Visit
Vivacious
Voice
Volcano
Vow

W

Wagon
Waistcoat
Wait
Wake
Walk
Wallet
Wallpaper
Walnut
Walrus
Want
War
Ward
Warm
Warmth
Wash
Washing
Watch
Water
Waterfall
Watering can
Watermelon
Wavy
Weak
Weakness
Wealth
Wealthy
Weapon
Weather
Weave
Wedding
Weep
Weird
Welcome
Well
Western
Wet
Whale
What
Wheel
When
Where
Which
Whispers
Whistle
White
Whole
Why
Wicked
Wicket
Wide
Wife
Wild
Win
Wind
Wine glass
Windmill
Winston
Wisdom
Wise
Witch
With
Withdraw
Withstand
Witness
Witty
Wonder
Wood
Woodworm
Work
World
Worm
Worst
Worth
Wrath
Wrist
Wristwatch
Write
Write (auditory)
Writer
Wrong

Y

Yard
Year
Yearn
Yellow
You
Young
Yours

Z

Zebra
Zip
Zoo

Association norms listed by semantic category

Category list

Nouns
Animals, Fish, and Insects
Birds
Body parts
Buildings
Clothing and Accessories
Food
Fruit, Vegetables, and Nuts
Games, Pastimes, and Equipment
Household Objects
Kitchen Objects
Landforms and Processes
Liquids
Material Substances
Measurements and Amounts
Medical
Musical Instruments
Occupations
Plants and Plant Parts
Proper Names
Social Relationships
Tools and Machinery
Vehicles
Weapons and War
Weather

Adjectives
Verbs
Compounds
Blends
Morphologically Complex Words
Adverbs
Closed Class

Note: Not all words in the norms appear in these categories, while other words may appear under more than one category.

Animals, Fish, and Insects

Alligator
Animal
Ape
Bat
Bear
Bee
Bug
Bull
Butterfly
Calf
Camel
Cat
Cob
Cod
Creature
Cricket
Cur
Dog
Dolphin
Donkey
Dragon
Dragonfly
Drone
Elephant
Feline
Fish
Fly
Frog
Giraffe
Goat
Gorilla
Grasshopper
Grub
Hamster
Hare
Hedgehog
Herring
Hog
Honeybee
Hound
Kangaroo
Kipper
Kippers
Kitten
Ladybird
Leopard
Lobster
Mammoth
Mongoose
Monkey
Mouse
Perch
Pet
Pig
Pike
Plaice
Pony
Queen
Rabbit
Raccoon
Racehorse
Rhino
Roach
Rodent
Seahorse
Seal
Sheep
Skunk
Sloth
Slug
Snail
Snake
Squirrel
Swordfish
Tadpole
Toad
Trout
Turtle
Walrus
Whale
Woodworm
Worm
Zebra

Birds

Cock
Cockerel
Crane
Dove
Duck
Falcon
Gull
Hawk
Hen
Kite
Lovebird
Parrot
Peacock
Pigeon
Raven
Rooster
Seabird
Stork
Swan

Body Parts

Abdomen
Ankle
Arm
Back
Backbone
Blood
Body
Bone
Calf
Chest
Crown
Ear
Elbow
Eye
Fat
Finger
Groin
Gut
Hair
Hand
Head
Heart
Leg
Lips
Lock
Mouth
Nose
Pigtail
Ribs
Shoulder
Skeleton
Skin
Spit
Stomach
Tear
Teeth
Thumb
Toe
Tongue
Torso
Tress
Tummy
Voice
Wrist

Buildings

Airport
Barn
Barrack
Bars
Building
Cabin
Cafe
Castle
Cathedral
Church
Cinema
Circus
College
Complex
Dairy
Delicatessen
Farm
Farmhouse
Flat
Gallery
Heliport
Home
Hospital
Hotel
House
Inn
Jail
Library
Market
Mill
Mine
Museum
Pension
Penthouse
Playschool
Prison
Pub
Saloon
Sawmill
School
Shop
Station
Stronghold
Tavern
Theatre
Windmill
Zoo

Clothing and Accessories

Apron
Bag
Basket
Belt
Bib
Bonnet
Boot
Briefcase
Button
Cane
Cap
Cape
Cigar
Clog
Clothing
Coat
Collar
Comb
Cravat
Crown
Dress
Dummy
Frock
Garment
Glasses
Glove
Habit
Handbag
Hat
Headscarf
Helmet
Jumper
Mitten
Muff
Necklace
Perfume
Pipe
Pocket
Pyjamas
Raincoat
Ring
Scarf
Scent
Skirt
Slide
Stay
Suitcase
Tartan
Tie
Toothbrush
Trousers
Turtleneck
Umbrella
Waistcoat
Wallet
Watch
Wristwatch
Zip

Food

Banquet
Batter
Biscuit
Bread
Broth
Brunch
Bun
Cake
Cereal
Chocolate
Chop
Cod
Cookie
Core
Cream
Crumble
Crust
Custard
Cutlet
Dip
Duck
Egg
Fat
Feast
Filling

Fish
Fishcake
Fondant
Food
Grain
Gravy
Grease
Grub
Gruel
Ham
Heart
Honey
Humbug
Ice
Kippers
Lobster
Margarine
Meat
Muffin
Noodles
Omelette
Paste
Pastry
Peppermint
Pie
Plaice
Pulp
Sandwich
Sausage
Savoury
Seafood
Shortbread
Shortcake
Stuffing
Sweet
Tart
Toffee
Tonic

Fruit, Vegetables, and Nuts

Apple
Apricot
Artichoke
Asparagus
Cabbage
Carrot
Celery
Cherry
Coconut
Currant
Date
Eggplant
Grape
Grapefruit
Honeydew
Kale
Lettuce
Lime
Mushroom
Nut
Orange
Pea
Peach
Peanut
Pepper
Pineapple
Pumpkin
Radish
Shallot
Tangerine
Walnut
Watermelon

Games, Pastimes, and Equipment

Badminton
Ballet
Bat
Billiard
Bingo
Boomerang
Bridge
Card
Cinema
Circus
Cricket
Dart
Doll
Fence
Football
Helmet
Hockey
Jack
Jog
Joker
Kite
Lacrosse
Motocross
Net
Paint
Puppet
Rugby
Sailboat
Skip
Sledge
Slide
Snooker
Surfboard
Swing
Tennis
Tennis racquet
Top
Toy
Wicket

Household Objects

Ashtray
Atlas
Basin
Bath
Bathtub
Bin
Birdcage
Blind
Book
Broom
Brush
Candle
Card
Carpet
Case
Chest
China
Cistern
Clothes-peg
Coal
Computer
Cooker
Cot
Cotton reel
Couch
Cup
Cupboard
Cushion
Desk
Dish
Door
Doorbell
Doorknob
Drain
Dresser
Duster
Envelope
Fire
Flannel
Fork
Fridge
Frying-pan
Glass
Glasses
Globe
Glue
Hairbrush
Hammock
Hamper
Hanger
Iron
Ironing board
Kennel
Ladder
Laundry
Light
Light bulb
Lock
Magazine
Mail
Nailfile
Nailbrush
Newspaper
Novel
Ornament
Oven
Parcel
Peg
Pencil
Pillow
Pin
Pipe
Pitcher
Plate
Plug
Pot
Pottery
Pram
Record-player
Rocking chair
Rolling pin
Rug
Salt shaker
Saucepan
Saucer
Screwdriver
Seat
Shampoo
Shelf
Silver
Sink
Snapshot
Sofa
Spoon
Stepladder
Stereo
Stopcock
Stove
String
Suitcase
Tablecloth
Tack
Telephone
Television
Thimble
Tile
Tin
Toaster
Tool
Toolbox
Toothbrush
Toothpaste
Trunk
Umbrella
Vase
Wallpaper
Wine glass

Kitchen Objects

Apron
Bowl
Chef
Cook
Cup
Cupboard
Dish
Fork
Fridge
Frying-pan
Glass
Glasses
Grater
Grill
Kitchen
Lid
Oven
Pan
Pitcher
Plate
Pot
Rolling pin
Salt shaker
Saucepan
Saucer
Shelf
Sink
Spit
Spoon
Store
Stove
Teaspoon
Vat

Landforms And Processes

Avalanche
Beach
Bog
Boulder
Canal
Canyon
Cape
Cliff
Coast
Country
Cove
Crater
Creek
Desert

Estuary
Farmland
Field
Flat
Forest
Fork
Galaxy
Hollow
Horizon
Key
Lagoon
Lake
Land
Landscape
Marine
Moor
Paradise
Park
Pasture
Peak
Plain
Polar
Pool
Sea
Shore
Slope
Swamp
Terrain
Trench
Volcano
Waterfall
Wood
World

Liquids

Alcohol
Beer
Beverage
Bitter
Brew
Broth
Buttermilk
Cocktail
Cola
Diesel
Effluent
Flood
Fluid
Gallon
Gin
Ice
Liquid
Milk
Milkshake
Orange
Port
Punch
Rain
Screwdriver
Soda
Spirit
Tea
Tonic
Water

Material Substances

Asbestos
Aspirin
Board
Bronze
Canvas
Cardboard
Cement
Chalk
Coal
Cotton
Diamond
Dust
Emerald
Enzyme
Fabric
Fire
Fluoride
Fur
Gas
Glass
Glue
Gold
Gravel
Iron
Lead
Log
Magnet
Marble
Material
Metal
Paint
Pebble
Rock
Ruby
Silver
Soda
Tar
Tarpaulin
Tin
Turf

Measurements and Amounts

Acre
Barrel
Batch
Billion
Bit
Bunch
Calorie
Carton
Case
Century
Chain
Cup
Date
Day
Decade
Double
Dram
Eight
Enormous
Equal
Even
Excess
Fat
Fathom
Few
First
Five
Four
Furlong
Gallon
Ginormous
Grain
Gram
Grand
Group
Half
Handful
Inch
Lot
Middle
Mile
Million
Month
Nine
Odd
One
Quid
Season
Second
Section
Segment
Senior
Seven
Six
Size
Slice
Solo
Surfeit
Surplus
Ten
Term
Three
Total
Two
Whole
Yard
Year

Medical

Ambulance
Antidote
Arthritis
Aspirin
Bacteria
Bandage
Birth
Blind
Boil
Cancer
Casualty
Childbirth
Cold
Cut
Death
Delirium
Depression
Disease
Distemper
Drug
Gauze
Germ
Gore
Graft
Graze
Gut
Hospital
Hygiene
Insane
Measles
Medic
Mumps
Pill
Plague
Quack
Sling
Suicide
Sunburn
Symptom
Tablet
Theatre
Tonic
Venom

Musical Instruments

Cello
Choir
Clarinet
French horn
Guitar
Horn
Keyboard
Lute
Music
Trombone
Trumpet
Violin

Occupations

Acrobat
Actor
Ambassador
Artist
Athlete
Auditor
Author
Bandit
Baron
Bishop
Boss
Bowler
Butcher
Captain
Caretaker
Carpenter
Chef
Chief
Clown
Comedian
Comic
Cook
Detective
Diplomat
Dresser
Duke
Fence
Fireman
Graduate
Grass
Guard
Guide
Janitor
Judge
King
Lieutenant
Magistrate
Major
Marshall
Minion
Monarch
Novice
Official
Organist
Painter
Parson
Pilot
Pimp
Pirate
Pope

Priest
Prince
Princess
Prisoner
Prompt
Quack
Queen
Rider
Schoolgirl
Sergeant
Skinhead
Sportsman
Tailor
Tart
Vagabond
Vagrant
Witch
Writer

Plants and Plant Parts

Bark
Birch
Blossom
Bough
Branch
Bud
Bush
Cane
Carnation
Daffodil
Dogwood
Dwarf
Flower
Grain
Grass
Honesty
Marigold
Orchard
Pine
Pip
Rose
Rosebud
Sprig
Stick
Sunflower
Teasel
Tree
Trunk
Tulip
Wood

Proper Names

Adolph
Africa
America
Anne
Arthur
Barbara
Billy
Boris
Brigitte
Carl
Cary
Christmas
Cliff
Dennis
Don
Edwina
Elizabeth
Elvis
Europe
Frank
Gary
George
Germanic
Glenda
Guy
Harrison
Helen
Holland
Interpol
Isaac
Jack
James
Jeffrey
Labour
Latin
Lawrence
Margaret
Marilyn
Maureen
Mel
Michael
Neil
New Zealand
Nigel
Norman
Oliver
Oscar
Pamela
Paul
Richard
Rick
Ronald
Sarah
Selina
Spanish
Steffi
Sue
Terry
Tina
Vanessa
Virginia
Winston

Social Relationships

Aunt
Baby
Boy
Boyfriend
Bride
Brother
Child
Couple
Cousin
Father
Friend
Gentleman
Granny
Husband
Infant
Lad
Lady
Man
Mate
Nephew
Person
Sister
Son
Uncle
Wife

Tools and Machinery

Anchor
Axe
Bell
Bit
Broom
Camera
Cauldron
Chisel
Claw
Computer
Crane
Dredge
Drill
Engine
Film
Fork
Furnace
Fuse
Gauge
Generator
Glue
Grease
Hatchet
Hook
Ignition
Implement
Iron
Jack
Ladder
Lantern
Lock
Magnet
Motor
Nut
Paintbrush
Peg
Pick
Pipe
Pliers
Plug
Press
Pulley
Pump
Punch
Pylon
Rake
Razor
Ruler
Saw
Screw
Screwdriver
Slide
Spade
Spanner
Stepladder
Swing
Tool
Trap
Watering can
Wheel
Windmill

Vehicles

Aeroplane
Ambulance
Automobile
Balloon
Barge
Bicycle
Bike
Boat
Bus
Car
Cart
Coach
Dodge
Helicopter
Lorry
Moped
Motor
Motorbike
Pillion
Raft
Rocket
Sailboat
Scooter
Ship
Sledge
Spitfire
Submarine
Tanker
Taxi
Thunderbird
Train
Tram
Trap
Truck
Wagon

Weapons and War

Armistice
Axe
Battle
Bayonet
Blitz
Bomb
Bullet
Cutlass
Dart
Firebomb
Hatchet
Helmet
Magazine
Pike
Pistol
Plunder
Spear
Sword
Weapon

Weather

Billow
Blizzard
Breeze
Climate
Cloud
Comet
Cyclone
Day
Daylight
Dew
Draft
Drought
Dusk
Flood
Foggy
Gale
Hurricane
Lightning
Misty
Monsoon

Night
Rain
Smog
Snow
Spring
Storm
Stormy
Sun
Sunshine
Weather
Wild
Wind

Adjectives

Able
Abrupt
Absolute
Active
Actual
Acute
Agile
Alike
Alive
Alone
Ancient
Animate
Another
Arid
Atrocious
Authentic
Authority
Avid
Awake
Awkward
Baby
Background
Bad
Bare
Basic
Beginner
Bent
Best
Big
Billion
Bitter
Black
Bland
Blank
Blatant
Blind
Blond
Blue
Blunt
Bony
Both
Bottom
Brave
Brief
Bright
Brisk
Brittle
Broad
Brown
Bull
Buoyant
Calm
Candid
Canine
Captive
Casual
Chaotic
Cherry
Choice
Clean
Clever
Closed
Clumsy
Coarse
Cold
Comic
Complex
Confidential
Content
Cool
Correct
Cosmetic
Cosy
Crimson
Cross
Cruel
Cryptic
Curly
Current
Cute
Damp
Dark
Dash
Deft
Delicate
Dense
Destitute
Difficult
Dingy
Dirty
Distant
Divine
Downward
Drab
Dread
Drunk
Dry
Dual
Dull
Dummy
Dwarf
Each
Eager
Early
Eastern
Easy
Effluent
Elastic
Elegant
Emerald
Empty
English
Enormous
Enthusiastic
Envious
Equal
Even
Evil
Excess
Expensive
Explosive
Express
Exquisite
Extra
Extreme
Fabulous
Facetious
Fallible
False
Famous
Fancy
Far
Fast
Fat
Feline
Fertile
Fervent
Few
Fierce
Fine
First
Flagrant
Flat
Flawless
Fluid
Foggy
Foreign
Formal
Former
Fragile
Fragrant
Frail
Frank
Free
Frivolous
Frolic
Front
Frontal
Fugitive
Full
Future
Gallant
Gentle
Genuine
Germanic
Ginormous
Gold
Good
Gradual
Grand
Grape
Grave
Great
Green
Grim
Grotesque
Guilty
Handsome
Happy
Hard
Head
Heathen
Heavy
High
Historic
Hollow
Horrid
Hot
Huge
Humble
Hypnotic
Idle
Immediate
Immoral
Inanimate
Incorrect
Infallible
Infant
Infantile
Infirm
Informal
Initial
Innate
Inner
Innocent
Inside
Insincere
Intense
Irate
Iron
Jealous
Jovial
Jumpy
Junior
Juvenile
Large
Late
Latin
Lazy
Lean
Left
Less
Light
Lightning
Like
Lime
Liquid
Little
Live
Lively
Long
Loose
Lost
Loud
Low
Lower
Magic
Maiden
Mammoth
Manic
Many
Marine
Married
Martian
Masculine
Mass
Mature
Mauve
Meagre
Mean
Median
Meek
Mere
Merry
Middle
Mild
Mingy
Misty
Modern
Moist
More
Much
Naked
Nasty
Native
Navy
Near
Neat
Needy
Neither
Net
New
Next
Nice
Nimble
Noisy
Novel
Obedient
Obese
Obnoxious

Obscure
Obvious
Odd
Off
Official
Old
Ominous
Open
Orange
Ornate
Outrageous
Oval
Own
Parallel
Passive
Past
Pat
Peach
Pensive
Perfect
Pet
Phantom
Pink
Pious
Plain
Pleasant
Plush
Polar
Polite
Powerful
Precious
Prehistoric
Previous
Prime
Private
Prompt
Public
Puny
Purple
Quick
Quiet
Rapid
Rare
Raw
Real
Recent
Rich
Rigid
Rose
Rough
Round
Ruby
Rural
Rush
Scarlet
Second
Secret
Sedate
Seedy
Senior
Separate
Serial
Serious
Shallow
Sharp
Shiny
Short
Shy
Sick
Silent
Silver
Simple
Single
Skinny
Slack
Slap
Sleepy
Slim
Slow
Small
Smart
Smooth
Snug
Sober
Soft
Solemn
Solid
Solo
Spicy
Steady
Stern
Stiff
Stormy
Straight
Strange
Stretch
Strict
Strong
Stubborn
Stupid
Subtle
Sudden
Super
Sweaty
Sweet
Swift
Tall
Tame
Teetotal
Tense
Tepid
Teutonic
Thick
Thin
Tidy
Tight
Timid
Tiny
Total
Tough
Tragic
Tranquil
True
Turbulent
Turquoise
Uncertain
Uncommon
Uneasy
Unique
Unkind
Unpopular
Unreal
Unsavoury
Unusual
Unwise
Upward
Urban
Urbane
Vacant
Vagrant
Valiant
Vicious
Virtual
Virtuous
Vivacious
Warm
Wavy
Weak
Wealthy
Weird
Welcome
Well
Western
Wet
White
Whole
Wicked
Wide
Wild
Wise
Witty
Worst
Worth
Wrong
Yellow
Young

Verbs

Abandon
Abate
Abduct
Accept
Accuse
Address
Admire
Admit
Age
Agree
Allow
Amaze
Amble
Amputate
Anger
Animate
Announce
Appeal
Appear
Appease
Argue
Arise
Arm
Array
Ascertain
Ask
Assist
Astonish
Attach
Attack
Attempt
Auction
Audition
Await
Awake
Award
Axe
Baby
Bag
Balance
Ball
Balloon
Ballot
Ban
Band
Bandage
Banish
Banquet
Baptise
Bare
Bargain
Barge
Bark
Bat
Batch
Bath
Batter
Battle
Bayonet
Beach
Bear
Beat
Become
Beg
Begin
Believe
Bell
Belt
Benefit
Bent
Beseech
Beseige
Best
Bet
Bias
Bike
Billow
Bind
Birch
Bite
Blame
Bleat
Bleed
Blend
Bless
Blind
Blitz
Blossom
Blot
Blunder
Blunt
Blush
Boast
Boat
Bog
Boil
Bond
Boo
Book
Boomerang
Boot
Boss
Bother
Bottom
Bounce
Bowl
Box
Brave
Brawl
Break
Breathe
Breed
Breeze
Brew
Bridge
Brief
Brisk
Broadcast
Bronze
Brown
Brush
Bubble
Bud
Bug
Build
Bull

Bully
Bump
Bunch
Burn
Burst
Bus
Bush
Butcher
Button
Buy
Cable
Cage
Calculate
Call
Cancel
Canvas
Cap
Cape
Capsize
Caption
Carol
Carpenter
Carry
Cart
Carve
Cash
Castle
Cause
Cave
Cellar
Cement
Chagrin
Chain
Chalk
Challenge
Chance
Change
Chase
Chat
Chew
Chisel
Choose
Chop
Chuckle
Church
Claim
Clamour
Clap
Clasp
Class
Clean
Cleanse
Climb
Cling
Clog
Clone
Cloud
Clown
Cluck

Clue
Coal
Coast
Coat
Cod
Coin
Collar
Collide
Comb
Come
Commence
Commend
Commute
Conceal
Concede
Conceive
Confess
Confide
Confine
Connect
Consent
Consume
Contend
Content
Converse
Convert
Cook
Cool
Cope
Copy
Core
Correct
Cost
Costume
Couch
Could
Couple
Cover
Crack
Craft
Cram
Crane
Crash
Crave
Crawl
Craze
Cream
Crease
Create
Creep
Cremate
Croak
Cross
Crow
Crowd
Crumble
Crush
Crust
Cry

Cuddle
Cup
Curse
Cushion
Custom
Cut
Cycle
Damage
Dance
Dangle
Dare
Dart
Dash
Dazzle
Deal
Declare
Demand
Dent
Depose
Devil
Devise
Dial
Die
Diet
Dig
Din
Dip
Disagree
Disappear
Disarray
Disclose
Discount
Discourse
Discover
Disgrace
Dish
Dismount
Disobey
Disorder
Dispatch
Distemper
Distress
Distrust
Divide
Do
Document
Dodge
Dog
Doll
Donate
Doss
Doubt
Draw
Dream
Drench
Dress
Drift
Drool
Drop

Drug
Dull
Dummy
Dust
Dwarf
Dwell
Earn
Eat
Educate
Elbow
Empty
Encrust
End
Endanger
Enfold
Engrave
Enlist
Entwine
Envelope
Envy
Estimate
Evade
Examine
Excel
Exchange
Excise
Exclaim
Excuse
Exile
Explain
Explore
Express
Extend
Eye
Fall
Famish
Fancy
Farm
Father
Fathom
Fault
Feed
Feel
Fence
Fetch
Fiddle
Fidget
Field
Fight
Fill
Film
Finger
Fire
Fish
Fix
Flag
Flannel
Flash
Fling

Float
Flood
Flower
Fly
Fold
Follow
Foot
Forbid
Force
Forest
Forget
Forgive
Fork
Form
Found
Free
Freeze
Frighten
Frock
Frolic
Frustrate
Fry
Furnish
Further
Fuse
Gag
Gain
Gallop
Gamble
Gape
Gasp
Gate
Gauge
Gaze
Gentle
Get
Ghost
Giggle
Give
Glance
Glass
Gleam
Glimpse
Glory
Gloss
Glove
Glow
Glue
Go
Gore
Gossip
Grab
Grace
Grade
Graduate
Graft
Grain
Grant
Grasp

Grass
Grave
Gravel
Graze
Grease
Grill
Grime
Grin
Grind
Grip
Groan
Group
Growl
Grub
Grumble
Grunt
Guard
Guess
Guide
Gut
Halt
Hamper
Hand
Handle
Harm
Have
Head
Heal
Hear
Help
Hesitate
Hide
Hire
Hiss
Hit
Hog
Hold
Home
Honour
Hoot
Hop
Hope
Hound
House
Howl
Hug
Hum
Humble
Hunt
Hurdle
Hurt
Ice
Idle
Ignore
Imagine
Impose
Inch
Incite
Increase
Infringe
Inhabit
Inhibit
Initial
Insist
Install
Instigate
Intend
Interview
Invite
Invoice
Jockey
Jog
Join
Journey
Judge
Jump
Keep
Kennel
Key
Kick
Kidnap
Kill
Kipper
Kiss
Kneel
Knit
Knock
Know
Labour
Lack
Ladder
Lament
Land
Laugh
Lay
Lead
Lean
Leap
Learn
Leather
Leave
Leg
Lend
Let
Lie
Light
Lime
Limit
Line
Link
List
Listen
Live
Lock
Loft
Log
Long
Look
Loose
Lose
Lost
Love
Low
Lower
Lubricate
Lust
Lute
Magnet
Mail
Make
Man
Manage
Manhandle
Marry
Massacre
Mature
Mean
Meet
Menace
Mend
Mess
Might
Mill
Mimic
Mine
Mislay
Mislead
Misplace
Miss
Mistake
Mix
Mouse
Munch
Name
Narrate
Narrow
Near
Need
Neglect
Neigh
Net
Nose
Notice
Nut
Obscure
Observe
Offer
Open
Order
Organise
Ornament
Own
Paint
Parcel
Park
Pass
Paste
Pat
Patch
Patter
Pause
Peak
Peek
Peer
Peg
Pelt
Pencil
Pension
Pepper
Perceive
Perch
Perfect
Perfume
Pet
Pick
Pig
Pillow
Pilot
Pimp
Pin
Pine
Pip
Pipe
Pirate
Pistol
Pity
Place
Plague
Plank
Plead
Please
Pledge
Plod
Plug
Poach
Pocket
Point
Poke
Pool
Pop
Post
Pot
Pounce
Pour
Power
Prank
Pray
Prejudice
Press
Pretend
Price
Prime
Print
Prize
Process
Prod
Profit
Promise
Prompt
Prop
Propose
Protect
Publish
Pull
Pulp
Pump
Pun
Punch
Pup
Purple
Put
Quack
Quarrel
Quit
Quiver
Rain
Rake
Rampage
Ran
Rang
Rate
Read
Rearrange
Reason
Rebuild
Recoil
Recollect
Record
Recycle
Redress
Reform
Refresh
Refund
Reign
Rejoice
Rejoin
Relax
Release
Remain
Remark
Remarry
Remember
Remind
Remove
Remodel
Rent
Repair
Repeal
Repeat
Report
Reprint
Request
Reside
Resign
Respect

Rest
Restore
Restrain
Result
Retail
Retreat
Retrieve
Return
Revolve
Rewrite
Rid
Ride
Ring
Rinse
Rise
Risk
Roar
Rob
Roller-skate
Rot
Rotate
Round
Row
Rub
Ruin
Rule
Run
Rush
Salute
Save
Saw
Say
Scent
Scheme
Scratch
Scream
Screw
Scrub
Seal
Search
Season
Seat
Section
Sedate
See
Seek
Seem
Segment
Sell
Send
Sense
Separate
Service
Set
Sew
Shake
Shall
Shampoo
Share

Shimmer
Shine
Ship
Shiver
Shock
Shoot
Shop
Shot
Shout
Shriek
Shut
Side
Sigh
Sin
Sing
Single
Sink
Sip
Sit
Size
Skin
Skip
Skirt
Slack
Slap
Sledge
Sleep
Slice
Slide
Slim
Sling
Slip
Slope
Slow
Slug
Smack
Smart
Smash
Smell
Smooth
Snake
Snap
Snarl
Snatch
Sneeze
Sniff
Snort
Soak
Sob
Spare
Speak
Spear
Speed
Spell
Spend
Spill
Spirit
Spit
Splash

Spoil
Spoon
Spring
Sprint
Squeeze
Squirrel
Stall
Stampede
Stand
Stare
Start
Starve
State
Stay
Steady
Steal
Sting
Stink
Stop
Storm
Stove
Stress
Stretch
Stride
Strike
String
Stroke
Stroll
Submerge
Suck
Suggest
Sun
Surface
Surfeit
Surprise
Swan
Swear
Sweep
Swim
Swing
Tack
Tailor
Take
Talk
Tame
Tangle
Tape
Tar
Target
Tarnish
Tart
Task
Taste
Taunt
Tax
Teach
Tear
Tease
Telephone

Tell
Tempt
Tend
Tense
Thin
Think
Thought
Throw
Thumb
Thump
Tie
Tile
Tin
Tip
Toe
Tolerate
Toll
Tongue
Top
Torment
Toss
Total
Touch
Tour
Toy
Track
Trade
Train
Trap
Trash
Travel
Trawl
Tread
Treat
Trek
Tremble
Trench
Trick
Trigger
Trill
Trip
Triumph
Trot
Trouble
Truck
Trumpet
Trust
Try
Tuck
Tumble
Turf
Turn
Twine
Twist
Twitch
Understand
Unhook
Up
Upset

Urge
Value
Visit
Voice
Vow
Wait
Wake
Walk
Want
Ward
Warm
Wash
Watch
Water
Weave
Weep
Welcome
Wet
Whale
Wheel
Whistle
Win
Wind
Witness
Wonder
Work
Worm
Worst
Write
Yearn
Zip

Compounds

Backbite
Backbone
Background
Bathroom
Bathtub
Become
Beehive
Birdcage
Birthday
Blueprint
Bootleg
Boyfriend
Briefcase
Broadcast
Butterfly
Buttermilk
Cardboard
Caretaker
Catchword
Childbirth
Classroom
Clothes-peg
Cobweb
Cocktail
Commonwealth

Cotton reel
Dashboard
Daylight
Dogcart
Dogwood
Doorbell
Doorknob
Downtown
Downward
Dragonfly
Eggplant
Fallout
Farmhouse
Farmland
Feedback
Firebomb
Fireman
Fishcake
Fishpond
Flashback
Football
French horn
Frying-pan
Gentleman
Grapefruit
Grasshopper
Greenhouse
Gunshot
Hairbrush
Handbag
Headlong
Headscarf
Hedgehog
Honeybee
Honeydew
Horseplay
Hotbed
Household
Humbug
Ironing board
Keyboard
Ladybird
Landscape
Light bulb
Lovebird
Manhandle
Milkshake
Millpond
Motorbike
Nailbrush
Necklace
Network
Newscast
Newspaper
Notebook
Outcome
Paintbrush
Peanut
Penthouse
Peppermint
Pigtail
Pineapple
Playroom
Playschool
Postcard
Racehorse
Raincoat
Record-player
Rocking chair
Roller-skate
Rolling pin
Rosebud
Rubbish bin
Sailboat
Salt shaker
Saucepan
Sawmill
Schoolgirl
Screwdriver
Sea Horse
Seabird
Seafood
Seaport
Shortbread
Shortcake
Skinhead
Snapshot
Snowman
Spitfire
Sportsman
Stepladder
Stockroom
Stopcock
Streamline
Stronghold
Suitcase
Sunburn
Sunflower
Sunshine
Surfboard
Sweetheart
Swordfish
Tablecloth
Teaspoon
Tennis racquet
Thumbnail
Thunderbird
Toolbox
Toothbrush
Toothpaste
Turtleneck
Waistcoat
Wallpaper
Waterfall
Watering can
Watermelon
Windmill
Withdraw
Withstand
Woodworm
Wristwatch

Blends

Aerobicise
Breathalyser
Brunch
Chocaholic
Chunnel
Electrocute
Eurosceptic
Franglais
Ginormous
Guesstimate
Heliport
Interpol
Mingy
Moped
Motocross
Paratroop
Pulsar
Sexploitation
Sitcom
Smog
Sprig
Technofear
Technophobic
Telecast
Telethon
Virtuality

Morphologically Complex Words

Abate
Abduct
Ability
Absolute
Accidental
Accordingly
Active
Aeroplane
Amazement
Annihilation
Annoyance
Applicant
Aptitude
Arise
Assistance
Authentic
Automobile
Await
Banish
Basement
Beginner
Beginning
Bent
Beseech
Beseige
Bicycle
Bigamy
Biology
Boredom
Bowler
Building
Buoyant
Casually
Cheerfulness
Classical
Cleanse
Closed
Clothing
Cockerel
Commend
Commerce
Commute
Competence
Conceal
Conceit
Conceive
Concept
Concern
Conclusion
Confess
Confide
Confidential
Consent
Consequence
Consume
Contend
Cooked
Correct
Courtship
Crooked
Curly
Cutlet
Death
Decoration
Defence
Demand
Depression
Destitute
Destruction
Detective
Did
Disagree
Disappear
Disarray
Disclose
Discord
Discount
Discourse
Disease
Disgrace
Dismount
Disobey
Disorder
Distemper
Distrust
Dresser
Drunken
Dullness
Duster
Education
Emergency
Encrust
Endanger
Enfold
Engrave
Enlist
Enthusiastic
Entwine
Envelope
Envious
Eventfully
Excel
Excise
Excitement
Exclaim
Expansion
Expensive
Explosive
Exposure
Express
Extend
Failure
Falsehood
Famous
Feeling
Flawless
Foggy
Formal
Formation
Former
Frailty
Freedom
Frighten
Frontal
Frontier
Generator
Germanic
Gradual
Grater
Growth
Guilty
Handful
Handsome
Hanger
Happiness
Hardship
Hasten
Hatred
Healthy
Heavy

Hesitation
Historic
Honesty
Humiliation
Hypnotic
Immoral
Importance
Impose
Impotence
Inanimate
Incorrect
Indifference
Infantile
Infirm
Informal
Infringe
Inhabit
Injustice
Innate
Inner
Insane
Inside
Interview
Irritation
Kingdom
Knowledge
Laziness
Learning
Leniency
Lightning
Lips
Lively
Lost
Lower
Married
Meant
Misfortune
Mislay
Mislead
Misplace
Mistake
Misty
Naked
Needy
Noisy
Obedient
Offence
Oriental
Outer
Outrageous
Painter
Painting
Parental
Passage
Payment
Perceive
Perfect
Pitcher
Plead
Pleasant
Powerful
Powerlessness
Prehistoric
Princess
Prisoner
Properly
Prosperity
Protect
Protection
Ran
Rang
Rearrange
Rebirth
Rebuild
Receipt
Recoil
Recollect
Recollection
Record
Recycle
Redress
Refill
Reform
Refresh
Refuge
Refund
Rejoice
Rejoin
Relax
Release
Remark
Remarry
Remind
Remodel
Remote
Remove
Rental
Repair
Repeat
Report
Reprint
Request
Reside
Resign
Respect
Restore
Restrain
Retail
Retreat
Retrieve
Return
Reunion
Revision
Revolve
Rewrite
Rider
Ruler
Sadness
Safety
Sagacity
Saw
Scenery
Security
Seedless
Seedy
Shiny
Shot
Sighted
Significance
Skinny
Sleepy
Spanish
Spicy
Stormy
Strength
Submerge
Successfully
Succession
Surplus
Sweaty
Tanker
Telephone
Telethon
Television
Thought
Toaster
Tragedy
Tranquillity
Truth
Truthfulness
Uncertain
Uncommon
Uneasy
Unhook
Unofficial
Unpopular
Unreal
Unsavoury
Unusual
Unwise
Upper
Upset
Upward
Victory
Virtuous
Warmth
Washing
Wavy
Weakness
Wealthy
Wedding
Western
Whispers
Wicked
Witness
Witty
Worst

Adverbs

Accordingly
Alike
Alone
Back
Best
Big
Both
Bright
Casually
Clean
Dead
Down
Downward
Early
Easy
Eventually
False
Far
Fast
First
Fit
Flat
Free
Full
Good
Half
Hard
High
Hollow
How
In
Inside
Late
Left
Less
Like
Long
Low
More
Much
Near
Neither
New
Next
Nor
Now
Off
On
Past
Plain
Previous
Quick
Right
Rough
Sharp
Soft
Solo
Straight
Successfully
True
Twice
Up
Upward
Welcome
Well
Why
Worst
Wrong

Closed Class

A
Also
And
At
Both
But
By
Each
For
Fro
From
Her
Here
Him
How
In
Me
Neither
Nor
Now
Of
Off
On
Out
Own
That
The
Them
Then
This
To
What
When
Where
Which
Why
With
You
Yours

BIRKBECK WORD ASSOCIATION NORMS DISK

The association norms contained in this book are available on disk in MS-DOS format and can be purchased from the publishers. The list is held in ASCII text. Please note that the disk does not contain the list of stimulus words or the category list. If you would like to purchase the disk please complete the order form below.

Please send me the disk for the *Birkbeck Word Association Norms* by Helen Moss and Lianne Older, ISBN No: 0-86377-405-9.

Price = £20.00 each
(inclusive of postage and packing)

Quantity:..................

Plus Value Added Tax @ 17.5%: **£**......................*(to be added to all UK orders and EU orders without VAT Registration No.).*

VAT Registration No. (if applicable):..

TOTAL AMOUNT PAYABLE: **£**..........................

Name:...

Delivery Address:..

....

....

I enclose a cheque for: **£**.................................

Cheques must be made payable to Direct Distribution and drawn on a UK bank. Eurocheques are not accepted.

I authorise you to debit my credit card with the amount of: **£**......................................

My Mastercard/American Express/Visa No. is:...

Expiry Date:...

Date:...

Signature:..

Credit Card Address (if different from delivery address above):

....

....

Please return this form to Direct Distribution, 27 Church Road, Hove, East Sussex, BN3 2FA, UK. (VAT Registration No. 233 4836 66).